Tokyo (p. 8)

East Tokyo
東京東部
1 : 70,000

8

64

65

1 : 100,000
Keiyō Area
京葉地区

TOKYO-TO
東京都

11

9

1 : 130,000
Central Tokyo (23 wards)
東京主部(23区)   7

13

Tamagawa
多摩川

KAWASAKI
川崎

Port of Tokyo
東京港

Tokyo Wan (bay)
東京湾

Central Tokyo   1 : 20,000
都心

Central
Yokohama
横浜中心部
1 : 20,000

63

KEY TO MAP PLATES (1)
索引図(1)

61

KISARAZU
木更津

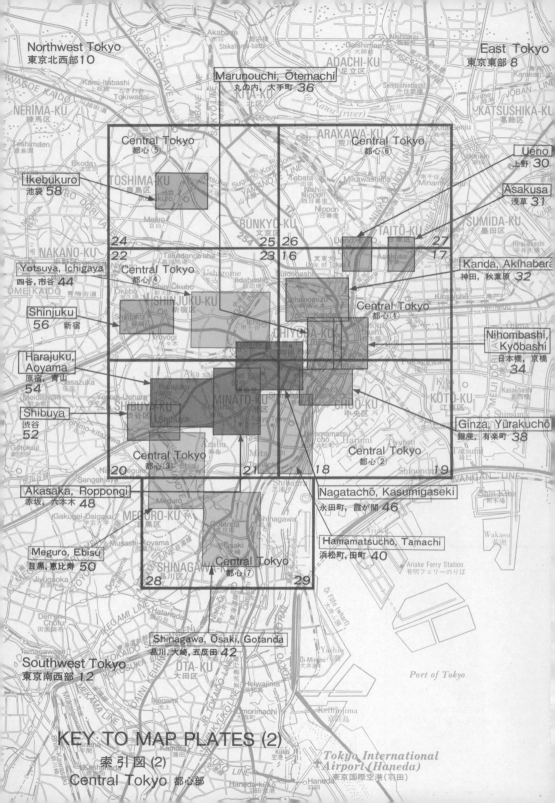

Northwest Tokyo
東京北西部 10

East Tokyo
東京東部 8

Marunouchi, Ōtemachi
丸の内、大手町 36

NERIMA-KU
練馬区

ADACHI-KU
足立区

KATSUSHIKA-KU
葛飾区

Central Tokyo
都心 ⑤

Central Tokyo
都心 ⑥

Ikebukuro
池袋 58

Ueno
上野 30

Asakusa
浅草 31

TOSHIMA-KU
豊島区

NAKANO-KU
中野区

BUNKYO-KU
文京区

TAITO-KU
台東区

SUMIDA-KU
墨田区

27

17

24

22

25 26

23 16

Yotsuya, Ichigaya
四谷、市谷 44

Central Tokyo
都心 ④

Kanda, Akihabara
神田、秋葉原 32

Shinjuku
56 新宿

SHINJUKU-KU
新宿区

CHIYODA-KU
千代田区

Central Tokyo
都心 ①

Nihombashi,
Kyōbashi
日本橋、京橋
34

Harajuku,
Aoyama
原宿、青山
54

KOTO-KU
江東区

Shibuya
渋谷 52

SHIBUYA-KU
渋谷区

MINATO-KU
港区

CHUO-KU
中央区

Ginza, Yūrakuchō
銀座、有楽町 38

20

21

18

19

Central Tokyo
都心 ③

Central Tokyo
都心 ②

Akasaka, Roppongi
赤坂、六本木 48

Nagatachō, Kasumigaseki
永田町、霞が関 46

MEGURO-KU
目黒区

Meguro, Ebisu
目黒、恵比寿 50

Hamamatsuchō, Tamachi
浜松町、田町 40

SHINAGAWA-KU
品川区

Central Tokyo
都心 ⑦

Ariake Ferry Station
有明フェリーのりば

28

29

Port of Tokyo

Shinagawa, Ōsaki, Gotanda
品川、大崎、五反田 42

OTA-KU
大田区

Southwest Tokyo
東京南西部 12

KEY TO MAP PLATES (2)

索引図 (2)
Central Tokyo 都心部

Tokyo International
Airport (Haneda)
東京国際空港(羽田)

THE NEW TOKYO

Bilingual Atlas

新東京ニヵ国語地図

講談社

KODANSHA

KEY　地域図凡例

—◇—◇— Prefectural Boundary　都県界
—·—··—·· City (*-shi*) Boundary　市町界
—··—··—·· Ward (*-ku*) Boundary　区界
———————— Town (*-machi/-chō*) Boundary　町界

▬■▬ J.R. Line　JR線

▬■▬ Other Railway　その他の鉄道

- - -▬- - - Subway　地下鉄

▬▬▬ Expressway　高速道路
▬●▬ Ramp　高速道路ランプ
(1) (2) (3)　*Chōme* Number　丁目番号
▭ Underground Arcade　地下街
▭ Shopping Area　ショッピング街
▭ Park 公園 Garden 庭園 Cemetery 霊園

⚥ Government Office　官公庁
Embassy　外国公館

• Tourist Spot or Place of
　Historic Interest　名所旧跡
丌 Shintō Shrine (Shr.) (*Jinja*)　神社
卍 Buddhist Temple (*-ji,-in*)　寺院
⛪ Church, Cathedral　教会
◎ City Office　市役所
⊙ Ward Office　区役所
⊗ Police Station (P.S.)　警察署
Y Fire Station　消防署
〒 Post Office (P.O.)　郵便局
☎ Telephone Office　NTT(支社、営業所)
♉ Bank　金融機関
⊞ Hospital (Hosp.)　病院
✕ School (Sch.)　学校
✿ Factory　工場
⚡ Power Plant　発電所
Ⓗ Hotel, Inn　ホテル、旅館
Ⓒ Cinema　映画館

Published by Kodansha Ltd., 12-21, Otowa 2-chome,
Bunkyo-ku, Tokyo 112, Japan.

Copyright Ⓒ 1993 Atsushi Umeda

All rights reserved.
Printed in Japan.
First edition, 1993.

ISBN 4-06-206590-8

Note: While every effort has been made by the Publisher to
ensure accuracy in this publication at the time of
going to press, the Publisher cannot be held res-
ponsible for any loss, damage or delay that may
ensue as a consequence of reference to this book.
The Publisher is interested in your comments, criti-
cisms and suggestions, especially if you find inac-
curacies.

目次 / CONTENTS

Major Roads　幹線道路図
　　Central Tokyo　都心 ‥‥‥‥‥‥‥‥ 4

PART Ⅰ

Central Tokyo : 23-ku(23 Wards) 東京主部(23区) ‥‥ 6
East Tokyo　東京都 ‥‥‥‥‥‥‥‥‥‥ 8
　　Sumida-ku, Kōtō-ku, Adachi-ku, Katsushika-ku, Edogawa-ku
　　墨田区、江東区、足立区、葛飾区、江戸川区
Northwest Tokyo　東京北西部 ‥‥‥‥‥ 10
　　Kita-ku, Itabashi-ku, Nerima-ku, Nakano-ku, Suginami-ku
　　北区、板橋区、練馬区、中野区、杉並区
Southwest Tokyo　東京南西部 ‥‥‥‥‥ 12
　　Ōta-ku, Meguro-ku, Setagaya-ku
　　大田区、目黒区、世田谷区
Tama Area　多摩地区 ‥‥‥‥‥‥‥‥‥ 14
Central Tokyo(1)　都心(1) ‥‥‥‥‥‥ 16
　　Chiyoda-ku(E), Chūō-ku(N), Bunkyō-ku(SE), Taitō-ku(S)
　　千代田区(東部)、中央区(北部)、文京区(南東部)、台東区(南部)
Central Tokyo(2)　都心(2) ‥‥‥‥‥‥ 18
　　Chiyoda-ku(S), Chūō-ku(S), Minato-ku(E)
　　千代田区(南部)、中央区(南部)、港区(東部)
Central Tokyo(3)　都心(3) ‥‥‥‥‥‥ 20
　　Chiyoda-ku(SW), Minato-ku(N), Shibuya-ku
　　千代田区(南西部)、港区(北部)、渋谷区
Central Tokyo(4)　都心(4) ‥‥‥‥‥‥ 22
　　Chiyoda-ku(NW), Shinjuku-ku
　　千代田区(北西部)、新宿区
Central Tokyo(5)　都心(5) ‥‥‥‥‥‥ 24
　　Toshima-ku, Bunkyō-ku(W)
　　豊島区、文京区(西部)
Central Tokyo(6)　都心(6) ‥‥‥‥‥‥ 26
　　Bunkyō-ku(NE), Taitō-ku(N), Arakawa-ku
　　文京区(北東部)、台東区(北部)、荒川区
Central Tokyo(7)　都心(7) ‥‥‥‥‥‥ 28
　　Minato-ku(S), Shinagawa-ku, Meguro-ku(E)
　　港区(南部)、品川区、目黒区(東部)

PART Ⅱ

Ueno　上野 ‥‥‥‥‥‥‥‥‥‥‥‥‥ 30
Asakusa　浅草 ‥‥‥‥‥‥‥‥‥‥‥‥ 31
Kanda, Akihabara　神田、秋葉原 ‥‥‥‥ 32
Nihombashi, Kyōbashi 日本橋、京橋 ‥‥‥ 34
Marunouchi, Ōtemachi　丸の内、大手町 ‥ 36
Ginza, Yūrakuchō　銀座、有楽町 ‥‥‥‥ 38
Hamamatsuchō, Tamachi　浜松町、田町 ‥ 40
Shinagawa, Ōsaki, Gotanda　品川、大崎、五反田 ‥ 42
Yotsuya, Ichigaya　四谷、市谷 ‥‥‥‥‥ 44
Nagatachō, Kasumigaseki　永田町、霞が関 ‥‥ 46
Akasaka, Roppongi　赤坂、六本木 ‥‥‥‥ 48
Meguro, Ebisu　目黒、恵比寿 ‥‥‥‥‥ 50
Shibuya　渋谷 ‥‥‥‥‥‥‥‥‥‥‥‥ 52
Harajuku, Aoyama　原宿、青山 ‥‥‥‥‥ 54
Shinjuku　新宿 ‥‥‥‥‥‥‥‥‥‥‥‥ 56

Ikebukuro　池袋 ‥‥‥‥‥‥‥‥‥‥‥ 58
Yokohama, Kawasaki　横浜、川崎 ‥‥‥‥ 60
　　Central Yokohama　横浜中心部 ‥‥‥‥ 62
Keiyō Area　京葉地区 ‥‥‥‥‥‥‥‥‥ 64

PART Ⅲ

Government Offices and Embassies ‥‥‥‥ 66
　　　　官公庁、外国公館
Medical and Telecommunication Facilities
　　　　厚生、通信施設
　　Central Tokyo　都心部 ‥‥‥‥‥‥‥ 68
　　Greater Tokyo　周辺部 ‥‥‥‥‥‥‥ 70
Universities and Libraries　大学、図書館
　　Central Tokyo　都心部 ‥‥‥‥‥‥‥ 72
　　Greater Tokyo　周辺部 ‥‥‥‥‥‥‥ 74
Foreign Companies and International Schools ‥ 76
　　　　外資系企業、国際スクール
　　Central Tokyo　都心部 ‥‥‥‥‥‥‥ 78
Tourist Spots and Places of Historic Interest
　　　　名所旧跡
　　Central Tokyo　都心部 ‥‥‥‥‥‥‥ 80
　　Greater Tokyo　周辺部 ‥‥‥‥‥‥‥ 82
Museums　博物館、美術館
　　Central Tokyo　都心部 ‥‥‥‥‥‥‥ 84
　　Greater Tokyo　周辺部 ‥‥‥‥‥‥‥ 86
Hotels and Japanese Inns　ホテル、旅館
　　Central Tokyo　都心部 ‥‥‥‥‥‥‥ 88
　　Greater Tokyo　周辺部 ‥‥‥‥‥‥‥ 90
Organizations (Political, Economic, Cultural, Sports, etc.) ‥ 92
　　　　各種団体(政治、経済、文化、スポーツ等)
Factories and Industrial Facilities　著名工場 ‥‥ 94
Tokyo Station　東京駅 ‥‥‥‥‥‥‥‥‥ 96
Routes to Airports　空港への交通 ‥‥‥‥ 97
Rail System　首都圏電車路線図 ‥‥‥‥‥ 98
Subway System　東京地下鉄路線図 ‥‥‥ 100
Map of Japan　日本全図 ‥‥‥‥‥‥‥‥ 102

INDEXES　索引(ＡＢＣ順) ‥‥‥‥‥‥‥ 103

SUPPLEMENTS　補遺

Japanese Index 各種機関、著名企業、博物館などの五十音順索引 131
Useful Telephone Numbers　各種電話番号
　　Government Offices　官公庁 ‥‥‥‥‥ 143
　　Embassies　外国公館 ‥‥‥‥‥‥‥‥ 144
　　Airlines　航空会社 ‥‥‥‥‥‥‥‥‥ 145
　　Hotels and Inns　ホテル、旅館 ‥‥‥‥ 146
　　Others　その他 ‥‥‥‥‥‥‥‥‥‥‥ 149
Useful Phrases　道のたずね方 ‥‥‥‥‥ 150

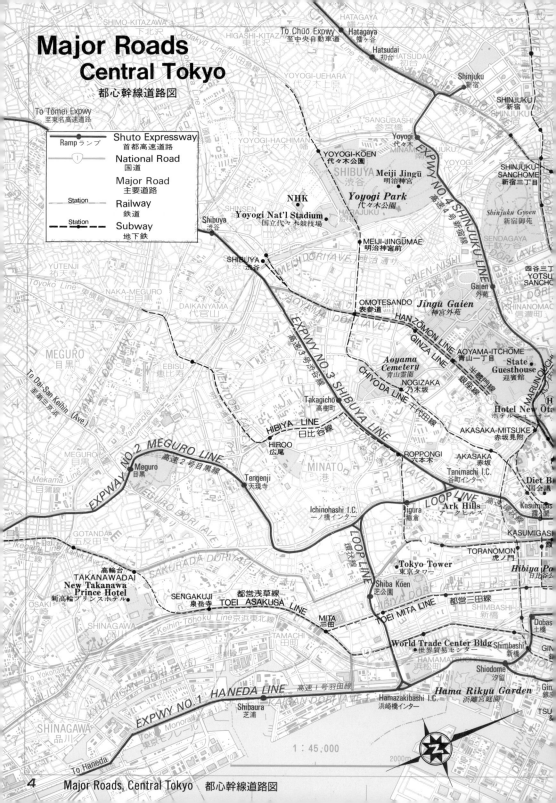

Major Roads
Central Tokyo
都心幹線道路図

Ramp ランプ
Shuto Expressway 首都高速道路
National Road 国道
Major Road 主要道路
Railway 鉄道
Subway 地下鉄
Station

1 : 45,000

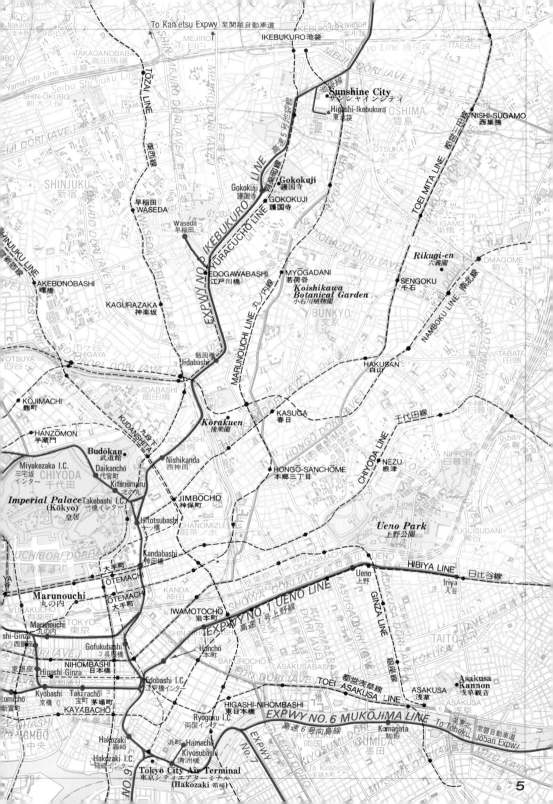

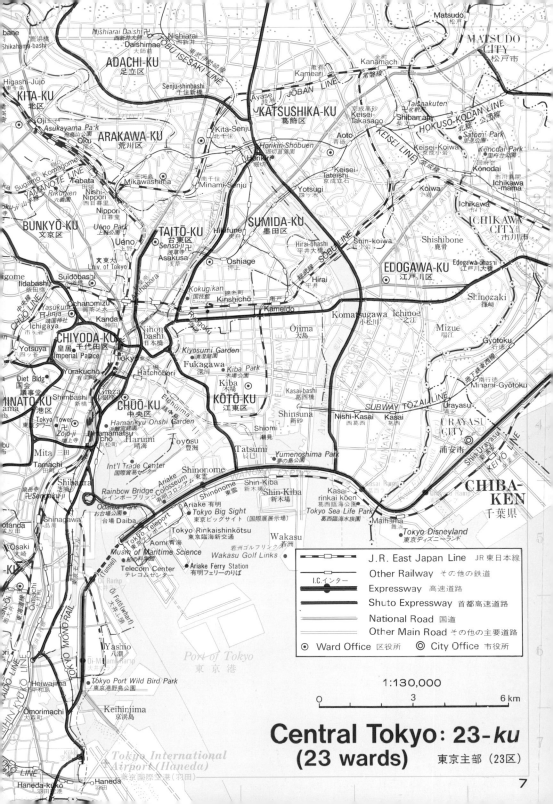

Nishiarai Dai-shi 西新井大師
Nishiarai 西新井
Shikahama-bashi 鹿浜橋
bane 鹿浜橋

Matsudo 松戸

MATSUDO CITY 松戸市

Higashi-Jūjō 東十条

ADACHI-KU 足立区

Kanamachi 金町

KITA-KU 北区

Senju-shinbashi 千住新橋

KATSUSHIKA-KU 葛飾区

JŌBAN LINE 常磐線

Ayase 綾瀬

Kameari 亀有

Keisei-Takasago 京成高砂

Takasakuten 高砂天

Shibamata 柴又

HOKUSŌ-KŌDAN LINE 北総・公団線

Satomi Park 里見公園

Oji 王子
Asukayama Park 飛鳥山公園
Oku 尾久
Kita-Senju 北千住

Aoto 青砥

Keisei-Koiwa 京成小岩

Kōnodai Park 国府台公園

Kōnodai 国府台

ARAKAWA-KU 荒川区

Horikiri-Shōbuen 堀切菖蒲園

Horikiri 堀切

Keisei-Tateishi 京成立石

KEISEI LINE 京成線

Ichikawa-mama 市川真間

YAMANOTE LINE 山手線
Tabata 田端
Mikawashima 三河島
Rikugien 六義園
Nishi-Nippori 西日暮里

Minami-Senju 南千住

Yotsugi 四ツ木

Koiwa 小岩

Ichikawa 市川

ICHIKAWA CITY 市川市

Nippori 日暮里
Ueno Park 上野公園
Univ. of Tokyo 東京大学

SUMIDA-KU 墨田区

Hikifune 曳舟

Shin-koiwa 新小岩

Shishibone 鹿骨

BUNKYŌ-KU 文京区

TAITŌ-KU 台東区

Ueno 上野

Hirai-ōhashi 平井大橋

SŌBU LINE 総武線

EDOGAWA-KU 江戸川区

Edogawa-ōhashi 江戸川大橋

Iidabashi 飯田橋
Suidōbashi 水道橋

Sensō-ji 浅草寺
Asakusa 浅草

Oshiage 押上

Hirai 平井

Shinozaki 篠崎

gome 駒込

CHŪŌ LINE 中央線
Ichigaya 市ヶ谷
Yotsuya 四ツ谷

Ochanomizu 御茶ノ水
Yasukuni Jinja 靖国神社
Kanda 神田

Kōkugikan 国技館
Kinshichō 錦糸町

Kameido 亀戸

Komatsugawa 小松川

Ichinoe 一之江

Mizue 瑞江

Gyōtoku 行徳

Diet Bldg. 国会議事堂

CHIYODA-KU 千代田区

Jimbōchō 神保町
Nihonbashi 日本橋

Kiyosumi Garden 清澄庭園
Fukagawa 深川

Ōjima 大島

Imperial Palace 皇居
Tōkyō 東京

Yurakuchō 有楽町
Hatchōbori 八丁堀

Kiba Park 木場公園
Kiba 木場

MINATO-KU 港区

Shimbashi 新橋

Ginza 銀座
Echūjima 越中島

KOTŌ-KU 江東区

Kasai-bashi 葛西橋

SUBWAY TŌZAI LINE 地下鉄東西線

Urayasu 浦安

Minami-Gyōtoku 南行徳

Tokyo Tower 東京タワー
Zōjō-ji 増上寺

CHŪŌ-KU 中央区

Hamamatsuchō 浜松町

Shinsuna 新砂

Nishi-Kasai 西葛西

Kasai 葛西

URAYASU CITY 浦安市 浦安市

Mita 三田
Tamachi 田町

Hamarikyū Onshi Garden 浜離宮恩賜庭園
Harumi 晴海
Toyosu 豊洲

Shiomi 潮見

KEIYŌ LINE 京葉線

Shibaura 芝浦

Int'l Trade Center 国際貿易センター

Shinonome 東雲

Tatsumi 辰巳

Yumenoshima Park 夢の島公園

CHIBA-KEN 千葉県 千葉県

Rainbow Bridge レインボーブリッジ

Ariake Colosseum 有明コロシアム
Shinonome 東雲
Shin-Kiba 新木場

Kasai-rinkai kōen 葛西臨海公園

Tokyo Sea Life Park 葛西臨海水族園

Maihama 舞浜

Odaiba Park お台場公園
Ariake 有明
Tokyo Teleport 東京テレポート

Ariake 有明
Tokyo Big Sight 東京ビッグサイト（国際展示場）

Shin-Kiba 新木場

Maihama 舞浜
Tokyo Disneyland 東京ディズニーランド

Aomi 青海
Tokyo Rinkaishinkōtsu 東京臨海新交通
Daiba 台場

Musm of Maritime Science 船の科学館

Wakasu 若洲

Telecom Center テレコムセンター

Wakasu Golf Links 若洲ゴルフリンクス

Ariake Ferry Station 有明フェリーのりば

J.R. East Japan Line JR東日本線

Other Railway その他の鉄道

I.C.インター

Expressway 高速道路

Shuto Expressway 首都高速道路

National Road 国道

Other Main Road その他の主要道路

⊙ **Ward Office** 区役所 ◎ **City Office** 市役所

1:130,000

0   3   6 km

Central Tokyo : 23-*ku*
(23 wards) 東京主部（23区）

Tokyo International Airport (Haneda) 東京国際空港（羽田）
Haneda 羽田
Haneda-kūko 羽田空港

Heiwajima 平和島
Omorimachi 大森町

Port of Tokyo 東京港

Tokyo Port Wild Bird Park 東京港野鳥公園

Keihinjima 京浜島

Yashio 八潮

7

East Tokyo 東京東部

Sumida-ku. Koto-ku. Adachi-ku. Katsushika-ku. Edogawa-ku
墨田区 江東区 足立区 葛飾区 江戸川区

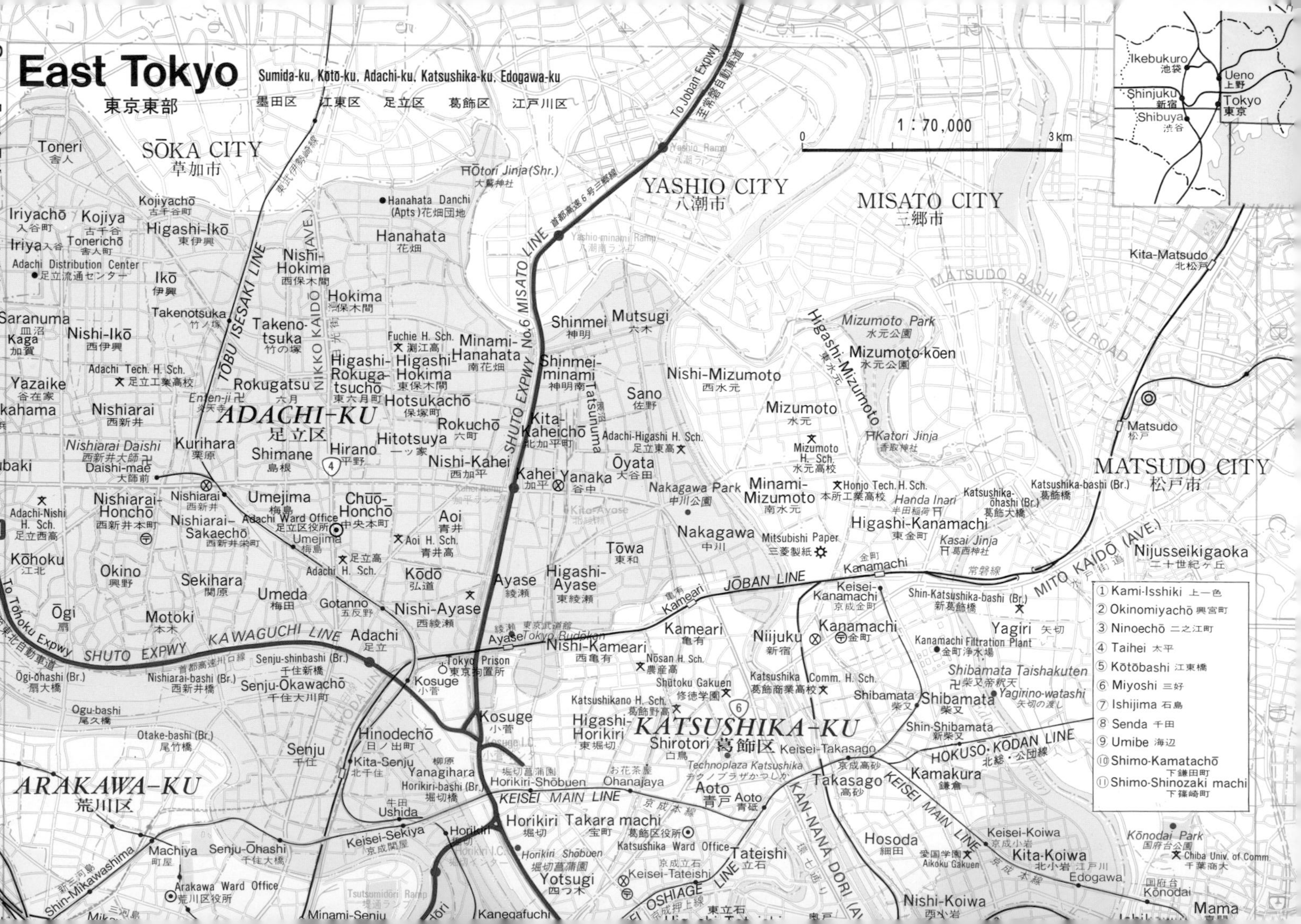

MATSUDO CITY 松戸市

MISATO CITY 三郷市

YASHIO CITY 八潮市

SŌKA CITY 草加市

ADACHI-KU 足立区

KATSUSHIKA-KU 葛飾区

ARAKAWA-KU 荒川区

Legend:
① Kami-Isshiki 上一色
② Okinomiyachō 興宮町
③ Ninoechō ニ之江町
④ Taihei 太平
⑤ Kotobashi 江東橋
⑥ Miyoshi 三好
⑦ Ishijima 石島
⑧ Senda 千田
⑨ Umibe 海辺
⑩ Shimo-Kamatachō 下鎌田町
⑪ Shimo-Shinozaki machi 下篠崎町

MITO KAIDŌ (AVE.) Nijusseikigaoka 二十世紀が丘

JOBAN LINE 常磐線

KEISEI MAIN LINE 京成本線

HOKUSŌ·KODAN LINE 北総・公団線

KEISEI MAIN LINE

TOBU ISESAKI LINE 東武伊勢崎線

CHIYODA LINE

KAWAGUCHI LINE 川口線

SHUTO EXPWY 首都高速

KAN-NANA DORI 環七通

Mizumoto Park 水元公園
Higashi-Mizumoto 東水元
Nishi-Mizumoto 西水元
Mizumoto 水元
Minami-Mizumoto 南水元
Nakagawa Park 中川公園

Shinmei Mutsugi 神明
Shinmei-minami 神明南
Sano 佐野
Ōyata 大谷田
Tatsunuma 辰沼
Yanaka 谷中
Tōwa 東和
Higashi-Ayase 東綾瀬
Ayase 綾瀬
Nishi-Ayase 西綾瀬
Kameari 亀有
Nishi-Kameari 西亀有
Higashi-Kanamachi 東金町
Kanamachi 金町
Niijuku 新宿
Shibamata 柴又
Kita-Shibamata 北柴又
Shin-Shibamata 新柴又
Takasago 高砂
Aoto 青戸
Shin-Koiwa 新小岩
Kita-Koiwa 北小岩
Nishi-Koiwa 西小岩
Hosoda 細田
Horikiri 堀切
Shirotori 白鳥
Yotsugi 四つ木
Tateishi 立石

Shin-Katsushika-bashi 新葛飾橋
Katsushika-Ōhashi 葛飾大橋
Yagiri 矢切
Kasai Jinja 葛西神社
Handa Inari 半田稲荷
Mitsubishi Paper 三菱製紙

Hanahata 花畑
Higashi-Hanahata 東花畑
Minami-Hanahata 南花畑
Hokima 保木間
Higashi-Hokima 東保木間
Nishi-Hokima 西保木間
Rokugatsu 六月
Rokuchō 六町
Hitotsuya 一ツ家
Nishi-Kahei 西加平
Kahei 加平
Aoi 青井
Kōdō 弘道
Chūō-Honchō 中央本町
Hirano 平野
Shimane 島根
Umejima 梅島
Umeda 梅田
Kurihara 栗原
Sekihara 関原
Motoki 本木
Okino 興野
Gotanno 五反野
Senju 千住
Senju-Okawachō 千住大川町
Hinodechō 日ノ出町

Adachi Ward Office 足立区役所
Katsushika Ward Office 葛飾区役所
Arakawa Ward Office 荒川区役所

Toneri 舎人
Iriyachō 入谷町
Iriya 入谷
Kojiya 古千谷
Higashi-Ikō 東伊興
Ikō 伊興
Nishi-Ikō 西伊興
Nishiarai 西新井
Nishiarai-Daishi 西新井大師
Nishiarai-Honchō 西新井本町
Takenotsuka 竹の塚
Nishi-Hokima
Saranuma 皿沼
Kaga 加賀
Yazaike 谷在家
Shikahama 鹿浜
Tsubaki 椿
Kōhoku 江北
Ōgi 扇

Senju-shinbashi (Br.) 千住新橋
Nishiara-bashi (Br.) 西新井橋
Kahei-Ōhashi (Br.) 加平大橋
Ogu-bashi (Br.) 尾久橋
Ōtake-bashi (Br.) 尾竹橋
Horikiri-bashi (Br.) 堀切橋
Senju-Ōhashi (Br.) 千住大橋
 Adachi-Ōhashi (Br.)

To Jōban Expwy 常磐自動車道
To Tōhoku Expwy 東北自動車道

SHUTO EXPWY No.6 MISATO LINE 首都高速6号三郷線

ZIKKO KAIDŌ (AVE.) 日光街道

Matsudo 松戸
Kita-Matsudo 北松戸

Mama 真間
Kōnodai 国府台
Kōnodai Park 国府台公園
Chiba Univ. of Comm. 千葉商科大

1:70,000
3 km

8 East Tokyo 東京東部

Northwest Tokyo
東京北西部

Kita-ku, Itabashi-ku, Nerima-ku, Nakano-ku, Suginami-ku
北区　板橋区　練馬区　中野区　杉並区

Ikebukuro 池袋
Ueno 上野
Tokyo 東京
Shinjuku 新宿
Shibuya 渋谷

Misono 三園
高島平ランプ Takashimadaira Ramp
Daimon 大門
Takashimadaira 高島平
Takashimadaira 高島平

Nat'l Saitama Hosp. 国立埼玉病院
Tokyo Daibutsu 東京大仏

ITABASHI 板橋
Akatsuka 赤塚
Tokumaru 徳丸
Shimo-Akatsuka 下赤塚
Akatsuka-shinmachi 赤塚新町
KAWAGOE KAIDO (AVE.) 川越街道 (254)
Tōbu-Ner
Kitamachi 北町

Ōizumi-Gakuenchō 大泉学園町
KAN-ETSU EXPWY. 関越自動車道
Ōizumimachi 大泉町

Hikarigaoka Park 光が丘公園
Hikarigaoka Park Town 光が丘パークタウン
Doshida 土支田
Hikarigaoka 光が丘

Tagara 田柄
Heiwa 平和

Nishi-Ōizumi 西大泉

Higashi-Ōizumi 東大泉
Miharadai 三原台
Nerima I.C. 練馬インター
Yahara 谷原

NERIMA-KU 練馬区
Kasugachō 春日町
Hayamiya 早宮

HŌYA CITY 保谷市
Hōya 保谷
Ōizumi-gakuen 大泉学園
Takamatsu 高松
MEJIRO DORI (AVE.) 目白通り
Nerima Ward Office 練馬区役所
Kasugachō
Nerima 練馬 (14)

Minami-Ōizumi 南大泉
Makino Mem. Garden 牧野記念庭園
Ōizumi H. Sch. 大泉高校
Shakujiimachi 石神井町
Takanodai 高野台
Chōmei-ji 長命寺
Toshimaen 豊島園
Toshimaen 豊島園
Sakura 桜台

Shakujidai 石神井台
Sanpōji-ike 三宝寺池
Shakuji Park 石神井公園
Takanodai 高野台
SEIBU IKEBUKURO LINE 西武池袋線
Fujimidai 富士見台
Nukui 貫井
Kōyama 向山
Nerima 練馬
Sakura

FUJI KAIDO (AVE.) 富士街道
Waseda H. Sch. 早稲田大学高等学院
Minamitanaka 南田中
Fujimidai 富士見台
Nakamurabashi 中村橋
Nakamura 中村
Toyotama-na 豊玉南

SHIN-ŌME KAIDO (AVE.) 新青梅街道
Shimo-Shakuji 下石神井
Ikuei Tech Coll. 郁英工業高校
Santa Maria School サンタマリアスクール
Igusa 井荻
Shimo-Igusa 下井草
Saginomiya 鷺宮
Kami-Saginomiya 上鷺宮
Nakamura-minami 中村南
Toyotama-minami 豊玉南

Higashi-Fushimi 東伏見
Musashi-Seki 武蔵関
Kami-Shakuji 上石神井
Kami-Igusa Field 上井草競技場
Kami-Igusa 上井草
Iogi 井荻
Shimo-Igusa 下井草
Saginomiya 鷺宮
Toritsu-Kasei 都立家政
Maruyama 丸山
Nur
buku
Nogata 野方

Sekimachi-Kita 関町北
OME KAIDO 青梅街道
Shirasagi 白鷺
Wakamiya 若宮
Nogata 野方

Sekimachi-Minami 関町南
Musashino City Office 武蔵野市役所
Tateno-chō 立野町
Zempukuji Park 善福寺公園
Kami-Igusa 上井草
Imagawa 今川
Momoi 桃井
Myōshō-ji 妙正寺
Shimizu 清水
Hon-Amanuma 本天沼
Yamatochō 大和町
NAKAN 中野

MUSASHINO CITY 武蔵野市
ITSUKAICHI KAIDO 五日市街道
Zempukuji 善福寺
Igusa Hachimangu 井草八幡宮
Zempukuji 善福寺
Kamiogi 上荻
Suginami Public Hall 杉並公会堂
Amanuma 天沼
Asagaya-Kita 阿佐谷北
Kawakita Hosp. 河北病院
Kōenji-Kita 高円寺北
Nakano Ward Office 中野区役

Tokyo Women's Univ. 東京女子大学
Nishiogi-Kita 西荻北
Asagaya 阿佐谷
Kōenji 高円寺

Mitaka 三鷹
Natural Cultural Garden 自然文化園
MITAKA CITY 三鷹市
Inokashira Park 井の頭恩賜公園
Kichijōji 吉祥寺
AVE.
Nishi-Ogikubo 西荻窪
Nishiogi-Minami 西荻南
Minami-Ogikubo 南荻窪
Ogikubo H. Sch. 荻窪高校
Ogikubo 荻窪
SUGINAMI-KU 杉並区
Asagaya-Minami 阿佐谷南
Suginami Ward Office 杉並区役所
Umezato 梅里
Kōenji-Minami 高円寺南
MARUNOUCHI LINE

① Sakaechō 栄町
② Higashiyamachō 東山町
③ Ōharachō 大原町
④ Izumichō 泉町
⑤ Inaridai 稲荷台
⑥ Jujo-Nakahara 十条仲原
⑦ Kishimachi 岸町
⑧ Ōji-Honchō 王子本町
⑨ Shōwamachi 昭和町
⑩ Higashi-Tabata 東田端
⑪ Tabata-Shimmachi 田端新町
⑫ Sekimachi-Higashi 関町東
⑬ Nakamura-Kita 中村北
⑭ Toyotama-Kami 豊玉上

Inokashira-kōen 井の頭公園
INOKASHIRA DORI (AVE.) 井の頭通り
INOKASHIRA LINE 井の頭線
Rikkyo Jogakuin 立教女学院
Shōan 松庵
Miyamae 宮前
Narita-Nishi 成田西
Narita-Higashi 成田東
Myōhō-ji 妙法寺
Horinouchi 堀ノ内
Wada 和田
Rissho-Kō 立正校

Mitakadai 三鷹台
Kugayama 久我山
Takaido-Nishi 高井戸西
Takaido-Higashi 高井戸東
Toyotama H. Sch. 豊多摩高校
Izumi 和泉
Hon
Takachiho Coll. of Commerce 高千穂商科大学
Ōmiya 大宮
Ōmiya Hachiman 大宮八幡

Mure 牟礼
Fujimigaoka 富士見ヶ丘
Takaido 高井戸
Hamadayama 浜田山
Hamadayama 浜田山
Daien-ji 大円寺
Nishi-Eifuku 西永福
Kama-de

Karasuyama Temple Town 烏山寺町
Takaido I.C. 高井戸インター
Eifukuchō 永福町
Eifuku 永福
Meiji Univ 明治大学
Kumano Jinja 熊野神社

CHŌFU CITY 調布市
CHŪŌ EXPWY. 中央自動車道
Kami-Takaido 上高井戸
Kita-Karasuyama 北烏山
Shimo-Takaido 下高井戸
Eifuku Ramp 永福ランプ
Meidaimae 明大前

Mitaka Toll Gate 三鷹料金所
Kyūden 給田
Minami-Karasuyama 南烏山
Rokakōen 芦花公園
Kami-Kitazawa 上北沢
Sakurajōsui 桜上水
Shimo-Takaido 下高井戸
Hanegi 羽根木

To Chofu I.C. 至調布インター
Shirayuri Women's Coll. 白百合女子大学
KŌSHŪ KAIDO (AVE.) 甲州街道
KEIO LINE 京王線
Chitose-Karasuyama 千歳烏山
Nihon Univ 日本大学
Matsubara 松原
Higashi-Matsubara 東松原

Roka Kōshun'en 芦花恒春園
Hachimanyama 八幡山
Hachimanyama 八幡山
SETAGAYA-KU 世田谷区

1 : 70,000

Southwest Tokyo
東京南西部
Ōta-ku, Meguro-ku, Setagaya-ku
大田区　目黒区　世田谷区

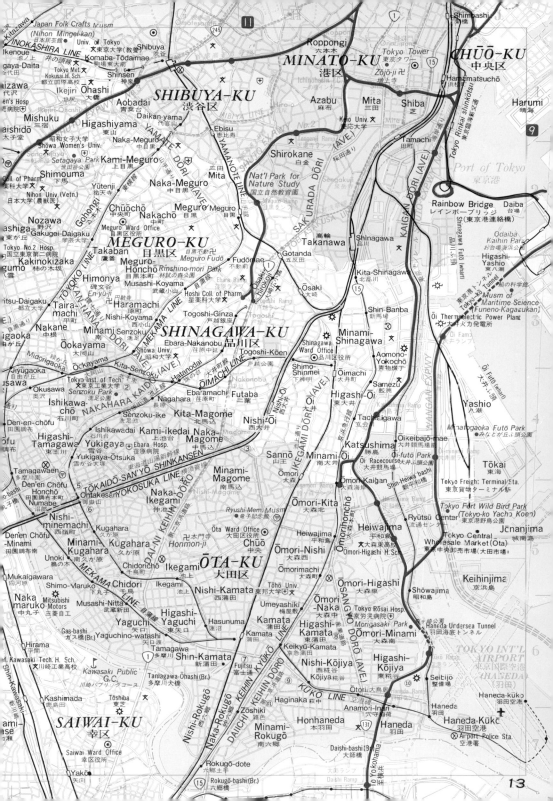

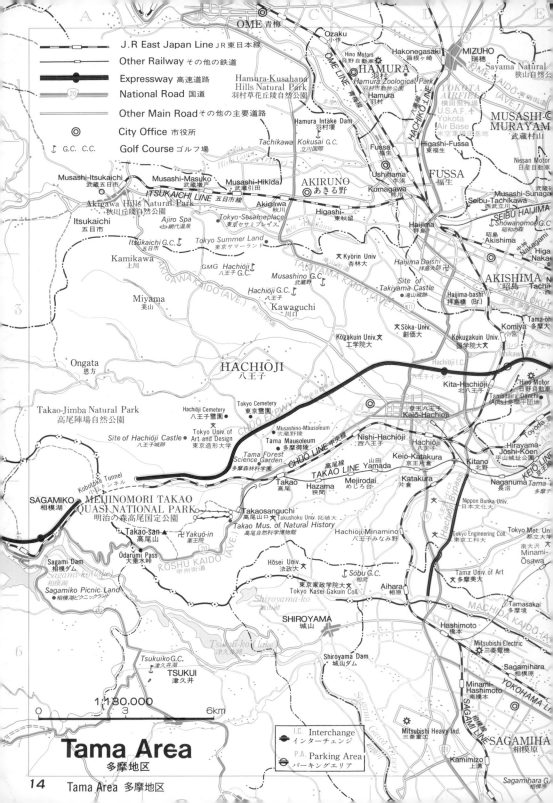

Tama Area
多摩地区

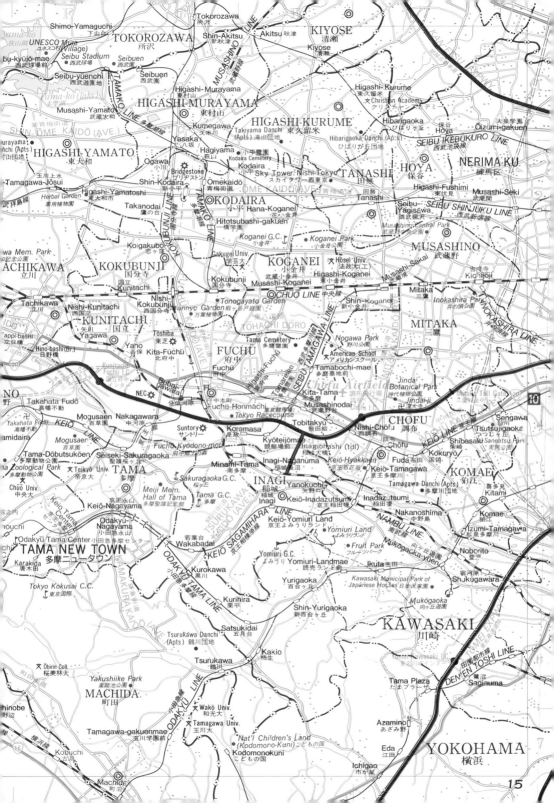

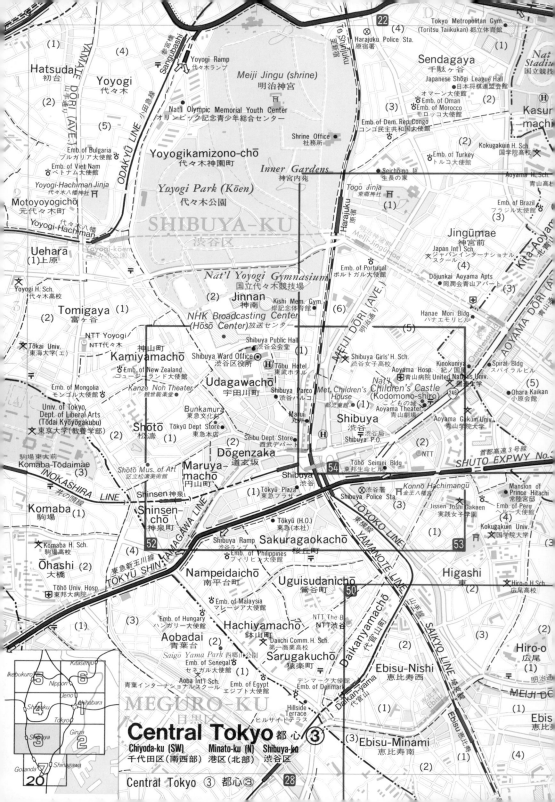

To Ikebukuro 至池袋

Takada 高田

(2) Nanzō-in 南蔵院

(3)

富士短大 Fuji Coll.

(2)

Omokagebashi 面影橋

(2) 戸塚署 Totsuka Police Sta.

Big Box Bldg ビッグボックス

早稲田通り WASEDA DŌRI (AVE.)

Braille Library 日本点字図書館

Nishi-Waseda 西早稲田

(1)

山手 YMCA Yamate YMCA

(3)

(2)

Suwa Jinja 諏訪神社

Waseda Casting Inst. 早大鋳物研究所

Takadano-baba 高田馬場

Plaza Citizen プラザシチズン (4)

Toyama Danchi (Apts) 都営戸山団地

Nishitoyama Park 西戸山公園

Shinjuku Fire Sta. 新宿消防署

Toyama Park Shinjuku-kita P.O. 戸山公園 新宿北

新宿北 Shinjuku-kita P.O.

Shinjuku Sports Center 新宿スポーツセンター

Yohan 洋販

Toyama H. Sch. 戸山高校

Gakushūin (Girls') Sch. 学習院

Hozen H. Sch. 保善高校

早稲田大(理工) Waseda Univ. (Sci. & Engn.)

Rehabilitation Center for the Physically and Mentally Handicapped 心身障害者福祉センター

Metropolitan Research Lab of Public Health 都立衛生研究所

タワーホーム Nishitoyama Tower Homes

(3) 西戸山

Social Insurance Central Hosp. 社会保険中央病院

Kaijo H. Sch. 海城学園

(3)

Ōkubo 大久保

Parking Bldg 駐車ビル (2)

Toyama 戸山

Toyama Park 戸山公園

Toyama Heights Apts 戸山ハイツ

Higashi-Nakano 東中野

Nihonkaku 日本閣

Kita-Shinjuku 北新宿

CHŪŌ LINE 中央線

(4)

(4)

(2)

Higashi-Nakano 東中野

(1)

(3)

Kita-shinjuku Lib 北新宿図書館

ŌKUBO DŌRI (AVE.) 大久保通り

Kita-Shinjuku 北新宿

(2)

Shinjuku Tax Office 新宿税務署

(1) NTT Shinjuku NTT新宿

Hyakuninchō 百人町

(2)

Shin-Ōkubo 新大久保

Lotte ロッテ

SEIBU SHINJUKU LINE 西武新宿線

YAMANOTE LINE 山手線

(1)

(3)

ŌKUBO DŌRI (AVE.) 大久保通り

NTT Ōkubo NTT大久保

(1)

MEIJI DŌRI (AVE.) 明治通り

SHINJUKU-KU 新宿区

Statistics Bu 統計局

Aikidō World H.Q. (Honbu Dōjō) 合気道本部道場

Nukebenten 抜弁天

Yochōmachi 余丁町

(7)

OME KAIDŌ (AVE.) 青梅街道

To Ōkubo 至大久保

NAKANO-KU 中野区

Naruko Tenjinsha 成子天神社

(8)

Shinjuku Public Employment Security Office 新宿職安

Shinjuku Red Cross Hosp. 新宿赤十字病院

(2)

NTV Golf Garden 日本テレビゴルフガーデン

Nishimuki Tenjin 西向天神

(6)

Health Center 新宿保健所

(7)

Nishi-shinjuku 西新宿

Seibu Shinjuku 西武新宿

Kabukichō 歌舞伎町

(1)

Shinjuku Culture Center 新宿文化センター

Shinjuku Ward Office 新宿区役所

Tokyo Med. Coll. 東京医科大学

Tomihisa 富久

Tokyo Med. Coll. Hosp. 東京医大病院

Nomura Bldg 野村ビル

(6)

Yasuda Kasai-kaijō Bldg 安田火災海上本社ビル

Hanazono Jinja 花園神社

Shinjuku 新宿

Kōsei Nenkin Hall 厚生年金会館

(5)

Tokyo Hilton Int'l 東京ヒルトンインターナショナル

Mitsui Bldg 三井ビル

Odakyū Dept Store 小田急デパート

紀伊国屋 Kinokuniya

伊勢丹 Isetan

Dai-ichi Seimei Bldg 第一生命ビル

Sumitomo Bldg 住友ビル

Mitsukoshi 三越

NTT Yotsuya NTT四谷

Hotel Century Hyatt ホテルセンチュリーハイアット

Kōgakuin Univ. 工学院大学

(1)

Marui 丸井

Kumano Jinja 熊野神社

Keio Plaza Hotel 京王プラザホテル

Shinjuku P.O. 新宿局

MY CITY マイシティー

Taisō-ji 太宗寺

(1)

Yotsuya-san 四谷三

MARUNŌUCHI LINE 丸ノ内線

Nishi-Shinjuku 西新宿

Tokyo Met. Gov't 東京都庁

Keio Dept Store 京王デパート

SHINJUKU DŌRI (AVE.) 新宿通り

(4)

(2)

Tenryū-ji 天龍寺

(4)

Shinjuku-gyoenmae 新宿御苑前

NS Bldg NSビル

KDD KDDビル

JR (HQ) JR本社

Shinjuku H. Sch. 新宿高校

Shinjuku Gyoen Tunn 新宿御苑トンネル

Kantō Int'l Senior H. Sch. 関東国際高校

56

Shinjuku Ramp 新宿ランプ

Washington Hotel ワシントンホテル

JR東京総合病院 JR Tokyo General Hosp.

20

Naitōchō 内藤町

YAMATE DŌRI (AVE.) 山手通り

Shinjuku Park Tower 新宿パークタワー

Shinjuku Park Hotel 新宿パークホテル

57

Shinjuku Gyoen (Shinjuku Imperial Gardens) 新宿御苑

Bunka Women's Coll. 文化女子大学

(2)

Japanese Garden 日本庭園

New Nat'l Theater Tokyo 東京第二国立劇場

NTT (HQ) NTT本社

KŌSHŪ KAIDŌ (AVE.) 甲州街道

Opera City オペラシティ

Bunka Gakuen Costume Mus. 文化学園服装博物館

ODAKYŪ LINE 小田急線

Western Garden 西洋庭園

Sendagaya 千駄ヶ谷

Hatsudai 初台

KEIO LINE 京王線

Yoyogi 代々木

Minami-Shinjuku 南新宿

(1)

Yoyogi 代々木

(5)

YOYOGI 代々木

SHIBUYA-KU 渋谷区

CHŪŌ LINE 中央線

Sendagaya 千駄ヶ谷

Japanese Sword Mus. (Tōken Hakubutsukan) 刀剣博物館

(4)

Communist Party of Japan 日本共産党

Nat'l Noh Theater 国立能楽堂

Yoyogi Hosp. 代々木病院

SHUTO EXPWY No. 4 首都高速4号線

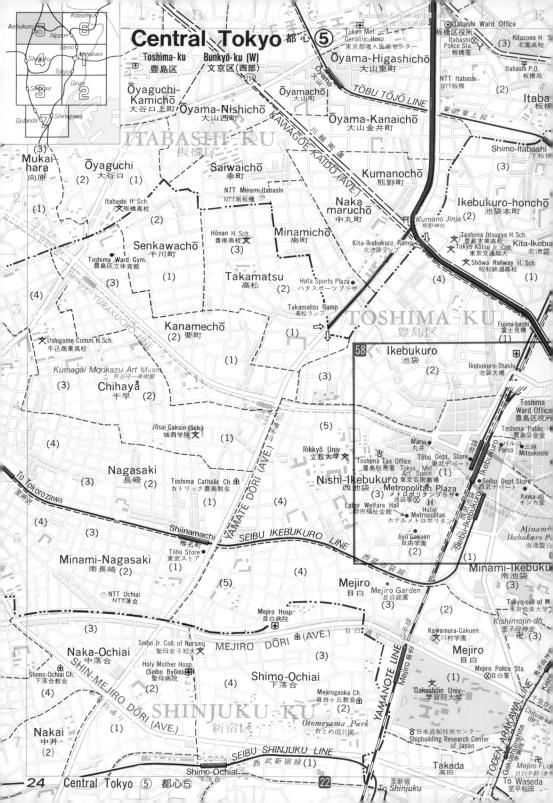

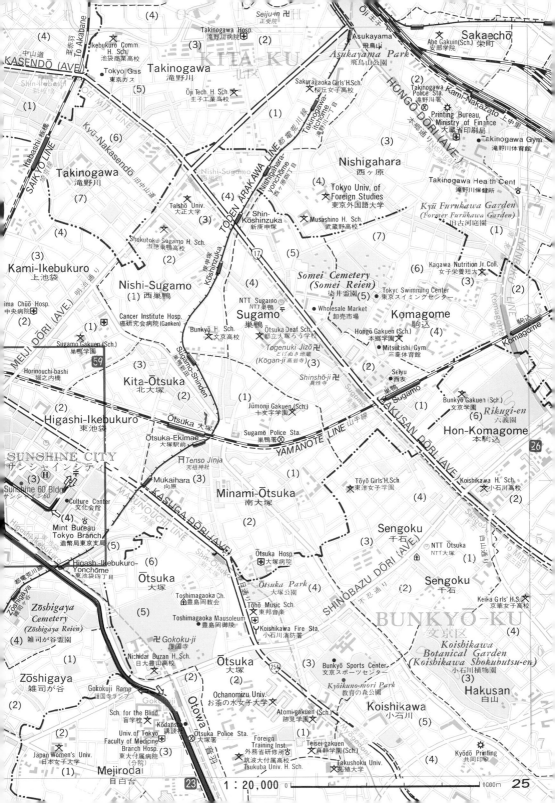

(4) To Akabane 赤羽 (4) Seiju-in 正受院 卍 王子 Ōji (4) Sakaechō 栄町

Ikebukuro Comm. H. Sch. 池袋商業高校 Takinogawa Hosp. 滝野川病院 (3) (2) Asukayama 飛鳥山 Abe Gakuin (Sch.) 安部学院

中山道 Nakasendō KASENDŌ (AVE.) Takinogawa 滝野川 KITA-KU 北区 Asukayama Park 飛鳥山公園

Shin-Itabashi 新板橋 Tokyo Gas 東京ガス (5) Sakuragaoka Girls' H.Sch. 桜丘女子高校 (2) Takinogawa Kami-Nakazato 滝野川上中里

(1) Itabashi 板橋 Ōji Tech. H. Sch. 王子工業高校 (1) Takinogawa-yonchōme 滝野川四丁目 Takinogawa Police Sta. 滝野川署

TOEI MITA LINE 都営三田線 Kyū-Nakasendō 旧中山道 (6) Nishigahara 西ヶ原 (3) Printing Bureau, Ministry of Finance 大蔵省印刷局

SAIKYO LINE 埼京線 Takinogawa 滝野川 Nishi-Sugamo 西巣鴨 TODEN ARAKAWA LINE 都電荒川線 HONGŌ DŌRI (AVE.) 本郷通り Takinogawa Gym 滝野川体育館

(7) Taishō Univ. 大正大学 (3) Nishigahara-yonchōme 西ヶ原四丁目 (4) Tokyo Univ. of Foreign Studies 東京外国語大学 (3) Kyū Furukawa Garden (Former Furukawa Garden) 旧古河庭園

(4) Shin-Kōshinzuka 新庚申塚 Musashino H. Sch. 武蔵野高校 (1)

(3) Shukutoku Sugamo H. Sch. 淑徳巣鴨高校 Kōshinzuka 庚申塚 (7) Kagawa Nutrition Jr. Coll. 女子栄養短大 (6)

Kami-Ikebukuro 上池袋 Somei Cemetery (Somei Reien) 染井霊園 Tokyo Swimming Center 東京スイミングセンター (2)

ima Chūō Hosp. 中央病院 (2) Nishi-Sugamo (1) 西巣鴨 NTT Sugamo NTT巣鴨 (5) Komagome 駒込

Cancer Institute Hosp. 癌研究会病院 (Ganken) (1) Sugamo 巣鴨 Wholesale Market 卸売市場 Komagome 駒込

MEIJI DŌRI (AVE.) 明治通り Sugamo Gakuen (Sch.) 巣鴨学園 (2) Bunkyō H. Sch. 文京高校 Ōtsuka Deaf Sch. 都立大塚ろう学校 Hongō Gakuen (Sch.) 本郷学園 (4)

Horinouchi-bashi 堀之内橋 (3) Kita-Ōtsuka 北大塚 Sugamo-Shinden 巣鴨新田 Tōgenuki Jizō とげぬき地蔵 (Kōgan-ji) 高岩寺 (3) Mitsubishi Gym 三菱体育館

59 (2) (3) (3) Shinshō-ji 真性寺 Seiyu 西友 (1)

Higashi-Ikebukuro 東池袋 Ōtsuka 大塚 Jūmonji Gakuen (Sch.) 十文字学園 Sugamo 巣鴨 Bunkyo Gakuen (Sch.) 文京学園 Rikugi-en 六義園

SUNSHINE CITY サンシャインシティ (2) Ōtsuka-Ekimae 大塚駅前 Sugamo Police Sta. 巣鴨署 YAMANOTE LINE 山手線 HAKUSAN DŌRI (AVE.) 白山通り Hon-Komagome 本駒込

H (4) Tenso Jinja 天祖神社 (1) Koishikawa H. Sch. 小石川高校

Sunshine 60 Bldg サンシャイン60 Mukaihara (3) 向原 Minami-Ōtsuka 南大塚 Tōyō Girls' H.Sch. 東洋女子学園 (4) 26

Culture Center 文化会館 MARUNOUCHI LINE 丸ノ内線 (2) (1) (2)

(4) Mint Bureau Tokyo Branch 造幣局東京支局 Sengoku 千石 NTT Ōtsuka NTT大塚 (1)

Higash-Ikebukuro-Yonchōme 東池袋四丁目 (6) KASUGA DŌRI (AVE.) 春日通り Shin-Ōtsuka 新大塚 Ōtsuka Hosp. 大塚病院 (3) Sengoku 千石 SHINOBAZU DŌRI (AVE.) 不忍通り BUNKYŌ-KU 文京区

(2) Zōshigaya Cemetery (Zōshigaya Reien) 雑司が谷霊園 Ōtsuka 大塚 Ōtsuka Park 大塚公園 (4) Keika Grls' H.S. 京華女子高校

(4) 雑司が谷 (5) Toshimagaoka Ch. 豊島岡教会 Tōhō Music Sch. 東邦音楽 Koishikawa Fire Sta. 小石川消防署 (2) Koishikawa Botanical Garden (Koishikawa Shokubutsu-en) 小石川植物園 (3)

Zōshigaya 雑司が谷 (1) Gokoku-ji 護国寺 Toshimagaoka Mausoleum 豊島岡御陵 Bunkyō Sports Center 文京スポーツセンター Koishikawa 小石川 Hakusan 白山

(2) Gokokuji Ramp 護国寺ランプ Ōtsuka 大塚 254 (3) Kyōikuno-mori Park 教育の森公園 (3)

Otowa 音羽 Nichidai Buzan H. Sch. 日大豊山高校 Ochanomizu Univ. お茶の水女子大学 Atomi-gakuen (Sch.) 跡見学園 Koishikawa 小石川 (5)

(2) Sch. for the Blind 音学校 Kōdansha 講談社 Ōtsuka Police Sta. 大塚署 Teisei-gakuen 貞静学園(Sch.) (1) Kyōdō Printing 共同印刷 (4)

(1) Japan Women's Univ. 日本女子大学 Univ. of Tokyo Faculty of Medicine Branch Hosp. 東大付属病院(分院) (3) Foreign Training Inst 外務省研修所 Takushoku Univ. 拓殖大学 Tsukuba Univ. H. Sch. 筑波大付属高校

(1) Mejiroda 目白台 23 1:20,000 0 1000m 25

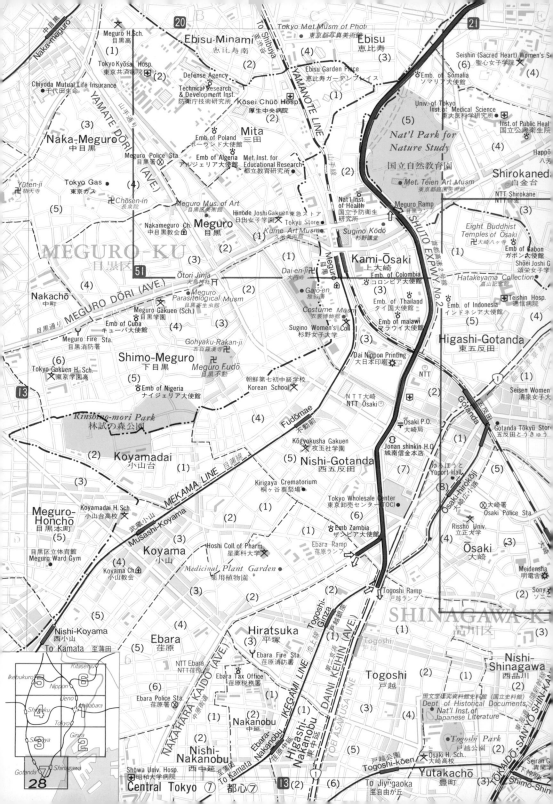

Meguro H. Sch.
目黒高
(1)

Tokyo Kyōsai Hosp.
東京共済病院 (2)

Ebisu-Minami
恵比寿南 (4)

Tokyo Met Musm of Photo
東京都写真美術館

Ebisu
恵比寿

Seishin (Sacred Heart) Women's S
(6) 聖心女子学院

Chiyoda Mutual Life Insurance
千代田生命

YAMATE DŌRI

Defense Agency
Technical Research
& Development Inst.
防衛庁技術研究所

Ebisu Garden Place
恵比寿ガーデンプレイス

YAMANOTE LINE

Emb. of Somalia
ソマリア大使館 (1)

Univ. of Tokyo
Inst. of Medical Science
東大医科学研究所

Inst. of Public Heal
国立公衆衛生院

Happō
八ヶ

Naka-Meguro
中目黒 (3)

Meguro Police Sta.
目黒署

Kosei Chūō Hosp.
厚生中央病院 (2)

Mita
三田

Emb. of Poland
ポーランド大使館

Emb. of Algeria
アルジェリア大使館

Met. Inst. for
Educational Research
都立教育研究所 (2)

Nat'l Park for
Nature Study
国立自然教育園 (5)

Met. Teien Art Musm
東京都庭園美術館

Shirokaned
白金台

NTT Shirokane
NTT白金 (4)

Tokyo Gas
東京ガス (4)

Yūten-ji
祐天寺 (5)

Chōsen-in
長泉院

Meguro Mus. of Art
目黒区美術館

Hinode Joshi Gakuen 東急ストア
日出女子学園 Tokyu Store

Nat'l Inst.
of Health
国立予防衛生
研究所

Meguro Ramp
目黒ランプ

Eight Buddhist
Temples of Ōsaki
大圓寺八ヶ寺 (3)

Nakameguro Ch.
中目黒教会

Meguro
目黒

Kume Art Musm
久米美術館 (1)

Sugino Kōdō
杉野講堂

Emb. of Gabon
ガボン大使館

Shōei Joshi G
頌栄女子学

MEGURO-KU
目黒区 51

Ōtori Jinja
大鳥神社

Meguro
Parasitological Musm
目黒寄生虫館

Dai-en-ji
大円寺 (1)

Kami-Ōsaki
上大崎

Emb. of Colombia
コロンビア大使館

Hatakeyama Collection
畠山記念館

Teishin Hosp.
逓信病院

Nakachō
中町

MEGURO DŌRI (AVE.)
目黒通り (4)

Meguro Gakuen (Sch.)
目黒学園 (3)

Gajō-en
雅叙園

Costume Musm
衣裳博物館

Emb. of Thailand
タイ王国大使館

Emb. of malawi
マラウイ大使館

Emb. of Indonesia
インドネシア大使館 (4)

Emb of Cuba
キューバ大使館 (3)

Meguro Fire Sta.
目黒消防署

Gohyaku-Rakan-ji
五百羅漢寺

Sugino Women's Coll
杉野女子大学

Dai Nippon Printing
大日本印刷

Higashi-Gotanda
東五反田

Tokyo Gakuen H. Sch.
東京学園高 (6)

Shimo-Meguro
下目黒 (5)

Meguro Fudō
目黒不動

朝鮮第七初中級学校
Korean School

NTT
NTT大崎
NTT Ōsaki

Seisen Women
清泉女子 (1)

Emb of Nigeria
ナイジェリア大使館

Fudōmae
不動前 (4)

Gotanda
五反田

Gotanda Tōkyū Stor
五反田とうきゅう

Rinshino-mori Park
林試の森公園

Kōgyokusha Gakuen
攻玉社学園

Ōsaki P.O.
大崎局 (1)

Koyamadai
小山台 (2)

MEKAMA LINE

目蒲線

Nishi-Gotanda
西五反田 (5)

Kirigaya Crematorium
桐ヶ谷葬祭場

Jonan shinkin H.Q
城南信金本店 (7)

Yūport Hall
ゆうぽうと
Yūport Hall (8)

Ōsaki-Hirokōji
大崎広小路

Ōsaki署
Ōsaki Police Sta.

Meguro-Honchō
目黒本町 (5)

Koyamadai H. Sch.
小山台高校

Musashi-Koyama
武蔵小山

Tokyo Wholesale Center
東京卸売センター(TOC)

Rissho Univ.
立正大学

Ōsaki
大崎

Meguro Ward Gym
目黒区立体育館

Koyama
小山 (3)

Hoshi Coll. of Pharm.
星薬科大学

Emb Zambia
ザンビア大使館 (6)

Ebara Ramp
荏原ランプ

(4)

Koyama Ch
小山教会 (4)

Medicinal Plant Garden
薬用植物園

Meidensha
明電舎

Sony
ソニー (2)

Nishi-Koyama
西小山 (5)

To Kamata 至蒲田

Ebara
荏原

Togoshi Ramp
戸越ランプ

SHINAGAWA-K
品川区

Nishi-
Shinagawa
西品川

Hiratsuka
平塚 (3)

Ebara Fire Sta.
荏原消防署

Togoshi
戸越

NTT Ebara
NTT荏原

Ebara Tax Office
荏原税務署

Togoshi
戸越 (2)

Ebara Police Sta.
荏原署 (6)

Nakanobu
中延

Nishi-
Nakanobu
西中延

Shōwa Univ. Hosp.
昭和大学病院

Higashi-
Nakanobu
東中延

Togoshi
戸越 (3)

Togoshi-kōen
戸越公園

Kokubungaku Shiryōkan 国立史料館
Dept of Historical Documents

Nat'l Inst. of
Japanese Literature

Togoshi Park
戸越公園 (2)

Ōsaki H. Sch.
大崎高校

Yutakachō
豊町 (3)

Shimo-Ōmo

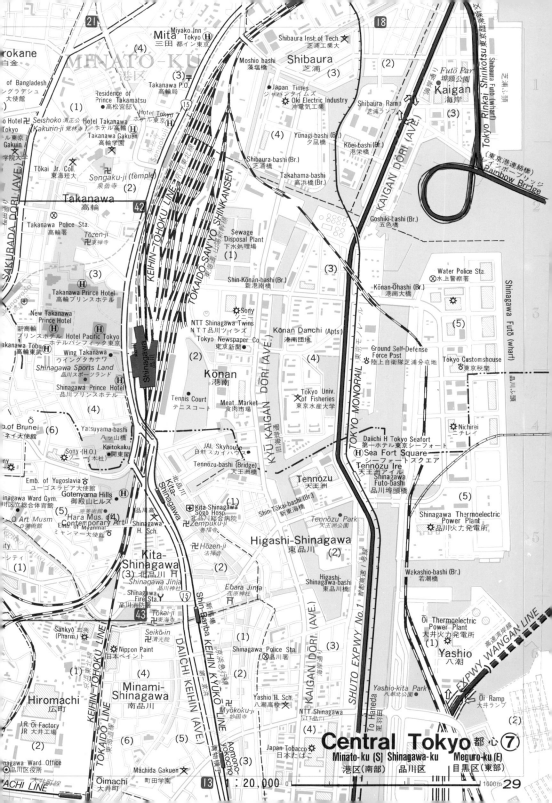

-okane
白金

of Bangladesh
ングラデシュ
大使館

MINATO-KU
港区

Mita
三田
Miyako Inn Tokyo
都イン東京 Ⓗ
(4)

(3)

Takanawa P.O.
高輪局

Residence of
Prince Takamatsu
高松宮邸

(1)

Hotel Tokyo
ホテル東京

Ⓗ (15)

Shibaura Inst. of Tech. ✪
芝浦工業大

Moshio bashi
藻塩橋

Shibaura
芝浦
(3)

Japan Times
ジャパンタイムズ
(2)

Oki Electric Industry
沖電気工業

Shibaura Ramp
芝浦ランプ

Futō Park
埠頭公園

Kaigan
海岸
(3)

Yūnagi-bashi (Br.)
夕凪橋

(4)

Kōei-bashi (Br.)
港栄橋

Tokyo Rinkai Shinkotsu 東京臨海高速鉄道

Shibaura Futō (wharf)

0 Hotel
ル東京
Gakuin

Seishoko 清正公
(Kakurin-ji) 覚林寺

Hotel Takanawa
ホテル高輪
Takanawa Gakuen
高輪学園

Tōkai Jr. Coll.
東海短大

Sengaku-ji (temple)
泉岳寺
(2)

Takanawa
高輪

Shibaura-bashi (Br.)
芝浦橋

Takahama-bashi (Br.)
高浜橋

(4)

Sewage
Disposal Plant
下水処理場
(1)

Shin-Kōnan-bashi (Br.)
新港南橋

(3)

Goshiki-bashi (Br.)
五色橋

Water Police Sta.
水上警察署 ✕

Kōnan-Ōhashi (Br.)
港南大橋

Rainbow Bridge
レインボーブリッジ
(東京港連絡橋)

KAIGAN DŌRI (AVE.)

Takanawa Police Sta.
高輪署
Tōzen-ji
東禅寺

(3)

Takanawa Prince Hotel
高輪プリンスホテル

New Takanawa
新高輪
Prince Hotel
プリンスホテル

Hotel Pacific Tokyo
ホテルパシフィック東京

Wing Takanawa
ウイングタカナワ

Shinagawa Sports Land
品川スポーツランド

Shinagawa Prince Hotel
品川プリンスホテル

(4)

Sony
ソニー

NTT Shinagawa Twins
NTT品川ツインズ

Tokyo Newspaper Co.
東京新聞

(2)

Kōnan
港南

Tennis Court
テニスコート

Meat Market
食肉市場

JAL Skyhouse
日航スカイハウス

Tennōzu-bashi (Bridge)
天王洲橋

Shinagawa
品川

Kōnan Danchi (Apts)
港南団地

(4)

Ground Self-Defense
Force Post
陸上自衛隊芝浦分屯地

Tokyo Univ.
of Fisheries
東京水産大学

Daiichi H Tokyo Seafort
第一ホテル東京シーフォート
Ⓗ Sea Fort Square
シーフォートスクエア

Tennōzu Ire
天王洲アイル

Tennōzu
天王洲

Tokyo Customshouse
東京税関

Nichirei
ニチレイ

Shinagawa Futō (wharf)

(5)

(5)

of Brunei
ネイ大使館
(6)

Yatsuyama-bashi
八ツ山橋

Sony (H.O.)
ソニー（本社）

Kaitokaku
開東閣

Emb. of Yugoslavia
ユーゴスラビア大使館

Gotenyama Hills
御殿山ヒルズ Ⓗ

Kita-Shinagawa
北品川

Kita-Shinagawa
Sōgō Hosp.
北品川総合病院
Zempuku-ji
善福寺

Shin-Tōkai-bashi (Br.)
新東海橋

Tennōzu Park
天王洲公園

Shinagawa
Futō-bashi
品川埠頭橋

Shinagawa Thermoelectric
Power Plant
品川火力発電所

(5)

-O Art Musm
美術館
(5)

Hara Mus. (4)
Contemporary Art
原美術館

Emb. of Myanmar
ミャンマー大使館

Shinagawa
H. Sch.
品川高

Hōzen-ji
法禅寺
(2)

Higashi-Shinagawa
東品川
(2)

Wakashio-bashi (Br.)
若潮橋

ity
(1)

Kita-
Shinagawa
北品川
(3)
Shinagawa Jinja
品川神社

Ebara Jinja
荏原神社

Higashi-
Shinagawa-bashi
東品川橋

Ōi Thermoelectric
Power Plant
大井火力発電所

EXPWY WANGAN LINE
高速湾岸線

Sankyo 三共
(Pharm.)
Nippon Paint
日本ペイント

Shinagawa
Fire Sta.
品川消防署

Tōkai-ji
東海寺

Seikō-in
清光院

Shin-Bamba KEIHIN KYŪKŌ
新馬場

(1)

Shinagawa Police Sta.
品川署 ✕

(1)

Ōi Ramp
大井ランプ

Yashio
八潮
(1)

(1)

J.R. Ōi Factory
JR 大井工場

(1)

Minami-
Shinagawa
南品川

(4)

Myōkoku-ji
妙国寺

(2)

Yashio H. Sch.
八潮高校 ✪

(2)

NTT Shinagawa
NTT品川

To Haneda
羽田

Hiromachi
広町

(1)

(6)

(5)

Aomono-
Yokochō
青物横丁

Japan Tobacco
日本たばこ

(4)

Central Tokyo 都心 ⑦
Minato-ku (S) Shinagawa-ku Meguro-ku (E)
港区（南部）　品川区　目黒区（東部）

nagawa Ward
Office
川区役所

Ōimachi
大井町

Māchida Gakuen
町田学園 ✪

　1 : 20,000　0

1000m 29

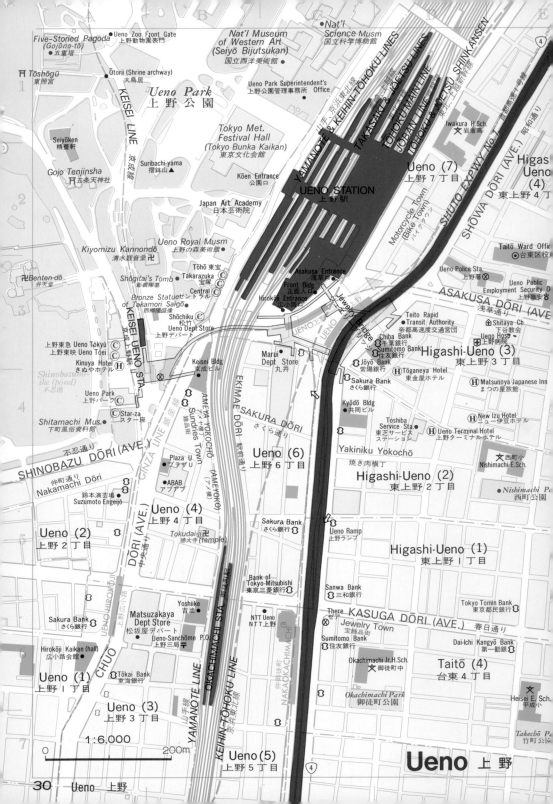

Asakusa 浅草

1:6,000

0 _____ 200m

Senzoku (1)
千束1丁目

Asakusa (3)
浅草3丁目

Asakusa
(6)
浅草6丁目

Dai-chi Kangyō Bank
第一勧銀

Fuji Bank
富士銀行

KOTOTOI DŌRI (AVE.)

Taito Traditional
Crafts Musm
台東区伝統工芸展示館

Kaminari Gorogoro Kaikan
雷5656会館

Nishi-Asakusa
(3)
西浅草3丁目

Banryu-ji
万隆寺

Lions Mansion
ライオンズマンション

Asahi Shinkin Bank
朝日信金

Sensō-ji Hosp.
浅草寺病院

Sensoji Welfare Hall
浅草寺福祉会館

engaku-in
天獄院

Asakusa View Hotel
浅草ビューホテル

Asakusa Tōei
浅草東映

Hanayashiki
Amusement Park
花やしき遊園地

Asakusa (2)
浅草2丁目

Asakusa Jinja (Shr.)
浅草神社

Hanakawado
(2)
花川戸2丁目

Nichirin-ji
日輪寺

Asakusa Shingekijō
浅草新劇場

Awashima-dō
淡島堂

Asakusa Kannondō
浅草観音堂

Niten-mon
二天門

Taitō Ward Hall
台東区民会館

Asakusa Ch.
浅草教会

WINS Asakusa
ウインズ浅草

Yakushi-dō
薬師堂

Tokyo Trade Center
(Taitō Hall)
都産業貿易センター

Asakusa Chūei
浅草中映

Nishi Sandō 西参道

Mokuba-kan
木馬館

Sensō-ji (temple) 浅草寺

Asakusa Tōhō
浅草東宝

Asakusa
Musm
浅草風俗歴史館

Five-Storied Pagoda
(Gojūno-tō)
五重塔

Hanakawado Park
花川戸公園

Rock-za Kaikan
ロック座会館

Asakusa Bowl
浅草ボウル

Hōzō-mon
宝蔵門

Asakusa E.Sch.
浅草小

Asakusa
ndicrafts Musm
浅草江戸工芸館

Denbōin Garden
伝法院庭園

Asakusa Park
浅草公園

Footwear,
Shoe Town

ishi-Asakusa
(2)
西浅草2丁目

Asakusa Engei Hall
浅草演芸ホール

Denbōin
伝法院

Sensoji Kindergarten
浅草寺幼稚園

Sukeroku
助六

Enten-dō
弁天堂

Hanakawado
(1)
花川戸1丁目

Rox Bldg
ロックスビル

Tokyo Club
東京クラブ

Kimuraya
木村屋

Sakura Bank
さくら銀行

Asakusa Shōchiku
浅草松竹

DENBŌIN DŌRI 伝法院通り

Drum Musm
太鼓館

SHIN NAKAMISE DŌRI
新仲見世通り

Asakusa Public Hall
浅草公会堂

Ryokan Mikawaya Bekkan
三河屋別館

TOBU ASAKUSA STA.
東武浅草駅

Sumida Park
隅田公園

ishi-
sakusa
(1)
浅草
1丁目

Asakusa (1)
浅草1丁目

Matsuya Dept Store
松屋デパート

Asakusa P.O.
浅草局

Religious Goods Town
神仏具店街

Mitsubishi
Bank
三菱銀行

Asakusa Plaza Hotel
浅草プラザホテル

Kamiya Bar
神谷バー

Waterbus Station
水上バスのりば

Tōkai Bank
東海銀行

Fuji Bank
富士銀行

Sumitomo Bank
住友銀行

Kaminarimon (1)
雷門1丁目

Tokyo Sōwa Bank
東京相和

Asakusa Tourist
Information Center
浅草文化観光センター

Kaminari-mon
雷門

Azuma-bashi (Br.)
吾妻橋

Tawara E.Sch.
田原小

Kaminarimon
(2)
雷門2丁目

Kaminarimon P.O.
雷門局

Metropolitan Tax Office
台東都税事務所

NTT Asakusa
NTT浅草

Kinryū-ji
金竜寺

Tokyo Toyota
東京トヨタ

Kaminarimon Skymansion
雷門スカイマンション

Mug toro むぎとろ

Komagata-dō
駒形堂

ARAMACHI GINZA LINE

Bank of Tokyo-Mitsubishi
東京三菱銀行

SHUTO EXPWY No.6
首都高速6号線

Kotobuki
寿

Komagata
駒形

Kurofune Jinja
黒船神社

Sanwa Bank
三和銀行

World Bags Musm
世界のカバン館

Komagata-bashi (Br.)
駒形橋

Azumabashi
吾妻橋

Kanda, Akihabara
神田　秋葉原

Yushima (2)
湯島2丁目

Tokyo Hitachi Hosp.
東京日立病院

Yushima (3)
湯島3丁目

Tsumagoi Jinja
妻恋神社

KURAMAE DORI (AVE.) 蔵前通り

Yushima 1 P.O.
湯島一局

Tokyo Garden Palace
東京ガーデンパレス

Denpa Bldg No.2
第2電波ビル

Sanwa Bank
三和銀行

Yamada Shōmei
山田照明

Hotel Silver Inn
ホテルシルバーイン

Akihabara
秋葉原

shima (1)
島1丁目

NGO DORI (AVE.)

Kanda Myōjin
神田明神

Soto-Kanda (2)
外神田2丁目

Kanda Ch.
神田教会

Soto-Kanda (4)
外神田4丁目

Tokyo Med. & Dent. Univ.
東京医科歯科大

Hōrin Park
芳林公園

Kanda-ji
神田寺

Kanda-Neribeichō
神田練堀町

Kanda-Matsunagachō
神田松永町

Ochanomizu P.O.
御茶ノ水局

Yushima Confucian
Shrine
(Yushima Seidō)
湯島聖堂

Shōhei E. Sch.
昌平小

Minami Art Musm
ミナミ美術館

anomizu-bashi　Hijiri-bashi
御茶ノ水橋　聖橋

OCHANOMIZU
STATION
御茶ノ水駅

Soto-Kanda (3)
外神田3丁目

Nippon Express
(Nittsu) Bldg
日通ビル

Yamagiwa
ヤマギワ

Kanda-Aioichō
神田相生町

KEIHIN-TOHOKU LINE 京浜東北線

AKIHABARA
ELECTRICAL STORES STREET
秋葉原電気器具街

Livina Yamagiwa
リビナヤマギワ

Ishimaru Denki
石丸電気

Sato Musen
サトー無線

Kanda-
Hanaokachō
神田花岡町

霊堂病院　Nippan
Nihondō Hosp.　日販

Sundai Prep. Sch.
駿台予備校 (4)

Hitachi (H.O.)
日立(本社)

SŌBU LINE 総武線

Akihabara Dept. Store
秋葉原デパート

Soto-
Kanda
(1)
外神田
1丁目

AKIHABARA STATION
秋葉原駅

Kanda-
Sakumachō
神田佐久間町

Kanda-Hirakawachō
神田平河町

Nikolai Cathedral
ニコライ堂

da Hosp.

Shōhei-bashi (Br.)
昌平橋

Laox
ラオックス

(17)

SHUTO EXPWY NO.1 首都高速1号線

Univ.
本大
Sci.&Engn)
理工)

Hotel Juraku
ホテル聚楽

Nagura Hosp.
名倉病院 (2)

Kanda Fire Sta.
神田消防署

Manseibashi Police Sta.
万世橋署

Kanda P.O.
神田局

Washington Hotel
ワシントンホテル

New Japan Securities
新日本証券

Shōhei E. Sch.
昌平小

Tokyo Green Hotel Awajichō
東京グリーンホテル淡路町

Hotel New Kanda
ホテルニュー神田

Transportation
Musm
交通博物館

Dōwa Hosp.
同和病院

Mansei-bashi (Br.)
万世橋

Mansei
万世

i Marine & Fire
rance (H.O.)
上(本社)

Kanda-Awajichō
神田淡路町

Kanda-Sudachō (2)
神田須田町2丁目

Zendentsu
Hall
全電通ホール

Sōhyō Kaikan
総評会館 (1)

YASUKUNI DORI (AVE.) 靖国通り

Kanda-Sudachō (1)
神田須田町1丁目

Kokumin Bank
国民銀行

nda-
rawamachi
神田小川町 (1)

OGAWAMACHI

(1)

Kanda-
Tachō
神田多町

Kanda
Kajichō
(3)
神田
鍛冶町
(3)

Shokusan Bank
殖産銀行

Kanda Higashi-
matsushitachō
神田東松下町

2)
EA

Sanwa Bank
三和銀行

Tōkai Bank
東海銀行

Kanda-
Tsukasamachi
神田司町

New Central Hotel
ニューセントラルホテル

Kandaekimae P.O.
神田駅前局

Kanda-Tomiyamachō
神田富山町

SOTOBORI DORI

Kanda-
Mitoshiro-
chō
神田
美土代町

OP Bldg
OPビル

YMCA
神田

Chiyoda E. Sch.
千代田小

Ohbayashi Corp.
大林組

NTT Kanda
NTT神田

Kanda-Konyachō
神田紺屋町

Kanda-Kita-
norimonochō
神田北乗物町

(1)

HONGO DORI (AVE.)

ri Gallery
ギャラリー
理ビル

Tokyo Royal Plaza
東京ロイヤルプラザ

Grand Central Hotel
グランドセントラル
ホテル

Central Hotel
セントラルホテル

Kajichō
(2)
鍛冶町
2丁目

Imagawa Jr.H.Sch
今川中

Kanda-Konya-
chō
神田紺屋町

Kanda-Nishi-
fukudachō
神田西福田町

Hyōgo Bank
兵庫銀行

MARUNOUCHI LINE

Uchi-Kanda
(1)
内神田
1丁目

Kanda Inst. of
Foreign Languages
神田外語学院

Uchi-Kanda
(3)
内神田
3丁目

KANDA STATION 神田駅

Kajichō-
(1)
鍛冶町
1丁目

Kanda-Mikurachō
神田美倉町

oman
マン

Hitachi Bldg
日立ビル

Kandabashi Ramp
神田橋ランプ

Kasahara Bldg
笠原ビル

Uchi-Kanda
(2)
内神田
2丁目

Imagawabashi P.O.
今川橋局

(17)

1:8,000

300m

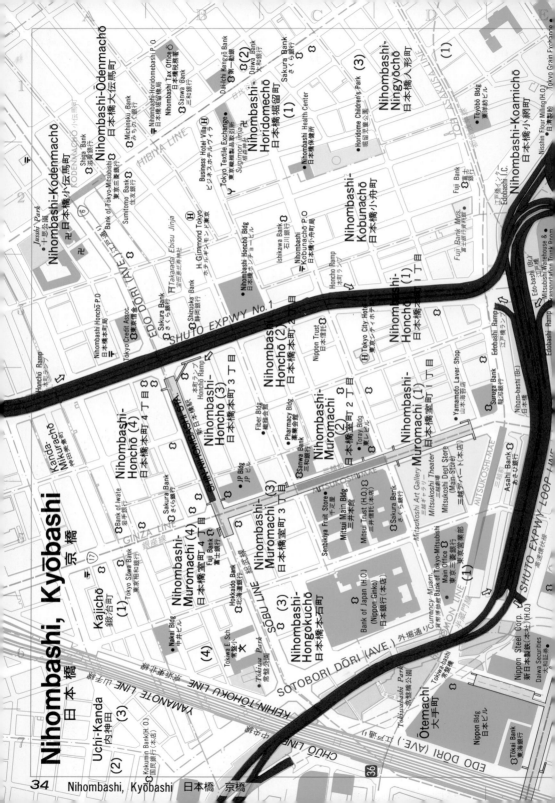

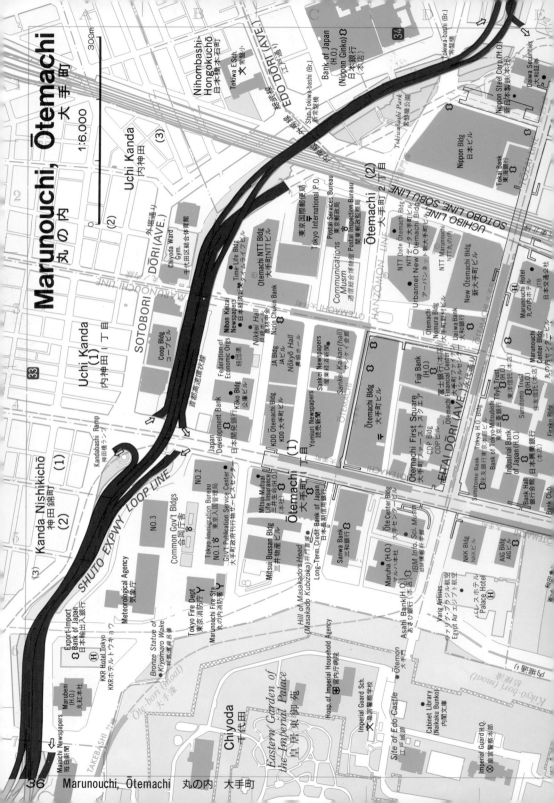

Marunouchi, Ōtemachi 丸の内

大手町

1:6,000

300m

Uchi Kanda (3) 内神田

Uchi Kanda 内神田 Ｉ丁目

Uchi Kanda (1) 内神田

Kanda Nishikichō (1) 神田錦町

Kanda Nishikichō (2) 神田錦町

(3)

(2)

(3)

SOTOBORI DŌRI (AVE.) 外堀通り

MARUNOUCHI LINE

SHUTO EXPWY LOOP LINE 首都高速都心環状線

Kandabashi Ramp 神田橋ランプ

Bronze Statue of Kiyomaro Wake 和気清麻呂像

Export-Import Bank of Japan 日本輸出入銀行

KKR Hotel Tokyo KKRホテルトウキョウ

Marubeni (H.O.) 丸紅本社

Mainichi Newspapers 毎日新聞社

TAKEBASHI 竹橋

Meteorological Agency 気象庁

Common Gov't Bldgs 合同庁舎

NO.2

NO.3

Tokyo Immigration Bureau NO.1 ☎ 東京入国管理局

Govt Publication Service Center 政府刊行物サービスセンター

Tokyo Fire Dept 東京消防庁

Marunouchi Fire Sta. 丸の内消防署

Coop Bldg コープビル

Japan Development Bank 日本開発銀行

Federation of Economic Orgs 経団連

Koko Bldg 公庫ビル

KDD Ōtemachi Bldg KDD大手町ビル

Yomiuri Newspapers 読売新聞

Nihon Keizai Newspapers 日本経済新聞社

Nikkei Hall 日経ホール

Time-Life Bldg タイムライフビル

Chiyoda Ward Gen'l Bldg 千代田区総合庁舎

Chiyoda Ward Gym.

Nikkō Shukin Bank 日興證券

Norin Chukin Bank 農林中金

JA Bldg JAビル

Nōkyō Hall 農協ホール

Sankei Newspapers 産業経済新聞社

Sankei Kaikan (hall) サンケイ会館

SOTOBORI DŌRI (AVE.)

HEITAI DŌRI (AVE.)

Mitsui Mutual Life Insurance 三井生命本社

Ōtemachi 大手町 Ｉ丁目

Long-Term Credit Bank of Japan 日本長期信用銀行

Mitsui Bussan Bldg 三井物産ビル

Hill of Masakado's Head (Masakado Kubizuka) 将門塚

Asahi Bank (H.O.) あさひ銀行本店

Maruha (H.O.) マルハ本社

Ōte Center Bldg 大手センタービル

IBM Info. Sci. Musm IBM情報科学館

Sanwa Bank 三和銀行

NKK Bldg NKKビル

Ōtemachi First Square 大手町ファーストスクエア

CDP Bldg CDPビル

Otemachi Nomura Bldg 大手町野村ビル

Ōtemachi Bldg 大手町ビル

Fuji Bank (H.O.) 富士銀行本店

Ōtemachi Financial Center 大手町フィナンシャルセンター

Bank of Tokyo-Mitsubishi (H.O.) 東京三菱銀行本店

Daiwa Bank 大和銀行

Tōyō Trust 東洋信託

Sumitomo Trust 住友信託

Sumitomo Bank (H.O.) 住友銀行本店

Industrial Bank of Japan 日本興業銀行

Bank Hall 銀行会館

Bank Club

Firaki Bldg

Marunouchi Hotel 丸の内ホテル

Marunouchi Center Bldg 丸の内センタービル

New Ōtemachi Bldg 新大手町ビル

NTT Marunouchi Bldg NTT丸の内ビル

Urbannet New Ōtemachi Bldg アーバンネット新大手町ビル

NTT Date Ōtemachi Bldg NTTデータ大手町ビル

Ōtemachi NTT Bldg 大手町NTTビル

Tokyo International P.O. 東京国際郵便局

Postal Services Bureau 郵政事業庁

Postal Inspection Bureau 関東郵政監察局

Communications Musm 逓信総合博物館

HANZOMON LINE

UCHIBO LINE, SOBU LINE

SOTOBO LINE, SOBU LINE

Ōtemachi (2) 大手町 ２丁目

Nihombashi-Hongokuchō 日本橋本石町

Tokiwa E.Sch. 常盤小

Shin-Tokiwa-bashi (Br.) 新常盤橋

Tokiwa-bashi (Br.) 常盤橋

Tokiwabashi Park 常盤橋公園

Bank of Japan (Nippon Ginko) (H.O.) 日本銀行本店

Nippon Steel Corp. (H.O.) 新日本製鐵本社

Daiwa Securities 大和証券

Nippon Bldg 日本ビル

Tokai Bank 東海銀行

EDO DŌRI (AVE.) 江戸通り

34

C

D

JTB 日本交通公社

Palace Hotel

Varig Airlines ヴァリグ・ブラジル航空

Egypt Air エジプト航空

Chiyoda 千代田

Eastern Garden of the Imperial Palace 皇居東御苑

Hosp. of Imperial Household Agency 宮内庁病院

Imperial Guard Sch. 皇宮警察学校

Imperial Guard HQ. 皇宮警察本部

Site of Edo Castle 江戸城跡

Cabinet Library (Naikaku Bunko) 内閣文庫

Ōteman 大手門

Ote-bori (moat) 大手濠

Kikyo-bori (moat) 桔梗濠

(H) Ryumeikan 竜名館

Fukuoka City Bank 福岡銀行 博多銀行

Yaesu (1) 八重洲 1丁目

Bank of Osaka 大阪銀行

Tekkō Bldg 鉄鋼ビル

Hotel Kokusai Kankō ホテル国際観光

Kokusai Kankō Kaikan 国際観光会館

(H)

Yaesu North Entrance 八重洲北口

Daimaru Dept.Store 大丸デパート

Taeguchi Kaikan (hall) 八重洲口会館

Yaesu Central Entrance 八重洲中央口

Yaesu Bldg 八重洲ビル

Yaesu South Entrance 八重洲南口

YAESU UNDERGROUND ARCADE 八重洲地下街

Yanmar Bldg ヤンマービル

Kyōbashi (1) 京橋 1丁目

Tokyo Tatemono Bldg 東京建物ビル

Dai-Ichi Kangyo Bank 第一勧銀

Yaesu Dai Bldg 八重洲ダイビル

Daiō E.Sch. 大岡山

Sumitomo Trust 住友信託

Yaesu Bldg (H.O.) 八重洲ビル

Kyō Bldg 京ビル

Kyōbashi (2) 京橋 2丁目

Kyōbashi Chiyoda Bldg 京橋千代田ビル

Meiji Seika 明治製菓

Kyōbashi Dai-Ichi Seimei Bldg 京橋第一生命ビル

CHUO-KU 中央区

Yaesu Book Center 八重洲ブックセンター

Yaesu (2) 八重洲 2丁目

Yaesu Mitsui Bldg 八重洲三井ビル

Yaesu Fuya Hotel 八重洲富士屋ホテル

Nittobō 日清紡

(H)

Shoko Chukin Bank (H.O.) 商工組合中央金庫(本店)

KEIYŌ LINE 京葉線

TOKYO STATION 東京駅

KEIHIN-TOHOKU LINE

CHUO LINE 中央線

TOKAIDO LINE

TOKAIDO SHINKANSEN 東海道新幹線

SHONAN LINE

Bus Terminal バスターミナル

Marunouchi North Entrance 丸の内北口

Marunouchi Bldg 丸の内ビル

Station Bldg ステーションビル

Tokyo Station Hotel 東京ステーションホテル

Marunouchi Central Entrance 丸の内中央口

(H)

Marunouchi South Entrance 丸の内南口

TOKYO STATION (Underground) 東京駅(地下)

YAMANOTE LINE 山手線

TOKYO STATION 東京駅

Bus Terminal バスターミナル

Tokyo Central Post Office 東京中央郵便局

Marunouchi (2) 丸の内 2丁目

Tokyo Bldg 東京ビル

Bank of Tokyo Mitsubishi (H.O.) 東京三菱銀行本店

Tokyo Int'l Forum 東京国際フォーラム

Marunouchi (1) 丸の内 1丁目

Tokyo Kaijō Bldg 東京海上ビル

New Marunouchi Bldg 新丸の内ビル

Yūsen Bldg 郵船ビル

Mitsubishi Shōji Bldg 三菱商事ビル

Mitsubishi Bldg 三菱ビル

Mitsui Bldg 三井ビル

Mitsubishi Heavy Industries Bldg 三菱重工ビル

Mitsubishi Electric Bldg 三菱電機ビル

Marunouchi Yaesu Bldg 丸の内八重洲ビル

Mitsubishi Shōji Bldg 三菱商事ビル

Banque Nationale de Paris パリ国立銀行

Chemical Bank ケミカル銀行

Bankers Trust バンカース・トラスト

Kishimoto Bldg 岸本ビル

Chiyoda Bldg 千代田ビル

Hongkong & Shanghai Bank 香港上海銀行

Furukawa Sōgō Bldg 古河総合ビル

Tokyo Bldg 東京ビル

Bank of Tokyo Mitsubishi 東京三菱銀行

YOKOSUKA LINE

Korean Air 大韓航空

Marunouchi (3) 丸の内 3丁目

Meiji Seimei Bldg 明治生命ビル

Tokyo Chamber of Commerce & Industry 東京商工会議所

Tokyo Kaikan 東京会館

Fuji Bldg 富士ビル

New Tokyo Bldg 新東京ビル

Shun Nisseki Bldg 新日石ビル

New Kokusai Bldg 新国際ビル

CHIYODA-KU 千代田区

Commemorative Fountain

Wadakura-mon 和田倉門

Kokusai Bldg 国際ビル

Idemitsu Art Gallery (9F)出光美術館

Imperial Theater (Teikoku Gekijō) 帝国劇場

Dai-Ichi Seimei Bldg 第一生命ビル

TOEI MITA LINE 都営三田線

Babasaki-bori (moat) 馬場先濠

Imperial Palace Outer Garden 皇居外苑

Babasaki-mon 馬場先門

Hibiya-bori (moat) 日比谷濠

Bronze Statue of Masashige Kusunoki 楠木正成像

UCHIBORI DORI (AVE.) 内堀通り

HIBIYA-CHO LINE 日比谷線

Ginza, Yūrakuchō
銀座　　　有楽町

1:6,000

300m

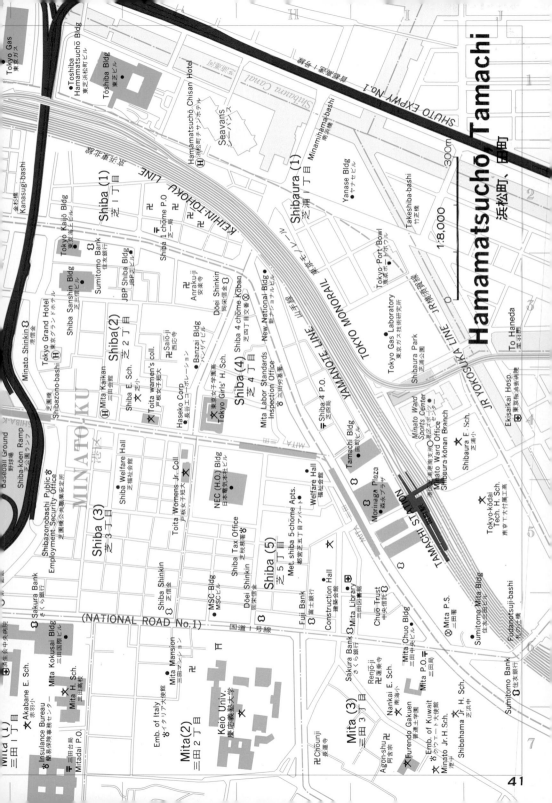

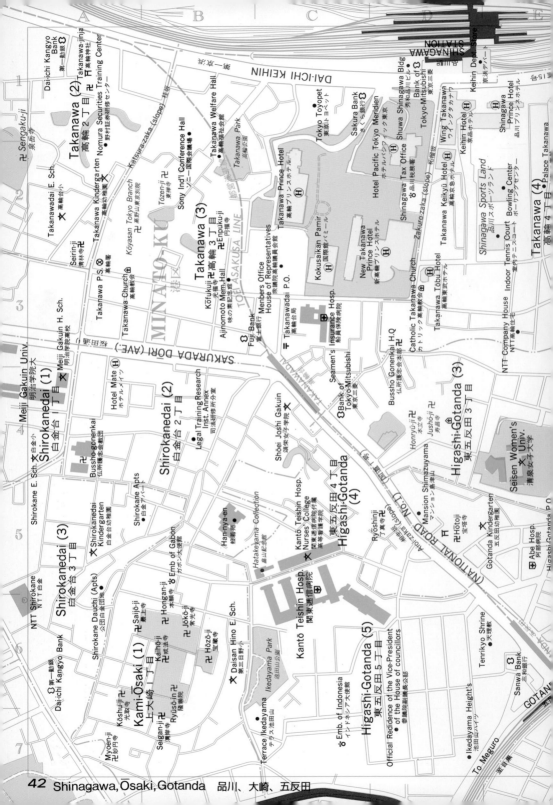

SHINAGAWA STATION
品川駅

Keihin Dept. Store
京急デパート

A B C D E

Dai-ichi Kangyo Bank 第一勧業銀行

Takanawa-jinja 高輪神社

Nomura Securities Training Center 野村証券研修センター

Takanawa (2) 高輪2丁目

Sengaku-ji 卍 泉岳寺

DAI-ICHI KEIHIN

Takanawadai/E. Sch. 高輪台小

Takanawadai/E. Sch. 高輪台小

Katsura-zaka (slope) 桂坂

Takanawa Kindergarten 高輪幼稚園

Kōyasan Tokyo Branch 卍 高野山東京別院

Seirin-ji 卍 清林寺

Tōzen-ji 卍 東禅寺

Takanawa Welfare Hall 高輪福祉会館

Tokyo Toyopet 東京トヨペット

Sakura Bank さくら銀行

Hotel Pacific Tokyo Meridien ホテルパシフィック東京

Shuwa Shinagawa Bldg 秀和品川ビル

Tokyo-Mitsubishi 東京三菱

Bank of 東京三菱銀行

Keihin Hotel H 京品ホテル

Wing Takanawa ウイング高輪

Shinagawa Prince Hotel 品川プリンスホテル

Takanawa (3) 高輪3丁目

Sony Int'l Conference Hall ソニー国際会議場

Takanawa Park 高輪公園

Takanawa Prince Hotel 高輪プリンスホテル

New Takanawa Prince Hotel 新高輪プリンスホテル

Zakurozaka (slope) 石榴坂

Takanawa Keikyū Hotel H 高輪京急ホテル

Takanawa Tōbu Hotel H 高輪東武ホテル

Shinagawa Sports Land 品川スポーツランド

Indoor Tennis Court 室内テニスコート

Bowling Center ボーリングセンター

Takanawa (4) 高輪4丁目

Palace Takanawa パレス高輪

MINATO-KU 港区

Takanawa P.S. 高輪警察署

Takanawa Church 高輪教会

Kōfuku-ji 卍 光福寺

Enpuku-ji 卍 円福寺

Ajinomoto Mem. Hall 味の素記念館

Fuji Bank 富士銀行

Members Office House of Representatives 衆議院議員会館

Takanawadai P.O. 高輪台局

Kokusaikan Pamir H 国際館パミール

Catholic Takanawa Church カトリック高輪教会

NTT Company House NTT高輪住宅

Seamen's Insurance Hosp. 船員保険病院

Bussho Gonenkai H.Q 仏所護念会本部

Bank of Tokyo-Mitsubishi 東京三菱

Meiji Gakuin Univ. 明治学院大

Shirokanedai E. Sch. 白金台小

Meiji Gakuin H. Sch. 明治学院高校

Shirokanedai (1) 白金台1丁目

Hotel Mate H ホテルメイ

Shirokanedai (2) 白金台2丁目

Legal Training Research Inst. Annex 司法研修所分室

Shōei Joshi Gakuin 頌栄女子学院

Higashi-Gotanda (3) 東五反田3丁目

Seisen Women's Univ. 清泉女子大学

SAKURADA DORI (AVE) 桜田通り

Shirokane E. Sch. 白金小

NTT Shirokane NTT白金

Dai-ichi Kangyo Bank 第一勧業銀行

Bussho-gonenkai 仏所護念会数団

Shirokanedai Kindergarten 白金台幼稚園

Shirokanedai Dauchi (Apts) 公園白金住宅

Shirokanedai Apts 白金台アパート

Han-nya-en 般若苑

Hatakeyama Collection 畠山記念館

Ryōshinji 卍 了真寺

Kantō Teishin Hosp. Nurses' College 関東逓信病院付属高等看護学院

Higashi-Gotanda (4) 東五反田4丁目

Mansion Shimazuyama マンション島津山

Jushō-ji 卍 寿昌寺

Honryū-ji 卍 本立寺

Arizaka (slope) 有坂

NATIONAL ROAD NO.1 (国道第1号)

Higashi-Gotanda (3) 東五反田3丁目

Gotanda Kindergarten 五反田幼稚園

Hōtoji 卍 宝塔寺

Abe Hosp. 阿部病院

Shirokanedai (3) 白金台3丁目

Shirokanedai (Apts) 白金台団地

Kami-Ōsaki (1) 上大崎1丁目

Kōshū-ji 卍 高秀寺

Seigan-ji 卍 清岸寺

Ryūsō-in 卍 隆崇院

Saijō-ji 卍 最上寺

Kaihō-ji 卍 開法寺

Hongan-ji 卍 本願寺

Jōkō-ji 卍 常光寺

Hōzō-ji 卍 宝蔵寺

Daisan Hino E./Sch. 第三日野小

Ikedayama Park 池田山公園

Higashi-Gotanda (5) 東五反田5丁目

Kantō Teishin Hosp. 関東逓信病院

Myōen-ji 卍 妙円寺

Terrace Ikedayama テラス池田山

Emb. of Indonesia インドネシア大使館

Official Residence of the Vice-President of the House of Councillors 参議院副議長公邸

Ikedayama Height's 池田山ハイツ

Tenrikyo Shrine 天理教

Sanwa Bank 三和銀行

Tenrikyo 天理教

GOTAN

To Meguro 至目黒

42 Shinagawa, Ōsaki, Gotanda 品川、大崎、五反田

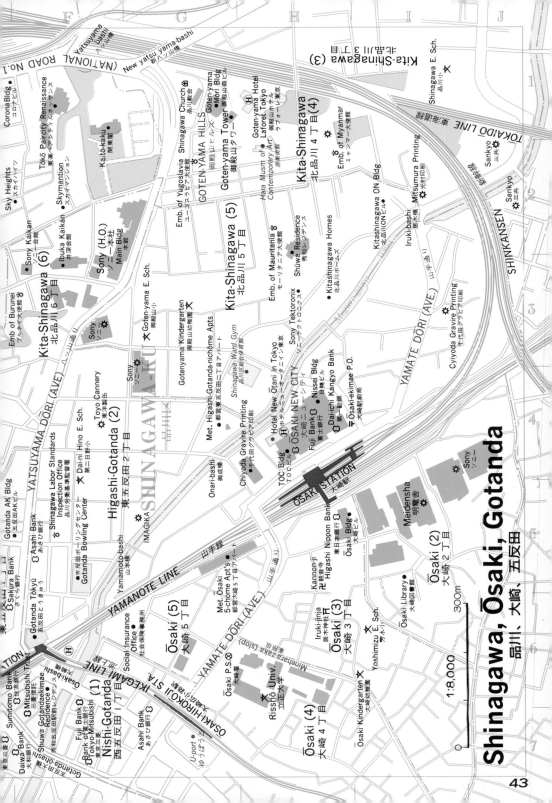

Yotsuya, Ichigaya
四谷、市谷

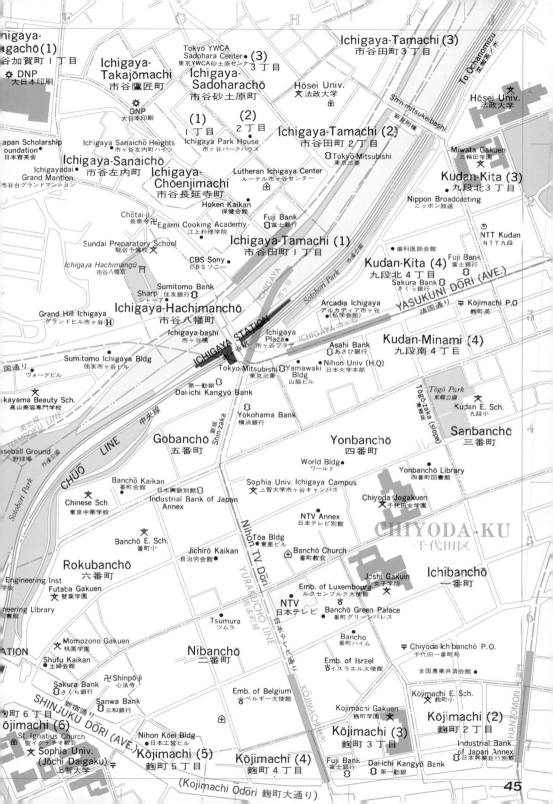

Ichigaya-Kagachō (1)
市谷加賀町 I 丁目
◆ DNP
大日本印刷

Ichigaya-
Takajōmachi
市谷鷹匠町
DNP
大日本印刷

Japan Scholarship
Foundation ●
日本育英会

Ichigaya-Sanaichō
市谷左内町
Ichigayadai
Grand Mantion
市谷台グランドマンション

Ichigaya Sanaichō Heights
市谷左内町ハイツ

Ichigaya-
Sadoharachō
市谷砂土原町

Tokyo YWCA
Sadohara Center (3)
東京YWCA砂土原センター 3 丁目

(1)
I 丁目

(2)
2 丁目

Ichigaya Park House
市ヶ谷パークハウス

Ichigaya-Tamachi (3)
市谷田町 3 丁目

Hōsei Univ.
法政大学

Shin-mitsuke-bashi
新見附橋

To Ochanomizu
御茶ノ水へ

Hōsei Univ.
法政大学

Ichigaya-Tamachi (2)
市谷田町 2 丁目

Tokyo-Mitsubishi
東京三菱

Miwata Gakuen
三輪田学園

Kudan-Kita (3)
九段北 3 丁目

Nippon Broadcasting
ニッポン放送

Ichigaya-
Chōenjimachi
市谷長延寺町

Lutheran Ichigaya Center
ルーテル市ヶ谷センター

Chōtai-ji
長泰寺

Hoken Kaikan
保健会館

Egami Cooking Academy
江上料理学院

Fuji Bank
富士銀行

Ichigaya-Tamachi (1)
市谷田町 I 丁目

NTT Kudan
NTT九段

Kudan-Kita (4)
九段北 4 丁目

歯科医師会館

Fuji Bank
富士銀行

Sakura Bank
さくら銀行

Sundai Preparatory School
駿台予備校

CBS Sony
CBSソニー

YASUKUNI DŌRI (AVE.)

Kōjimachi P.O.
麹町局

Ichigaya Hachimangū
市谷八幡宮

Sumitomo Bank
住友銀行

Sharp
シャープ

Arcadia Ichigaya
アルカディア市ヶ谷
(私学会館)

Kudan-Minami (4)
九段南 4 丁目

Grand Hill Ichigaya
グランドヒル市谷 Ⓗ

Ichigaya-Hachimanchō
市谷八幡町

Ichigaya-bashi
市ヶ谷橋

Ichigaya
Plaza
市ヶ谷プラザ

Asahi Bank
あさひ銀行

Togō Park
東郷公園

Kudan E. Sch.
九段小

Sanbanchō
三番町

Sumitomo Ichigaya Bldg
住友市ヶ谷ビル

国通り

Vogue Bldg
ヴォーグビル

ICHIGAYA STATION

Tokyo-Mitsubishi
東京三菱

Dai-ichi Kangyō Bank
第一勧銀

Yamawaki
Bldg
山脇ビル

Nihon Univ. (H.Q)
日本大学本部

Togō-zaka (slope)
東郷坂

Kayama Beauty Sch.
高山美容専門学校

CHUO LINE
中央線

Shin-zaka
新坂

Yokohama Bank
横浜銀行

Baseball Ground
野球場

Gobanchō
五番町

Yonbanchō
四番町

World Bldg
ワールド

Yonbanchō Library
四番町図書館

NAMBOKU LINE

Sotobori Park
外濠公園

Bancho Kaikan
番町会館

日本興銀別館

Sophia Univ. Ichigaya Campus
上智大学市ヶ谷キャンパス

Chiyoda Jogakuen
千代田女学園

Chinese Sch.
東京中華学校

Industrial Bank of Japan
Annex

NTV Annex
日本テレビ別館

CHIYODA-KU
千代田区

Bancho E. Sch.
番町小

Jichirō Kaikan
自治労会館

Tōa Bldg
東亜ビル

Bancho Church
番町教会

Rokubanchō
六番町

Engineering Inst

Futaba Gakuen
雙葉学園

neering Library

Nihon TV Dōri

Joshi Gakuin
女子学院

Ichibanchō
一番町

Emb. of Luxembourg
ルクセンブルク大使館

NTV
日本テレビ

Bancho Green Palace
番町グリーンパレス

Tsumura
ツムラ

Momozono Gakuen
桃園学園

STATION

Shufu Kaikan
主婦会館

Shinpō-ji
心法寺

Sakura Bank
さくら銀行

Sanwa Bank
三和銀行

Nibanchō
二番町

Bancho
番町ハイム

Emb. of Israel
イスラエル大使館

Chiyoda-Ichibanchō P.O.
千代田一番町局

全国農業共済会館

Kōjimachi E. Sch.
麹町小

Kōjimachi (2)
麹町 2 丁目

SHINJUKU DŌRI (AVE.)
新宿通り

麹町 6 丁目

ōjimachi (5)

St. Ignatius Church
聖イグナチオ教会

Sophia Univ.
(Jōchi Daigaku)
上智大学

Nihon Kōei Bldg
日本工営ビル

Kōjimachi (5)
麹町 5 丁目

Emb. of Belgium
ベルギー大使館

Kōjimachi (4)
麹町 4 丁目

Kōjimachi Gakuen
麹町学園

Kōjimachi (3)
麹町 3 丁目

Fuji Bank
富士銀行

Dai-ichi Kangyo Bank
第一勧銀

Industrial Bank
of Japan Annex
日本興業銀行別館

(Kōjimachi Ōdōri) 麹町大通り

(5)
Kōsai Kaikan
弘済会館
(4)
Sophia (Jōchi) Univ.
上智大学

Kōjimachi Dai Bldg
麹町ダイビル

Shuwa TBR Bldg
秀和TBRビル

Fukudaya, Japanese Restaurant
福田家

Kōjimachi
麹町
(3)

Wacoal Kōjimachi Bldg
ワコール麹町ビル
(2)
(1)

FM Tok
エフエム東京

Hanzōmon Kaik
半蔵門会

Kioichō Bldg
紀尾井町ビル

Bungeishunju
文芸春秋

Park Bldg
パークビル

(1)

Hirakawa Tenjin
平河天神

Hirakawachō
平河町

Hayabusac
隼町

Nat'l
Theat
国立劇

Kioichō
紀尾井町

Shimizudani Park
清水谷公園

Kōjimachi Kaikan
麹町会館

Nihon Toshi Center
日本都市センター

(2)

Hōchi Newspaper
報知新聞

Engei Hall
演芸場

Hotel New Ōtani
ホテルニューオータニ

Nihon Toshi Center Hall
日本都市センターホール

Zenkyōren Bldg
全共連ビル

Supr
最

Hotel New Ōtani Tower
ホテルニューオータニタワー

Kōjimachi Jr.H.Sch.
麹町中

Japan Junior Chamber
日本青年会議所

New Ōtani Garden Court
ニューオータニガーデンコート

Guest House
旧館

Akasaka Prince Hotel
赤坂プリンスホテル

Sabō-kaikan Hall
砂防会館ホール

Sabō Kaikan
砂防会館

Miyakezaka
三宅坂イン

Tower
新館

Benkei-bashi
井慶橋

Metropolitan District Hall
(To-do-fu-ken Kaikan)
都道府県会館

Towns & Villages Kaikan
全国町村会館

首都高速4号線

IBM

Liberal-Democratic Party
H.Q
自由民主党本部

SHUTO EXPWY NO. 4

Maeda Surgery Hosp
前田外科医院

Akasaka-mituke
赤坂見附

NAGATACHŌ 永田町

Official Residence of the Speaker of the House of Representatives
衆議院議長公邸

Official Residence of the President of the House of Councillors
参議院議長公邸

Embs of Lebanon, Jordan
レバノン、ヨルダン大使館

Members' Office
House of Councillors
参議院議員会館

Moto-Akasaka
元赤坂

Suntory Bldg
サントリービル

Suntory Mus. of Art
サントリー美術館

Kajima Bldg
鹿島ビル

AIU Akasaka Bldg
AIU赤坂ビル

Belle Vie Akasaka
ベルビー赤坂

Akasaka Tokyu Hotel
赤坂東急ホテル

Emb. of Mexico
メキシコ大使館

Nagatachō
永田町

(2)
(1)

Akasaka Center Bldg
赤坂センタービル

Toyokawa Inari
豊川稲荷

Fuji Bank
富士

Sannō Grand Bldg
山王グランドビル

Hibiya H. Sch.
日比谷高校

Bldg two Members' Office
House of Representa
衆議院第二議員会館

Aoyama-fudōson
赤坂不動尊

Continental Airlines
コンチネンタル航空

Philippine Airlines
フィリピン航空

AOYAMA DŌRI (AVE.) 青山通り

(3)

HITOTSUGI DŌRI

Toraya
虎屋

Akasaka Police Sta.
赤坂署

Sumitomo Seimei
Akasaka Bldg
住友生命赤坂ビル

Hie Jinja (shrine)
日枝神社

Bldg one Members' Office
House of Representa
衆議院第一議員会館

Akasaka Public Hall
赤坂公会堂

Kokusai Sannō Bldg
国際山王ビル

(4)

Jōdo-ji
浄土寺

MINATO-KU
港区

Yamawaki Gakuen (Sch.)
山脇学園

Capitol Tokyo Hotel
キャピトル東急ホテル

Jōgen-ji
浄玄寺

Sannō Hanten
山王飯店

Science Bldg
サイエンスビル

Nippon Colombia
日本コロムビア

Akasaka
赤坂

Sanyō Akasaka Bldg
サンヨー赤坂ビル

Sannōshita
山王下

Prime Minis
Official Resid
首相官

TBS Kaikan
TBS会館

TBS Hall
TBSホール

Yachiyo Bldg
八千代ビル

Entsu-ji
円通寺

Gadelius Bldg
ガデリウスビル

Minato Shinkin Bank (H.O.)
港信金(本店)

East Bldg 東館

Kokusai Shin Akasaka Bldgs
国際新赤坂ビル

Kokusai Akasaka Bldg
国際赤坂ビル

Tokyo Isuzu Motor
東京いすゞ

Sabena Airlines
サベナ航空

Green Park Akasaka
グリーンパーク赤坂

West Bldg 西館

Nisshō Iwai
日商岩井

Akasaka Shanpia Hotel
赤坂シャンピアホテル

TBS Broadcasting Center
TBS放送センター

Toshiba EM
東芝EM

Komatsu Bldg
小松ビル

GINZA LINE

KOKKAI-GIJIDO

Nagatachō, Kasumigaseki
永田町　霞が関

1:8,000

300m

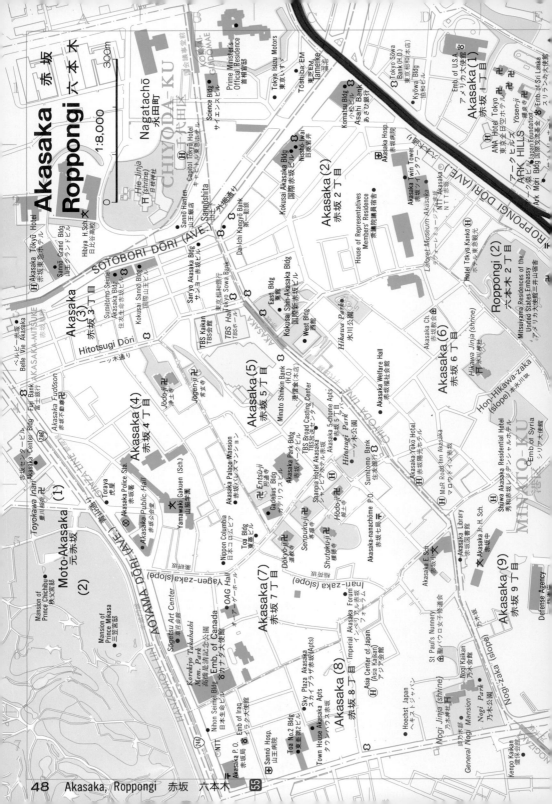

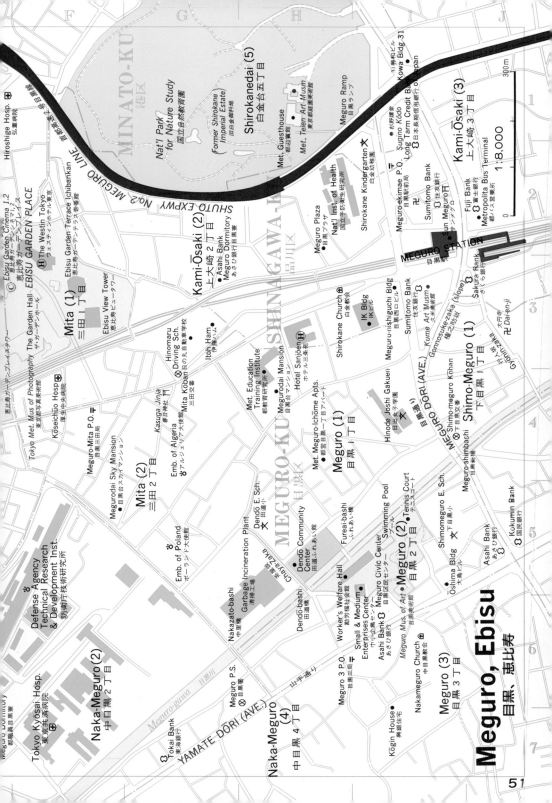

Kamiyamachō
神山町

PL Hosp.
PL病院

Shibuya Creston Hotel
渋谷クレストンホテル

Kyōdō Bldg
共同ビル

Shibuya Video Studio
渋谷ビデオスタジオ

Kanze Noh Theater
観世能楽堂

Toguri Mus. of Art
戸栗美術館

Shōtō Jr. H. Sch.
松濤中

Shōtō (1)
松濤 I 丁目

Official Residence,
Governor of Tokyo
東京都知事公館

Bunkamura
東急文化村

Orchard Hall (3F)
オーチャードホール
The Museum
ザ・ミュージアム

Shōtō P.O.
松濤局

Shōtō Art Musm
松濤美術館

SAKAE DŌRI (AVE.)
栄通り

Sakaedōri Danchi (Apts)
栄通り団地

Kokusai Bunka Barber
& Beauty Coll.
国際文化理容美容専門学校

Maruyamachō
円山町

INOKASHIRA LINE
井の頭線

SHINSEN STA.
神泉駅

Shinsenchō
神泉町

Myōhō-ji
妙法寺

To Sangenjaya

Tokyo Gas
東京ガス

NHK Broadcasting Center
N H K放送センター

Jinnan (2)
神南 2 丁目

Shibuya Tax Office
渋谷税務署

Legal Affairs
法務局(出)

Shibuya Health Center
渋谷保健所

Shibuya Public Hall
渋谷公会堂

Shibuya Ward Office
渋谷区役所

Shibuya Homes
渋谷ホームズ

Jinnan E. Sch.
神南小

Tōbu Hotel
東武ホテル

Parco Part II
パルコパート 2

Jinnan Bldg
神南ビル

Tobacco & Salt
たばこと塩の博物館

Jinnan
神南

Workers' Welfare
勤労福祉会

Shibuya Parco Store
渋谷パルコ

Tōkyū Hands
東急ハンズ

Parco Part III
パルコパート 3

Parco Theater
パルコ劇場

Yamate Ch.
山手教会

Marui
Main
丸井本

Udagawachō
宇田川町

Quattro by Parco

Tokyo Tomin Bank
東京都民銀行

ONE-OH-NINE 30S

Seibu Dept Store
西武デパート(シー
Seibu Dept. Store
(SEED Bldg)
Joypack Bldg
ジョイパックビル

Seibu Dept Store
(Loft Bldg)
西武デパートロフト館

Palace P.
パレス座

(C)

(B Bldg)
B 館

BUNKAMURA DŌRI (AVE.)
文化村通り

Sakura Bank
さくら銀行

Manyō Kaikan
万葉会館

西武デパ
Seibu Dept S

Tōkyū Dept Store
(main store)
東急デパート(本店)

Center-gai
センター街

Shibuya Takarazuka
渋谷宝塚

Dai-ichi Kangyō Bank
第一勧銀

Tōkai Bank
東海銀行

Dōgenzaka (2)
道玄坂 2 丁目

109 Fashion
Community

The Prime
ザ・プライム

Dogenzaka Center Bldg
道玄坂センタービル

(C)

Ekimae Bldg
駅前ビル

Daiwa Bank
大和銀行

SHIB

Statue of Dog Ha

Yachiyo Bank
八千代銀行

Interior Imon
インテリア井門

Shibutō Cinetower
渋東シネタワー

Tōkyū D
東急東横店
Sto

SHIBUYA STA.
渋谷駅

DŌGEN-ZAKA (SLOPE)
道玄坂

Noa Dōgenzaka
ノア道玄坂

Kita Nippon Bank
北日本銀行

Shin Taiso Bldg
新大宗ビル

Ekimae Kaikan
駅前会館

三菱ビル
Mitsubishi Bldg

Tōkyū Plaza
東急プラザ

Tram Depot
電車

Dōgenzaka (1)
道玄坂 I 丁目

Dōgenzaka P.O.
道玄坂局

SHUTO EXPWY No.3

Hotel P & A Plaza
ホテルP & Aプラザ

Suruga Bank
駿河銀行

Tōkyū Bldg
東急ビル

TAMAGAWA DŌRI (AVE.)
玉川通り

Hotel Sunroute Shibuya
ホテルサンルート渋谷

Japan Tobacco
(Nihon Tobacco)
日本たばこ

Shibuya Ramp
渋谷ランプ

Nanpeidaichō
南平台町

Ōwada Hosp.
大和田病院

Hill Port
ヒルポート

Sakuragaoka

SHIN-TAMAGAWA LINE

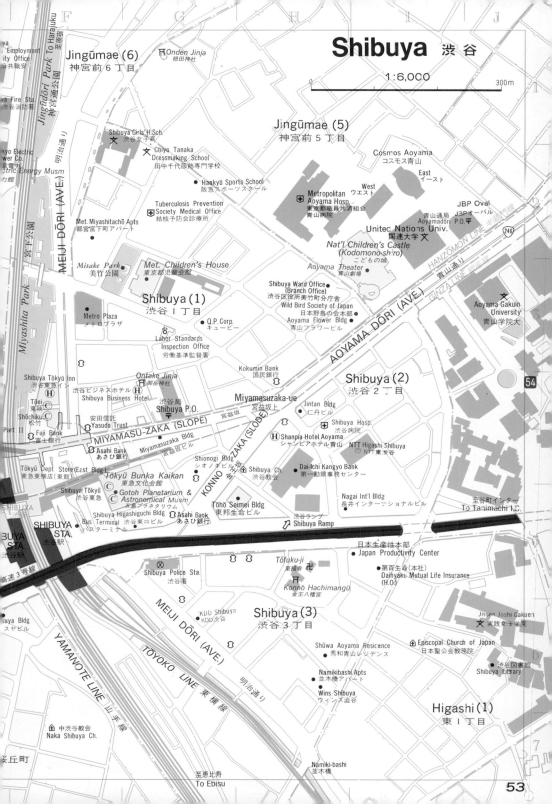

Meiji Jingū (shrine)
明治神宮

HARAJUKU STATION
原宿駅

TAKESHITA DŌRI
竹下通り

☆ Yoyogi Seminar
代々木ゼミナール(分校)

● Seichōno-ie
生長の家

Tōgō Jinja (shrine)
東郷神社

● Tōgō Mem. Hall
東郷記念館

● Boutique Kansai
ブティック寛斎

Rehabilitation Center for the Mentally and
Physically Handicapped
心身障害者福祉センター

● Harajuku Danchi (Apts)
原宿団地

Myōen-ji 卍
妙円寺

Chōar 卍
長寿

FLAG

Palais France
パレフランス

Jingūmae (1)
神宮前1丁目

Jingūmae (3)
神宮前3丁目

☆ Harajuku Jr. H. Sch.
原宿中

原宿クエスト
Harajuku Quest

Ota Mem. Mus. of Art
太田記念美術館

Kokumin Bank
国民銀行

Laforet Harajuku
ラフォーレ原宿

Tin Toy Musm
おもちゃの博物館

● Japan Int'l Sch.
ジャパン インターナショナル スクール

Jingūmae (4)
神宮前4丁目

● Corp Olympia
コープ オリンピア

卍 Jingumae
神宮前

駐車場

MEIJI DŌRI (AVE.) 明治通り

Kyū Shibuya River Promenade
旧渋谷川遊歩道

Nat'l
Gymnasium
国立競技場

Harajuku Tower Height
原宿タワーハイツ

Emb. of Portugal
ポルトガル大使館

OMOTE SANDŌ (AVE.)

Jingūmae E. Sch.
☆ 神宮前小

● Omote-Sandō City House
表参道シティハウス

Kita-Aoyama
北青山3丁

Harajuku-ekimae P.O.
原宿駅前局

Kiddy Land
キディランド

Dōjunkai Aoyama Apts
同潤会青山アパート

● Tokyo Central Bldg
東京セントラルビル

Jingūmae (6)
神宮前6丁目

Jingubashi Bldg
神宮橋ビル

VIVRE 21

Oriental Bazaar
オリエンタルバザール

✚ Itō Hosp.
伊藤病院

Zenkō-ji 卍
善光寺

Kirin Brewery (H.O.)
キリンビール(本社)

Nurse's Agency
看護協会

Kyōcera Bldg
京セラビル

Tokyo Union Ch.
東京ユニオン教会

Cafe des Pre's

卍 Chōsen-ji
長泉寺

Corp Inn Shibuya
コープイン渋谷

Kyū Shibuya River Promenade
旧渋谷川遊歩道

● Tenriism Shrine
天理教教会

Hanae Mori Bldg
ハナエモリビル

Fuji Bank
富士銀行

Kishi Mem.
Hall
岸記念体育会館

卍 Onden Jinja
穏田神社

Jingūmae (5)
神宮前5丁目

Kita-Aoyama Hosp.
北青山病院

Natural House
ナチュラルハウス

Sanwa
三和

SHIBUYA-KU
渋谷区

Spiral
(Wacoal Aoyama Bl
スパイラル
(ワコール青山ビ

Jingūdōri Park
神宮通公園

Shibuya Girls' H. Sch.
渋谷女子高

Cosmos Aoyama
コスモス青山

Kinokuniya International
紀ノ国屋

MEIJI DŌRI (AVE.) 明治通り

☆ Chiyo Tanaka Dressmaking Sch.
東京田中千代服飾専門学校

Aoyama Book Center
青山ブックセンター

Aoyama 5-chome
青山五丁目

Max Mara

Met. Aoyama Hosp.
✚ 東京都職員共済組合青山病院

JBP Oval
JBPオーバル

Miyashita Park
宮下公園

Tokyo Met.
Children's House
東京都児童会館

Nat'l Children's Castle
(Kodomono-shiro)
こどもの城

Aoyama Theater
青山劇場

United Nations Univ.
国連大学 ☆

Aoyamadōri P.O.
青山通局

Ohara Bldg
小原ビル

☆ Shibuya E. Sch.
渋谷小

Gymnasium
体育館

Chateau 1
シャトー

Metro Plaza
メトロプラザ

Shibuya (1)
渋谷1丁目

Aogaku Kaikan Hall
青学会館

52

YAMANOTE LINE 山手線

Ontake Jinja
卍 御嶽神社

Kokumin
国民銀行

HANZOMON LINE

Aoyama Gakuin University
青山学院大学

Shibuya Tōkyū Inn
渋谷東急イン

Shibuya P.O.
渋谷局

Miyamasuzaka-ue
宮益坂上

Jintan Bldg
仁丹ビル

☆ Women's Jr. Coll.
女子短大

Fuji Bank
富士銀行

Jōnan Denki
城南電気

Shibuya (2)
渋谷2丁目

Shibuya (4)
渋谷4丁目

☆ Junior H. Sch.
中等部

SHIBUYA STA.
渋谷駅

Asahi Bank
あさひ銀行

Shanpia Hotel Aoyama
シャンピアホテル青山

NTT Higashi Shibuya
NTT東渋谷

High School
高等部

GINZA LINE

Shionogi Bldg
シオノギビル

Tōkyū Bunka Kaikan
東急文化会館

Tōhō Seimei Bldg
東邦生命ビル

Japan Coca-Cola (H.O.)
日本コカコーラ

54 Harajuku, Aoyama　原宿　青山

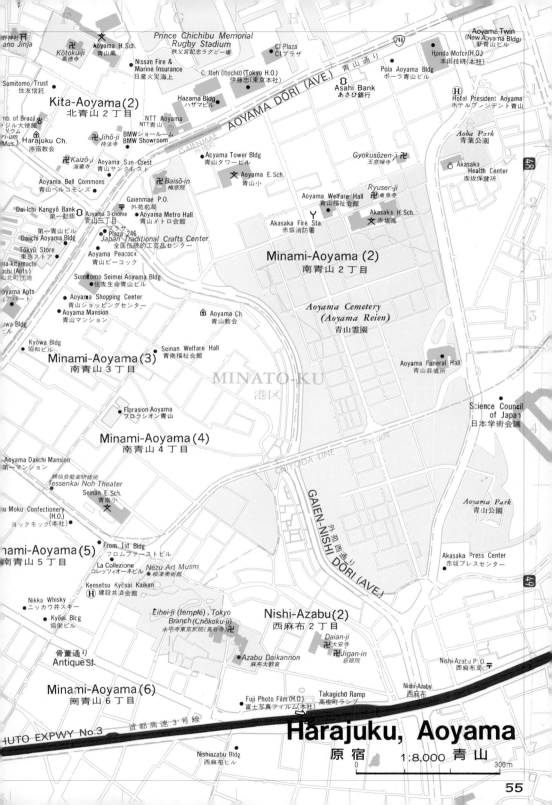

Harajuku, Aoyama
原宿　　1:8,000　　青山

Shinjuku 新宿

Underground Arcade & Passage
地下街と地下道路

✤ Kojimaya Confectionery
小島屋乳業製菓

Kashiwagi Bldg
柏木ビル

Shinjuku Health Center
新宿保健所

Jōon-ji
浄恩寺

Naruko Tenjinsha
成子天神社

☆ Yodobashi Daiichi E. Sch.
淀橋一小

Tokyo Language Center
東京外語専門学校

Shōko Chukin Bank
商工中金

Yamaguchi Bank
山口銀行

Nishi-Shinjuku (8)
西新宿 8 丁目

Yodobashi Daiichi Kindergarten
淀橋第一幼稚園

Nishi-Shinjuku (7)
西新宿 7 丁目

Kashiwagi Park
柏木公園

Tōhō
東邦

Wakashio Bank
わかしお銀行

Tenriism Central Shr.
天理教中央教会

Tokyo Cookery Academy
東京調理師専門学校

Daikan Plaza
ダイカンプラ

Nishi-shinjuku KB Bldg
西新宿KBビル

Hyōgo Bank
兵庫銀行

Rōsai Kaikan (hall)
労済会館

Jōen-ji
常円寺

Star Hotel Tokyo
スターホテル東京

Tokyo
東京

Tokyo Medical College Hospital
東京医科大学病院

Yamagata Shiawase Bank
山形しあわせ銀行

Jōsen-in
常泉院

Nishi-Shinjuku (6)
西新宿 6 丁目

Shinjuku Police Sta.
新宿署

Heiwa Credit Union
平和信組

Shōwa Shinkin
昭和信金

Shinjuku I-Land
新宿アイランド

Shinjuku Nomura Bldg (50Fl)
新宿野村ビル

Yasuda Kasai-Kaijo Bldg (43Fl)
安田火災海上本社ビル

Odakyū Dep.
小田急デ

Tokyo Hilton Int'l
東京ヒルトンインターナショナル

Shinjuku Cookery Scl
新宿調理師専門学校

Free Observatory
無料展望ロビー (50Fl)
Nomura Hall
野村ホール (B1)

Tōgo Seiji Art Museum
東郷青児美術館 (42Fl)

Jōfū-ji
浄風寺

Green Tower Bldg
グリーンタワービル

Shinjuku Kokusai Bldg
新宿国際ビル

Shinjuku i-Land Hall
新宿アイランドホール

Sanwa Bank
三和銀行

Shinjuku L Tower
新宿Lタワー

Shinjuku Water Recycle Center
新宿副都心 水リサイクルセンター

KITA DŌRI (AVE.) 北通り

Shinjuku Mitsui Bldg
新宿三井ビル (55Fl)
Observation Restaurant
展望レストラン (54〜55Fl)

Shinjuku Center Bldg
新宿センタービル (54Fl)
Free Observatory
無料展望台 (53Fl)

Sumitomo Bank
住友銀行

Matsuoka Centra
松岡セントラ

Asahi Mutual Life
Insurance (H.O.)
朝日生命本社ビル/Dai-Ichi
朝日生命・第一

Subaru Bldg
スバルビル

Do Sports Plaza
ドゥスポーツプラザ

Shinjuku Daiichi
Seimei Bldg
新宿第一生命ビル

Shinjuku Sumitomo Bldg
新宿住友ビル (52Fl)
Free Observatory (51Fl)
無料展望台ロビー

Asahi Seimei Hall
朝日生命ホール

Nishi-Shinjuku (1)
西新宿 1 丁目

Hotel Century Hyatt
ホテルセンチュリーハイアット

Asahi Culture Center
朝日カルチャーセンター
Sumitomo Hall (B1)
住友ホール

CHŪŌ DŌRI (AVE.)
中央通り

Nishi-Shinjuku (1)
西新宿 1 丁目

West L
West L

Hiroshima Bank
広島銀行

Shinjuku Bldg
新宿ビル

Fuji Bank
富士銀行

Keio Plaza Hotel (47Fl)
京王プラザホテル

Kōgakuin Univ
工学院大学

S-TEC
Joho Bldg
エステック
情報ビル

Meiji Seimei Bldg
明治生命ビル

Yasuda Seimei Bldg
安田生命ビル

Yasuda Seimei Hall
安田生命ホール

Shinjuku
Central Park
新宿中央公園

Met. Assembly Hall
都議会議事堂

Plaza Dōri

Shinjuku P.O.
新宿局

Hokkaido Bank
北海道銀行

Asa
あき

Keiō Plaza Hotel
(South Tower)
京王プラザホテル南館

Kadoya Hotel
かどやホテル

Highway Bus Terminal
高速バスターミナル

Yodobashi Camera
ヨドバシカメラ Mitsubishi

Nishi-Shinjuku (2)
西新宿 2 丁目
No. 1

Yamanashi Chūō Bank
山梨中央銀行

Tōyō Trust
東洋信託

Metropolitan
Government Office
東京都庁

☐ NTT

San'ei Bldg
サンエービル

Industrial Bank of Japan
興銀

Sakuraya Camera
カメラのさくらや

Shinjuku Monolith
新宿モノリス

Doi Camera
カメラのドイ

People's Finance Corp.
国民金融公庫

Kokusai Dōri
新宿スカイビル

Shinjuku Sky Bldg
新宿スカイビル

No. 2

Meihō Bldg
明宝ビル

Sakura Bank
さくら銀行

Kubo Bl
久保ビ

Shinjuku
NS Bldg (30Fl)
新宿NSビル

KDD Bldg (32Fl)
KDDビル

Taihei Bldg
太平ビル

Fukutoku Bank
福徳銀行

Tokyo Kaijo Bldg
東京海上ビル

Sakakibara Mem.
榊原記念病院

KDD P.O.
KDD内局

Tsunohazu-bashi (Br.) 角筈橋

MINAMI DŌRI (AVE.) 南通り

KEIŌ SHIN-SEN (NEW LINE) 京王新線

KEIŌ LINE
京王線

Hotel Sunr
ホテルサン

Shinjuku Washington Hotel
新宿ワシントンホテル

Yoyogi
代々木

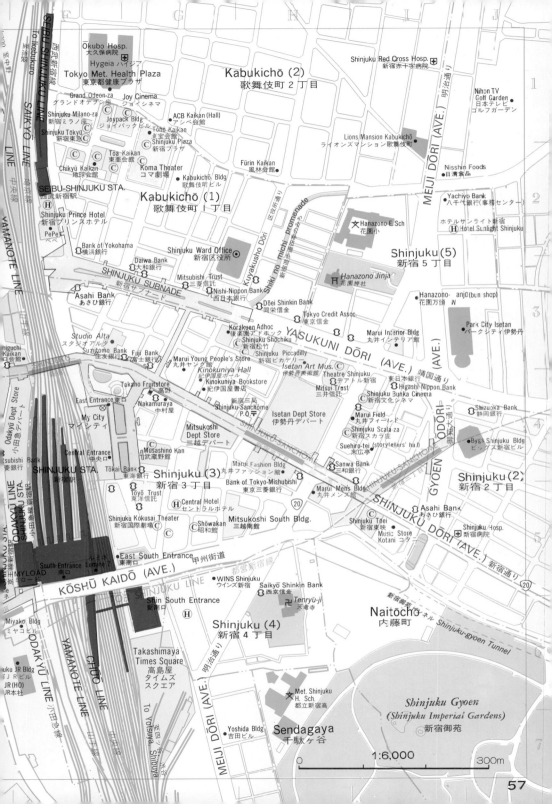

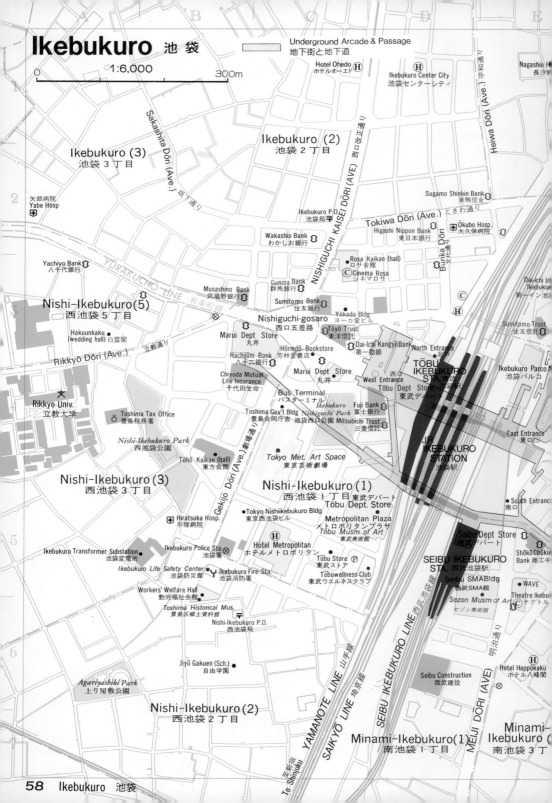

Ikebukuro 池袋

1:6,000

0   300m

Underground Arcade & Passage
地下街と地下道

Hotel Ohedo
ホテルオーエド

Ikebukuro Center City
池袋センターシティ

Nagashio Inn
長汐ホテル

Ikebukuro (2)
池袋2丁目

Ikebukuro (3)
池袋3丁目

Sakashita Dōri (Ave.)
坂下通り

Heiwa Dōri (Ave.)
平和通り

Yabe Hosp
矢部病院

Sugamo Shinkin Bank
巣鴨信金

Ikebukuro P.O.
池袋局

Tokiwa Dōri (Ave.)
ときわ通り

Higashi Nippon Bank
東日本銀行

Ōkubo Hosp.
大久保病院

Wakashio Bank
わかしお銀行

Dai-ichi Inn
Ikebukuro
第一イン池袋

Yachiyo Bank
八千代銀行

Rosa Kaikan (hall)
ロサ会館

Cinema Rosa
シネマロサ

YURAKUCHO-LINE

Nishi-Ikebukuro(5)
西池袋5丁目

Musashino Bank
武蔵野銀行

Gunma Bank
群馬銀行

Sumitomo Bank
住友銀行

Yōkado Bldg
ヨーカ堂ビル

Sumitomo Trust
住友信託

Hakuunkaku
(wedding hall) 白雲閣

Nishiguchi-gosaro
西口五差路

Marui Dept Store
丸井

Tōyō Trust
東洋信託

Rikkyō Dōri (Ave.)

Hōrindō Bookstore
芳林堂書店

Dai-Ichi Kangyō Bank
第一勧銀

North Entrance
北口

Ikebukuro Parco
池袋パルコ

Hachijūni Bank
八十二銀行

Marui Dept Store
丸井

TŌBU
IKEBUKURO
STA. 東武

Chiyoda Mutual
Life Insurance
千代田生命

West Entrance
西口

Tōbu Dept Store
東武デパート

Bus Terminal
バスターミナル

Fuji Bank
富士銀行

East Entrance
東口

Rikkyo Univ.
立教大学

Toshima Tax Office
豊島税務署

Toshima Gov't Bldg
豊島会同庁舎

Ikebukuro
Nishiguchi Park
池袋西口公園

Mitsubishi Trust
三菱信託

JR
IKEBUKURO
STATION
池袋駅

Nishi-Ikebukuro Park
西池袋公園

Nishi-Ikebukuro (3)
西池袋3丁目

Tōhō Kaikan (hall)
東方会館

Tokyo Met. Art Space
東京芸術劇場

Nishi-Ikebukuro (1)
西池袋1丁目

Tōbu Dept Store
東武デパート

Tokyo Nishiikebukuro Bldg
東京西池袋ビル

Metropolitan Plaza
メトロポリタンプラザ

South Entrance
南口

Hiratsuka Hosp.
平塚病院

Hotel Metropolitan
ホテルメトロポリタン

Tōbu Musm of Art
東武美術館

Seibu Dept Store
西武デパート

Shōkō Chūkin
Bank 商工中金

Ikebukuro Transformer Substation
池袋変電所

Ikebukuro Police Sta.
池袋署

Tobu Store
東武ストア

SEIBU IKEBUKURO
STA. 西武池袋駅

WAVE

Ikebukuro Life Safety Center
池袋防災館

Ikebukuro Fire Sta.
池袋消防署

Tobuwellness Club
東武ウエルネスクラブ

Seibu SMABldg
西武SMA館

Theatre Inst
テアトル

Workers' Welfare Hall
勤労福祉会館

Sezon Musm of Art
セゾン美術館

Toshima Historical Mus.
豊島区郷土資料館

Nishi-Ikebukuro P.O.
西池袋局

Jiyū Gakuen (Sch.)
自由学園

Agariyashiki Park
上り屋敷公園

Seibu Construction
西武建設

Hotel Happakaku
ホテル八峰閣

Nishi-Ikebukuro (2)
西池袋2丁目

Minami-Ikebukuro(1)
南池袋1丁目

Minami-
Ikebukuro (3)
南池袋3丁目

YAMANOTE LINE 山手線

SAIKYŌ LINE 埼京線

SEIBU IKEBUKURO LINE 西武池袋線

MEIJI DŌRI (AVE)
明治通り

To Shinjuku
新宿

NISHIGUCHI KAISEI DŌRI (AVE)
西口改正通り

BUNKA DŌRI
文化通り

Gekijō Dōri (Ave.)
劇場通り

有楽町線

立教通り

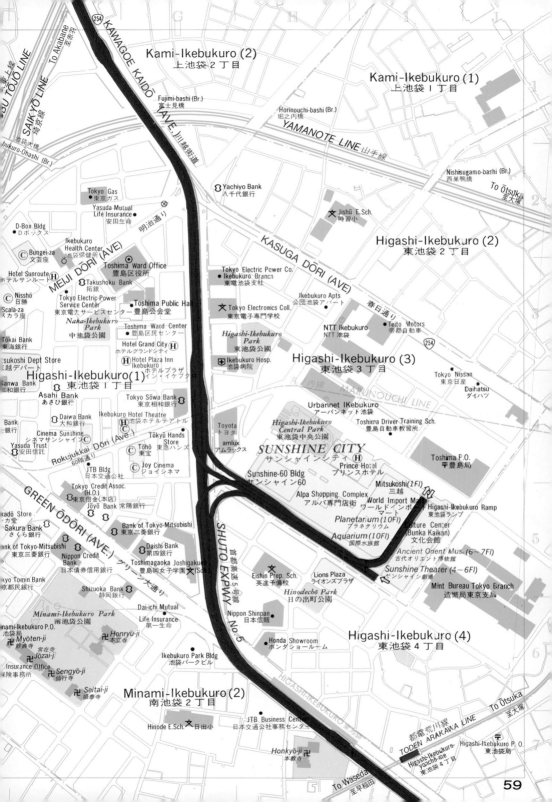

Kami-Ikebukuro (2)
上池袋2丁目

Kami-Ikebukuro (1)
上池袋1丁目

KAWAGOE KAIDŌ (AVE.) 川越街道

Fujimi-bashi (Br.)
富士見橋

Horinouchi-bashi (Br.)
堀之内橋

YAMANOTE LINE 山手線

Nishisugamo-bashi (Br.)
西巣鴨橋

To Ōtsuka
至大塚

Yachiyo Bank
八千代銀行

Jishū E.Sch.
時習小

Higashi-Ikebukuro (2)
東池袋2丁目

Tokyo Gas
東京ガス

Yasuda Mutual
Life Insurance
安田生命

D-Box Bldg
D ボックス

Bungei-za
文芸座

Ikebukuro
Health Center
池袋保健所

Hotel Sunroute
ホテルサンルート

Toshima Ward Office
豊島区役所

Takushoku Bank
拓銀

Nisshō
日勝

Scala-za
スカラ座

Tokyo Electric Power
Service Center
東京電力サービスセンター

Toshima Public Hall
豊島区公会堂

KASUGA DŌRI (AVE) 春日通り

Tokyo Electric Power Co.
Ikebukuro Branch
東電池袋支社

Ikebukuro Apts
公団池袋アパート

Teito Motors
帝都自動車

Tōkai Bank
東海銀行

Naka-Ikebukuro
Park
中池袋公園

Toshima Ward Center
豊島区民センター

Tokyo Electronics Coll.
東京電子専門学校

NTT Ikebukuro
NTT 池袋

Higashi-Ikebukuro
Park
東池袋公園

Hotel Grand City
ホテルグランドシティ

Ikebukuro Hosp.
池袋病院

Higashi-Ikebukuro (3)
東池袋3丁目

Tokyo Nissan
東京日産

Daihatsu
ダイハツ

tsukoshi Dept Store
越デパート

Hotel Plaza Inn
Ikebukuro
ホテルプラザ
イン イケブク

Higashi-Ikebukuro (1)
東池袋1丁目

nwa
Bank

Asahi Bank
あさひ銀行

Tokyo Sōwa Bank
東京相和銀行

Urbannet Ikebukuro
アーバンネット池袋

MARUNOUCHI LINE

Toshima Driver Training Sch.
豊島自動車教習所

SUNSHINE CITY
サンシャインシティ

Toshima P.O.
豊島局

Prince Hotel
プリンスホテル

Mitsukoshi(1Fl)
三越

Higashi-Ikebukuro Ramp
東池袋ランプ

Bank

Daiwa Bank
大和銀行

Ikebukuro Hotel Theatre
池袋ホテルテアトル

Cinema Sunshine
シネマサンシャイン

Yasuda Trust
安田信託

Tōkyū Hands
Store
東急ハンズ

Tōhō
東宝

Joy Cinema
ジョイシネマ

JTB Bldg
日本交通公社

Toyota
トヨタ

amlux
アムラックス

Higashi-Ikebukuro
Central Park
東池袋中央公園

Sunshine-60 Bldg
サンシャイン60

Alpa Shopping Complex
アルパ専門店街

Planetarium(10Fl)
プラネタリウム

Aquarium (10Fl)
国際水族館

World Import Mart
ワールドインポート
マート

Culture Center
(Bunka Kaikan)
文化会館

Ancient Orient Mus. (6-7Fl)
古代オリエント博物館

Sunshine Theater (4-6Fl)
サンシャイン劇場

Mint Bureau Tokyo Branch
造幣局東京支局

ROKUJUKKAI Dōri (AVE.)
60階通り

Tokyo Credit Assoc. (H.O.)
東京信金(本店)

Jōyō Bank
常陽銀行

GREEN ŌDORI (AVE.) グリーン大通り

kadō Store
カ丸

Sakura Bank
さくら銀行

Bank of Tokyo-Mitsubishi
東京三菱銀行

Bank of Tokyo-Mitsubishi
東京三菱銀行

Daishi Bank
第四銀行

Nippon Credit Bank
日本債券信用銀行

Toshimagaoka
Joshigakuen
豊島女子学園

SHUTO EXPWY. NO.5 首都高速5号線

Eishin Prep. Sch.
英進予備校

Lions Plaza
ライオンズプラザ

kyo Tomin Bank
京都民銀行

Shizuoka Bank
静岡銀行

Dai-ichi Mutual
Life Insurance
第一生命

Hinodechō Park
日の出町公園

Higashi-Ikebukuro (4)
東池袋4丁目

Minami-Ikebukuro Park
南池袋公園

nami-Ikebukuro P.O.
池袋局

Myōten-ji
妙典寺

Honryū-ji
本立寺

Nippon Shinpan
日本信販

Honda Showroom
ホンダショールーム

Jōzai-ji
常在寺

Insurance Office
保険事務所

Sengyō-ji
仙行寺

Ikebukuro Park Bldg
池袋パークビル

Seitai-ji
盛泰寺

Minami-Ikebukuro (2)
南池袋2丁目

HIGASHI-IKEBUKURO

JTB Business Center
日本交通公社事務センター

Hinode E.Sch.
日出小

Honkyō-ji
本教寺

TODEN ARAKAWA LINE 都電荒川線

To Ōtsuka
至大塚

Higashi-Ikebukuro
yonchō-me
東池袋4丁目

Higashi-Ikebukuro P.O.
東池袋局

To Waseda
至早稲田

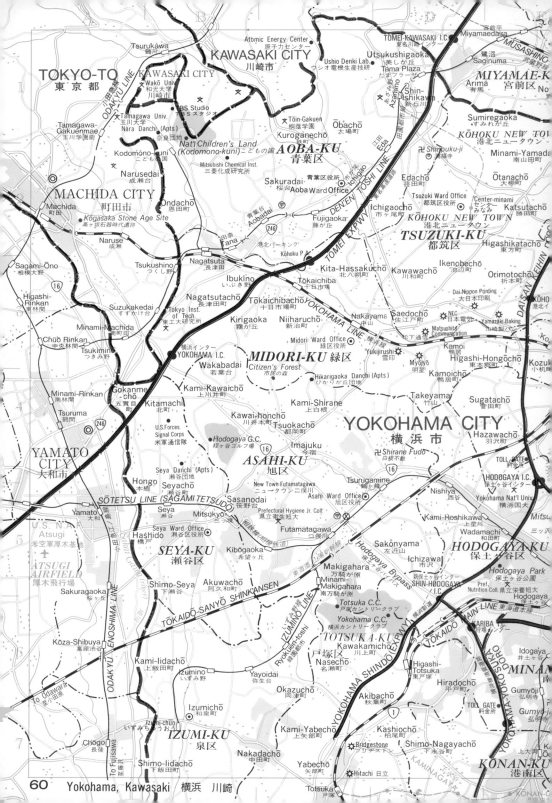

Yokohama, Kawasaki

横浜　　　　　　川崎

KANAGAWA

Miyagaya
宮ヶ谷

Mitsuzawa High Town
三ツ沢バイタウン

Nishiguchi Ramp
西口ランプ

Kusunokichō
楠町

Mitsukoshi
三越

Kinko I.C.
金港インター

Central Whl
中央卸売

Ōnochō
大野町

Kinkochō
金港町

Yokohama City
Air Terminal
横浜シティエアターミナル

Kita-Saiwai
北幸

Hotel Rich
ホテルリッチ

Tōkyū Hotel
東急ホテル

Hotel/Sunroute
Yokohama
ホテルサンルート横浜

Sōtetsu Bldg
相鉄ビル

Takashimaya
高島屋

Yokohama Kokusai Hotel
横浜国際ホテル

Sōgo Dept Store
横浜そごうデパート

Sky Bldg
スカイビル

Higashiguchi Ramp
東口ランプ

MOVIL

Yokohama Central P.O
横浜中央局

Daiei
ダイエー

Sengen Jinja
浅間神社

Sengendai
浅間台

Minami-Saiwai
南幸

Takashima
高島

Okano
岡野

Okano Park
岡野公園

Hiranuma H. Sch.
平沼高校

Park Heights
パークハイツ

Yokohama Golf Dome
横浜ゴルフドーム

Sengenchō
浅間町

Miyata-
chō
宮田町

NISHI-KU
西区

Hiranumabashi
平沼橋

Hira-
numa
平沼

Tobe Sta.
戸部

Midorichō
緑町

Yokohama Musm of Art
横浜美術館

Mitsubishi
三菱

Kyū-Tōkaidō
旧東海道

SŌTETSU LINE
相鉄本線

Tobe-
honchō
戸部本町

Tobechō
戸部町

Sakuragichō

The Landmark Tow

Bank of Yokohama
(H.O.)
横浜銀行本店

Minami-
Sengenchō
南浅間町

Nishi-Hiranuma-
bashi
西平沼橋

Tennōchō
天王町

Furukawa-
denkō
Field
古河電工
グラウンド

Chūō
中央

Gosho-
yamachō
御所山町

Kamonyama
Park
掃部山公園

Ushidachō

Nippon-i
Mem. Hall

To Ebina
至海老名

Nishi-Yokohama
西横浜

Ōwada-bashi

Nishi Ward Office
西区役所

Isechō
伊勢町

Prefectural
Youth Center
県立青少年センター

Miyazakichō
宮崎町

Iseyama Kōdaijingū
伊勢山皇大神宮

To Hodogaya
至保土ヶ谷

Hama-
matsuchō
浜松町

Nishi Public Hall
西公会堂

Nishimaechō
西前町

Narita Fudo
成田不動

Hanasakichō

Kubochō
久保町

Nagasakiya
長崎屋

Baptist Ch.
バプテスト教会

Uehara Ch.
上原教会

Nogechō
野毛町

Miya-
gawachō
宮川町

Fuku-
tomichō
福富町

Fujioka Gakuen (Sch.)
富士見丘学園

Fujidana-chō
藤棚町

Prefectural Apts
県営アパート

Nishi-Tobechō
西戸部町

Oimatsuchō
老松町

City Library
市立図書館

Nogeyama Zoo
野毛山動物園

Higashi-Kubochō
東久保町

Ipponmatsu E. Sch.
一本松小

Nogeyama Park
野毛山公園

RF Radio Nippon
ラジオ日本

Matsuzakaya
松坂屋デパート

Chōjamachi

Motokubochō
元久保町

Sakainotani
境ノ谷

Sakainotani Ch.
境ノ谷教会

Kasumigaoka
霞ヶ丘

Nogeyama Swimming Pool
野毛山プール

Azumagaoka
東ヶ丘

Hino-
dechō
日ノ出町

Kuboyama Cemetery
久保山墓地

Crematorium
斎場

Kuboyama Mausoleum
久保山霊堂

Church of
the Nazarene
ナザレン教会

Isezakichō

Wakabachō

Fushimichō
伏見町

Aka-
monchō
赤門町

Hatsu-
nechō
初音町

Yokohama-higashi Nat'l Hosp.
国立横浜東病院

Miharudai
三春台

Kantō Gakuin
関東学院

MINAMI-KU
南区

Kanoedai
庚台

Nishinakachō
西中町

Sueyoshichō
末吉町

Akebonochō
曙町

Eiraku-
chō
永楽町

Yam

Shimizugaoka Danchi (Apts)
清水ヶ丘団地

Shimizugaoka Ch.
清水ヶ丘教会

Maesatochō
前里町

Koganechō
黄金町

Magane-
chō
真金町

Shimizugaoka
清水ヶ丘

Shimizugaoka H. Sch.
清水ヶ丘高校

Minamiōta
南太田

Hiechō
日枝町

Minami-
Yoshidachō
南吉田町

Sannochō
山王町

Yoshinochō
吉野町

Takanechō
高根町

Shirotaechō
白妙町

Manseichō
万世町

Chitos

Miyosh

Minami-
Otamachi
南太田町

To Kami-ōoka
至上大岡

Hie Jinja
日枝神社

Futabachō
二葉町

Yokohama City Univ. (Med.)
横浜市立大学

Nakamura
中村町

KEIHIN KYŪKŌ LINE
京浜急行線

Yokohama Comm.
H. Sch.
横浜商業高校

Maita Park
蒔田公園

Yokohama City Univ. Hosp
市立大病院

Urafunechō

Tax Office
税務署

Keiyō Area
京葉地区

Makuhari 幕張

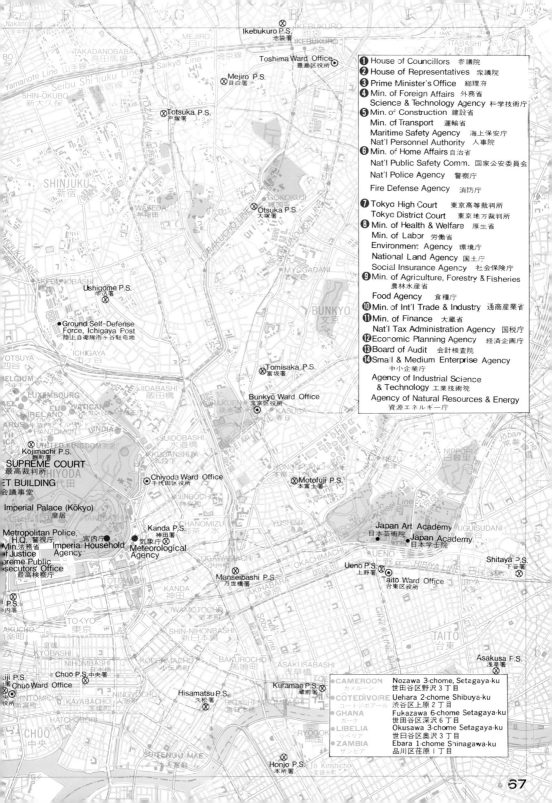

❶	House of Councillors	参議院
❷	House of Representatives	衆議院
❸	Prime Minister's Office	総理府
❹	Min. of Foreign Affairs	外務省
	Science & Technology Agency	科学技術庁
❺	Min. of Construction	建設省
	Min. of Transport	運輸省
	Maritime Safety Agency	海上保安庁
	Nat'l Personnel Authority	人事院
❻	Min. of Home Affairs	自治省
	Nat'l Public Safety Comm.	国家公安委員会
	Nat'l Police Agency	警察庁
	Fire Defense Agency	消防庁
❼	Tokyo High Court	東京高等裁判所
	Tokyo District Court	東京地方裁判所
❽	Min. of Health & Welfare	厚生省
	Min. of Labor	労働省
	Environment Agency	環境庁
	National Land Agency	国土庁
	Social Insurance Agency	社会保険庁
❾	Min. of Agriculture, Forestry & Fisheries	農林水産省
	Food Agency	食糧庁
❿	Min. of Int'l Trade & Industry	通商産業省
⓫	Min. of Finance	大蔵省
	Nat'l Tax Administration Agency	国税庁
⓬	Economic Planning Agency	経済企画庁
⓭	Board of Audit	会計検査院
⓮	Small & Medium Enterprise Agency	中小企業庁
	Agency of Industrial Science & Technology	工業技術院
	Agency of Natural Resources & Energy	資源エネルギー庁

CAMEROON カメルーン	Nozawa 3-chome, Setagaya-ku	世田谷区野沢3丁目
CÔTEDIVOIRE コートジボアール	Uehara 2-chome Shibuya-ku	渋谷区上原2丁目
GHANA ガーナ	Fukazawa 6-chome Setagaya-ku	世田谷区深沢6丁目
LIBELIA リベリア	Okusawa 3-chome Setagaya-ku	世田谷区奥沢3丁目
ZAMBIA ザンビア	Ebara 1-chome Shinagawa-ku	品川区荏原1丁目

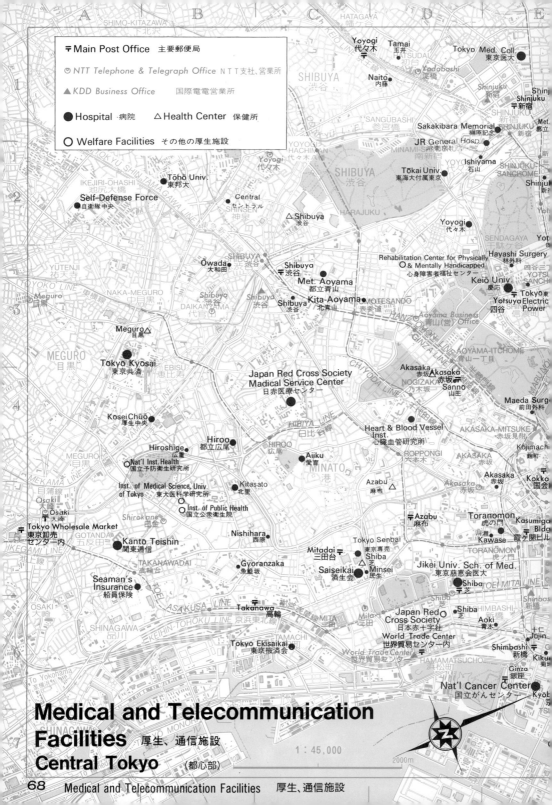

Medical and Telecommunication
Facilities 厚生、通信施設
Central Tokyo （都心部）

1 : 45,000

2000m

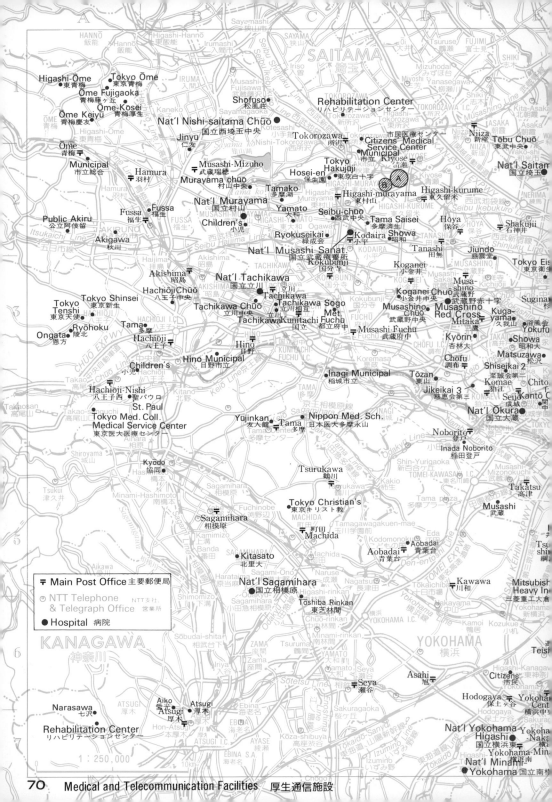

KIYOSE 清瀬

1. Tokyo Hosp. Nat'l Sanatorium　国立療養所東京
2. Met. Kiyose Children's　都立清瀬小児
3. Hosp. in affiliation with T.B. Inst.　結核研究所付属
4. Kiyose Hosp. Salvation Army　救世軍清瀬
5. Shin-ai　信愛
6. Bethlehem Garden　ベトレヘムの園
7. Kunpū-en　薫風園
8. Seikōkai　生光会
9. Takeoka　竹丘
10. Met. Staff Association　東京都職員共済組合

HIGASHI-MURAYAMA 東村山

1. Tama Zensei-en Nat'l Sanatorium　国立療養所多摩全生園
2. Sankei　三恵
3. Akitsu Ryōikuen　秋津療育園

Medical and Telecommunication Facilities

厚生，通信施設

Greater Tokyo 　（周辺部）

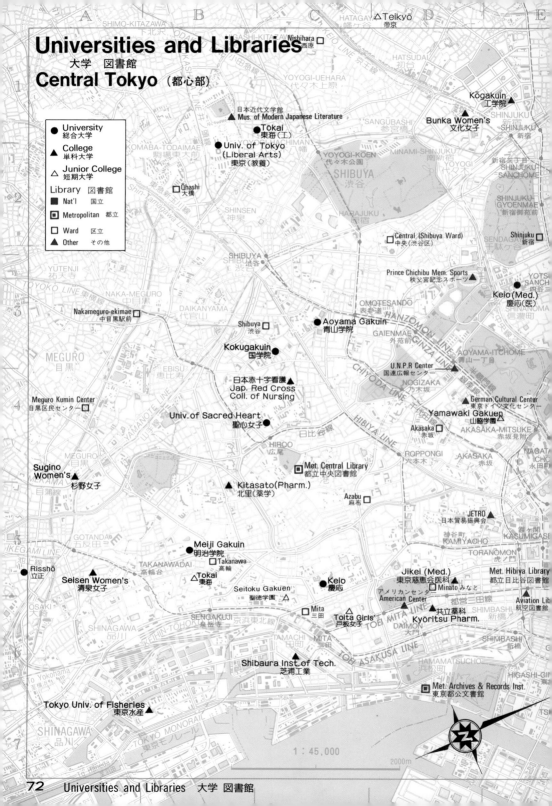

Universities and Libraries
大学　図書館
Central Tokyo（都心部）

Legend:
- ● University 総合大学
- ▲ College 単科大学
- △ Junior College 短期大学

Library 図書館
- ■ Nat'l 国立
- ▣ Metropolitan 都立
- □ Ward 区立
- ▲ Other その他

△ Teikyō 帝京

Nishihara 西原

△ Kōgakuin 工学院

Bunka Women's 文化女子

日本近代文学館 Mus. of Modern Japanese Literature

Tokai 東海（工）

Univ. of Tokyo (Liberal Arts) 東京（教養）

Ōhashi 大橋

YOYOGI-KOEN 代々木公園

SHIBUYA 渋谷

Central (Shibuya Ward) 中央（渋谷区）

Prince Chichibu Mem. Sports 秩父宮記念スポーツ

Keio (Med.) 慶應（医）

Nakameguro-ekimae 中目黒駅前

Shibuya 渋谷

Aoyama Gakuin 青山学院

Kokugakuin 国学院

U.N.P.R Center 国連広報センター

日本赤十字看護 Jap. Red Cross Coll. of Nursing

German Cultural Center 東京ドイツ文化センター

Meguro Kumin Center 目黒区民センター

Univ. of Sacred Heart 聖心女子

Yamawaki Gakuen 山脇学園

Akasaka 赤坂

Sugino Women's 杉野女子

Met. Central Library 都立中央図書館

Kitasato (Pharm.) 北里（薬学）

Azabu 麻布

JETRO 日本貿易振興会

Meiji Gakuin 明治学院

Takanawa 高輪

Jikei (Med.) 東京慈恵会医科

Met. Hibiya Library 都立日比谷図書館

Risshō 立正

Seisen Women's 清泉女子

Tokai 東海

Seitoku Gakuen 聖徳学園

Keio 慶應

American Center アメリカンセンター

Minato みなと

Aviation Lib 航空図書館

Mita 三田

Toita Girls' 戸坂女子

共立薬科 Kyoritsu Pharm.

Shibaura Inst. of Tech. 芝浦工業

Met. Archives & Records Inst. 東京都公文書館

Tokyo Univ. of Fisheries 東京水産

1 : 45,000

2000m

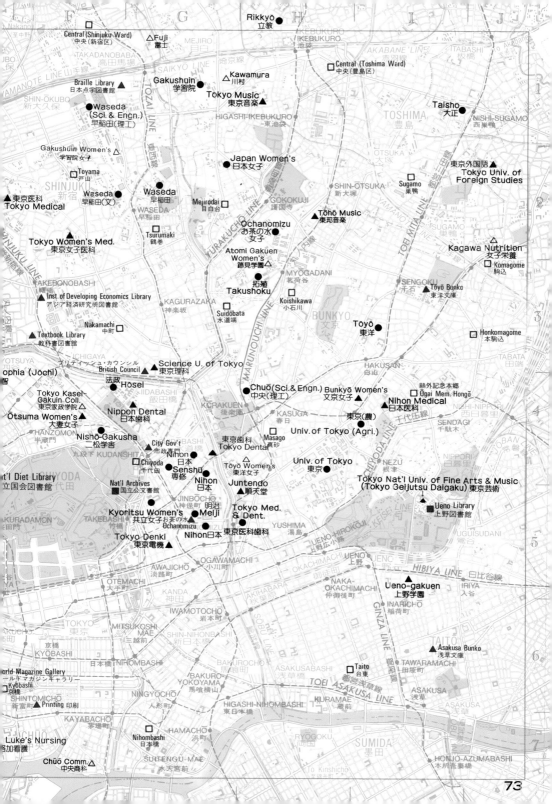

Rikkyō
立教

Central (Shinjuku Ward)
中央 (新宿区)

△Fuji
富士

Kawamura
川村

Central (Toshima Ward)
中央 (豊島区)

Braille Library
日本点字図書館 ▲

Gakushuin
学習院

Tokyo Music
東京音楽

Taisho
大正

Waseda
(Sci. & Engn.)
早稲田 (理工)

Japan Women's
日本女子

Gakushuin Women's
学習院女子 △

東京外国語 ▲
Tokyo Univ. of
Foreign Studies

Toyama
戸山

Sugamo
巣鴨

Waseda
早稲田 (文)

Waseda
早稲田

Mejirodai
目白台

Tōhō Music
東邦音楽

▲東京医科
Tokyo Medical

Tsurumaki
鶴巻

Ochanomizu
お茶の水女子

Kagawa Nutrition
女子栄養
Komagome
駒込 △

Tokyo Women's Med.
東京女子医科

Atomi Gakuen
Women's
跡見学園 △

Takushoku
拓殖

Tōyō Bunko
東洋文庫

Inst. of Developing Economics Library
アジア経済研究所図書館

Suidobata
水道端

Koishikawa
小石川

▲ Textbook Library
教科書図書館

Nakamachi
中町

Tōyō
東洋

Honkomagome
本駒込

British Council
ブリティッシュ・カウンシル

Science U. of Tokyo
東京理科

Chuō(Sci.&Engn.)
中央 (理工)

Bunkyō Women's
文京女子 ▲

鷗外記念本郷

Nihon Medical
日本医科

ophia (Jōchi)

Hōsei
法政

Nippon Dental
日本歯科 ▲

Ōgai Mem. Hongō

Tokyo Kasei-
Gakuin Coll. △
東京家政学院

Ōtsuma Women's ▲
大妻女子

Nishō-Gakusha
二松学舎 ▲

City Gov't
市政会館

Univ. of Tokyo (Agri.)
東京(農)

Chiyoda
千代田

Nihon
日本

Senshū
専修

Tokyo Dental
東京歯科

Masago
真砂

Univ. of Tokyo
東京

t'l Diet Library
立国会図書館

Nat'l Archives
国立公文書館

Nihon
日本

Juntendo
順天堂 ▲

Tōyō Women's
東洋女子 △

Tokyo Nat'l Univ. of Fine Arts & Music
(Tokyo Geijutsu Daigaku) 東京芸術

Kyoritsu Women's
共立女子

Meiji
明治

Ochanomizu
お茶の水

Tokyo Med.
& Dent.
東京医科歯科

Ueno Library
上野図書館 ■

Tokyo Denki
東京電機 ▲

Nihon 日本

Ueno-gakuen
上野学園

Asakusa Bunko
浅草文庫 ▲

world Magazine Gallery
ールドマガジンギャラリー
Kyobashi
京橋

Taito
台東

Printing 印刷 ▲

Luke's Nursing
加看護

Nihombashi
日本橋

Chūō Comm. △
中央商科

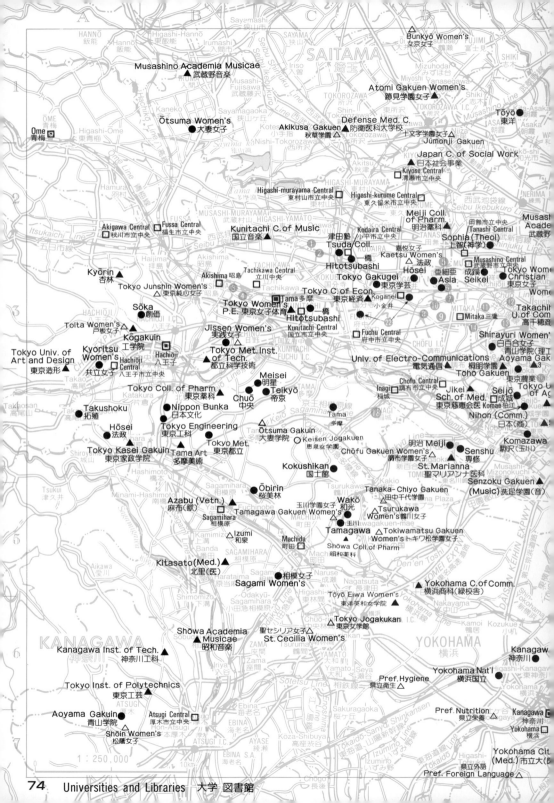

Musashino Academia Musicae
武蔵野音楽

Atomi Gakuen Women's
跡見学園女子

Bunkyō Women's
女子女子

Tōyō
東洋

Ōtsuma Women's
大妻女子

Defense Med. C.
防衛医科大学校

十文字学園女子
Jūmonji Gakuen

Akikusa Gakuen
秋草学園

Japan C. of Social Work
日本社会事業

Kiyose Central
清瀬市立中央

Akigawa Central
秋川市立中央

Fussa Central
福生市立中央

Kunitachi C.of Music
国立音楽

Tsuda Coll.
津田塾

Higashi-murayama Central
東村山市立中央

Higashi-kurume Central
東久留米市立中央

Kodaira Central
小平市立中央

Tanashi Central
田無市立中央

Meiji Coll. of Pharm.
明治薬科

Musash
Acade
武蔵野

Sophia (Theol)
上智(神学)

Kyōrin
杏林

Tokyo Junshin Women's
東京純心女子

Akishima
昭島

Tachikawa Central
立川中央

Hitotsubashi
一橋

Kaetsu Women's
嘉悦女子

Hōsei
法政

Musashino Women's
武蔵野女子

Tokyo Wome
Christian
東京女

Sōka
創価

Tama
多摩

Tokyo Gakugei
東京学芸

Asia
亜細亜

Seikei
成蹊

Seijo
成城

Tōita Women's
戸板女子

Tokyo Women's P.E.
東京女子体育

Tokyo C. of Econ.
東京経済

Koganei
小金井

Mitaka
三鷹

Takachi
U.of Com
高千穂商

Kōgakuin
工学院

Jissen Women's
実践女子

Hitotsubashi
一橋

Shirayuri Women's
白百合女子

Tokyo Univ. of Art and Design
東京造形

Kyoritsu Women's
共立女子

Hachiōji Central
八王子市立中央

Tokyo Met.Inst. of Tech.
都立科学技術

Kunitachi Central
国立市立中央

Fuchu Central
府中市立中央

Univ. of Electro-Communications
電気通信

Aoyama Gak
青山学院(理工

Meisei
明星

Teikyō
帝京

Chofu Central
調布市立中央

Toho Gakuen
桐朋学園

Tokyo U.
of Ag
東京農業

Tokyo Coll. of Pharm.
東京薬科

Chuō
中央

Inagi
稲城

Jikei Sch.of Med.
東京慈恵会医

Seijo
成城

Takushoku
拓殖

Nippon Bunka
日本文化

Tama
多摩

Komae
狛江

Nihon (Comm.)
日本(商)

Hōsei
法政

Tokyo Engineering
東京工科

Tokyo Met.
東京都立

Meiji
明治

Senshu
専修

Komazawa
駒沢(玉川)

Tokyo Kasei Gakuin
東京家政学院

Tama Art
多摩美術

Otsuma Gakuin
大妻学院

Keisen Jogakuen
恵泉女学園

Chōfu Gakuen Women's
調布学園女子

St. Marianna
聖マリアンナ医科

Azabu (Vetn.)
麻布(獣)

Kokushikan
国士館

Tanaka-Chiyo Gakuen
田中千代学園

Tsurukawa
鶴川

Senzoku Gakuen
(Music)洗足学園(音)

Ōbirin
桜美林

Tamagawa Gakuen Women's
玉川学園女子

Wakō
和光

Tsurukawa Women's鶴川女子

Izumi
和泉

Sagamihara
相模原

Machida
町田

Tamagawa
玉川

Tokiwamatsu Gakuen Women'sトキワ松学園女子

Kitasato(Med.)
北里(医)

Shōwa Coll.of Pharm
昭和薬科

Sagami Women's
相模女子

Naruse

Yokohama C.of Comm.
横浜商科(緑校舎)

Shōwa Academia Musicae
昭和音楽

St. Cecilia Women's
聖セシリア女子

Tōyō Eiwa Women's
東洋英和女学院

Tokyo Jogakukan
東京女学館

Kanagawa Inst. of Tech.
神奈川工科

Kanagaw
神奈川

Tokyo Inst. of Polytechnics
東京工芸

Yokohama Nat'l
横浜国立

Pref. Hygiene
県立衛生

Aoyama Gakuin
青山学院

Atsugi Central
厚木市立中央

Kanagawa
神奈川
Yokohama
横浜

Shōin Women's
松蔭女子

Pref. Nutrition
県立栄養

Yokohama Cit
(Med.)市立大(医)

1:250,000

県立外語
Pref. Foreign Language

Yokohama
横浜

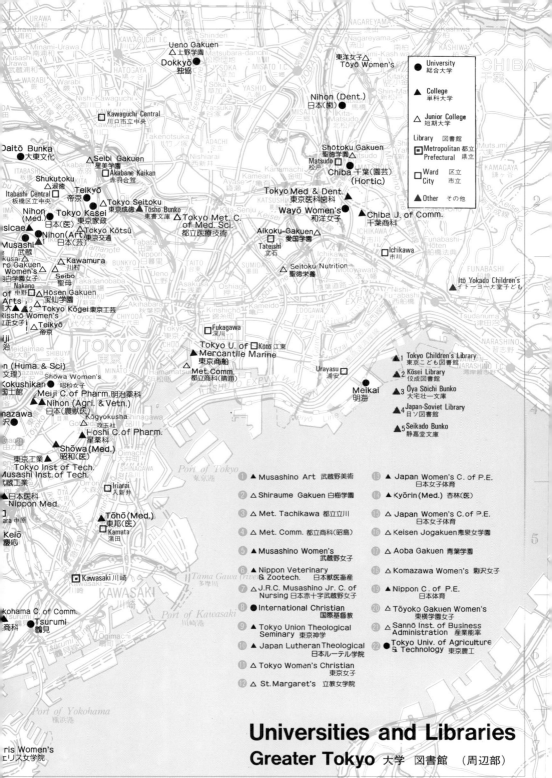

Universities and Libraries
Greater Tokyo 大学 図書館 （周辺部）

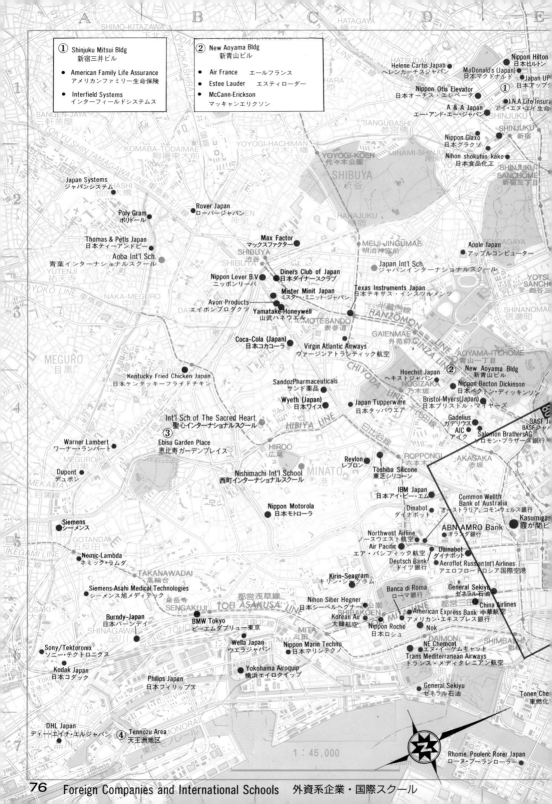

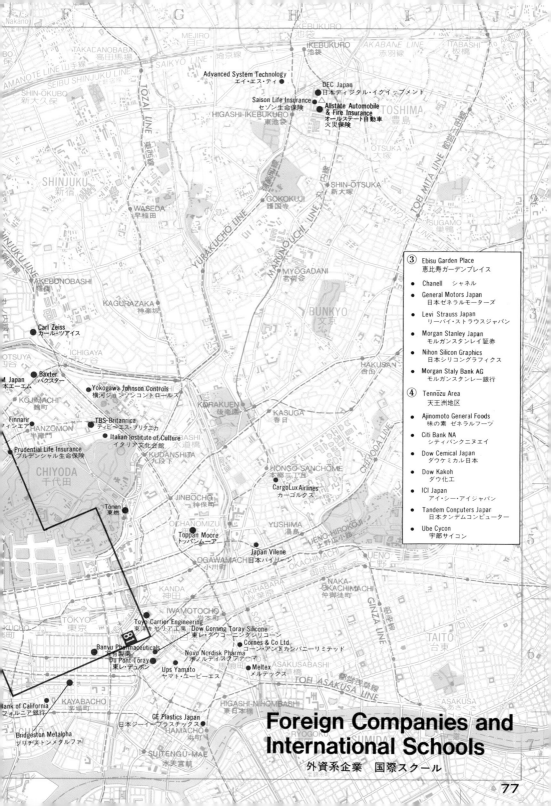

Foreign Companies and International Schools

外資系企業　国際スクール

① Palace Bldg　パレスビル
▼ VARIG Brazilian Airlines
ヴァリグ・ブラジル航空
▼ Egypt Air
エジプト航空

・ICI Japan
アイ・シー・アイ ジャパン

② AIU Bldg　ＡＩＵビル
・AIU Insurance
AIU保険会社
・American Life Insurance
アリコジャパン

・Midland Bank
ミッドランド銀行

・First Nat'l Bank of Boston
ファースト・ボストン銀行

・First Commercial Bank
第一商業銀行

③ Togin Bldg　東銀ビル
・Int'l Commercial Bank of China
中国国際商業銀行
・Bayerische Vereinsbank
バイエリッシュ フェラインス銀行
・NBD Bank N.A
エヌビーディバンクエヌエー

④ Mitsubishi Bldg　三菱ビル
・Monsant Kasei
モンサント化成
・Mitsubishi Petrochemical
三菱油化

⑤ Fuji Bldg　富士ビル
・Cargill Japan
カーギルジャパン
・Standard Chartered Bank
スタンダード チャータード銀行
・Republic Nat'l Bank of New York
リパブリック・ニューヨーク銀行
・Nippon Roche
日本ロシュ
・State Street Bank of Trust
ステートストリート銀行
・Korean Development Bank
韓国産業銀行

⑥ Shin Tokyo Bldg.　新東京ビル
・Skandinaviska Enskilda Bank
スカンジナビスカエンシルダ銀行
・Oversea Chinese Banking
オーバーシー・チャイニーズ銀行

⑦ Kokusai Bldg　国際ビル
・Westdeutsche Landesbank
西ドイツ銀行
・Kleinwort Benson
クラインオートベンソン証券
・Bank Negara Indonesia 1946
バンク ネガラ インドネシア 1946年
・ING Bank NV
アイエヌジーバンクエヌ・ヴイ
・American Airlines
アメリカン航空
・United Airlines
ユナイテッド航空

⑧ Shin Kokusai Bldg　新国際ビル
・Korea Exchange Bank
韓国外換銀行
・Banco de Brasil
ブラジル銀行
・United Overseas Bank
ユナイテッド・オーバーシーズ銀行
・Morgan Trust
モルガン信託
・Air New Zealand
ニュージーランド航空
・Nihon Siber Hegner
日本シイベル・ヘグナー

⑨ Urbannet Otemachi Bldg アーバンネット
大手町ビル
・Barclays Trust & Banking
バークレイズ信託銀行
・Union Bank of Switzerland
スイス・ユニオン信託銀行
・Solomon Brothers Asia
ソロモン・ブラザーズ・アジア証券
・BZW Securities
BZWジャパン証券
・UBS Securities
UBS証券

⑩ Yūrakuchō Bldg　有楽町ビル
・Singapore Airlines
シンガポール航空
・Pakistan Int'l Airlines
パキスタン国際航空

⑪ Ōte Center Bldg　大手センタービル
・Merrill Lynch Japan
メリルリンチ証券

⑫ Hibiya Park Bldg　日比谷パークビル
・Credit Lyonnais
クレディ・リヨネ
▼ Canadian Airlines Int'l
カナディアン航空
▼ Swiss Air
スイス航空
▼ Air India
エア・インディア
・Korea First Bank
第一銀行

Delta Airlines ▼
デルタ航空
Dover Japan
日本ドーバー
Iraqi Airways
イラク航空 ▼

Hotel New Ōtani
ホテルニューオータニ
Oracle Corp.
日本オラクル
Akasaka Prince Hotel
赤坂プリンスホテル
Ranco Japan
日本ランコ
Nationale-Nederlanden Life
ナショナーレネーデルランデン生命保険

Hirakawachō
平河町

Kiōichō
紀尾井町

NAGATACHŌ LINE 永田町

HANZOMON LINE 半蔵門線

GINZA LINE 銀座線

Air Canada ▼
エア・カナダ

Akasaka Tōkyū Hotel
赤坂東急ホテル

⑳ Sannō Grand Bldg
山王グランドビル
CIGNA Insurance
シグナル保険会社
Fuji Xerox
富士ゼロックス

Hie Jinja (Shr.)
日枝神社

Morgan Guaranty Trust
モルガン銀行
Esso Sekiyu
エッソ石油
ABB

Kokusai Shin Akasaka Bldg
国際新赤坂ビル

Akasaka
赤坂

Toshiba Electronic Systems
東芝テスコ

⑳ Ark Mori Bldg　アーク森ビル
・Monsanto Japan
日本モンサント
・Bank of America
バンクオブアメリカ
・Lehman Brothers Bankhaus
リーマンブラザース証券
・Goldman Sachs (Japan)
ゴールドマンサックス証券
▼ Asiana Airlines
アシアナ航空

㉒ CS Tower Bldg
ＣＳタワー
・Credit Suisse
クレディ・スイス
・Volvo Cars Japan
ボルボ・カーズ・ジャパン

Hecchst Marione Russel Japan
日本ヘキストマリオンルセル

ANA Hotel Tokyo
東京全日空ホテル

Ark Mori Bldg
アーク森ビル
ARK HILLS
アークヒルズ

Hotel Ōkura
ホテルオークラ

Roppongi
六本木

IBM Japan
日本アイ・ビー・エム

Mercedes Benz Japan
メルセデスベンツ日本

Nat'l Diet Library
国立国会図書館

YŪRAKUCHŌ LINE

Parliamentary Mus.
憲政記念館

Sakurada-m
桜田門

Nat'l Diet Bldg
国会議事堂

Nagatachō
永田町

KŌKKAI-GIJIDŌMAE
国会議事堂前

Capitol Tōkyū Hotel
キャピトル東急ホテル

Prime Minister's
Official Residence
首相官邸

Ministry of Foreign Affairs
外務省

MARUNOUCHI LINE

Kasumigaseki
霞ヶ関

Sabena Airlines
サベナ航空
Fuji Valve 富士バルブ
Toshiba EMI
東芝イーエムアイ
P.T. Garuda Indonesia
ガルーダインドネシア航空

Kasumigaseki Bldg
⑱ 霞が関ビル

Banco Central Hispano Americano
セントラルスペインアメリカ銀行
Lloyds Bank
ロイド銀行 Iran Air
イラン航空

Tokyo Club Bldg
⑲ 東京倶楽部ビル
NCR Japan アール
日本エヌ・シー・アール
Hanil Bank
韓一銀行
China Eastern Airlines
中国東方航空

Bank of Hawaii
バンク・オブ・ハワイ

Emb. of U.S.A.
アメリカ大使館

Bank Bumiputra Malaysia
ブミプトラ・マレーシア銀行

Banque Nationale de Paris
パリ国立銀行
British Airways
英国航空

Ford Motor (Japan)
フォード自動車（日本）

Dainabot
ダイナボット

Teisan
テイサン

Turkish Airlines
トルコ航空

Nippon Polyurethane
Industry
日本ポリウレタン工業

Scandinavian Airlines System
スカンジナビア航空

Nat'l Bank of Pakistan
パキスタン・ナショナル銀行
Qantas Airways ▼
カンタスオーストラリア航空
Cho Hung Bank
朝興銀行
Bangkok Bank
バンコック銀行

Nippon Petroleum
Refining 日本石油精製

Commerzbank
コメルツ銀行

Hibiya Kokusai Bldg
日比谷国際ビル
Hibiya Central Bldg
日比谷セントラルビル

GINZA
銀座

Shimbashi
新橋

Malaysian A
マレーシア

Sakuradamon
桜田門

Tokyo Metropolitan
Police Dept.
警視庁

Nippon Press Center
日本プレスセンター

TORANOMON
虎ノ門

⑮ ⑯ ⑰

1 : 15000
0　　　　500m

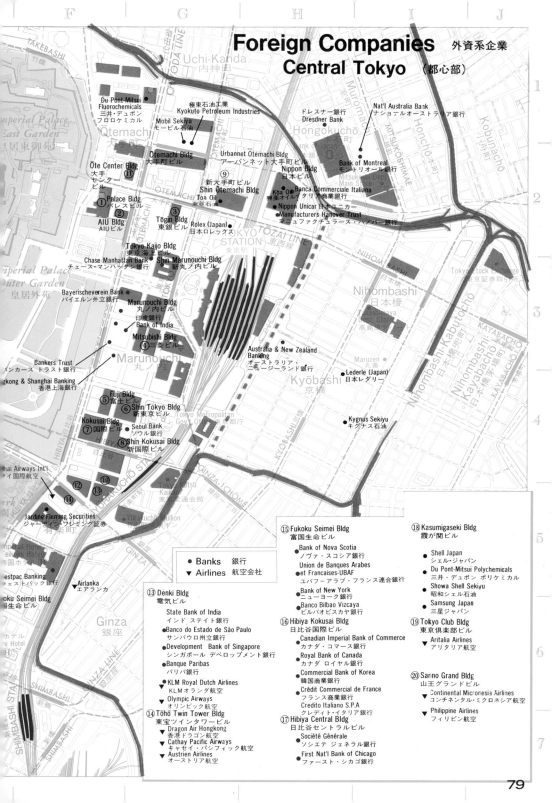

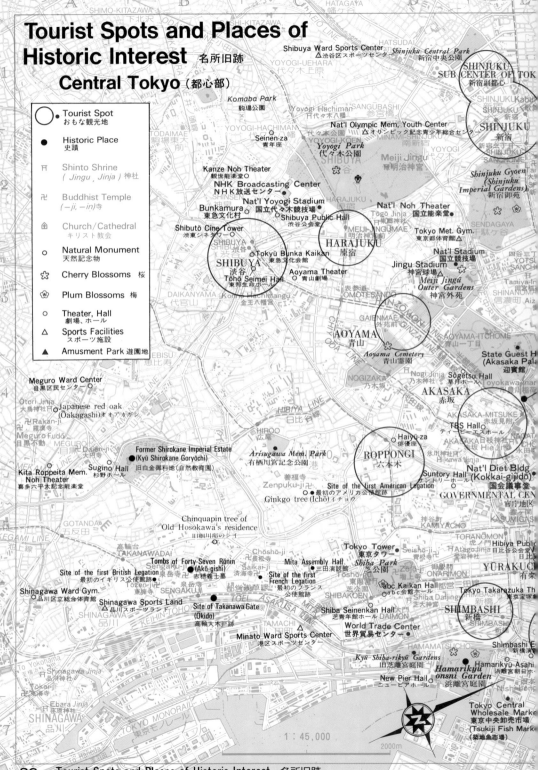

Tourist Spots and Places of Historic Interest 名所旧跡

Central Tokyo（都心部）

Legend:
- ◯ Tourist Spot おもな観光地
- ● Historic Place 史蹟
- 卉 Shinto Shrine (Jingū , Jinja) 神社
- 卍 Buddhist Temple (−ji, −in)寺
- ⛪ Church/Cathedral キリスト教会
- ○ Natural Monument 天然記念物
- ☆ Cherry Blossoms 桜
- ✿ Plum Blossoms 梅
- ○ Theater, Hall 劇場、ホール
- △ Sports Facilities スポーツ施設
- ▲ Amusement Park 遊園地

Shibuya Ward Sports Center △渋谷区スポーツセンター
Shinjuku Central Park 新宿中央公園
SHINJUKU SUB CENTER OF TOK 新宿副都心
SHINJUKU Kabu 新宿歌
SHINJUKU 新宿

Komaba Park 駒場公園
Yoyogi Hachiman 代々木八幡
Nat'l Olympic Mem, Youth Center △オリンピック記念青少年総合センター
Seinen-za 青年座
Yoyogi Park 代々木公園
Meiji Jingu 明治神宮
Shinjuku Gyoen (Shinjuku Imperial Gardens) 新宿御苑

Kanze Noh Theater 観世能楽堂
NHK Broadcasting Center NHK放送センター
Nat'l Yoyogi Stadium 国立代々木競技場
Nat'l Noh Theater 国立能楽堂
Togo Jinja 東郷神社
Tokyo Met. Gym. 東京都体育館
Bunkamura 東急文化村
Shibuya Public Hall 渋谷公会堂
Shibutō Cine Tower 渋東シネタワー
MEIJI-JINGUMAE 明治神宮前
HARAJUKU 原宿
SENDAGAYA
Nat'l Stadium 国立競技場

Tōkyū Bunka Kaikan 東急文化会館
Aoyama Theater 青山劇場
Jingu Stadium 神宮球場
Meiji Jingū Outer Gardens 神宮外苑
SHIBUYA 渋谷
Tōhō Seimei Hall 東邦生命ホール
GAIENMAE 外苑前
AOYAMA-ITCHOME 青山一丁目

DAIKANYAMA 代官山
Konno Hachimangu 金王八幡宮
OMOTESANDO 表参道
AOYAMA 青山
Aoyama Cemetery 青山霊園
State Guest H (Akasaka Pal 迎賓館

EBISU 恵比寿
NOGIZAKA 乃木坂
Nogi Jinja 乃木神社
Sōgetsu Hall 草月ホール
AKASAKA 赤坂
AKASAKA-MITSUKE 赤坂見附

Meguro Ward Center 目黒区民センター
Otori Jinja 大鳥神社
Japanese red oak (Oakagashi) オオアカガシ
Rakan-ji 羅漢寺
Meguro Fudō 目黒不動
HIROO 広尾
Arisugawa Mem. Park 有栖川宮記念公園
TBS Hall ティービーエスホール
AKASAKA 赤坂
Akasaka Hie 赤坂日枝
Hikawa Jinja 氷川神社
Nat'l Diet Bldg (Kokkai-gijidō) 国会議事堂

MEKAMA
Daien-ji 大円寺
Sugino Hall 杉野ホール
Former Shirokane Imperial Estate (Kyū Shirokane Goryōchi) 旧白金御料地（自然教育園）
ROPPONGI 六本木
Haiyū-za 俳優座
Suntory Hall サントリーホール
GOVERNMENTAL CEN 官庁地区

Kita Roppeita Mem. Noh Theater 喜多六平太記念能楽堂
Zenpuku-ji 善福寺
Site of the first American Legation 最初のアメリカ公使館跡
Ginkgo tree (Ichō) イチョウ
KAMIYACHO
KASUMIGAS

GOTANDA 五反田
TAKANAWADAI 高輪台
Chinquapin tree of Old Hosokawa's residence 旧細川邸のシイ
Chōshō-ji 長松寺
Zuishō-ji 瑞聖寺
Saikai-ji 済海寺
Tokyo Tower 東京タワー
Shiba Park 芝公園
Seishō-ji 青松寺
Atago Jinja 愛宕神社
Hibiya Publ 日比谷公会堂
TORANOMON 虎ノ門
YURAKUC 有楽

IKEGAMI LINE 池上線
Tombs of Forty-Seven Rōnin (Akō-gishi) 赤穂義士
Mita Assembly Hall 三田演説堂
Site of the first French Legation 最初のフランス公使館跡
SHIBAKOEN 芝公園
Zōjō-ji 増上寺
abc Kaikan Hall abc会館ホール
Shiba Daijingu 芝大神宮
ONARIMON 御成門
Tokyo Takarazuka Th 東京宝塚
SHIMBASHI 新橋

Site of the first British Legation 最初のイギリス公使館跡
Tōzen-ji 東禅寺
Sengaku-ji 泉岳寺
Shinagawa Ward Gym. 品川区立総合体育館
Shinagawa Sports Land △品川スポーツランド
Site of Takanawa Gate (Ōkido) 高輪大木戸
Shiba Seinenkan Hall 芝青年館ホール
DAIMON 大門
World Trade Center 世界貿易センター

Minato Ward Sports Center 港区スポーツセンター
HAMAMATSUCHO
Shimbashi E 新橋

Shinagawa Jinja 品川神社
Kyū-Shiba-rikyū Gardens 旧芝離宮庭園
Hamarikyū Asahi 浜離宮朝日
Hamarikyū Onshi Garden 浜離宮庭園

Tokari-ji 東海寺
New Pier Hall ニューピアホール

Ebara Jinja 荏原神社
SHINAGAWA 品川
TOKYO MONORAIL 東京モノレール
Tokyo Central Wholesale Marke 東京中央卸売市場 (Tsukiji Fish Mark 築地魚市場)
Tokyo Central Wholesale Marke

1 : 45,000
2000m

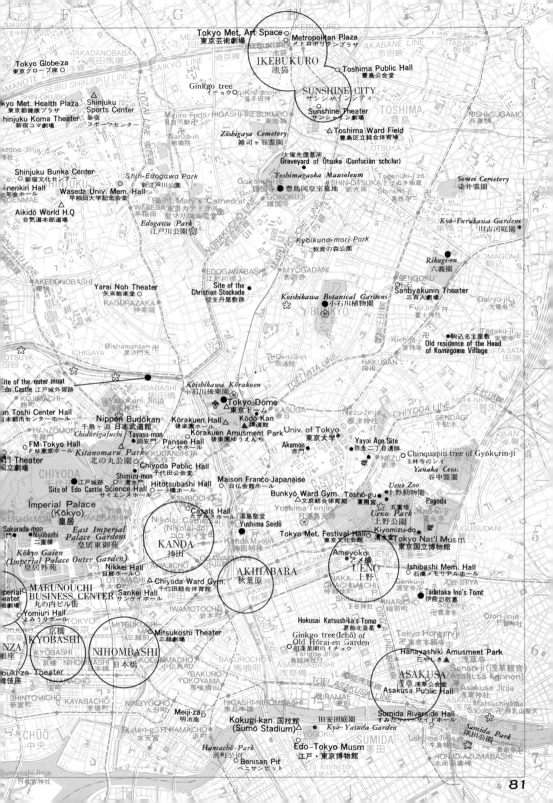

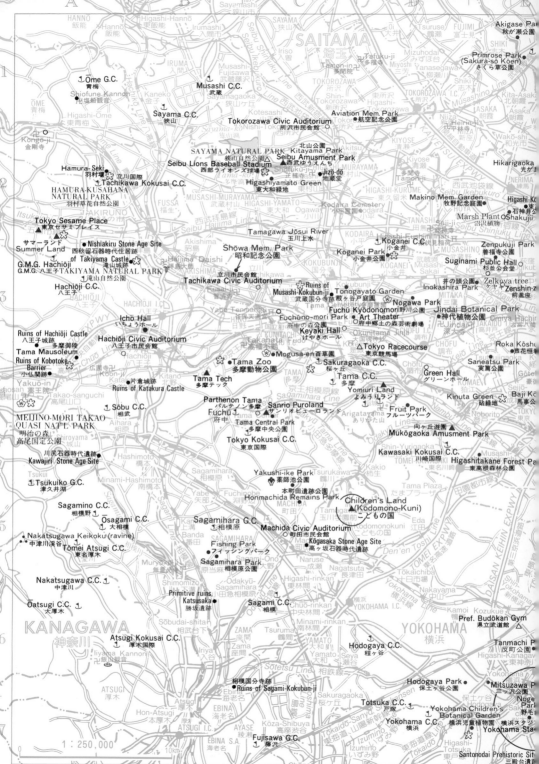

Tourist Spots and Places of Historic Interest 名所旧跡

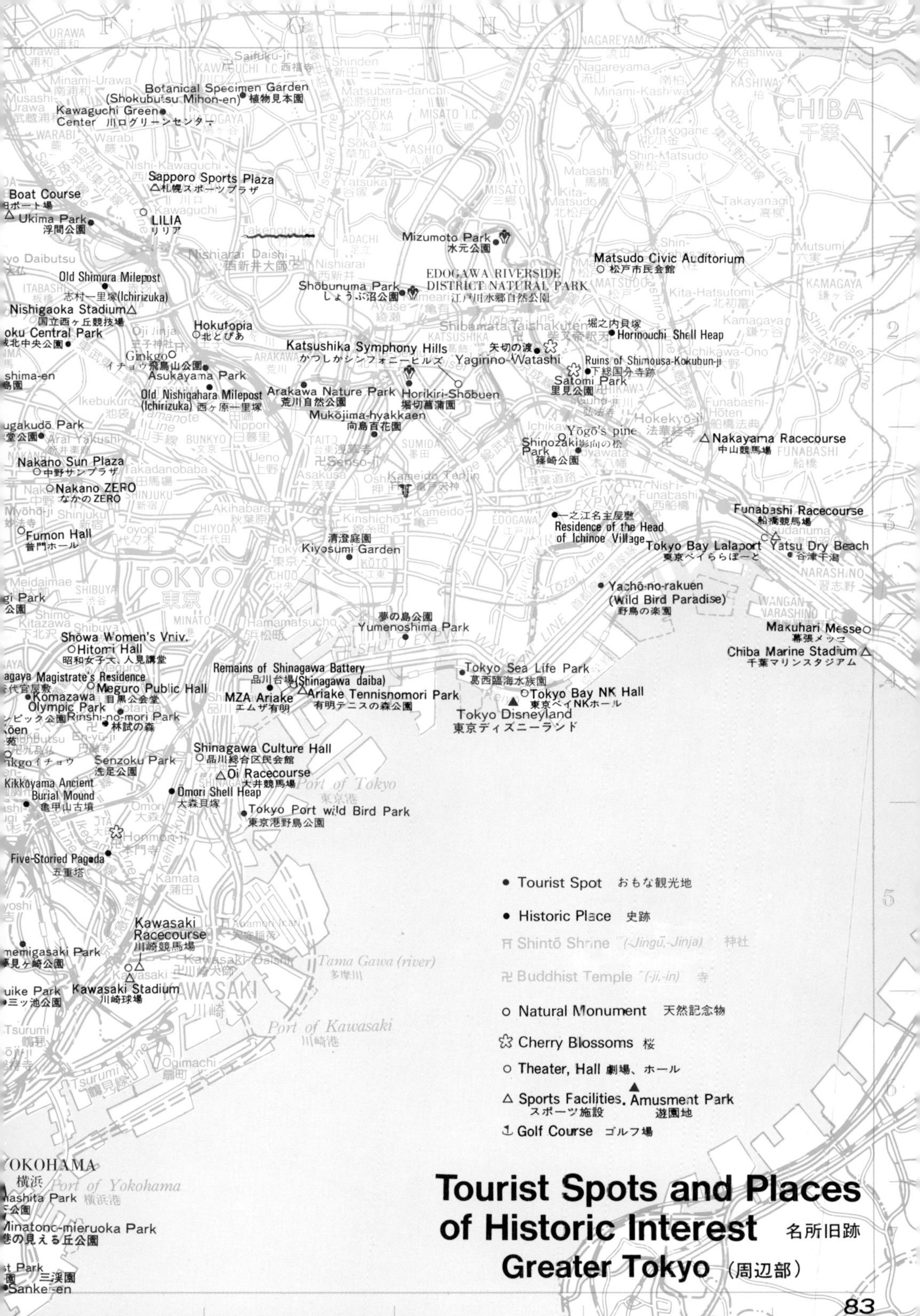

Urawa
URAWA
Saifuku-ji
Shinden
KAWAGUCHI I.C. 西福寺
Minami-Urawa
南浦和
Nagareyama
NAGAREYAMA
Nagareyama
Minami-Kashiwa
CHIBA
千葉

Botanical Specimen Garden
(Shokubutsu Mihon-en) 植物見本園
Kawaguchi Green
Center 川口グリーンセンター

Sapporo Sports Plaza
△札幌スポーツプラザ

Boat Course
ボート場
△ Ukima Park
浮間公園
○ LILIA
リリア

Mizumoto Park
水元公園

Matsudo Civic Auditorium
○ 松戸市民会館

Old Shimura Milepost
志村一里塚(Ichirizuka)
Nishigaoka Stadium△
国立西ヶ丘競技場
oku Central Park
北口中央公園

Shōbunuma Park
しょうぶ沼公園

EDOGAWA RIVERSIDE
DISTRICT NATURAL PARK
江戸川水郷自然公園

Shibamata Taishakuten
堀之内貝塚
○ Horinouchi Shell Heap

Hokutopia
北とぴあ

矢切の渡
Yagirino-Watashi

Ruins of Shimousa-Kokubun-ji
下総国分寺跡

Katsushika Symphony Hills
かつしかシンフォニーヒルズ

Satomi Park
里見公園

Asukayama Park
イチョウ飛鳥山公園

Arakawa Nature Park
荒川自然公園

Horikiri-Shōbuen
堀切菖蒲園

Old Nishigahara Milepost
(Ichirizuka) 西ヶ原一里塚

Mukōjima-hyakkaen
向島百花園

Yōgo's pine
法華経寺
Nakayama Racecourse
中山競馬場

Nakano Sun Plaza
中野サンプラザ

Shinozaki
Park
篠崎公園

FUNABASHI
船橋

Nakano ZERO
なかのZERO

一之江名主屋敷
Residence of the Head
of Ichinoe Village

Funabashi Racecourse
船橋競馬場

Fumon Hall
普門ホール

Tokyo Bay Lalaport
東京ベイららぽーと

Yatsu Dry Beach
谷津干潟

Kiyosumi Garden
清澄庭園

Yachō-no-rakuen
(Wild Bird Paradise)
野鳥の楽園

NARASHINO

Shōwa Women's Univ.
昭和女子大
△ Hitomi Hall
人見講堂

Yumenoshima Park
夢の島公園

Makuhari Messe
幕張メッセ
Chiba Marine Stadium △
千葉マリンスタジアム

agaya Magistrate's Residence
Meguro Public Hall
目黒公会堂
Komazawa
Olympic Park
オリンピック公園 Rinshi-no-mori Park
林試の森

Remains of Shinagawa Battery
品川台場(Shinagawa daiba)
MZA Ariake
エムザ有明
Ariake Tennisnomori Park
有明テニスの森公園

Tokyo Sea Life Park
葛西臨海水族園

Tokyo Bay NK Hall
東京ベイNKホール

Tokyo Disneyland
東京ディズニーランド

Shinagawa Culture Hall
品川総合区民会館
Oi Racecourse
大井競馬場

Senzoku Park
洗足公園

Kikkōyama Ancient
Burial Mound
亀甲山古墳

Omori Shell Heap
大森貝塚
Tokyo Port Wild Bird Park
東京港野鳥公園

Five-Storied Pagoda
五重塔

Kawasaki
Racecourse
川崎競馬場

Tama Gawa (river)
多摩川

emigasaki Park
見ヶ崎公園

Kawasaki Stadium
川崎球場
KAWASAKI
川崎

uike Park
三ツ池公園

Port of Kawasaki
川崎港

YOKOHAMA
横浜

Minatono-mieruoka Park
港の見える丘公園

Sankei-en
三渓園

• Tourist Spot　おもな観光地

• Historic Place　史跡

卄 Shintō Shrine　(-Jingū,-Jinja)　神社

卍 Buddhist Temple　(-ji,-in)　寺

○ Natural Monument　天然記念物

✿ Cherry Blossoms　桜

○ Theater, Hall　劇場、ホール

△ Sports Facilities.　▲ Amusement Park
スポーツ施設　　　　遊園地

⛳ Golf Course　ゴルフ場

Tourist Spots and Places
of Historic Interest 名所旧跡
Greater Tokyo （周辺部）

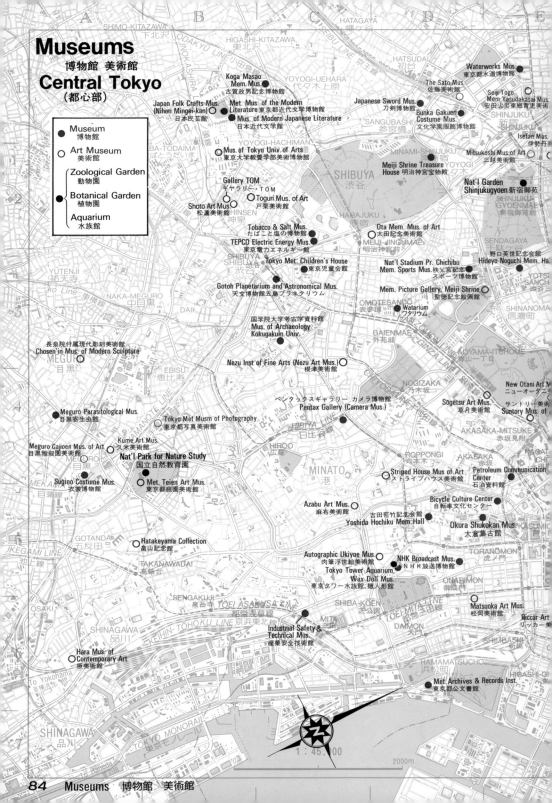

Museums
博物館 美術館
Central Tokyo
（都心部）

| | | Museum 博物館 |
| Art Museum 美術館 |
| Zoological Garden 動物園 |
| Botanical Garden 植物園 |
| Aquarium 水族館 |

Koga Masao
Mem. Mus.
古賀政男記念博物館

Japan Folk Crafts Mus.
(Nihon Mingei-kan)
日本民芸館

Met. Mus. of the Modern
Literature 東京都近代文学博物館
Mus. of Modern Japanese Literature
日本近代文学館

Japanese Sword Mus.
刀剣博物館

Waterworks Mus.
東京都水道博物館

The Sato Mus.
佐藤美術館

Seiji Togo
Mem Yasudakasai Mus.
安田火災東郷青児美術館

Bunka Gakuen
Costume Mus.
文化学園服飾博物館

Isetan Mus.
伊勢丹

Mus. of Tokyo Univ. of Arts
東京大学教養学部美術館

Mitsukoshi Mus of Art
三越美術館

Meiji Shrine Treasure
House 明治神宮宝物殿

Nat'l Garden
Shinjukugyoen 新宿御苑

Gallery TOM
ギャラリー・TOM

Toguri Mus. of Art
戸栗美術館

Shoto Art Mus.
松濤美術館

Tobacco & Salt Mus.
たばこと塩の博物館

TEPCO Electric Energy Mus.
東京電力エネルギー館

Ota Mem. Mus. of Art
太田記念美術館

Nat'l Stadium Pr. Chichibu
Mem. Sports Mus.
秩父宮記念
スポーツ博物館

Hideyo Noguchi Mem. Ha
野口英世記念会館

Tokyo Met. Children's House
東京児童会館

Gotoh Planetarium and Astronomical Mus.
天文博物館五島プラネタリウム

Mem. Picture Gallery, Meiji Shrine
聖徳記念絵画館

Mus. of Archaeology
Kokugakuin Univ.
国学院大学考古学資料館

Watarium
ワタリウム

Chosen in Mus. of Modern Sculpture
長泉院付属現代彫刻美術館

Nezu Inst of Fine Arts (Nezu Art Mus.)
根津美術館

New Otani Art M
ニューオータニ美

Sogetsu Art Mus.
草月美術館

Suntory Mus. of
サントリー美術

Pentax Gallery (Camera Mus.)
ペンタックスギャラリー カメラ博物館

Meguro Parasitological Mus.
目黒寄生虫館

Tokyo Met Musm of Photography
東京都写真美術館

Kume Art Mus.
久米美術館

Meguro Gajioen Mus. of Art
目黒雅叙園美術館

Nat'l Park for Nature Study
国立自然教育園

Striped House Mus of Art
ストライプハウス美術館

Petroleum Communication
Center
石油資料館

Sugino Costume Mus.
衣裳博物館

Met. Teien Art Mus.
東京都庭園美術館

Azabu Art Mus.
麻布美術館

Bicycle Culture Center
自転車文化センター

Okura Shukokan Mus.
大倉集古館

Hatakeyama Collection
畠山記念館

Yoshida Hochiku Mem. Hall
吉田苞竹記念会館

Autographic Ukiyoe Mus.
肉筆浮世絵美術館

NHK Broadcast Mus.
NHK放送博物館

Tokyo Tower Aquarium
Wax Doll Mus.
東京タワー水族館、蝋人形館

Matsuoka Art Mus.
松岡美術館

Riccar Art
リッカー美

Hara Mus. of
Contemporary Art
原美術館

Industrial Safety &
Technical Mus.
産業安全技術館

Met. Archives & Records Inst.
東京都公文書館

1：45,000

2000m

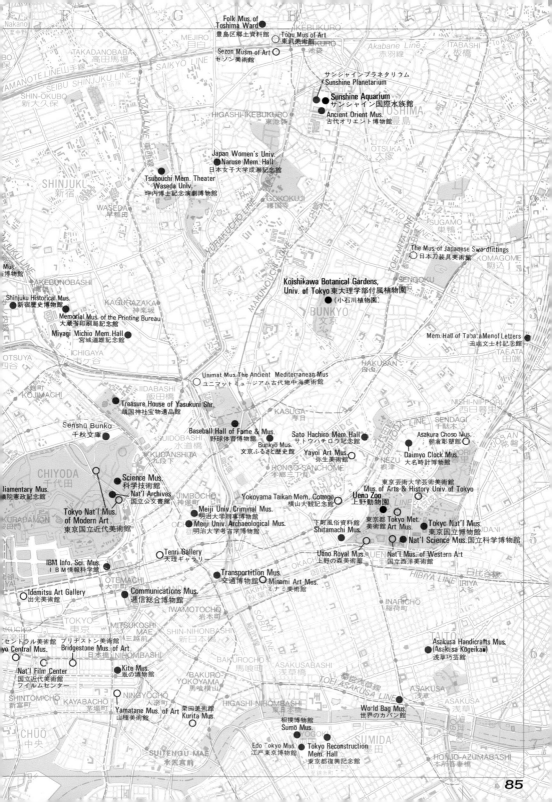

Folk Mus. of
Toshima Ward
豊島区郷土資料館

Tobu Mus. of Art
東武美術館

Sezon Musm of Art
セゾン美術館

サンシャインプラネタリウム
Sunshine Planetarium

Sunshine Aquarium
サンシャイン国際水族館

Ancient Orient Mus.
古代オリエント博物館

Japan Women's Univ.
Naruse Mem. Hall
日本女子大学成瀬記念館

Tsubouchi Mem. Theater
Waseda Univ.
坪内博士記念演劇博物館

The Mus. of Japanese Swordfittings
日本刀装具美術館

Koishikawa Botanical Gardens,
Univ. of Tokyo 東大理学部付属植物園
（小石川植物園）

Shinjuku Historical Mus.
新宿歴史博物館

Memorial Mus. of the Printing Bureau
大蔵省印刷局記念館

Miyagi Michio Mem. Hall
宮城道雄記念館

Mem. Hall of Tabata Menof Letters
田端文士村記念館

Unimat Mus. The Ancient Mediterranean Mus
ユニマットミュージアム古代地中海美術館

Treasure House of Yasukuni Shr.
靖国神社宝物遺品館

Senshu Bunko
千秋文庫

Baseball Hall of Fame & Mus.
野球体育博物館

Bunkyo Mus.
文京ふるさと歴史館

Sato Hachiro Mem. Hall
サトウハチロウ記念館

Yayoi Art Mus.
弥生美術館

Asakura Choso Mus.
朝倉彫塑館

Daimyo Clock Mus.
大名時計博物館

Science Mus.
科学技術館

Nat'l Archives
国立公文書館

Yokoyama Taikan Mem. Cottege
横山大観記念館

Mus. of Arts & History Univ. of Tokyo

Ueno Zoo
上野動物園

liamentary Mus.
議院憲政記念館

Tokyo Nat'l Mus.
of Modern Art
東京国立近代美術館

Meiji Univ. Criminal Mus.
明治大学刑事博物館

Meiji Univ. Archaeological Mus.
明治大学考古学博物館

下町風俗資料館
Shitamachi Mus.

東京都
美術館 Tokyo Met.
Art Mus.

Tokyo Nat'l Mus.
東京国立博物館

Nat'l Science Mus. 国立科学博物館

IBM Info. Sci. Mus.
ＩＢＭ情報科学館

Tenri Gallery
天理ギャラリー

Transportation Mus.
交通博物館

Minami Art Mus.
ミナミ美術館

Ueno Royal Mus.
上野の森美術館

Nat'l Mus. of Western Art
国立西洋美術館

Idemitsu Art Gallery
出光美術館

Communications Mus.
通信総合博物館

Asakusa Handicrafts Mus.
（Asakusa Kogeikan）
浅草巧芸館

yo Central Mus.
セントラル美術館

ブリヂストン美術館
Bridgestone Mus. of Art
日本橋

Kite Mus.
凧の博物館

Nat'l Film Center
国立近代美術館
フィルムセンター

Yamatane Mus. of Art
山種美術館

栗田美術館
Kurita Mus.

World Bag Mus.
世界のカバン館

相撲博物館
Sumo Mus.

Edo Tokyo Mus.
江戸東京博物館

Tokyo Reconstruction
Mem. Hall
東京都復興記念館

Nakano

MEJIRO
目白

IKEBUKURO
池袋

Akabane Line
赤羽線

ITABASHI
板橋

TAKADANOBABA
高田馬場

SAIKYO LINE

TOZAI LINE

HIGASHI-IKEBUKURO
東池袋

OTSUKA
大塚

SUGAMO
巣鴨

SHIN-OKUBO
新大久保

SEIBU SHINJUKU LINE

GOKOKUJI
護国寺

YAMANOTE LINE

KOMAGOME
駒込

SHINJUKU
新宿

WASEDA
早稲田

YURAKUCHO LINE

SENGOKU
千石

MARUNOUCHI LINE

BUNKYO
文京

HAKUSAN
白山

TABATA
田端

AKEBONOBASHI
曙橋

KAGURAZAKA
神楽坂

NISHI-NIPPORI
西日暮里

SENDAGI
千駄木

OTSUYA

ICHIGAYA
市ヶ谷

KASUGA
春日

NEZU
根津

KOJIMACHI
麹町

IIDABASHI
飯田橋

SUIDOBASHI
水道橋

KUDANSHITA
九段下

HONGO-SANCHOME
本郷三丁目

UENO
上野

IRIYA
入谷

CHIYODA
千代田

JIMBOCHO
神保町

OCHA

HIBIYA LINE

INARICHO
稲荷町

KURADAMON

TOKYO
東京

OTEMACHI
大手町

IWAMOTOCHO
岩本町

AKIHABARA
秋葉原

MITSUKOSHI
三越前

SHIN-NIHOMBASHI
新日本橋

SOBU LINE

BAKUROCHO
馬喰町

ASAKUSABASHI
浅草橋

ASAKUSA
浅草

KUCHO

NIHOMBASHI
日本橋

BAKURO-
YOKOYAMA
馬喰横山

HIGASHI-NIHOMBASHI
東日本橋

TOEI ASAKUSA LINE

SHINTOMICHO
新富町

NINGYOCHO
人形町

KAYABACHO
茅場町

SUITENGU-MAE
水天宮前

CHUO
中央

SUMIDA
隅田

HONJO-AZUMABASHI
本所吾妻橋

85

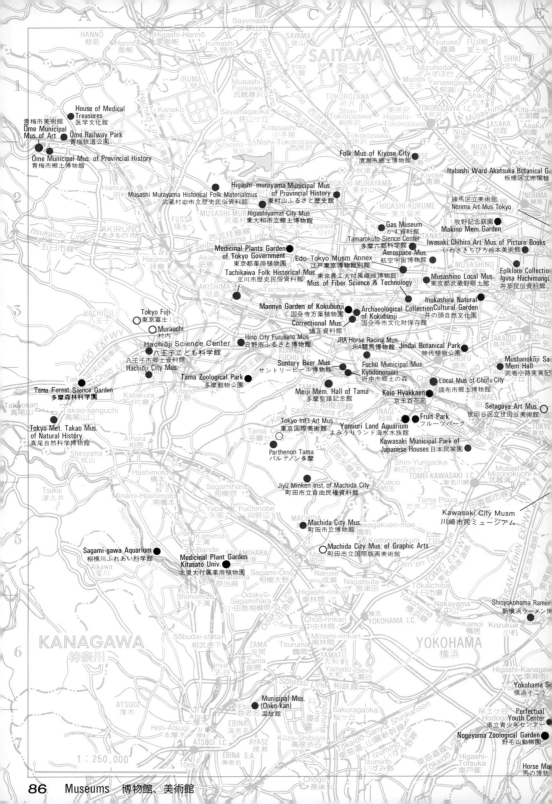

House of Medical
Treasures
医学文化館

青梅市美術館
Ōme Municipal
Mus. of Art

Ōme Railway Park
青梅鉄道公園

Ōme Municipal Mus. of Provincial History
青梅市郷土博物館

Folk Mus of Kiyose City
清瀬市郷土博物館

Itabashi Ward Akatsuka Botanical G.
板橋区立赤塚植

練馬区立美術館
Nerima Art Mus Tokyo

Higashi-murayama Municipal Mus.
of Provincial History
東村山ふるさと歴史館

Musashi Murayama Historical Folk Materialmus
武蔵村山市立歴史民俗資料館

Higashiyamat City Mus
東大和市立郷土博物館

牧野記念庭園
Makino Mem. Garden

Gas Museum
かす資料館

Tamarokuto Sience Center
多摩六都科学館

Iwasaki Chihiro Art Mus. of Picture Books
いわさきちひろ絵本美術館

Medicinal Plants Garden
of Tokyo Government
東京都薬用植物園

Aerospace Mus.
航空宇宙博物館

Edo-Tokyo Musm Annex
江戸東京博物館別館

Musashino Local Mus.
東京都武蔵野郷土館

Folklore Collectio
Igusa Hachimangu
井草民俗資料館

Tachikawa Folk Historical Mus.
立川市歴史民俗資料館

東京農工大付属繊維博物館
Mus. of Fiber Science & Technology

Tokyo Fuji
東京富士

Murauchi
村内

Hachiōji Science Center
八王子こども科学館

Mannyo Garden of Kokubunji
国分寺万葉植物園

Archaeological Collection
of Kokubunji
国分寺市文化財保存館

Cultural Garden
井の頭自然文化園

Inokashira Natural

Correctional Mus.
矯正資料館

JRA Horse Racing Mus.
JRA競馬博物館

Jindai Botanical Park
神代植物公園

Mushanokōji Sa
Mem. Hall
武者小路実篤記

八王子市郷土資料館
Hachiōji City Mus.

Hino City Furusato Mus.
日野市ふるさと博物館

Suntory Beer Mus.
サントリービール博物館

Fuchū Municipal Mus.
Kyōdonomori
府中市郷土の森

Local Mus of Chofu City
調布市郷土博物館

Tama Forest Science Garden
多摩森林科学園

Tama Zoological Park
多摩動物公園

Meiji Mem. Hall of Tama
多摩聖蹟記念館

Keio Hyakkaen
京王百花苑

Setagaya Art Mus.
世田谷区立世田谷美術館

Tokyo Met. Takao Mus.
of Natural History
高尾自然科学博物館

Tokyo Int'l Art Mus
東京国際美術館

Fruit Park
フルーツパーク

Yomiuri Land Aquarium
よみうりランド海水水族館

Parthenon Tama
パルテノン多摩

Kawasaki Municipal Park of
Japanese Houses 日本民家園

Sagami-gawa Aquarium
相模川ふれあい科学館

Jiyū Minken Inst. of Machida City
町田市立自由民権資料館

Kawasaki City Musm
川崎市民ミュージアム

Medicinal Plant Garden
Kitasato Univ.
北里大付属薬用植物園

Machida City Mus.
町田市立博物館

Machida City Mus. of Graphic Arts
町田市立国際版画美術館

Shinyokohama Ramer
新横浜ラーメン

KANAGAWA
神奈川

YOKOHAMA
横浜

Yokohama S
横浜こ

Municipal Mus.
(Onko-kan)
温故館

Perfectual
Youth Center
県立青少年センター

Nogeyama Zoological Garden
野毛山動物園

Horse Mu
馬の博物

1 : 250,000

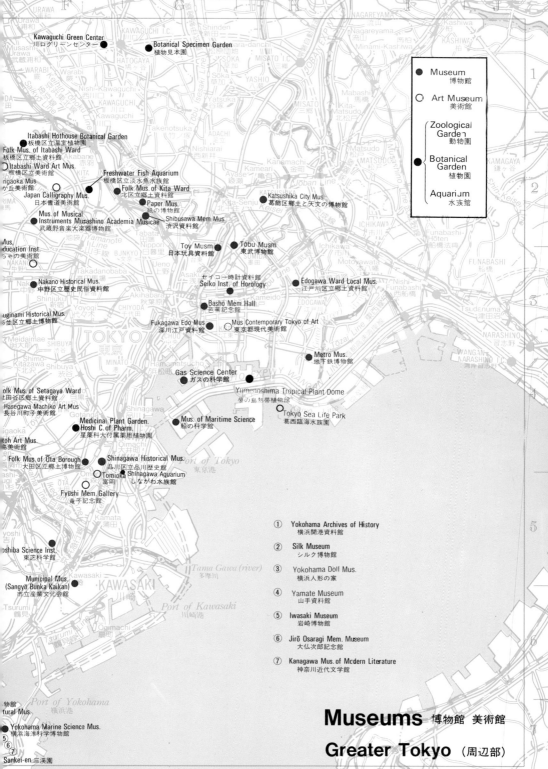

Kawaguchi Green Center
川口グリーンセンター

Botanical Specimen Garden
植物見本園

Itabashi Hothouse Botanical Garden
板橋区立温室植物園
Folk Mus. of Itabashi Ward
板橋区立郷土資料館
Itabashi Ward Art Mus.
板橋区立美術館
rigaoka Mus
が丘美術館
Japan Calligraphy Mus.
日本書道美術館
Mus. of Musical
Instruments Musashino Academia Musicae
武蔵野音楽大楽器博物館

Freshwater Fish Aquarium
板橋区立淡水魚水族館
Folk Mus. of Kita Ward
北区立郷土資料館
Paper Mus.
紙の博物館
Shibusawa Mem Mus
渋沢資料館

Katsushika City Mus
葛飾区郷土と天文の博物館

Mus,
ducation Inst.
ちゃの美術館

Nakano Historical Mus.
中野区立歴史民俗資料館

uginami Historical Mus.
区立郷土博物館

Toy Musm
日本玩具資料館
Tōbu Musm
東武博物館

Seiko Inst. of Horology
セイコー時計資料館

Edogawa Ward Local Mus.
江戸川区立郷土資料館

Bashō Mem Hall
芭蕉記念館

Fukagawa Edo Mus.
深川江戸資料館
Mus Contemporary Tokyo of Art
東京都現代美術館

Metro Mus.
地下鉄博物館

Gas Science Center
ガスの科学館

olk Mus. of Setagaya Ward
田谷区郷土資料館
Hasegawa Machiko Art Mus
長谷川町子美術館
igaoka
toh Art Mus.
島美術館
Folk Mus. of Ōta Borough
大田区立郷土博物館

Medicinal Plant Garden.
Hoshi C. of Pharm.
星薬科大付属薬用植物園

Mus. of Maritime Science
船の科学館

Yumenoshima Tropical Plant Dome
夢の島熱帯植物館

Tokyo Sea Life Park
葛西臨海水族園

Shinagawa Historical Mus.
品川区立品川歴史館
Tomioka Shinagawa Aquarium
富岡 しながわ水族館
Fyūshi Mem Gallery
竜子記念館

oshiba Science Inst.
東芝科学館

Municipal Mus.
(Sangyō Bunka Kaikan)
市立産業文化会館

Tama Gawa (river)
多摩川

KAWASAKI

Port of Kawasaki
川崎港

Port of Tokyo
東京港

Port of Yokohama
横浜港

物館
tural Mus.

Yokohama Marine Science Mus.
横浜海洋科学博物館

Sankei-en 三溪園

① Yokohama Archives of History
横浜開港資料館

② Silk Museum
シルク博物館

③ Yokohama Doll Mus.
横浜人形の家

④ Yamate Museum
山手資料館

⑤ Iwasaki Museum
岩崎博物館

⑥ Jirō Osaragi Mem. Museum
大仏次郎記念館

⑦ Kanagawa Mus. of Modern Literature
神奈川近代文学館

● Museum
博物館

○ Art Museum
美術館

Zoological Garden
動物園

● Botanical Garden
植物園

Aquarium
水族館

Museums 博物館 美術館

Greater Tokyo (周辺部)

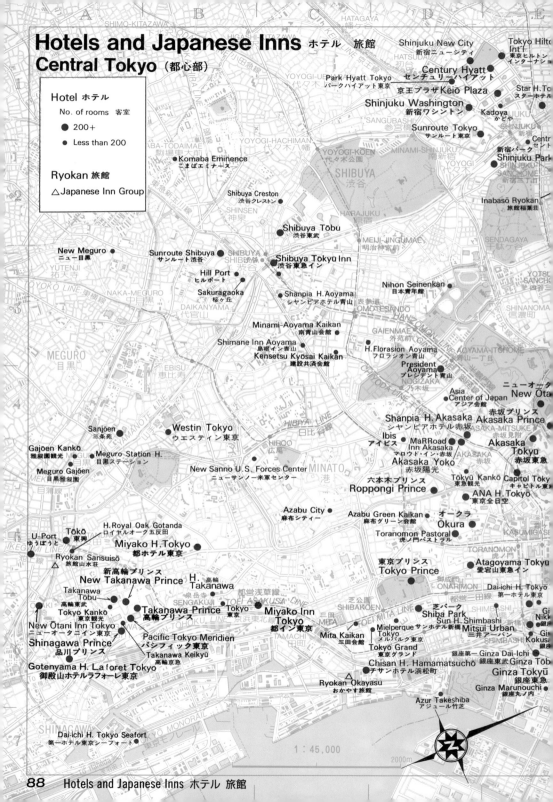

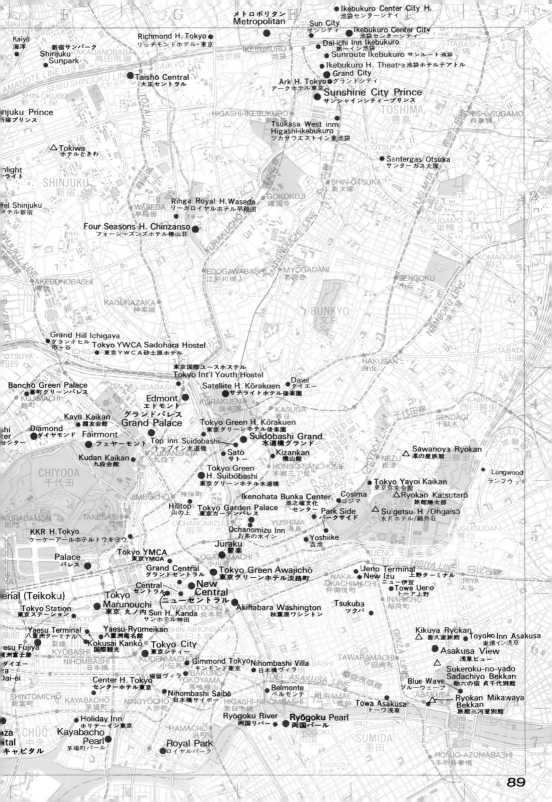

メトロポリタン
Metropolitan

Ikebukuro Center City H.
Sun City
サンシティ

Richmond H. Tokyo
リッチモンドホテル・東京

Ikebukuro Center City
池袋センターシティ

Dai-ichi Inn Ikebukuro
第一イン池袋

Sunroute Ikebukuro サンルート池袋

Kaiyō
海洋

新宿サンパーク
Shinjuku
Sunpark

Ikebukuro H. Theatre 池袋ホテルテアトル

Grand City
グランドシティ

Taisho Central
大正セントラル

Ark H. Tokyo
アークホテル東京

Sunshine City Prince
サンシャインシティープリンス

njuku Prince
宿プリンス

Tsukasa West inm
Higashi-ikebukuro
ツカサウエストイン東池袋

Santergas Otsuka
サンターガス 大塚

△ Tokiwa
ホテルときわ

nlight
ライト

el Shinjuku
テル新宿

Rihga Royal H. Waseda
リーガロイヤルホテル早稲田

Four Seasons H. Chinzanso
フォーシーズンズホテル椿山荘

Grand Hill Ichigaya
グランドヒル
市ヶ谷

Tokyo YWCA Sadohara Hostel
東京YWCA砂土原寮ホステル

東京国際ユースホステル
Tokyo Int'l Youth Hostel

Bancho Green Palace
番町グリーンパレス
番町グリーンパレス

Satellite H. Kōrakuen
サテライトホテル後楽園

Daiei
ダイエー

Edmont
エドモント

Kayu Kaikan
霞友会館

Grand Palace
グランドパレス

Tokyo Green H. Kōrakuen
東京グリーンホテル後楽園

Suidobashi Grand
水道橋グランド

Sawanoya Ryokan
澤の屋旅館

Diamond
ダイヤモンド

Fairmont
フェヤーモント

Top inn Suidobashi
トップイン水道橋

Kizankan
喜山館

Lungwood
ラングウッド

Kudan Kaikan
九段会館

Satō
サトー

Tokyo Green
H. Suibōbashi
東京グリーンホテル水道橋

Tokyo Yayoi Kaikan
東京弥生会館

Cosima
コジマ

Ryokan Katsutarō
旅館勝太郎

CHIYODA
千代田

Ikenohata Bunka Center
池之端文化
センター

Park Side
パークサイド

△ Suigetsu H / Ohgaisō
水月ホテル/鴎外荘

KKR H.Tokyo
ケーケーアールホテルトウキョウ

Hilltop
山の上

Tokyo Garden Palace
東京ガーデンパレス

Ochanomizu Inn
お茶の水イン

Yoshiike
吉池

Palace
パレス

Tokyo YMCA
東京YMCA

Juraku
聚楽

Ueno Terminal
New Izu
ニュー伊豆

perial (Teikoku)

Grand Central
グランドセントラル

Tokyo Green Awajichō
東京グリーンホテル淡路町

Towa Ueno
東和上野

Kikuya Ryokan
△喜久屋旅館

Toyoko Inn Asakusa
東横イン浅草

Central
セントラル

New
Central
ニューセントラル

Tsukuba
ツクバ

Tokyo Station
東京ステーション

Tokyo
Marunouchi
東京 丸ノ内

Sun H. Kanda
サンホテル神田

Akihabara Washington
秋葉原ワシントン

Asakusa View
浅草ビュー

Yaesu Terminal
八重洲ターミナル

Yaesu-Ryūmeikan
八重洲竜名館

Sukeroku-no-yado
Sadachiyo Bekkan
助六の宿 貞千代別館

su Fujiya
洲富士屋

Kokusai Kankō
国際観光

Tokyo City
東京シティー

Gimmond Tokyo
キンモンド東京

Nihombashi Villa
日本橋ヴィラ

Blue Wave
ブルーウェーブ

Ryokan Mikawaya
Bekkan
旅館三河屋別館

Dai-ei

Center H. Tokyo
センターホテル東京

Nihombashi Saibo
日本橋サイボー

Belmonte
ベルモンテ

Towa Asakusa
トーワ浅草

za
tal

Holiday Inn
ホリデーイン東京

Kayabacho
Pearl
茅場町パール

Ryōgoku River
両国リバー

Ryōgoku Pearl
両国パール

Royal Park
ロイヤルパーク

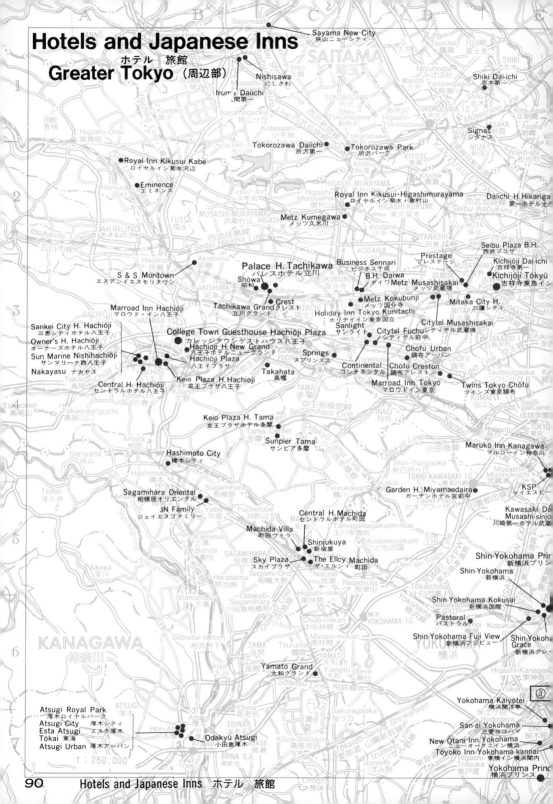

Hotels and Japanese Inns
ホテル　旅館
Greater Tokyo （周辺部）

Sayama New City
狭山ニューシティ

Nishisawa
にしさわ

Irumu-Daiichi
入間第一

Shiki Dai-ichi
志木第一

Tokorozawa Daiichi
所沢第一

Tokorozawa Park
所沢パーク

Signas
シグナス

Royal Inn Kikusui Kabe
ロイヤルイン菊水河辺

Eminence
エミネンス

Royal Inn Kikusui・Higashimurayama
ロイヤルイン菊水・東村山

Daiichi H. Hikariga
第一ホテル光ヶ

Metz Kumegawa
メッツ米川

Seibu Plaza B.H.
西武プラザ

S & S Moritown
エスアンドエスモリタウン

Palace H. Tachikawa
パレスホテル立川

Business Sennari
ビジネス千成

Prestage
プレステージ

Kichijōji Dai-ichi
吉祥寺第一

Kichijōji Tōkyū
吉祥寺東急イン

Shōwa
昭和

B.H. Daiwa
ダイワ

Metz Musashisakai
メッツ武蔵境

Crest
クレスト

Metz Kokubunji
メッツ国分寺

Mitaka City H.
三鷹シティ

Marroad Inn Hachiōji
マロウド・イン八王子

Tachikawa Grand
立川グランド

Holiday Inn Tokyo Kunitachi
ホリディイン東京国立

Citytel Musashisakai
シティテル武蔵境

Sankei City H. Hachiōji
三恵シティホテル八王子

College Town Guesthouse Hachiōji Plaza
カレッジタウンゲストハウス八王子

Sanlight
サンライト

Citytel Fuchū
シティテル府中

Chōfu Urban
調布アーバン

Owner's H. Hachiōji
オーナーズホテル八王子

Hachiōji H. New Grand
八王子ホテルニューグランド

Sun Marine Nishihachiōji
サンマリーン西八王子

Hachiōji Plaza
八王子プラザ

Springs
スプリングス

Continental
コンチネンタル

Chōfu Creston
調布クレストン

Nakayasu
ナカヤス

Keio Plaza H. Hachiōji
京王プラザ八王子

Takahata
高幡

Marroad Inn Tokyo
マロウドイン東京

Twins Tokyo Chōfu
ツインズ東京調布

Central H. Hachiōji
セントラルホテル八王子

Keio Plaza H. Tama
京王プラザホテル多摩

Marukō Inn Kanagawa
マルコーイン神奈川

Hashimoto City
橋本シティ

Sunpier Tama
サンピア多摩

KSP
ケイエスピー

Sagamihara Oriental
相模原オリエンタル

Garden H. Miyamaedaira
ガーデンホテル宮前平

JN Family
ジェイエヌファミリー

Central H. Machida
セントラルホテル町田

Kawasaki Da
Musashi-shinjo
川崎第一ホテル武蔵

Machida Villa
町田ヴィラ

Shinjukuya
新宿屋

Sky Plaza
スカイプラザ

The Ellcy Machida
ザ・エルシィ町田

Shin-Yokohama Prir
新横浜プリン

Shin-Yokohama
新横浜

Shin-Yokohama Kokusai
新横浜国際

Pastoral
パストラル

Shin-Yokohama Fuji View
新横浜フジビュー

Shin-Yokoha
Grace
新横浜グレ

Yamato Grand
大和グランド

Yokohama Kaiyōtei
横浜開洋亭

Atsugi Royal Park
厚木ロイヤルパーク

Atsugi City 厚木シティ

San-ai Yokohama
三愛ヨコハマ

Esta Atsugi エスタ厚木

New Ōtani Inn Yokohama
ニューオータニイン横浜

Tōkai 東海

Odakyū Atsugi
小田急厚木

Tōyoko Inn Yokohama kannai
東横イン横浜駅内

Atsugi Urban 厚木アーバン

1 : 250,000

Yokohama Princ
横浜プリンス

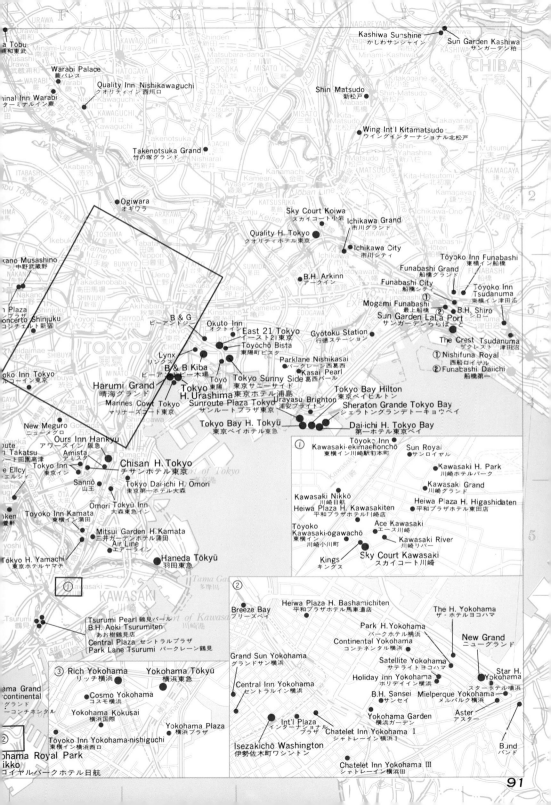

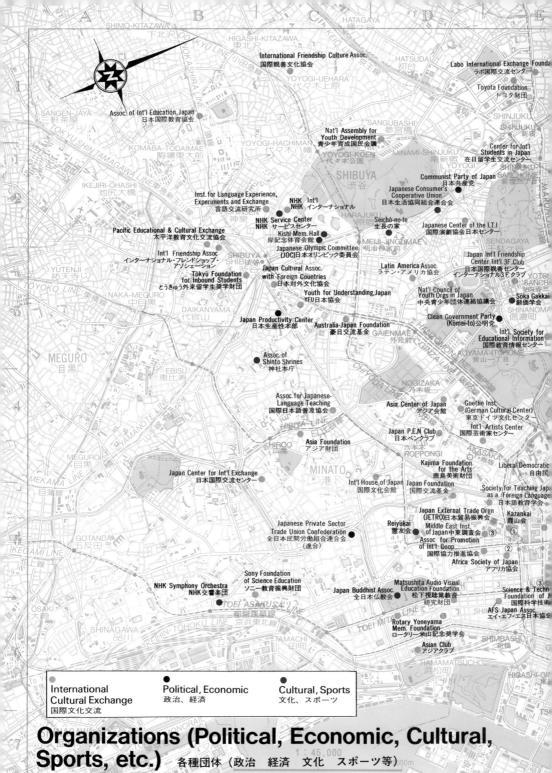

International Friendship Culture Assoc.
国際親善文化協会

Labo International Exchange Foundation
ラボ国際交流センター

Toyota Foundation
トヨタ財団

Assoc. of Int'l Education, Japan
日本国際教育協会

Nat'l Assembly for Youth Development
青少年育成国民会議

Center for Int'l Students in Japan
在日留学生センター

Communist Party of Japan
日本共産党

Japanese Consumer's Cooperative Union
日本生活協同組合連合会

Inst. for Language Experience, Experiments and Exchange
言語交流研究所

NHK Int'l
NHK インターナショナル

Seichô-no-Ie
生長の家

Japanese Center of the I.T.I.
国際演劇協会日本センター

NHK Service Center
NHK サービスセンター

Kishi Mem. Hall
岸記念体育会館

Pacific Educational & Cultural Exchange
太平洋教育文化交流協会

Japanese Olympic Committee
(JOC)日本オリンピック委員会

Japan Int'l Friendship Center Int'l 3F Club
日本国際親善センター インターナショナル3Fクラブ

Int'l Friendship Assoc
インターナショナル・フレンドシップ・アソシエーション

Japan Cultural Assoc. with Foreign Countries
日本対外文化協会

Latin America Assoc.
ラテン・アメリカ協会

Tôkyû Foundation for Inbound Students
とうきゅう外来留学生奨学財団

Youth for Understanding,Japan
YFU日本協会

Nat'l Council of Youth Orgs in Japan
中央青少年団体連絡協議会

Sôka Gakkai
創価学会

Japan Productivity Center
日本生産性本部

Australia-Japan Foundation
豪日交流基金

Clean Government Party (Komei-to)公明党

Int'l Society for Educational Information
国際教育情報センター

Assoc. of Shinto Shrines
神社本庁

Assoc. for Japanese-Language Teaching
国際日本語普及協会

Asia Center of Japan
アジア会館

Goethe Inst. (German Cultural Center)
東京ドイツ文化センター

Int'l Artists Center
国際芸術家センター

Asia Foundation
アジア財団

Japan P.E.N Club
日本ペンクラブ

Kajima Foundation for the Arts
鹿島美術財団

Liberal-Democratic
自由党

Japan Center for Int'l Exchange
日本国際交流センター

Int'l House of Japan
国際文化会館

Japan Foundation
国際交流基金

Society for Teaching Japanese as a Foreign Language
日本語教育学会

Japan External Trade Orgn (JETRO)日本貿易振興会

Kazankai
霞山会

Japanese Private Sector Trade Union Confederation
全日本民間労働組合連合会 (連合)

Reiyûkai
霊友会

Middle East Inst. of Japan中東調査会

Assoc. for Promotion of Int'l Coop.
国際協力推進協会

Africa Society of Japan
アフリカ協会

Sony Foundation of Science Education
ソニー教育振興財団

NHK Symphony Orchestra
NHK交響楽団

Japan Buddhist Assoc.
全日本仏教会

Matsushita Audio Visual Education Foundation
松下視聴覚教育研究財団

Science & Technology Foundation of Japan
国際科学技術財団

AFS Japan Assoc.
エイ・エフ・エス日本協会

Rotary Yoneyama Mem. Foundation
ロータリー米山記念奨学会

Asian Club
アジアクラブ

● International Cultural Exchange
国際文化交流

● Political, Economic
政治、経済

● Cultural, Sports
文化、スポーツ

Organizations (Political, Economic, Cultural, Sports, etc.) 各種団体（政治　経済　文化　スポーツ等）

1 : 45,000

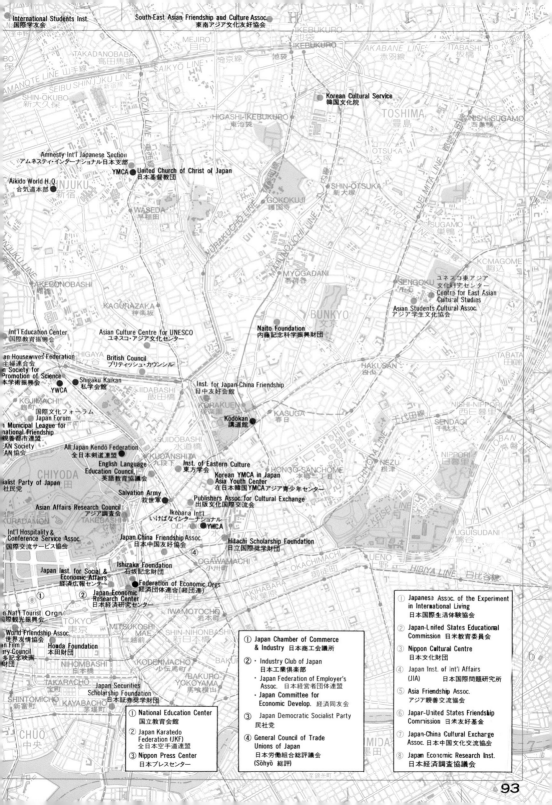

大日本印刷
DNP

Kawaguchi Metal
川口金属

Sôka
草加

Yashio 八潮

Shingō
新郷

Kitamatsudo
北松戸

Sharp
シャープ

Matsuhi-dai
松飛台

Sapporo Breweries
サッポロビール

on Metal
本金属

ppon Steel
新日本製鉄

Toshiba Chemical
東芝ケミカル

Snow Brand Milk
雪印乳業

Rengo
レンゴー

Nisshin Spinning
日清紡績

DNP
大日本印刷

Toppan
凸版印刷

Toppan
凸版印刷

Kirin Brewery
キリンビール

Japan Paper
日本紙業

Mitsubishi Paper
三菱製紙

Sumitomo Metal
住友金属

Japan Tobacco
日本たばこ

Printing Bureau
印刷局

Morinaga Milk
森永乳業

Iwaki Glass
岩城硝子

Nihon Kentetsu
日本建鉄

Asahi Glass
旭硝子

Kyōdo
共同印刷

Toppan
凸版印刷

Japan Tobacco
日本たばこ

Kao
花王

Seikosha
精工舎

Honshū Paper
本州製紙

Lotte
ロッテ

DNP
大日本印刷

Kubota
クボタ

Nisshin Steel
日新製鋼

Sapporo Breweries
サッポロビール

Ishikawajima-Harima
石川島播磨

Tokyo Oil Mills
東京油脂

Shin Tokyo Thermoelectric Power Plant
新東京火力発電所

Nippon Roller
日本ロール

Tokyo Gas
東京瓦斯

DNP
大日本印刷

Meidensha
明電舎

Sony
ソニー

Sankyō (Pharmaceutical)
三共

Japan Tobacco
日本たばこ

JR
JR大井工場

Matsushita Electric Ind.
松下電器

Mitsubishi Motors
三菱自動車

Canon
キャノン

Nippon Seikō
日本精工

NEC
日本電気

Mitsubishi Motors
自動車

Mitsui Seiki 三井精機

Fujitsū
富士通

Komatsu

Isuzu Motors
いすゞ自動車

Ajinomoto
味の素

Toshiba
東芝

Columbia
日本コロムビア

Tōyō Glass
東洋ガラス

Toshiba 東芝

General Sekiyu
(Petrol.) ゼネラル石油

o Auto Body
日野車体

NKK

Nippon Oil
日本石油

oshiba
東芝

aga&
永製菓

Shōwa
Electric Wire
昭和電線

Hitachi Zosen
日立造船

Mitsubishi Oil
三菱石油

NKK

urumi

Shōwa Denkō 昭和電工

Brewery

ssan 日産

Shōwa Shell Sekiyu 昭和シェル石油

Toshiba Turbine 東芝タービン

Tsurumi Soda 鶴見曹達

NKK

Asia Oil アジア石油

Shōwa Denkō 昭和電工

(Japan)

Port of Yokohama
横浜港

Port of Tokyo
東京港

Tokyo Wan (bay)
東京湾

Port of Kawasaki
川崎港

● Metalworking Industry
金属工業

○ Machine Industry
機械工業

◌ Chemical Industry
化学工業

◯ Petroleum Industry
石油工業

□ Printing Industry 印刷

● Food Industry 食品工業

○ Others その他

△ Laboratory 研究所

Industrial Park 工業団地

① Nisshin Flour 日清製粉

② Nippon Casting 日本鋳造

③ Fuji Electric 富士電機

④ Tokyo Gas 東京瓦斯

⑤ Asahi Glass 旭硝子

⑥ Yokohama Thermoelectric
Power Plant 横浜火力発電所

Factories and Industrial Facilities
著名工場

95

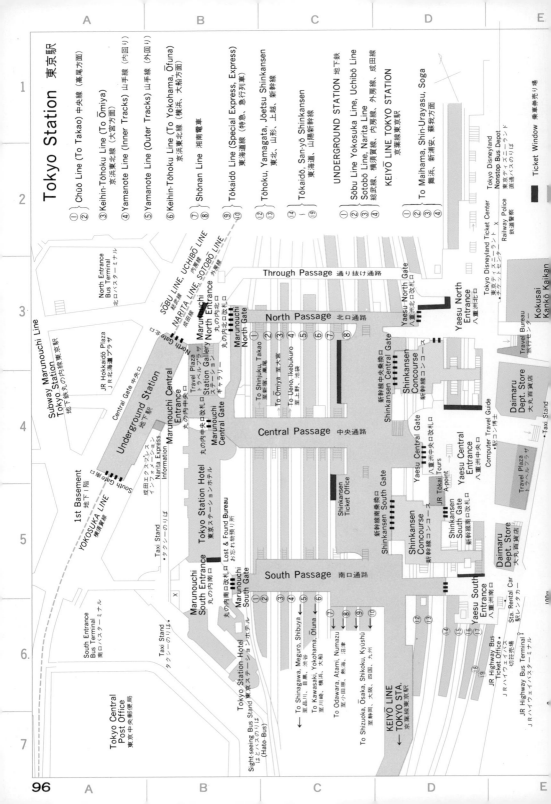

Routes to Airports
空港への交通

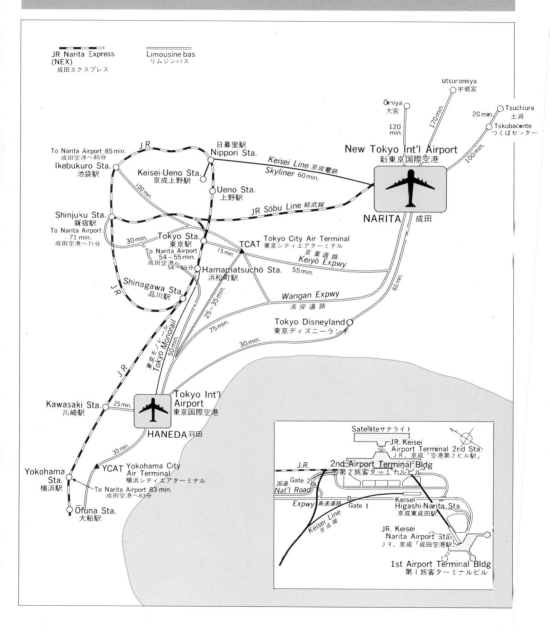

JR Narita Express (NEX)
成田エクスプレス

Limousine bas
リムジンバス

utsuromiya 宇都宮

Ōmiya 大宮
120 min.
170 min.
20 min.
Tsuchiura 土浦
Tsukubacente つくばセンター

New Tokyo Int'l Airport
新東京国際空港
NARITA 成田

100 min.

To Narita Airport 85 min.
成田空港へ85分
Ikebukuro Sta. 池袋駅

JR

日暮里駅 Nippori Sta.

Keisei Line 京成電鉄
Skyliner 60 min.

Keisei-Ueno Sta.
京成上野駅

Ueno Sta. 上野駅

100 min.

JR Sōbu Line 総武線

Shinjuku Sta. 新宿駅
To Narita Airport 71 min.
成田空港へ71分

30 min.

Tokyo Sta. 東京駅
To Narita Airport 54~55 min.
成田空港へ54~55分

TCAT Tokyo City Air Terminal
東京シティエアターミナル

15 min.

Keiyo Expwy
京葉道路

Hamamatsuchō Sta. 浜松町駅

55 min.

60 min.

Shinagawa Sta. 品川駅

JR

25~35 min.

Wangan Expwy
湾岸道路

Tokyo Disneyland
東京ディズニーランド

Tokyo Monorail
東京モノレール

50 min.

75 min.

30 min.

JR

Kawasaki Sta. 川崎駅

25 min.

Tokyo Int'l Airport
東京国際空港
HANEDA 羽田

30 min.

Yokohama Sta. 横浜駅

YCAT Yokohama City Air Terminal
横浜シティエアターミナル
To Narita Airport 83 min.
成田空港へ83分

Ōfuna Sta. 大船駅

Satellite サテライト

JR. Keisei
Airport Terminal 2nd Sta.
JR、京成「空港第2ビル駅」

J.R.

2nd Airport Terminal Bldg
第2旅客ターミナルビル

Gate 2
Nat'l Road
国道

Keisei
Higashi-Narita Sta.
京成東成田駅

Expwy 高速道路
Gate 1

JR. Keisei
Narita Airport Sta.
JR、京成「成田空港駅」

Keisei Line
京成線

1st Airport Terminal Bldg
第1旅客ターミナルビル

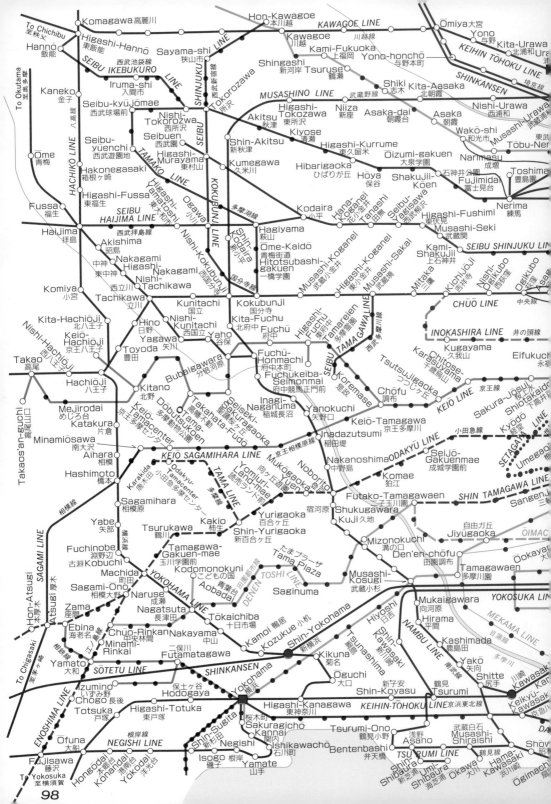

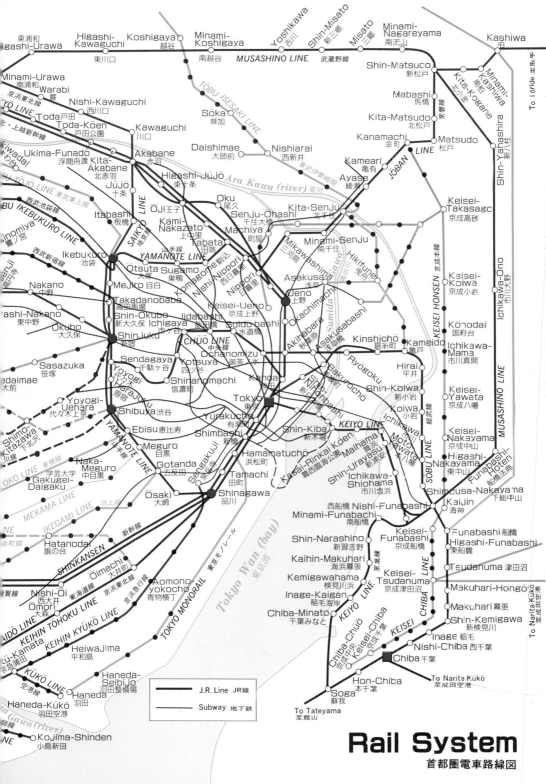

Rail System
首都圏電車路線図

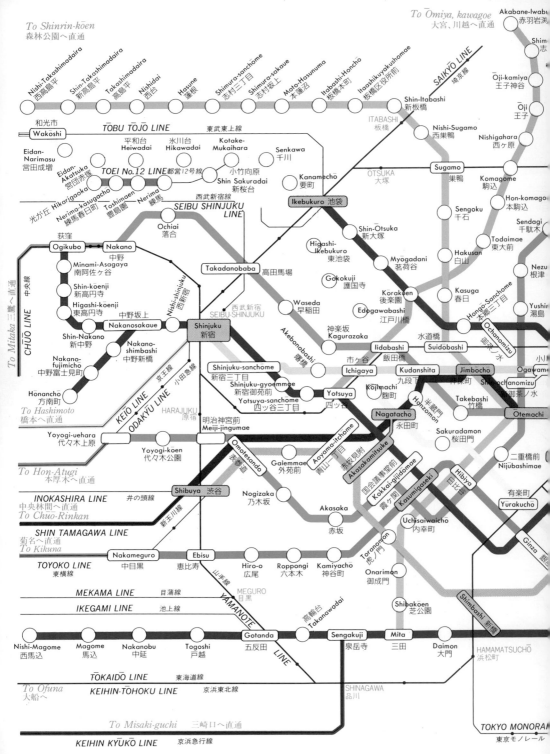

Subway System

東京地下鉄路線図

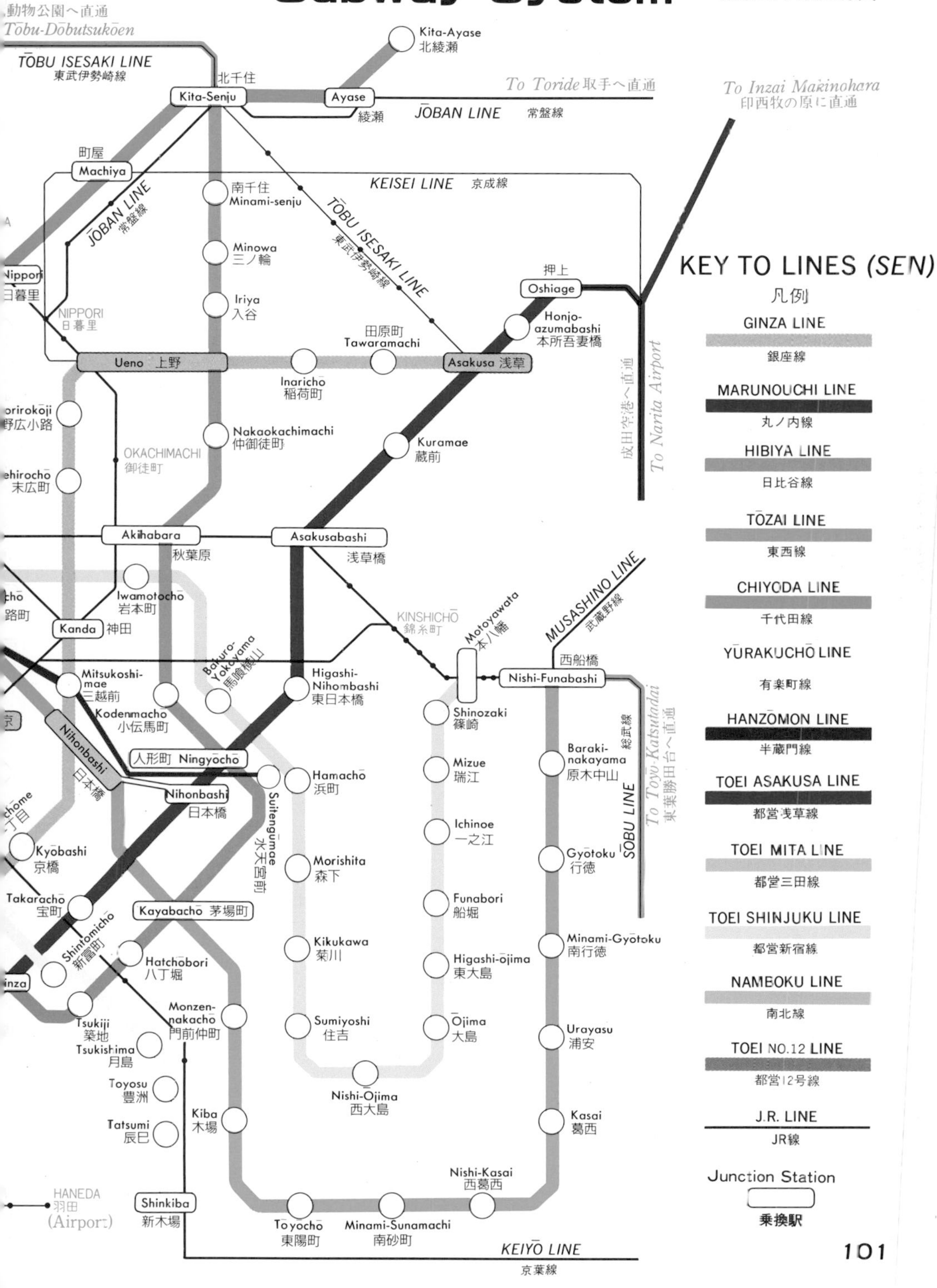

動物公園へ直通
Tōbu-Dōbutsukōen

TŌBU ISESAKI LINE
東武伊勢崎線

Kita-Ayase
北綾瀬

Kita-Senju
北千住

Ayase
綾瀬

To Toride 取手へ直通

To Inzai Makinohara
印西牧の原に直通

JŌBAN LINE 常磐線

Machiya
町屋

KEISEI LINE 京成線

Minami-senju
南千住

TŌBU ISESAKI LINE
東武伊勢崎線

Oshiage
押上

JŌBAN LINE
常磐線

Minowa
三ノ輪

Iriya
入谷

Honjo-
azumabashi
本所吾妻橋

Nippori
日暮里

NIPPORI
日暮里

Tawaramachi
田原町

Asakusa 浅草

成田空港へ直通

To Narita Airport

KEY TO LINES (SEN)
凡例

Ueno 上野

Inaricho
稲荷町

orirokoji
野広小路

OKACHIMACHI
御徒町

Nakaokachimachi
仲御徒町

Kuramae
蔵前

GINZA LINE
銀座線

ehirocho
末広町

Akihabara
秋葉原

Asakusabashi
浅草橋

MARUNOUCHI LINE
丸ノ内線

MUSASHINO LINE
武蔵野線

HIBIYA LINE
日比谷線

cho
路町

Iwamotocho
岩本町

KINSHICHO
錦糸町

Motoyawata
本八幡

TŌZAI LINE
東西線

Kanda 神田

Bakuro-
Yokoyama
馬喰横山

Higashi-
Nihombashi
東日本橋

Nishi-Funabashi
西船橋

CHIYODA LINE
千代田線

Mitsukoshi-
mae
三越前

Shinozaki
篠崎

Baraki-
nakayama
原木中山

YŪRAKUCHŌ LINE
有楽町線

Kodenmacho
小伝馬町

人形町 Ningyōcho

Mizue
瑞江

SŌBU LINE 総武線

HANZŌMON LINE
半蔵門線

Nihonbashi
日本橋

Nihonbashi
日本橋

Hamacho
浜町

Ichinoe
一之江

Gyōtoku
行徳

TOEI ASAKUSA LINE
都営浅草線

chome
一丁目

Kyōbashi
京橋

Suitengumae
水天宮前

Morishita
森下

Funabori
船堀

To Tow-Katsutadai
東葉勝田台へ直通

TOEI MITA LINE
都営三田線

Takaracho
宝町

Kayabachō 茅場町

Kikukawa
菊川

Minami-Gyōtoku
南行徳

TOEI SHINJUKU LINE
都営新宿線

Higashi-ojima
東大島

Shintomicho
新富町

Hatchōbori
八丁堀

Urayasu
浦安

NAMBOKU LINE
南北線

nza

Tsukiji
築地

Tsukishima
月島

Monzen-
nakacho
門前仲町

Sumiyoshi
住吉

Ōjima
大島

TOEI NO.12 LINE
都営12号線

Toyosu
豊洲

Kiba
木場

Nishi-Ojima
西大島

Kasai
葛西

J.R. LINE
JR線

Tatsumi
辰巳

Nishi-Kasai
西葛西

Junction Station

HANEDA
羽田
(Airport)
羽田

Shinkiba
新木場

Tōyochō
東陽町

Minami-Sunamachi
南砂町

乗換駅

KEIYŌ LINE
京葉線

101

Map of Japan 日本全図

INDEX
索　引（ABC順）

Please refer to the Useful Telephone Numbers section for government offices, embassies, airlines, hotels and inns.
官公庁、外国公館、航空会社、ホテル／旅館は、各種電話番号のページをご参照下さい。

Airlines　航空会社 ················ 145
Embassies　外国公館 ············ 144
Government Offices　官公庁 ···· 143
Hotels and Inns　ホテル、旅館 ······· 146

ABAB　アブアブ················ 30　B 4
ABC Kaikan Hall　abc 会館ホール···· 80　D 6
Adachi 1〜4 (Adachi-ku)　足立 1〜4丁目(足立区)··· 8　D 5
Adachi-ku　足立区············ 7　F 1
Adachi Ward Office　足立区役所··········· 8　C 5
Agebachō (Shinjuku-ku)　揚場町(新宿区)··· 23　I 3
Aihara Sation　相原駅········· 14　D 5
Aikidō World H. Q.　合気道本部道場··· 22　E 4
Aioichō (Itabashi-ku)　相生町(板橋区)··· 11　F 1
AIU Akasaka Bldg　AIU 赤坂ビル······ 46　B 4
AIG Bldg　AIG ビル············ 36　E 5
Aizumichō (Shinjuku-ku)　愛住町(新宿区)··· 23　F 5
Ajinomoto (H. O.)　味の素(本社)··· 37　I 1
Akabane 1〜3 (Kita-ku)　赤羽 1〜3丁目(北区)··· 11　H 1
Akabanedai 1〜4 (Kita-ku)　赤羽台 1〜4丁目(北区)··· 11　G 1
Akabane-Kita 1〜3 (Kita-ku)　赤羽北 1〜3丁目(北区)··· 11　G 1
Akabane-Minami 1〜2 (Kita-ku)　赤羽南 1〜2丁目(北区)··· 11　H 1
Akabane-Nishi 1〜6 (Kita-ku)　赤羽西 1〜6丁目(北区)·· 11　H 1
Akabane Station　赤羽駅······ 11　H 1
Akagimotomachi (Shinjuku-ku)　赤城元町(新宿区)·· 23　H 3
Akagishitamachi (Shinjuku-ku)　赤城下町(新宿区)··· 23　H 2
Akamon (gate)　赤門········· 16　B 1
Akasaka 1〜9 (Minato-ku)　赤坂 1〜9丁目(港区)··· 21　H 2
Akasaka Center Bldg　赤坂センタービル······ 46　A 4
Akasaka-mitsuke Station (subway)　赤坂見附駅(地下鉄)··· 46　C 4
Akasaka Palace (Akasaka Gosho)　赤坂御所········· 21　G 1
Akasaka Post Office　赤坂郵便局·········· 48　B 7
Akasaka Public Hall　赤坂公会堂······· 46　A 5
Akasaka Station (subway)　赤坂駅(地下鉄)······ 46　B 6
Akashichō (Chūō-ku)　明石町(中央区)··· 18　E 2
Akatsuka 1〜8 (Itabashi-ku)　赤塚 1〜8丁目(板橋区)··· 10　D 1
Akatsukashinmachi 1〜3 (Itabashi-ku)　赤塚新町1〜8丁目(板橋区)··· 10　D 1
Akatsutsumi 1〜5 (Setagaya-ku)　赤堤 1〜5丁目(世田谷区)··· 12　D 1
Akebonobashi Station (subway)　曙橋駅(地下鉄)···· 23　F 5
Akigawa Station　秋川駅······· 14　C 2

Akihabara (Taitō-ku)　秋葉原(台東区)··· 33　I 1
Akihabara Electrical Stores Street　秋葉原電気器具街··· 33　H 3
Akihabara Station　秋葉原駅··· 16　D 4
Akiruno City　あきる野市····· 14　C 2
Akishima City　昭島市········· 14　E 3
Akishima Station　昭島駅······ 14　E 2
Akitsu Station　秋津駅········· 15　H 1
All Japan Kendō Federation　全日本剣道連盟 ··· 93　F 4
Alpa Shopping Complex　アルパ専門店街··· 59　H 5
Amanuma 1〜3 (Suginamii-ku)　天沼 1〜3丁目(杉並区)··· 10　C 5
American Club　アメリカンクラブ··· 49　I 2
Ameya-Yokochō　アメヤ横丁··· 30　B 4
Ana Hachiman Jinja (shrine)　穴八幡神社 ·········· 23　E 3
Anamori-inari Station　穴守稲荷駅····· 13　I 7
Ancient Orient Museum　古代オリエント博物館 ··· 59　I 5
Anzen Station　安善駅········· 61　H 4
Aobadai 1〜4 (Meguro-ku)　青葉台 1〜4丁目(目黒区)·· 20　B 6
Aobadai Station　青葉台駅····· 60　B 2
Aoba Int'l Sch.　青葉インターナショナルスクール ··· 20　B 6
Aoi 1〜6 (Adachi-ku)　青井 1〜6丁目(足立区)··· 8　C 5
Aoi Kaikan (hall)　葵会館···· 88　E 5
Aomi 1〜2 (Kōtō-ku)　青海 1〜2丁目(江東区)··· 7　G 5
Aomi Station　青海駅········· 7　G 5
Aomono-yokochō Station　青物横丁駅··· 29　G 7
Aoto 1〜8 (Katsushika-ku)　青戸 1〜8丁目(葛飾区)····· 8　D 3
Aoto Station　青砥駅········· 8　D 3
Aoyama Cemetery　青山霊園··· 55　H 3
Aoyama Gakuin Univ.　青山学院大学······ 54　D 6
Aoyama Gakuin Univ. (Atsugi)　青山学院大学(厚木)··· 74　A 7
Aoyama Gakuin Univ. (Sci. & Engn.)　青山学院大学(理工)··· 74　E 3
Aoyama-itchōme Station (subway)　青山一丁目駅(地下鉄)··· 21　F 2
Aoyama Theater　青山劇場···· 54　C 5
Arai 1〜5 (Nakano-ku)　新井 1〜5丁目(中野区)··· 10　E 4
Arai Yakushi (temple)　新井薬師··· 11　F 4
Arai-yakushimae Station　新井薬師前駅··· 11　F 4
Arakawa 1〜8 (Arakawa-ku)　荒川 1〜8丁目(荒川区)··· 27　F 3
Arakawa-ku　荒川区·········· 7　F 1
Arakawa Natural Park　荒川自然公園··· 27　F 2
Arakawa Post Office　荒川郵便局··· 27　F 3
Arakawa Sports Center　荒川総合スポーツセンター ··· 27　G 3

Arakawa Ward Office　荒川区役所 …………… 27　F 3

Arakichō (Shinjuku-ku)　荒木町(新宿区) …… 23　F 5

Ariake1〜4 (Kōtō-ku)　有明1〜4丁目(江東区) … 7　G 5

Ariake Colosseum　有明コロシアム ………… 83　G 4

Ariake Station　有明駅 ……………………… 7　G 5

Ariake Tennis-no-mori Park　有明テニスの森公園 ……… 7　G 5

Arisugawa Mem. Park　有栖川宮記念公園 … 21　F 6

Ark Hills　アークヒルズ ……………………… 48　E 2

Asagaya-Kita1〜6 (Suginami-ku)　阿佐谷北1〜6丁目(杉並区) … 10　D 4

Asagaya-Minami1〜3 (Suginami-ku)　阿佐谷南1〜3丁目(杉並区) … 10　D 5

Asagaya Station　阿佐ケ谷駅 ……………… 10　D 5

Asahi Bank (H. O.)　あさひ銀行本店 ……… 36　D 5

Asahichō1〜3 (Nerima-ku)　旭町1〜3丁目(練馬区) …… 10　C 1

Asahigaoka1〜2 (Nerima-ku)　旭丘1〜2丁目(練馬区) … 11　F 3

Asahi Hall (Yūrakuchō)　朝日ホール(有楽町) … 38　E 2

Asahi Mutual Life Insurance (H. O.)　朝日生命(本社) … 56　D 4

Asahi Newspapers　朝日新聞社 …………… 18　C 3

Asahi Seimei Hall　朝日生命ホール ………… 56　D 4

Asakura Choso Museum　朝倉彫塑館 ……… 26　D 5

Asakusa1〜7 (Taitō-ku)　浅草1〜7丁目(台東区) … 27　H 7

Asakusabashi1〜5 (Taitō-ku)　浅草橋1〜5丁目(台東区) … 17　F 3

Asakusabashi Station　浅草橋駅 …………… 17　F 4

Asakusa Engei Hall　浅草演芸ホール ……… 31　F 4

Asakusa Handicrafts Museum　浅草巧芸館 … 31　F 3

Asakusa Jinja (shrine)　浅草神社 ………… 31　I 3

Asakusa Kannon-dō (temple)　浅草観音堂 … 31　H 3

Asakusa Museum　浅草風俗歴史館 ………… 31　H 3

Asakusa Post Office　浅草郵便局 ………… 31　F 6

Asakusa Public Hall　浅草公会堂 ………… 31　H 4

Asakusa Shōchiku (cinema)　浅草松竹(映) … 31　G 4

Asakusa Station (subway)　浅草駅(地下鉄) … 31　I 6

Asakusa Tōei (cinema)　浅草東映(映) …… 31　G 2

Asakusa Tōhō (cinema)　浅草東宝(映) …… 31　G 3

Asakusa Tourist Info. Center　浅草文化観光センター … 31　H 5

Asano Station　浅野駅 ……………………… 61　H 4

Asia Center of Japan　アジア会館 ………… 48　C 6

Asian Students Cultural Assoc.　アジア学生文化協会 … 93　I 3

Asia University　亜細亜大学 ……………… 74　D 3

Assoc. of Int'l Education Japan　日本国際教育協会 … 92　B 1

Asukayama Park　飛鳥山公園 ……………… 25　I 1

Atago1〜2 (Minato-ku)　愛宕1〜2丁目(港区) … 18　A 3

Atago Jinja (shrine)　愛宕神社 …………… 80　D 5

Atomi Gakuen Women's Univ.　跡見学園女子大学 … 74　D 1

Atsugi Airfield　厚木飛行場 ……………… 60　A 5

Australia-Japan Foundation　豪日交流基金 … 92　C 3

Autographic Ukiyoe Mus.　肉筆浮世絵美術館 … 84　D 5

Aviation Bldg　航空会館 …………………… 38　A 5

Awajichō Station (subway)　淡路町駅(地下鉄) … 33　G 5

Axis Bldg　アクシスビル …………………… 49　H 3

Ayase1〜7 (Adachi-ku)　綾瀬1〜7丁目(足立区) … 9　C 4

Ayase Station　綾瀬駅 ……………………… 8　D 4

Azabudai1〜3 (Minato-ku)　麻布台1〜3丁目(港区) … 21　I 5

Azabu Green Kaikan (hall)　麻布グリーン会館 ……… 49　G 1

Azabujūban1〜4 (Minato-ku)　麻布十番1〜4丁目(港区) … 21　H 5

Azabu-Mamianachō (Minato-ku)　麻布狸穴町(港区) … 21　I 4

Azabu-Nagasakachō (Minato-ku)　麻布永坂町(港区) … 49　I 3

Azabu Post Office　麻布郵便局 …………… 49　H 1

Azabu Univ. (Veterinary)　麻布大学(獣医) … 74　B 5

Azamino Station　あざみ野駅 ……………… 60　D 1

Azumabashi1〜3 (Sumida-ku)　吾妻橋1〜3丁目(墨田区) … 17　I 2

Azusawa1〜4 (Itabashi-ku)　小豆沢1〜4丁目(板橋区) … 11　G 1

Babashitachō (Shinjuku-ku)　馬場下町(新宿区) … 23　F 2

Baji Kōen (park)　馬事公苑 ……………… 12　D 2

Bakurochō Station　馬喰町駅 ……………… 17　F 5

Bakuro-Yokoyama Station (subway)　馬喰横山駅(地下鉄) … 17　F 5

Bank of Japan (H. O.)　日本銀行(本店) …… 34　C 6

Bank of Tokyo-Mitsubishi (H. O.)　東京三菱銀行(本店) … 37　H 5

Baseball Hall of Fame & Museum　野球体育博物館 … 85　G 4

Bashō Memorial Hall　芭蕉記念館 ………… 17　H 6

Belle Vie Akasaka　ベルビー赤坂 ………… 46　B 4

Bentenbashi Station　弁天橋駅 …………… 61　H 4

Bentenchō (Shinjuku-ku)　弁天町(新宿区) … 23　G 3

Bicycle Culture Center　自転車文化センター … 84　E 5

Big Box Bldg　ビッグボックスビル ………… 22　D 1

Bishamonten (temple) (Kagurazaka)　毘沙門天(神楽坂) … 23　I 3

Botan1〜3 (Kōtō-ku)　牡丹1〜3丁目(江東区) … 19　H 2

Braille Library　日本点字図書館 ………… 22　D 1

Bridgestone Museum of Art　ブリヂストン美術館 …… 35　H 5

British Council, Japan　ブリティッシュ・カウンシル … 93　G 3

Bubaigawara Station　分倍河原駅 ………… 15　G 4

Bungeishunju　文芸春秋 …………………… 46　C 1

Bungei-za　文芸座 ………………………… 59　F 2

Bunka1〜3 (Sumida-ku)　文花1〜3丁目(墨田区) … 9　F 5

Bunka Broadcasting (NCB)　文化放送 …… 23　F 6

Bunka Gakuen Costume Musm　文化学園服飾博物館 … 22　B 6

Bunkamura　東急文化村 …………………… 52　B 4

Bunka Women's Univ.　文化女子大学 …… 22　B 6

Bunkyō-ku　文京区 ………………………… 7　F 2

Bunkyō Museum　文京ふるさと歴史館 …… 16　B 2

Bunkyō Ward Gym.　文京総合体育館 …… 16　C 2

Bunkyō Ward Office　文京区役所 ………… 16　A 2

Cabinet Library (Naikaku Bunko)　内閣文庫 … 36　D 7

Cancer Institute Hosp.　癌研究会付属病院 … 25　F 3

Casals Hall　カザルスホール ……………… 32　E 4

Central Plaza Bldg.　セントラルプラザ …… 23　I 3

Chichibu Mem. Rugby Stadium　秩父宮記念ラグビー場 … 21　F 2

Chidori1〜3 (Ōta-ku)　千鳥1〜3丁目(大田区) … 13　F 5

Chidorichō Station　千鳥町駅 …………… 13　G 5

Chidorigafuchi Nat'l Mem. Garden　千鳥ケ淵戦没者墓苑 … 23　J 5

Chihayachō1〜4 (Toshima-ku)　千早町1〜4丁目(豊島区) … 24　A 4

China Town (Yokohama)　中華街(横浜) …… 63　G 5

Chinzan-sō　椿山荘 ………………………… 23　G 1

Chitose1〜3 (Sumida-ku) 千歳1〜3丁目(墨田区)········ 17 H5
Chitosedai1〜6 (Setagaya-ku) 千歳台1〜6丁目(世田谷区)··· 12 C1
Chitose-Funabashi Station 千歳船橋駅········ 12 C1
Chitose-Karasuyama Station 千歳烏山駅········ 10 C7
Chiyoda (Chiyoda-ku) 千代田(千代田区)········ 16 A6
Chiyoda Bldg 千代田ビル········ 35 I6
Chiyoda-ku 千代田区········ 7 F1
Chiyoda Mutual Life Insurance (H. O.) 千代田生命(本社)··· 28 A1
Chiyoda Ward Gym. 千代田区総合体育館········ 36 B2
Chiyoda Ward Office 千代田区役所········ 32 A5
Chōfu City 調布市········ 15 I4
Chōfu Station 調布駅········ 15 I4
Chōgo Station 長後駅········ 60 A7
Chōmei-ji (temple) 長命寺········ 10 C3
Chōsen-in (temple) 長泉院········ 28 A2
Christian Academy クリスチャンアカデミー········ !5 I1
Chūō1〜4 (Edogawa-ku) 中央1〜4丁目(江戸川区)···· 9 F2
Chūō1〜5 (Nakano-ku) 中央1〜5丁目(中野区)····· 11 E5
Chūō1〜8 (Ōta-ku) 中央1〜8丁目(大田区)········ 13 H5
Chūōchō1〜2 (Meguro-ku) 中央1〜2丁目(目黒区)··· 13 F2
Chūō-Honchō1〜5 (Adachi-ku) 中央本町1〜5丁目(足立区)··· 8 C5
Chūō-ku 中央区········ 7 G4
Chūō-Rinkan Station 中央林間駅········ 60 A3
Chūō Trust Bank (H. O.) 中央信託銀行(本店)········ 35 I6
Chūō University 中央大学········ 15 F5
Chūō Univ. (Sci. & Engn.) 中央大学(理工)········ 16 A2
Chūō Ward Office 中央区役所········ 39 I4
Cine Vivant シネヴィヴァン········ 49 H6
Common Gov't Bldgs (Ōtemachi) 合同庁舎(大手町)··· 36 B5
Common Gov't Bldg (Kasumigaseki) 合同庁舎(霞が関)··· 47 G6
Communications Museum 逓心総合博物館········ 36 C3
Costume Museum 杉野学園衣裳博物館········ 28 C3

Daiba (Minato-ku) 台場(港区)········ 13 J2
Daiba Station 台場駅········ 7 F5
Daien-ji (temple) 大円寺········ 28 C3
Dai-Ichi Kangyō Bank (H. O.) 第一勧業銀行(本店)····· 38 B4
Dai-ichi Mutual Life Insurance 第一生命········ 38 C1
Daikanyamachō (Shibuya-ku) 代官山町(渋谷区)··· 20 C6
Daikan-yama Station 代官山駅········ 20 C6
Daikyōchō (Shinjuku-ku) 大京町(新宿区)········ 23 F6
Daimaru Dept Store 大丸デパート········ 23 G7
Daimon (Itabashi-ku) 大門(板橋区)········ 6 D1
Daimon Station (subway) 大門駅(地下鉄)········ 18 B5
Daimyō Clock Museum 大名時計博物館········ 26 C6
Dai Nippon Printing (H. O.) 大日本印刷(本社)········ 23 H4
Daishimae Station 大師前駅········ 8 C6
Daita1〜6 (Setagaya-ku) 代田1〜6丁目(世田谷区)··· 12 E1
Daitabashi Station 代田橋駅········ 10 E6
Daito Bunka University 大東文化大学········ 11 F1
Daizawa1〜5 (Setagaya-ku) 代沢1〜5丁目(世田谷区)··· 12 E1
Defense Medical College 防衛医科大学校········ 74 C1

Denbōin (temple) 伝法院········ 31 H4
Den'enchōfu1〜5 (Ōta-ku) 田園調布1〜5丁目(大田区)··· 12 E4
Den'enchōfu-Honchō (Ōta-ku) 田園調布本町(大田区)··· 13 F5
Den'enchōfu-Minami (Ōta-ku) 田園調布南(大田区)···· 13 F5
Den'enchōfu Station 田園調布駅········ 13 E4
Dentsū Inc. (H. O.) 電通(本社)········ 39 H5
Denzū-in (temple) 伝通院········ 23 J1
Diplomatic Record Office 外交史料館········ 49 H2
DN Tower 21 DNタワー21········ 38 D1
Dōgenzaka1〜2 (Shibuya-ku) 道玄坂1〜2丁目(渋谷区)··· 20 B4
Dokkyo Univ. 独協大学········ 75 G1
Doshida1〜4 (Nerima-ku) 土支田1〜4丁目(練馬区)··· 1C C2
Drum Museum 太鼓館········ 31 F5

Eastern Garden of the Imperial Palace 皇居東御苑··· 16 B6
Ebara1〜7 (Sinagawa-ku) 荏原1〜7丁目(品川区)··· 28 B6
Ebara Jinja (Shrine) 荏原神社········ 29 G5
Ebaramachi Station 荏原町駅········ 13 G4
Ebara-Nakanobu Station 荏原中延駅········ 28 C7
Ebisu Garden place 恵比寿ガーデンプレイス··· 5l F3
Ebisu1〜4 (Shibuya-ku) 恵比寿1〜4丁目(渋谷区)··· 20 E7
Ebisu-Minami1〜3 (Shibuya-ku) 恵比寿南1〜3丁目(渋谷区)··· 20 D7
Ebisu-Nishi1〜2 (Shibuya-ku) 恵比寿西1〜2丁目(渋谷区)··· 20 D6
Ebisu Station 恵比寿駅········ 20 D7
Edagawa1〜3 (Kōtō-ku) 枝川1〜3丁目(江東区)··· 19 I5
Eda Station 江田駅········ 60 D2
Edogawa1〜6 (Edogawa-ku) 江戸川1〜6丁目(江戸川区)··· 9 H2
Edogawabashi Station (subway) 江戸川橋駅(地下鉄)··· 23 H2
Edogawa-ku 江戸川区········ 7 I3
Edogawa Recreation Park 江戸川総合レクリエーション公園··· 9 J2
Edogawa Station 江戸川駅········ 8 E1
Edogawa Ward Office 江戸川区役所········ 9 G3
Edo-Tokyo Musm 江戸・東京博物館········ 17 H4
Egota1〜4 (Nakano-ku) 江古田1〜4丁目(中野区)··· 11 F3
Eharachō1〜3 (Nakano-ku) 江原町1〜3丁目(中野区)··· 11 F3
Eidan-Akatsuka Station (subway) 営団赤塚駅(地下鉄)··· 10 D1
Eidan-Narimasu Station (subway) 営団成増駅(地下鉄)··· 10 D1
Eifuku1〜4 (Suginami-ku) 永福1〜4丁目(杉並区)··· 20 D6
Eifukuchō Station 永福町駅········ 10 D6
Eitai1〜2 (Kōtō-ku) 永代1〜2丁目(江東区)··· 19 G2
Eitai-bashi (bridge) 永代橋········ l9 F1
Ekoda Station 江古田駅········ 1l F3
Ekō-in (temple) (Minami-Senju) 回向院(南千住)··· 27 H4
Ekō-in (temple) (Ryōgoku) 回向院(両国)··· 17 G5
Enokichō (Shinjuku-ku) 榎町(新宿区)··· 23 G2
Enten-ji (temple) 炎天寺········ 8 B6
En'yū-ji (temple) 円融寺········ 13 F3
Etchūjima1〜3 (Kōtō-ku) 越中島1〜3丁目(江東区)··· 19 G3
Etchūjima Station 越中島駅········ 38 G3
Etchūjima Park 越中島公園········ 19 G2
Export-Import Bank of Japan 日本輸出入銀行··· 36 A6

105

Federation of Economic Orgs　経団連	36	B	3
Ferris Women's Coll.　フェリス女学院大学	63	G	7
FM Tokyo Hall　FM東京ホール	47	E	1
Folk Musm of Itabashi Ward　板橋区立郷土資料館	87	E	2
Fuchinobe Station　淵野辺駅	15	E	7
Fuchū City　府中市	15	G	3
Fuchū-Honmachi Station　府中本町駅	15	G	4
Fuchū Municipal Musm Kyōdonomori　府中市郷土の森	86	C	4
Fuchū Station　府中駅	15	G	4
Fuda Station　布田駅	15	I	4
Fudōmae Station　不動前駅	28	C	4
Fuji Bank（H. O.）　富士銀行(本店)	36	D	4
Fuji Bank Musm　富士銀行資料館	34	D	2
Fujigaoka Station　藤が丘駅	60	C	2
Fuji Jinja（shrine）　富士神社	26	A	4
Fujimi1～2（Chiyoda-ku）　富士見1～2丁目(千代田区)	23	J	4
Fujimichō（Itabashi-ku）　富士見町(板橋区)	11	G	2
Fujimidai1～4（Nerima-ku）　富士見台1～4丁目(練馬区)	10	C	3
Fujimidai Station　富士見台駅	10	D	3
Fujimigaoka Station　富士見ケ丘駅	10	C	6
Fuji Photo Film　富士写真フィルム	55	H	6
Fuji Television　フジテレビジョン	23	F	4
Fujitsū General　富士通ゼネラル	12	D	5
Fukagawa1～2（Kōtō-ku）　深川1～2丁目(江東区)	19	H	1
Fukagawa Edo Musm　深川江戸資料館	87	G	3
Fukagawa Fudō（temple）　深川不動	19	H	2
Fukasawa1～8（Setagaya-ku）　深沢1～8丁目(世田谷区)	12	E	3
Fukoku Mutual Life Insurance　富国生命	38	A	4
Fukuromachi（Shinjuku-ku）　袋町(新宿区)	23	I	3
Fukuzumi1～2（Kōtō-ku）　福住1～2丁目(江東区)	19	G	1
Fumon Hall　普門ホール	83	F	3
Funabashi1～7（Setagaya-ku）　船橋1～7丁目(世田谷区)	12	C	1
Funabori1～7（Edogawa-ku）　船堀1～7丁目(江戸川区)	9	H	3
Funabori Station（subway）　船堀駅(地下鉄)	9	H	3
Funamachi（Shinjuku-ku）　舟町(新宿区)	23	F	5
Funeno-Kagakukan（see Musm of Maritime Sci.）　船の科学館	13	J	3
Furniture Museum　家具の博物館	18	E	5
Furuishiba1～3（Kōtō-ku）　古石場1～3丁目(江東区)	19	H	3
Furukawa Sōgō Bldg　古河総合ビル	37	H	5
Fussa City　福生市	14	D	2
Fussa Station　福生駅	14	D	2
Futaba1～4（Shinagawa-ku）　二葉1～4丁目(品川区)	13	H	4
Futabachō（Itabashi-ku）　双葉町(板橋区)	11	G	2
Futako-Shinchi Station　二子新地駅	12	D	4
Futako-Tamagawaen Station　二子玉川園駅	12	D	3
Futamatagawa Station　二俣川駅	60	C	5
Fuyuki（Kōtō-ku）　冬木(江東区)	19	H	1
Gaienmae Station（subway）　外苑前駅(地下鉄)	55	G	1
Gakugei-Daigaku Station　学芸大学駅	13	F	2
Gakushi Kaikan　学士会館	32	D	6
Gakushūin Univ.　学習院大学	24	D	6
Gas Hall　ガスホール	38	E	5
Gas Museum　がす資料館	86	D	2
Gas Science Center　ガスの科学館	87	G	4
Geihinkan（see State Guesthouse）　迎賓館	21	G	1
Geijutsu-za（theater）　芸術座	38	C	3
Genkū-ji（temple）　源空寺	17	F	1
German Culture Center　ドイツ文化会館	48	B	5
Ginza1～8（Chūō-ku）　銀座1～8丁目(中央区)	18	C	2
Ginza Core　銀座コア	39	F	4
Ginza-itchōme Station（subway）　銀座一丁目駅(地下鉄)	39	F	1
Ginza Komatsu　銀座小松	38	E	4
Ginza Melsa　銀座メルサ	39	G	2
Ginza Miyuki-kan Theater　銀座みゆき館劇場	38	D	3
Ginza Noh Theater　銀座能楽堂	38	D	4
Ginza Station（subway）　銀座駅(地下鉄)	38	E	3
Gobanchō（Chiyoda-ku）　五番町(千代田区)	23	H	5
Goethe Inst. Tokyo（see German Culture Center）　東京ドイツ文化センター	48	B	6
Gohongi1～3（Meguro-ku）　五本木1～3丁目(目黒区)	13	F	2
Gohyaku-Rakan-ji（temple）　五百羅漢寺	28	B	3
Gokoku-ji（temple）　護国寺	25	G	6
Gokokuji Station（subway）　護国寺駅(地下鉄)	25	G	6
Gotanda Station　五反田駅	28	E	4
Gotanno Station　五反野駅	8	C	5
Gotenyama Hills　御殿山ヒルズ	29	F	5
Gotoh Art Museum　五島美術館	12	D	3
Gotoh Planetarium　五島プラネタリウム	53	G	5
Gōtokuji1～2（Setagaya-ku）　豪徳寺1～2丁目(世田谷区)	12	E	1
Gōtoku-ji（temple）　豪徳寺	12	E	1
Gōtokuji Station　豪徳寺駅	12	E	1
Grand Hill Ichigaya　グランドヒル市ケ谷	23	H	5
Green Hall　グリーンホール	82	D	4
Green Tower Bldg　グリーンタワービル	56	A	4
Gumyō-ji（temple）　弘明寺	60	E	7
Hachimanyama1～3（Setagaya-ku）　八幡山1～3丁目(世田谷区)	12	C	1
Hachimanyama Station　八幡山駅	10	C	7
Hachiōji City　八王子市	14	B	4
Hachiōji City Musm　八王子市郷土資料館	86	A	3
Hachiōji-minamino Station　八王子みなみ野駅	14	D	5
Hachiōji Science Center　八王子こども科学館	86	B	4
Hachiōji Station　八王子駅	14	D	4
Hachiyamachō（Shibuya-ku）　鉢山町(渋谷区)	20	B	6
Haginaka1～3（Ōta-ku）　萩中1～3丁目(大田区)	13	H	6
Hagiyama Station　萩山駅	15	G	2
Haijima Daishi（temple）　拝島大師	14	D	3
Haijima Station　拝島駅	14	D	2
Haiyū-za Theater　俳優座劇場	49	G	5
Hakonegasaki Station　箱値ケ崎駅	14	D	1
(Hakozaki) Tokyo City Air Terminal　(箱崎)東京シティエアターミナル	14	G	7
Hakuhinkan Theater　博品館劇場	38	D	6
Hakuhōdō（H. O.）　博報堂(本社)	32	D	6
Hakuraku Station　白楽駅	61	F	4
Hakusan1～5（Bunkyō-ku）　白山1～5丁目(文京区)	26	A	6

Hakusan Station (subway)　白山駅（地下鉄）・・・・・・26　A6
Hamachō Park　浜町公園・・・・・・17　G6
Hamachō Station (subway)　浜町駅（地下鉄）・・・・・・17　F5
Hamadayama1〜4 (Suginami-ku)　浜田山1〜4丁目（杉並区）・・・10　D6
Hamadayama Station　浜田山駅・・・・・・10　D6
Hama-Kawasaki Station　浜川崎駅・・・・・・61　I3
Hamarikyū Onshi Garden　浜離宮恩賜庭園・・・・・・18　C4
Hamamatsuchō1〜2 (Mirato-ku)　浜松町1〜2丁目（港町）・・・18　B5
Hamamatsuchō Station　浜松町駅・・・・・・18　B5
Hamarikyū Asahi Hall　浜離宮朝日ホール・・・・・・18　C4
Hamura Station　羽村駅・・・・・・14　C1
Hamura City　羽村市・・・・・・14　C1
Hanae Mori Bldg　ハナエ・モリビル・・・・・・54　D4
Hanahata1〜8 (Adachi-ku)　花畑1〜8丁目（足立区）・・・・・・8　B5
Hanakawado1〜2 (Taitō-ku)　花川戸1〜2丁目（台東区）・・・17　H1
Hana-Koganei Station　花小金井駅・・・・・・15　H2
Hanayashiki (amusement park)　花やしき・・・・・・31　G2
Hanazono Jinja (shrine)　花園神社・・・・・・57　H3
Haneda1〜6 (Ōta-ku)　羽田1〜6丁目（大田区）・・・13　I7
Haneda Airport (see Tokyo Int'l Airport)　羽田空港・・・13　J6
Haneda-Asahichō (Ōta-ku)　羽田旭町（大田区）・・・13（I6）
Haneda-kūkō1〜2 (Ōta-ku)　羽田空港1〜2丁目（大田区）・・・13　I7
Haneda-kūkō Station　羽田空港駅・・・・・・13　I7
Haneda Station　羽田駅・・・・・・13　I7
Hanegi1〜2 (Setagaya-ku)　羽根木1〜2丁目（世田谷区）・・・10　E7
Hankyū Dept Store (Yūrakuchō)　阪急デパート（有楽町店）・・・38　D2
Hanzōmon Kaikan　半蔵門会館・・・・・・46　E1
Hanzōmon Station (subway)　半蔵門駅（地下鉄）・・・23　I6
Hara Mus. of Contemporary Art　原美術館・・・・・・29　F5
Haraikatamachi (Shinjuku-ku)　払方町（新宿区）・・・23　H4
Harajuku Quest　原宿クエスト・・・・・・54　B2
Harajuku Station　原宿駅・・・・・・20　C2
Haramachi1〜2 (Meguro-ku)　原町1〜2丁目（目黒区）・・・13　G3
Haramachi1〜3 (Shinjuku-ku)　原町1〜3丁目（新宿区）・・・23　F3
Haruechō1〜5 (Edogawa-ku)　春江町1〜5丁目（江戸川区）・・・9　H2
Harumi1〜5 (Chūō-ku)　晴海1〜5丁目（中央区）・・・19　F5
Harumi Futō (wharf)　晴海ふ頭・・・・・・18　E6
Hashiba1〜2 (Taitō-ku)　橋場1〜2丁目（台東区）・・・27　I5
Hashimoto Station　橋本駅・・・・・・14　D6
Hasune1 (Itabashi-ku)　蓮根1〜3丁目（板橋区）・・・11　F1
Hasune Station (subway)　蓮根駅（地下鉄）・・・11　F1
Hasunumachō (Itabashi-ku)　蓮沼町（板橋区）・・・11　G1
Hasunuma Station　蓮沼駅・・・・・・13　G6
Hatagaya1〜3 (Shibuya-ku)　幡ケ谷1〜3丁目（渋谷区）・・・11　F6
Hatagaya Station　幡ケ谷駅・・・・・・11　F6
Hatakeyama Collection　畠山記念館・・・・・・28　E3
Hatanodai1〜6 (Shinagawa-ku)　旗の台1〜6丁目（品川区）・・・13　G4
Hatanodai Station　旗の台駅・・・・・・13　G4
Hatchōbori1〜4 (Chūō-ku)　八丁堀1〜4丁目（中央区）・・・18　E1
Hatchōbori Station (J. R.)　八丁堀駅（JR）・・・・・・18　E2
Hatchōbori Station (subway)　八丁堀駅（地下鉄）・・・18　E1
Hatchōnawate Station　八丁畷駅・・・・・・61　H3

Hatsudai1〜2 (Shibuya-ku)　初台1〜2丁目（渋谷区）・・・20　A1
Hatsudai Station　初台駅・・・・・・11　F6
Hayabusachō (Chiyoda-ku)　隼町（千代田区）・・・・・・23　J7
Hayamiya1〜4 (Nerima-ku)　早宮1〜4丁目（練馬区）・・・10　E2
Hazama Bldg　ハザマビル・・・・・・55　G1
Hazama Station　狭間駅・・・・・・14　C5
Hazama1〜3 (Nerima-ku)　羽沢1〜3丁目（練馬区）・・・11　E3
Heiwadai1〜4 (Nerima-ku)　平和台1〜4丁目（練馬区）・・・10　E2
Heiwadai Station (subway)　平和台駅（地下鉄）・・・10　E2
Heiwajima1〜6 (Ōta-ku)　平和島1〜6丁目（大田区）・・・13　I5
Heiwajima Station　平和島駅・・・・・・13　H5
Hibarigaoka Station　ひばりケ丘駅・・・・・・15　I1
Hibiya Chanter　日比谷シャンテ・・・・・・38　C2
Hibiya City　日比谷シティ・・・・・・38　A4
Hibiya Dai Bldg　日比谷ダイビル・・・・・・33　A4
Hibiya Eiga (cinema)　日比谷映画・・・・・・38　C2
Hibiya-Kōen (Chiyoda-ku)　日比谷公園（千代田区）・・・38　A2
Hibiya Kōkaidō (see Hibiya Public Hall)　日比谷公会堂・・・38　A3
Hibiya Kokusai Bldg　日比谷国際ビル・・・・・・38　A4
Hibiya Library　日比谷図書館・・・・・・38　A3
Hibiya Public Hall　日比谷公会堂・・・・・・38　A3
Hibiya Park　日比谷公園・・・・・・38　A1
Hibiya Park Bldg　日比谷パークビル・・・・・・38　C1
Hibiya Station (subway)　日比谷駅（地下鉄）・・・38　C1
Hie Jinja (shrine)　日枝神社・・・・・・46　D5
Higashi1〜4 (Shibuya-ku)　東1〜4丁目（渋谷区）・・・20　D5
Higashi-Akiru Station　東秋留駅・・・・・・14　C2
Higashi-Asakusa1〜2 (Taitō-ku)　東浅草1〜2丁目（台東区）・・・27　H5
Higashi-Ayase1〜3 (Adachi-ku)　東綾瀬1〜3丁目（足立区）・・・8　C4
Higashi-Azabu1〜3 (Minato-ku)　東麻布1〜3丁目（港区）・・・21　I5
Higashi-Azuma Station　東あずま駅・・・・・・9　G4
Higashi-Enokichō (Shinjuku-ku)　東榎町（新宿区）・・・23　G3
Higashi-Fuchū Station　東府中駅・・・・・・15　H4
Higashi-Fushimi Station　東伏見駅・・・・・・15　I2
Higashi-Fussa Station　東福生駅・・・・・・19　D2
Higashigaoka1〜2 (Meguro-ku)　東が丘1〜2丁目（目黒区）・・・12　E2
Higashi-Ginza Station (subway)　東銀座駅（地下鉄）・・・37　G4
Higashi-Gokenchō (Shinjuku-ku)　東五軒町（新宿区）・・・23　I2
Higashi-Gotanda1〜5 (Shinagawa-ku)　東五反田1〜5丁目（品川区）・・・29　D3
Higashi-Hokima1〜2 (Adachi-ku)　東保木間1〜2丁目（足立区）・・・8　B5
Higashi-Horikiri1〜3 (Katsushika-ku)　東堀切1〜3丁目（葛飾区）・・・8　D4
Higashi-Ikebukuro1〜5 (Toshima-ku)　東池袋1〜5丁目（豊島区）・・・25　F1
Higashi-Ikebukuro Station (subway)　東池袋駅（地下鉄）・・・59　H3
Higashi-Ikōchō (Adachi-ku)　東伊興町（足立区）・・・8　A6
Higashi-Jūjo1〜6 (Kita-ku)　東十条1〜6丁目（北区）・・・11　H1
Higashi-Jūjo Station　東十条駅・・・・・・11　H2
Higashi-Kamata1〜2 (Ōta-ku)　東蒲田1〜2丁目（大田区）・・・13　H6
Higashi-Kanagawa Station　東神奈川駅・・・・・・61　F4
Higashi-Kanamachi1〜8 (Katsushika-ku)　東金町1〜8丁目（葛飾区）・・・8　C2
Higashi-Kanda1〜3 (Chiyoda-ku)　東神田1〜3丁目（千代田区）・・・17　E4
Higashi-Kasai1〜9 (Edogawa-ku)　東葛西1〜9丁目（江戸川区）・・・9　I2
Higashi-Kitazawa Station　東北沢駅・・・・・・11　F7

Higashi-Kōenji Station （subway） 東高円寺駅(地下鉄)	10	E 5	Higashi-Yukigaya1～5 （Ōta-ku） 東雪谷1～5丁目(大田区)	13	F 4
Higashi-Koganei Station 東小金井駅	15	H 3	Hikarigaoka1～7 （Nerima-ku） 光が丘1～7丁目(練馬区)	10	D 2
Higashi-Koiwa1～6 （Edogawa-ku） 東小岩1～6丁目(江戸川区)	8	E 3	Hikarigaoka Park 光が丘公園	10	D 1
Higashi-Kōjiya1～6 （Ōta-ku） 東糀谷1～6丁目(大田区)	13	I 6	Hikawachō （Itabashi-ku） 氷川町(板橋区)	11	G 2
Higashi-Komagata1～4 （Sumida-ku） 東駒形1～4丁目(墨田区)	17	I 2	Hikawadai1～4 （Nerima-ku） 氷川台1～4丁目(練馬区)	11	E 2
Higashi-Komatsugawa1～4 （Edogawa-ku） 東小松川1～4丁目(江戸川区)	9	G 3	Hikawadai Station （subway） 氷川台駅(地下鉄)	11	E 2
Higashi-Kurume City 東久留米市	15	H 2	Hikawa Jinja （shrine） （Akasaka） 氷川神社(赤坂)	48	C 3
Higashi-Kurume Station 東久留米駅	15	I 1	Hikifune Station 曳舟駅	9	F 5
Higashi-Magome1～2 （Ōta-ku） 東馬込1～2丁目(大田区)	13	(H 4)	Hill of Masakado's Head （Masakado Kubizuka） 将門首塚	36	C 5
Higashi-Matsubara Station 東松原駅	12	E 1	Himon'ya1～6 （Meguro-ku） 碑文谷1～6丁目(目黒区)	13	F 3
Higashi-Minemachi （Ōta-ku） 東嶺町(大田区)	13	(F 5)	Hino City 日野市	15	E 4
Higashi-Mizue 2 （Edogawa-ku） 東瑞江2丁目(江戸川区)	9	G 1	Hinodechō （Adachi-ku） 日ノ出町(足立区)	8	D 5
Higashi-Mizumoto1～6 （Katsushika-ku） 東水元1～6丁目(葛飾区)	8	B 3	Hinode Sanbashi （pier） 日の出桟橋	18	B 7
Higashi-Mukōjima1～6 （Sumida-ku） 東向島1～6丁目(墨田区)	9	F 5	Hinode Station 日の出駅	18	B 6
Higashi-Mukōjima Station 東向島駅	9	F 5	Hino Station 日野駅	15	E 4
Higashi-Murayama City 東村山市	15	G 2	Hirai1～7 （Edogawa-ku） 平井1～7丁目(江戸川区)	9	G 4
Higashi-Murayama Station 東村山駅	15	G 1	Hirai Station 平井駅	9	G 4
Higashi-Nagasaki Station 東長崎駅	11	F 3	Hirakawachō1～2 （Chiyoda-ku） 平河町1～2丁目(千代田区)	23	I 7
Higashi-Nakagami Station 東中神駅	14	E 3	Hirama Station 平間駅	61	G 2
Higashi-Nakano1～5 （Nakano-ku） 東中野1～5丁目(中野区)	22	A 3	Hirano1～3 （Adachi-ku） 平野1～3丁目(足立区)	8	C 5
Higashi-Nakanobu1～2 （Shinagawa-ku） 東中延1～2丁目(品川区)	28	C 7	Hirano1～4 （Kōtō-ku） 平野1～4丁目(江東区)	19	I 1
Higashi-Nakano Station 東中野駅	11	F 5	Hiranumabashi Station 平沼橋駅	62	B 2
Higashi-Nihombashi1～3 （Chūō-ku） 東日本橋1～3丁目(中央区)	17	F 5	Hiratsuka1～3 （Shinagawa-ku） 平塚1～3丁目(品川区)	28	B 6
Higashi-Nihombashi Station （subway） 東日本橋駅(地下鉄)	17	F 5	Hirayama-Jōshikōen Station 平山城址公園駅	14	E 4
Higashi-Nippon Bank （H. O.） 東日本銀行(本店)	35	H 4	Hiromachi1～2 （Shinagawa-ku） 広町1～2丁目(品川区)	29	F 7
Higashi-Nippori1～6 （Arakawa-ku） 東日暮里1～6丁目(荒川区)	27	F 4	Hiro-o1～5 （Shibuya-ku） 広尾1～5丁目(渋谷区)	20	E 5
Higashi-Oku1～8 （Arakawa-ku） 東尾久1～8丁目(荒川区)	26	D 1	Hiro-o Hosp. 広尾病院	21	F 6
Higashi-Ōi1～6 （Shinagawa-ku） 東大井1～6丁目(品川区)	13	H 4	Hiro-o Station （subway） 広尾駅(地下鉄)	21	F 6
Higashi-Ōizumi1～7 （Nerima-ku） 東大泉1～7丁目(練馬区)	10	B 2	Hitachi （H. O.） 日立(本社)	33	F 3
Higashi-Ōjima Station （subway） 東大島駅(地下鉄)	9	H 4	Hitotsubashi1～2 （Chiyoda-ku） 一ツ橋1～2丁目(千代田区)	16	B 5
Higashi-Rinkan Station 東林間駅	60	A 3	Hitotsubashi-Gakuen Station 一橋学園駅	15	G 2
Higashi-Rokugatsuchō （Adachi-ku） 東六月町(足立区)	8	B 5	Hitotsubashi Kōdō （hall） 一ツ橋講堂	32	C 6
Higashi-Rokugō1～3 （Ōta-ku） 東六郷1～3丁目(大田区)	13	(H 6)	Hitotsubashi Univ. 一橋大学	74	C 3
Higashi-Sakashita1～2 （Itabashi-ku） 東坂下1～2丁目(板橋区)	11	F 1	Hitotsubashi Univ. （Kodaira） 一橋大学(小平)	15	G 2
Higashi-Shimbashi1～2 （Minato-ku） 東新橋1～2丁目(港区)	18	B 4	Hitotsuya1～4 （Adachi-ku） 一ツ家1～4丁目(足立区)	8	C 5
Higashi-Shinagawa1～5 （Shinagawa-ku） 東品川1～5丁目(品川区)	29	H 5	Hiyoshi Station 日吉駅	61	F 2
Higashi-Shinkoiwa1～8 （Katsushika-ku） 東新小岩1～8丁目(葛飾区)	9	F 3	Hōchiku Yoshida Mem. Hall 吉田苞竹記念館	49	B 1
Higashi-Shinozakimachi （Edogawa-ku） 東篠崎町(江戸川区)	9	G 1	Hodogaya-ku （Yokohama City） 保土ケ谷区(横浜市)	60	D 5
Higashi-Sumida1～3 （Sumida-ku） 東墨田1～3丁目(墨田区)	9	F 4	Hodogaya Park 保土ケ谷公園	60	E 5
Higashi-Suna1～8 （Kōtō-ku） 東砂1～8丁目(江東区)	9	H 4	Hodogaya Station 保土ケ谷駅	60	E 6
Higashi-Tabata1～2 （Kita-ku） 東田端1～2丁目(北区)	26	B 2	Hokekyō-ji （temple） 法華経寺	83	I 3
Higashi-Tamagawa1～2 （Setagaya-ku） 東玉川1～2丁目(世田谷区)	13	F 4	Hokima1～5 （Adachi-ku） 保木間1～5丁目(足立区)	8	B 5
Higashi-Tateishi1～4 （Katsushika-ku） 東立石1～4丁目(葛飾区)	8	E 3	Hon-Amanuma1～3 （Suginami-ku） 本天沼1～3丁目(杉並区)	10	D 4
Higashi-Totsuka Station 東戸塚駅	60	D 6	Hōnan1～2 （Suginami-ku） 方南1～2丁目(杉並区)	10	E 6
Higashi-Ueno1～6 （Taitō-ku） 東上野1～6丁目(台東区)	17	E 2	Hōnanchō Station （subway） 方南町駅(地下鉄)	10	E 6
Higashi-Yaguchi1～3 （Ōta-ku） 東矢口1～3丁目(大田区)	13	G 6	Honchō （Itabashi-ku） 本町(板橋区)	11	G 2
Higashiyama1～3 （Meguro-ku） 東山1～3丁目(目黒区)	13	F 1	Honchō1～6 （Nakano-ku） 本町1～6丁目(中野区)	11	F 5
Higashiyamachō （Itabashi-ku） 東山町(板橋区)	11	(F 2)	Honda Motor 本田技研工業	55	I 1
Higashi-Yamato City 東大和市	15	F 2	Honda Theater 本多劇場	80	B 1
Higashi-Yamatoshi Station 東大和市駅	15	F 2	Hongō1～7 （Bunkyō-ku） 本郷1～7丁目(文京区)	16	B 2
Higashi-Yashio （Shinagawa-ku） 東八潮(品川区)	13	J 3	Hongō Post Office 本郷郵便局	16	B 1
Higashi-Yotsugi1～4 （Katsushika-ku） 東四つ木1～4丁目(葛飾区)	8	E 4	Hongō-sanchōme Station （subway） 本郷三丁目駅(地下鉄)	16	B 2

108

Hon-Haneda1〜3（Ōta-ku）　本羽田1〜3丁目（大田区）‥	13	H 7
Hon-Isshiki1〜3（Edogawa-ku）　本一色1〜3丁目（江戸川区）‥	9	F 3
Honjo1〜4（Sumida-ku）　本所1〜4丁目（墨田区）‥‥‥	17	I 3
Honjo-Azumabashi Station（subway）　本所吾妻橋駅（地下鉄）‥	17	I 2
Hon-Komagome1〜6（Bunkyō-ku）　本駒込1〜6丁目（文京区）‥	26	A 5
Honmachi1〜6（Shibuya-ku）　本町1〜6丁目（渋谷区）‥‥	11	F 6
Honmoku Citizen's Park　本牧市民公園‥‥‥‥‥‥‥	61	G 7
Honmon-ji（temple）　本門寺‥‥‥‥‥‥‥‥‥‥	13	G 4
Honshiochō（Shinjuku-ku）　本塩町（新宿区）‥‥‥‥	23	G 5
Honshū Paper（H. O.）　本州製紙（本社）‥‥‥‥‥	39	F 5
Horifune1〜4（Kita-ku）　堀船1〜4丁目（北区）‥‥‥	11	I 1
Horikiri1〜8（Katsushika-ku）　堀切1〜8丁目（葛飾区）‥	8	E 4
Horikiri Shōbuen（iris garden）　堀切菖蒲園‥‥‥‥	8	E 4
Horikiri Shōbuen Station　堀切菖蒲園駅‥‥‥‥‥	8	D 4
Horikiri Station　堀切駅‥‥‥‥‥‥‥‥‥‥‥‥	8	E 5
Horinouchi1〜2（Adachi-ku）　堀之内1〜2丁目（足立区）‥‥	11	I 1
Horinouchi1〜3（Suginami-ku）　堀ノ内1〜3丁目（杉並区）‥	10	E 5
Hosei Univ.（Ichigaya）　法政大学（市ケ谷）‥‥‥	23	I 4
Hosei Univ.（Koganei）　法政大学（小金井）‥‥‥	74	D 3
Hosei Univ.（Tama）　法政大学（多摩）‥‥‥‥‥	74	A 4
Hoshi Coll. of Pharmacy　星薬科大学‥‥‥‥‥‥	13	G 3
Hoshikawa Station　星川駅‥‥‥‥‥‥‥‥‥‥	60	E 5
Hōshō Noh Theater　宝生能楽堂‥‥‥‥‥‥‥‥	32	B 1
Hosoda1〜5（Katsushika-ku）　細田1〜5丁目（葛飾区）‥	8	E 2
House of Medical Treasures　医学文化館‥‥‥‥‥	86	A 1
Hōya City　保谷市‥‥‥‥‥‥‥‥‥‥‥‥‥‥	15	I 2
Hōya Station　保谷駅‥‥‥‥‥‥‥‥‥‥‥‥	15	I 1
Hozukachō（Adachi-ku）　保塚町（足立区）‥‥‥‥	8	B 5
Hyakuninchō1〜4（Shinjuku-ku）　百人町1〜4丁目（新宿区）‥‥	22	B 3
Hygeia（Tokyo Met. Health Plaza）　ハイジア（東京都健康プラザ）‥	57	F 1
IBM Japan（H. O.）　日本IBM（本社）‥‥‥‥‥‥	49	F 3
Ichibancyō（Chiyoda-ku）　一番町（千代田区）‥‥‥‥	23	I 6
Ichigao Station　市が尾駅‥‥‥‥‥‥‥‥‥‥	60	C 2
Ichigaya-Chōenjimachi（Shinjuku-ku）　市谷長延寺町（新宿区）‥	23	H 4
Ichigaya-Daimachi（Shinjuku-ku）　市谷台町（新宿区）‥	23	F 4
Ichigaya-Funagawaramachi（Shinjuku-ku）　市谷船河原町（新宿区）‥	23	I 4
Ichigaya Hachiman（shrine）　市谷八幡神社‥‥‥	23	H 5
Ichigaya-Hachimanchō（Shinjuku-ku）　市谷八幡町（新宿区）‥	23	H 5
Ichigaya-Honmurachō（Shinjuku-ku）　市谷本村町（新宿区）‥	23	G 4
Ichigaya-Kagachō1〜2（Shinjuku-ku）　市谷加賀町1〜2丁目（新宿区）‥	23	G 4
Ichigaya-Kōrachō（Shinjuku-ku）　市谷甲良町（新宿区）‥	23	G 4
Ichigaya-Nakanochō（Shinjuku-ku）　市谷仲之町（新宿区）‥	23	F 4
Ichigaya-Sadoharachō1〜3（Shinjuku-ku）　市谷砂土原町1〜3丁目（新宿区）‥	23	H 4
Ichigaya-Sanaichō（Shinjuku-ku）　市谷左内町（新宿区）‥	23	H 4
Ichigaya Station　市ケ谷駅‥‥‥‥‥‥‥‥‥‥	23	H 5
Ichigaya-Takajōmachi（Shinjuku-ku）　市谷鷹匠町（新宿区）‥	23	H 4
Ichigaya Tamachi1〜3（Shinjuku-ku）　市谷田町1〜3丁目（新宿区）‥	23	I 4
Ichigaya-Yakuōjimachi（Shinjuku-ku）　市谷薬王寺町（新宿区）‥	23	G 4
Ichigaya-Yamabushichō（Shinjuku-ku）　市谷山伏町（新宿区）‥	23	G 3
Ichigaya-Yanagichō（Shinjuku-ku）　市谷柳町（新宿区）‥	23	G 4
Ichikawa-Mama Station　市川真間駅‥‥‥‥‥‥	9	E 1
Ichikawa Station　市川駅‥‥‥‥‥‥‥‥‥‥	9	E 1
Ichinoe1〜7（Edogawa-ku）　一之江1〜7丁目（江戸川区）‥	9	G 2
Ichinoechō（Edogawa-ku）　一之江町（江戸川区）‥‥	9	H 3
Ichinoe Station（subway）　一之江駅（地下鉄）‥‥	9	H 2
Ichiyō Memorial Hall　一葉記念館‥‥‥‥‥‥‥	27	G 5
Idemitsu Art Gallery　出光美術館‥‥‥‥‥‥‥	37	J 6
Igusa1〜5（Suginami-ku）　井草1〜5丁目（杉並区）‥	10	C 2
Igusa Hachimangū（shrine）　井草八幡宮‥‥‥‥	10	B 4
Iidabashi1〜4（Chiyoda-ku）　飯田橋1〜4丁目（千代田区）‥	16	A 3
Iidabashi Post Office　飯田橋郵便局‥‥‥‥‥‥	23	I 3
Iidabashi Station　飯田橋駅‥‥‥‥‥‥‥‥‥	23	I 3
Iino Bldg　飯野ビル‥‥‥‥‥‥‥‥‥‥‥‥	47	I 7
Iino Hall　イイノホール‥‥‥‥‥‥‥‥‥‥‥	47	I 7
Ikebukuro1〜4（Toshima-ku）　池袋1〜4丁目（豊島区）‥	24	D 3
Ikebukuro-Honchō1〜4（Toshima-ku）　池袋本町1〜4丁目（豊島区）‥	24	E 2
Ikebukuro Parco Store　池袋パルコ‥‥‥‥‥‥	58	E 4
Ikebukuro Scala-za（cinema）　池袋スカラ座‥‥‥	59	E 3
Ikebukuro Station　池袋駅‥‥‥‥‥‥‥‥‥‥	24	E 4
Ikebukuro Tōhō（cinema）　池袋東宝‥‥‥‥‥‥	59	G 4
Ikebukuro Tōkyō（cinema）　池袋東急‥‥‥‥‥	59	E 3
Ikegami1〜8（Ōta-ku）　池上1〜8丁目（大田区）‥	13	G 5
Ikegami Station　池上駅‥‥‥‥‥‥‥‥‥‥‥	13	G 5
Ikejiri1〜4（Setagaya-ku）　池尻1〜4丁目（世田谷区）‥	13	F 1
Ikejiri-Ōhashi Station　池尻大橋駅‥‥‥‥‥‥	13	F 1
Ikenohata1〜4（Taitō-ku）　池之端1〜4丁目（台東区）‥	16	D 1
Ikenoue Station　池ノ上駅‥‥‥‥‥‥‥‥‥‥	13	F 1
Ikō（Adachi-ku）　伊興（足立区）‥‥‥‥‥‥‥	8	B 6
Ikuta Green　生田緑地‥‥‥‥‥‥‥‥‥‥‥	82	D 4
Ikuta Station　生田駅‥‥‥‥‥‥‥‥‥‥‥‥	15	I 5
Imado1〜2（Taitō-ku）　今戸1〜2丁目（台東区）‥	27	I 6
Imagawa1〜4（Suginami-ku）　今川1〜4丁目（杉並区）‥	10	C 4
Imperial Palace Outer Garden（Kōkyo Gaien）　皇居外苑‥	37	G 7
Imperial Theater（Teikoku Gekijō）　帝国劇場‥‥	37	J 6
Inadazutsumi Station　稲田堤駅‥‥‥‥‥‥‥‥	15	I 5
Inagi City　稲城市‥‥‥‥‥‥‥‥‥‥‥‥‥	15	H 5
Inagi-Naganuma Station　稲城長沼駅‥‥‥‥‥	15	H 4
Inagi Station　稲城駅‥‥‥‥‥‥‥‥‥‥‥‥	15	H 5
Inarichō Station（subway）　稲荷町駅（地下鉄）‥‥	17	F 1
Inaridai（Itabashi-ku）　稲荷台（板橋区）‥‥‥‥	11	(G 2)
Industrial Bank of Japan（H. O.）　日本興業銀行（本店）‥	36	E 4
Industrial Safety & Technical Musm　産業安全技術館‥	84	C 6
Industry Club of Japan　日本工業倶楽部‥‥‥‥	37	E 4
Inokashira-Kōen Station　井の頭公園駅‥‥‥‥	10	B 5
Inokashira Natural Cultural Garden　井の頭自然文化園‥	10	A 5
Inokashira Park　井の頭公園‥‥‥‥‥‥‥‥‥	10	A 5
Int'l Christian Univ.　国際基督教大学‥‥‥‥‥	74	(C 3)
Int'l House of Japan（Kokusai Bunka Kaikan）　国際文化会館‥	49	4
Int'l Students Institute　国際学友会‥‥‥‥‥	93	(E 1)
Int'l Trade Center　東京国際貿易センター‥‥‥	18	D 6
Iogi Station　井荻駅‥‥‥‥‥‥‥‥‥‥‥‥	10	C 4
Irifune1〜3（Chūō-ku）　入船1〜3丁目（中央区）‥	18	E 2
Iriya3〜9（Adachi-ku）　入谷3〜9丁目（足立区）‥‥	8	B 7

Iriya1～2 （Taitō-ku） 入谷1～2丁目（台東区）········· 27　F 6
Iriyachō （Adachi-ku） 入谷町（足立区）··············· 8　A 7
Iriya Station （subway） 入谷駅（地下鉄）··············· 27　F 6
Isetan Art Museum 伊勢丹美術館············· 57　H 3
Isetan Dept Store 伊勢丹デパート ············· 57　H 4
Isezakichō （Yokohama City） 伊勢佐木町（横浜市）······· 62　D 6
Ishibashi Memorial Hall 石橋メモリアルホール ········· 17　F 1
Ishijima （Kōtō-ku） 石島（江東区）··············· 9　(H5)
Ishikawachō1～2 （Ōta-ku） 石川町1～2丁目（大田区）··· 13　F 4
Ishikawachō Station 石川町駅············· 63　G 6
Ishikawadai Station 石川台駅··············· 13　F 4
Ishiwara1～4 （Sumida-ku） 石原1～4丁目（墨田区）····· 17　I 3
Isogo-ku （Yokohama City） 磯子区（横浜市）··········· 61　F 7
Isogo Station 磯子駅··············· 61　F 7
Itabashi1～4 （Itabashi-ku） 板橋1～4丁目（板橋区）··· 24　E 1
Itabashi-Honchō Station （subway） 板橋本町駅（地下鉄区）·· 11　G 2
Itabashi-ku 板橋区 ··············· 6　D 1
Itabashi-Kuyakushomae Station （subway） 板橋区役所前駅（地下鉄）···· 24　D 1
Itabashi-Post Office 板橋郵便局··············· 24　E 1
Itabashi Station 板橋駅··············· 25　F 2
Itabashi Ward Office 板橋区役所··············· 24　D 1
Iwabuchimachi （Kita-ku） 岩淵町（北区）············· 11　H 1
Iwamotochō1～3 （Chiyoda-ku） 岩本町1～3丁目（千代田区）··· 16　E 5
Iwamotochō Station （subway） 岩本町駅（地下鉄）········· 16　D 4
Iwanami Hall 岩波ホール··············· 32　C 4
Iwasaki Museum 岩崎博物館··············· 63　(H6)
Iwatochō （Shinjuku-ku） 岩戸町（新宿区）··········· 23　H 3
Izumi1～4 （Suginami-ku） 和泉1～4丁目（杉並区）····· 10　E 6
Izumichō （Itabashi-ku） 泉町（板橋区）············· 11　G 1
Izumi-ku （Yokohama City） 泉区（横浜市）············· 60　B 7
Izumino Station いずみ野駅··············· 60　B 6
Izumi-Tamagawa Station 和泉多摩川駅··············· 12　A 2

JA Bldg JAビル ··············· 36　C 3
Japan Calligraphy Museum 日本書道美術館············· 87　F 2
Japan China Friendship Assoc. 日本中国友好協会 ········· 93　G 5
Japan Coll. of Social Work 日本社会事業大学········· 74　D 2
Japan Development Bank 日本開発銀行··············· 36　B 4
Japan External Trade Orgn （see JETRO） 日本貿易振興会··· 21　J 2
Japan Folk Crafts Musm （Nihon Mingei-kan） 日本民芸館··· 13　F 1
Japan Forum 国際文化フォーラム ········· 93　F 4
Japan Foundation 国際交流基金 ··············· 48　E 2
Japan Int'l Sch. ジャパンインターナショナルスクール ··· 20　D 3
Japan Karatedo Federation 全日本空手道連盟 ········· 92　(E5)
Japan Lutheran Theol. Coll. 日本ルーテル学院大学 ··· 74　D 3
Japan Nat'l Tourist Orgn 国際観光振興会 ··········· 93　F 6
Japan Press Center （see Nippon Press Center） ··········· 47　I 7
Japan Red Cross Coll. of Nursing 日本赤十字看護大学 ··· 72　C 4
JR （H. O） JR本社 ··············· 22　C 6
J. R. C. Medical Service Center 日赤医療センター ··· 21　F 5
Japan Red Cross Society （Nippon Sekijūjisha） 日本赤十字社··· 18　A 4
Japan Society for the Promotion of Science 日本学術振興会··· 93　F 4

Japan Times, The ジャパンタイムズ··············· 29　H 1
Japan Traditional Crafts Center 全国伝統的工芸品センター ··· 55　F 2
Japan-United States Friendship Commission 日米友好基金 ····· 92　(E5)
Japan Women's University 日本女子大学··············· 25　E 7
Japanese Sake Center 日本酒センター··············· 39　F 4
Japanese Sword Museum 刀剣博物館··············· 22　A 7
JBP Oval JBPオーバル··············· 54　D 5
JETRO 日本貿易振興会··············· 21　J 2
Jiji Press （Jiji Tsūshin） 時事通信社··············· 47　J 7
Jikei Univ. Hosp. 東京慈恵会医大病院··· 18　A 4
Jikei Univ. School of Medicine 東京慈恵会医大大学··· 18　A 4
Jimbōchō Station （subway） 神保町駅（地下鉄）········· 32　C 4
Jindai Botanical Park 神代植物公園 ··········· 15　I 4
Jindai-ji （temple） 深大寺··············· 15　I 4
Jingū Gaien （see Meiji Jingū Outer Gardens） 神宮外苑··········· 21　F 1
Jingūmae1～6 （Shibuya-ku） 神宮前1～6丁目（渋谷区）········· 20　D 2
Jinnan1～2 （Shibuya-ku） 神南1～2丁目（渋谷区）········· 20　B 3
Jirō Osaragi Mem. Hall 大仏次郎記念館··········· 63　(H6)
Jissen Women's University 実践女子大学··············· 74　B 3
Jiyūgaoka1～3 （Meguro-ku） 自由が丘1～3丁目（目黒区）··· 12　E 3
Jiyūgaoka Station 自由が丘駅··············· 13　F 4
Jiyū Theater 自由劇場··············· 21　F 4
Jōhoku Central Park 城北中央公園··············· 11　F 2
Jōnanjima1～2 （Ōta-ku） 城南島1～2丁目（大田区）··· 13　J 5
Jōshin-ji （Kuhonbutsu） （temple） 浄真寺（九品仏）··· 12　E 3
JTB （H. O.） 日本交通公社（本社）··············· 36　E 3
Jūjōdai1～2 （Kita-ku） 十条台1～2丁目（北区）··· 11　H 2
Jūjō-Nakahara1～4 （Kita-ku） 十条仲原1～4丁目（北区）··· 11　(H1)
Jūjō Station 十条駅··············· 11　H 2
Juntendō （Univ.）Hosp. 順天堂医院··············· 32　E 1
Juntendō University 順天堂大学··············· 32　D 1

Kabukichō1～2 （Shinjuku-ku） 歌舞伎町1～2丁目（新宿区）····· 22　C 4
Kabukichō Tōei （cinema） 歌舞伎町東映··············· 57　F 2
Kabuki-za （theater） 歌舞伎座··············· 39　G 4
Kachidoki1～6 （Chūō-ku） 勝どき1～6丁目（中央区）··· 18　E 4
Kachidoki-bashi （bridge） 勝鬨橋··············· 18　D 4
Kaga1～2 （Adachi-ku） 加賀1～2丁目（足立区）··· 8　B 7
Kaga1～2 （Itabashi-ku） 加賀1～2丁目（板橋区）··· 11　G 2
Kagaku Gijutsukan （see Science Museum） 科学技術館··· 16　A 5
Kagawa Nutrition Junior Coll. 女子栄養短大··· 25　J 3
Kaguragashi （Shinjuku-ku） 神楽河岸（新宿区）··· 23　I 3
Kagurazaka1～6 （Shinjuku-ku） 神楽坂1～6丁目（新宿区）··· 23　I 3
Kagurazaka Station （subway） 神楽坂駅（地下鉄）··· 23　H 3
Kahei1～3 （Adachi-ku） 加平1～3丁目（足立区）··· 8　C 4
Kaiga-kan （see Meiji Memorial Picture Gallery） （聖徳記念）絵画館··· 21　F 1
Kaigan1～3 （Minato-ku） 海岸1～3丁目（港区）··· 18　B 6
Kaitaichō （Shinjuku-ku） 改代町（新宿区）··· 23　H 2
Kajichō1～2 （Chiyoda-ku） 鍛冶町1～2丁目（千代田区）··· 16　D 5
Kajigaya Station 梶が谷駅··············· 12　C 4
Kajima Corp. Bldg 鹿島ビル··············· 46　B 4
Kakinokizaka1～3 （Meguro-ku） 柿の木坂1～3丁目（目黒区）··· 13　F 3

Kakio Station　柿生駅 ·············· 15　H 6

Kamakura1〜4 (Katsushika-ku)　鎌倉1〜4丁目(葛飾区)　8　D 2

Kamata1〜5 (Ōta-ku)　蒲田1〜5丁目(大田区)　13　H 6

Kamata1〜4 (Setagaya-ku)　鎌田1〜4丁目(世田谷区)　12　C 3

Kamata-Honchō1〜2 (Ōta-ku)　蒲田本町1〜2丁目(大田区) ··· 13　(H 6)

Kamata Station　蒲田駅 ·············· 13　H 6

Kameari1〜5 (Katsushika-ku)　亀有1〜5丁目(葛飾区)　8　D 4

Kameari Station　亀有駅·············· 8　C 4

Kameido1〜9 (Kōtō-ku)　亀戸1〜9丁目(江東区)　9　G 5

Kameido Station　亀戸駅 ·············· 9　G 5

Kameido-Suijin Station　亀戸水神駅 ········· 9　G 4

Kameido Tenjin (shrine)　亀戸天神 ········· 9　G 5

Kamezawa1〜4 (Sumida-ku)　亀沢1〜4丁目(墨田区)　17　I 4

Kami-Hoshikawa Station　上星川駅 ·········· 62　D 5

Kami-Igusa1〜4 (Suginami-ku)　上井草1〜4丁目(杉並区)　10　C 4

Kami-Igusa Station　二井草駅 ··········· 10　C 4

Kami-Ikebukuro1〜4 (Toshima-ku)　上池袋1〜4丁目(豊島区) ······ 24　F 3

Kami-Ikedai1〜5 (Ōta-ku)　上池台1〜5丁目(大田区)　13　G 4

Kami-Isshiki1〜3 (Edogawa-ku)　一色1〜3丁目(江戸川区) ··· (9 (F 2)

Kami-Itabashi1〜3 (Itabashi-ku)　上板橋1〜3丁目(板橋区)　11　F 2

Kami-Itabashi Station　上板橋駅 ·········· 11　F 2

Kami-Jūjō1〜5 (Kita-ku)　上十条1〜5丁目(北区) ······ 11　H 2

Kami-Kitazawa1〜5 (Setagaya-ku)　上北沢1〜5丁目(世田谷区)　10　C 7

Kami-Kitazawa Station　上北沢駅 ·········· 10　C 7

Kamimachi Station　上町駅 ············ 12　D 2

Kami-Meguro1〜5 (Meguro-ku)　上目黒1〜5丁目(目黒区)　13　F 2

Kamimizo Station　上溝駅 ············ 14　D 7

Kami-Nakazato1〜3 (Kita-ku)　上中里1〜3丁目(北区)　26　A 2

Kami-Nakazato Station　上中里駅 ·········· 11　I 3

Kaminarimon1〜2 (Taitō-ku)　雷門1〜2丁目(台東区) ··· 17　G 1

Kaminari-mon (gate)　雷門 ············· 31　H 5

Kami-Noge1〜4 (Setagaya-ku)　上野毛1〜4丁目(世田谷区) ··· 12　D 3

Kaminoge Station　上野毛駅 ··········· 12　D 3

Kami-Ochiai1〜3 (Shinjuku-ku)　上落合1〜3丁目(新宿区) ··· 11　F 4

Kamiogi1〜4 (Suginami-ku)　上荻1〜4丁目(杉並区)　10　C 4

Kami-Osaki1〜4 (Shinagawa-ku)　上大崎1〜4丁目(品川区)　28　C 3

Kami-Saginomiya1〜5 (Nakano-ku)　上鷺宮1〜5丁目(中野区)　10　D 3

Kami-Shakujii1〜4 (Nerima-ku)　上石神井1〜4丁目(練馬区)　10　B 3

Kamishakujii-Minamichō (Nerima-ku)　上石神井南町(練馬区)　10　B 4

Kami-Shakujii Station　上石神井駅 ········· 10　B 4

Kami-Shinozakimachi1〜4 (Edogawa-ku)　上篠崎町1〜4丁目(江戸川区) ······· 9　F 1

Kami-Soshigaya1〜7 (Setagaya-ku)　上祖師谷1〜7丁目(世田谷区)　12　B 1

Kami-Takada1〜5 (Nakano-ku)　上高田1〜5丁目(中野区)　11　F 4

Kami-Takaido1〜3 (Suginami-ku)　上高井戸1〜3丁目(杉並区)　10　C 6

Kamiuma1〜5 (Setagaya-ku)　上馬1〜5丁目(世田谷区)　13　E 4

Kamiya1〜3 (Kita-ku)　神谷1〜3丁目(北区) ······ 11　H 1

Kamiyachō Station (subway)　神谷町駅(地下鉄) ········· 21　J 4

Kamiyamachō (Shibuya-ku)　神山町(渋谷区) ········· 20　A 3

Kami-Yōga1〜6 (Setagaya-ku)　上用賀1〜6丁目(世田谷区)　12　D 2

Kamoi Station　鴨居駅 ············· 60　D 3

Kamon'yama Park　掃部山公園 ·········· 62　D 3

Kanagawa Inst. of Tech.　神奈川工科大学 ······· 74　A 6

Kanagawa Kenmin Hall　神奈川県民ホール ······ 63　G 5

Kanagawa-ku (Yokohama City)　神奈川区(横浜市) ···· 61　F 4

Kanagawa Pref. Budōkan Gym.　神奈川県立武道館 ···· 82　E 6

Kanagawa Pref. Concert Hall　神奈川県立音楽堂 ···· 62　(D 4)

Kanagawa Pref. Library　神奈川県立図書館 ····· 52　(D 4)

Kanagawa Pref. Museum　神奈川県立博物館 ····· 63　E 4

Kanagawa Pref. Musm of Modern Literature　神奈川近代文学館 ··· 63　(I 6)

Kanagawa Pref. Youth Center　神奈川県立青少年センター ··· 62　D 4

Kanagawa University　神奈川大学 ········· 61　F 4

Kanamachi1〜6 (Katsushika-ku)　金町1〜6丁目(葛飾区)　8　D 3

Kanamachi Station　金町駅 ··········· 8　C 3

Kanamechō1〜3 (Toshima-ku)　要町1〜3丁目(豊島区)　24　B 3

Kanamechō Station (subway)　要町駅(地下鉄) ······· 24　C 4

Kanda-Aioichō (Chiyoda-ku)　神田相生町(千代田区) ··· 33　I 3

Kanda-Awajichō1〜2 (Chiyoda-ku)　神田淡路町1〜2丁目(千代田区) ··· 33　G 4

Kanda Bookshops Area　神田書店街 ········ 32　C 4

Kanda-Hanaokachō (Chiyoda-ku)　神田花岡町(千代田区)　33　I 3

Kanda-Higashikon'yachō (Chiyoda-ku)　神田東紺屋町(千代田区)　33　I 6

Kanda-Higashimatsushitachō (Chiyoda-ku)　神田東松下町(千代田区)　33　I 5

Kanda-Hirakawachō (Chiyoda-ku)　神田平河町(千代田区)　33　J 3

Kanda Inst. of Foreign Languages　神田外語学院 ··· 33　G 6

Kanda-Iwamotochō (Chiyoda-ku)　神田岩本町(千代田区)　16　E 5

Kanda-Izumichō (Chiyoda-ku)　神田和泉町(千代田区)　16　E 3

Kanda-Jimbōchō1〜3 (Chiyoda-ku)　神田神保町1〜3丁目(千代田区)　16　B 4

Kanda-Kajichō3 (Chiyoda-ku)　神田鍛冶町3丁目(千代田区)　33　H 5

Kanda-Kitanorimonochō (Chiyoda-ku)　神田北乗物町(千代田区)　33　I 6

Kanda-Kon'yachō (Chiyoda-ku)　神田紺屋町(千代田区)　33　I 6

Kanda-Matsunagachō (Chiyoda-ku)　神田松永町(千代田区)　33　J 2

Kanda-Mikurachō (Chiyoda-ku)　神田美倉町(千代田区)　33　I 7

Kanda-Mitoshirochō (Chiyoda-ku)　神田美土代町(千代田区)　33　F 5

Kanda Myōjin (shrine)　神田明神 ········· 33　G 1

Kanda-Neribeichō (Chiyoda-ku)　神田練塀町(千代田区)　33　I 2

Kanda-Nishifukudachō (Chiyoda-ku)　神田西福田町(千代田区)　33　I 7

Kanda-Nishikichō1〜3 (Chiyoda-ku)　神田錦町1〜3丁目(千代田区)　16　B 5

Kanda-Ogawamachi1〜3 (Chiyoda-ku)　神田小川町1〜3丁目(千代田区)　16　C 4

Kanda Post Office　神田郵便局 ·········· 33　G 4

Kanda-Sakumachō1〜4 (Chiyoda-ku)　神田佐久間町1〜4丁目(千代田区)　16　E 4

Kanda-Sakumagashi (Chiyoda-ku)　神田佐久間河岸(千代田区)　16　E 4

Kanda Station　神田駅 ············· 33　H 6

Kanda-Sudachō1〜2 (Chiyoda-ku)　神田須田町1〜2丁目(千代田区)　16　D 4

Kanda-Surugadai1〜4 (Chiyoda-ku)　神田駿河台1〜4丁目(千代田区)　16　C 4

Kanda-Tachō2 (Chiyoda-ku)　神田多町2丁目(千代田区)　16　D 4

Kanda-Tomiyamachō (Chiyoda-ku)　神田富山町(千代田区)　33　I 5

Kanda-Tsukasamachi2 (Chiyoda-ku)　神田司町2丁目(千代田区)　33　G 4

Kanegafuchi Station　鐘ヶ淵駅 ·········· 8　E 5

Kan'ei-ji (temple)　寛永寺 ············ 26　E 6

Kannai Hall　関内ホール ············ 63　F 5

Kannai Station　関内駅 ············· 63　E 5

Kanze Noh Theater　観世能楽堂 ········· 52　A 2

Kaō Corp. (H. O.)　花王(本社) ········· 35　G 1

Kappabashi Kitchenware Town　かっぱ橋道具街 ···· 17　G 1

Kasai-rinkaikōen Station　葛西臨海公園駅 ········ 7　I 5

Kasai-rinkai Park　葛西臨海公園･･････････････　7　I 5

Kasai Station（subway）　葛西駅（地下鉄）･･････　9　I 2

Kashimada Station　鹿島田駅･･････････････････　6　G 2

Kasuga I〜2（Bunkyo-ku）　春日 I〜2丁目（文京区）･･････　23　I 1

Kasugachō I〜6（Nerima-ku）　春日町 I〜6丁目（練馬区）･･････　10　D 2

Kasuga Station（subway）　春日駅（地下鉄）･･････　16　A 2

Kasumigaokamachi（Shinjuku-ku）　霞岳町（新宿区）･･････　20　E 1

Kasumigaseki I〜3（Chiyoda-ku）　霞が関（千代田区）･･････　18　A 1

Kasumigaseki Bldg　霞が関ビル･･････････････　47　F 6

Kasumigaseki Station（subway）　霞ケ関駅（地下鉄）･･････　47　H 5

Kasuya I〜4（Setagaya-ku）　粕谷 I〜4丁目（世田谷区）･･　12　C 1

Katakura Station　片倉駅･･････････････････････　14　D 4

Katamachi（Shinjuku-ku）　片町（新宿区）･･････　23　G 5

Katsushika-ku　葛飾区･･････････････････････････　7　H 1

Katsushika Ward Office　葛飾区役所･･････････　8　F 4

Katsushima I〜3（Shinagawa-ku）　勝島 I〜3丁目（品川区）･･　13　I 7

Kawadachō（Shinjuku-ku）　河田町（新宿区）･･････　23　F 4

Kawasaki City Museum　川崎市民ミュージアム･･････　86　E 5

Kawasaki City　川崎市･･････････････････････････　61　I 3

Kawasaki Daishi（temple）　川崎大師･･････････　61　I 3

Kawasaki-Daishi Station　川崎大師駅･･････････　61　I 2

Kawasaki-ku（Kawasaki City）　川崎区（川崎市）･･････　61　H 2

Kawasaki Municipal Park of Japanese Houses　日本民家園･･････　15　I 5

Kawasaki Racecourse　川崎競馬場･･････････････　83　F 5

Kawasaki-Shinmachi Station　川崎新町駅･･････　61　H 3

Kawasaki Stadium　川崎球場･･････････････････　61　H 3

Kawasaki Station　川崎駅･･････････････････････　61　H 2

Kayabachō Station（subway）　茅場町駅（地下鉄）･･････　35　G 2

KDD Bldg KDD　（国際電信電話）ビル･･････････　56　C 6

Keihinjima I〜3（Ōta-ku）　京浜島 I〜3丁目（大田区）･･　13　J 5

Keikyū-Kamata Station　京急蒲田駅･･････････　13　H 6

Keikyū-Kawasaki Station　京急川崎駅･･････････　61　H 2

Keiō Dept Store　京王デパート･･････････････････　57　E 5

Keiō-Hachiōji Station　京王八王子駅･･････････　14　D 4

Keiō-Horinouchi Station　京王堀之内駅･･････････　15　F 5

Keiō（Univ.）Hospital　慶応病院･･････････････　23　F 7

Keiō-Inadazutsumi Station　京王稲田堤駅･･････　19　H 5

Keiō-Katakura Station　京王片倉駅･･････････････　14　D 4

Keiō Mall　京王モール･･････････････････････････　56　E 5

Keiō-Nagayama Station　京王永山駅･･････････････　15　F 5

Keiō-Tama Center Station　京王多摩センター駅･･････　15　F 5

Keiō-Tamagawa Station　京王多摩川駅･･････････　15　I 4

Keiō University（Hiyoshi）　慶応大学（日吉）･･････　61　G 2

Keiō University（Mita）　慶応大学（三田）･･････　21　I 6

Keiō University（Yotsuya）　慶応大学（四ツ谷）･･････　23　F 7

Keiō-Yomiuri Land Station　京王よみうりランド駅･･････　15　H 5

Keisei-Hikifune Station　京成曳舟駅･･････････････　9　F 5

Keisei-Kanamachi Station　京成金町駅･･････････　8　C 3

Keisei-Koiwa Station　京成小岩駅･･････････････　8　E 2

Keisei-Sekiya Station　京成関屋駅･･････････････　8　E 5

Keisei-Takasago Station　京成高砂駅･･････････････　8　D 3

Keisei-Tateishi Station　京成立石駅･･････････････　8　E 3

Keisei-Ueno Station　京成上野駅･･････････････　30　A 3

Keisen Jogakuen Univ.　恵泉女学園大学･･････････　74　C 4

Kensetsu Kyōsai Kaikan（hall）　建設共済会館･･････　55　F 5

Keyaki Hall　けやきホール･･････････････････････　82　D 3

Kiba I〜6（Kōtō-ku）　木場 I〜6丁目（江東区）･･････　19　I 2

Kiba Park　木場公園･･････････････････････････････　9　H 5

Kiba Station（subway）　木場駅（地下鉄）･･････　19　I 2

Kibōgaoka Station　希望ケ丘駅･･････････････････　60　B 5

Kichijōji Station　吉祥寺駅･･････････････････････　15　J 3

Kikuichō（Shinjuku-ku）　喜久井町（新宿区）･･････　23　F 3

Kikukawa I〜3（Sumida-ku）　菊川 I〜3丁目（墨田区）･･････　17　I 5

Kikukawa Station（subway）　菊川駅（地下鉄）･･････　9　H 5

Kikuna Station　菊名駅･･････････････････････････　61　F 3

Kinokuniya Bookstore　紀伊国屋書店･･････････　57　G 4

Kinokuniya Hall　紀伊国屋ホール･･････････････　57　G 4

Kinokuniya International　紀ノ国屋（スーパーマーケット）･･････　54　D 5

Kinshi I〜4（Sumida-ku）　錦糸 I〜4丁目（墨田区）･･････　17　J 4

Kinshichō Station　錦糸町駅･･････････････････････　9　G 5

Kinuta I〜8（Setagaya-ku）　砧 I〜8丁目（世田谷区）･･　12　C 2

Kinuta Park　砧公園･･････････････････････････････　12　C 2

Kioichō（Chiyoda-ku）　紀尾井町（千代田区）･･････　23　H 7

Kioichō Bldg　紀尾井町ビル･････････････････････　46　B 1

Kirigaoka I〜2（Kita-ku）　桐ケ丘 I〜2丁目（北区）･･････　11　G 1

Kirin Breweries（H. O.）　キリンビール（本社）･･････　54　A 3

Kishimachi I〜2（Kita-ku）　岸町 I〜2丁目（北区）･･････　11（H 2）

Kishi Mem. Gym.　岸記念体育館･･････････････　20　C 3

Kishimojin-dō（temple）（Shitaya）　鬼子母神堂（下谷）･･　27　F 6

Kishimojin-dō（temple）（Zōshigaya）　鬼子母神堂（雑司が谷）･･　24　E 6

Kita-Aoyama I〜3（Minato-ku）　北青山 I〜3丁目（港区）･･････　20　E 2

Kita-Ayase Station（subway）　北綾瀬駅（地下鉄）･･････　8　C 4

Kita-Hachiōji Station　北八王子駅･･････････････　14　D 4

Kita-Ikebukuro Station　北池袋駅･･････････････　24　E 2

Kita-Kaheichō（Adachi-ku）　北加平町（足立区）･･････　8　C 4

Kita-Karasuyama I〜9（Setagaya-ku）　北烏山 I〜9丁目（世田谷区）･･････　10　B 6

Kita-Kasai I〜5（Edogawa-ku）　北葛西 I〜5丁目（江戸川区）･･　9　H 3

Kita-Koiwa I〜8（Edogawa-ku）　北小岩 I〜8丁目（江戸川区）･･　9　E 2

Kita-Kōjiya I〜2（Ota-ku）　北糀谷 I〜2丁目（大田区）･･････　13（H 6）

Kita-ku　北区･･････････････････････････････････････　7　F 1

Kitamachi I〜8（Nerima-ku）　北町 I〜8丁目（練馬区）･･････　10　E 2

Kitamachi（Shinjuku-ku）　北町（新宿区）･･････　23　H 3

Kita-Magome I〜2（Ōta-ku）　北馬込 I〜2丁目（大田区）･･････　13　G 4

Kitami I〜9（Setagaya-ku）　喜多見 I〜9丁目（世田谷区）･･　12　B 2

Kita-Minemachi（Ōta-ku）　北嶺町（大田区）･･････　13（F 5）

Kitami Station　喜多見駅･･････････････････････　12　B 2

Kitanomaru-Kōen（Chiyoda-ku）　北の丸公園（千代田区）･･････　16　A 5

Kitanomaru Nat'l Garden　北の丸公園･･････････　16　A 5

Kitano Station　北野駅･･････････････････････････　14　D 4

Kita-Ōtsuka I〜3（Toshima-ku）　北大塚 I〜3丁目（豊島区）･･　25　G 4

Kita Roppeita Mem. Noh Theater　喜多六平太記念能楽堂･･････　80　A 5

Kitasato University　北里大学･･････････････････　21　G 7

Kitasato Univ.（Sagamihara）　北里大学（相模原）･･････　74　B 5

Kita-Senju Station　北千住駅･･････････････････　27　I 1

Kita-Senzoku 1～3 (Ōta-ku) 北千束1～3丁目(大田区) ········· 13 G 4
Kita-Senzoku Station 北千束駅 ·········· 13 G 4
Kita-Shinagawa 1～6 (Shinagawa-ku) 北品川1～6丁目(品川区) ··· 29 G 5
Kita-Shinagawa Station 北品川駅 ·········· 29 G 5
Kita-Shinjuku 1～4 (Shinjuku-ku) 北新宿1～4丁目(新宿区) ··· 22 A 3
Kita-Shinozakimachi 1～2 (Edogawa-ku) 北篠崎町1～2丁目(江戸川区) ··· 9 F 1
Kita-Suna 1～7 (Kōtō-ku) 北砂1～7丁目(江東区) ··· 9 H 4
Kita-Tama Station 北多磨駅 ·········· 15 H 4
Kita-Ueno 1～2 (Taitō-ku) 北上野1～2丁目(台東区) ··· 27 F 7
Kita Ward Office 北区役所 ·········· 11 H 2
Kita-Yamabushichō (Shinjuku-ku) 北山伏町(新宿区) ··· 23 G 3
Kitazawa 1～5 (Setagaya-ku) 北沢1～5丁目(世田谷区) ··· 11 E 7
Kite Museum 凧の博物館 ·········· 35 F 3
Kiyokawa 1～2 (Taitō-ku) 清川1～2丁目(台東区) ··· 27 I 5
Kiyomizu Kannondō 清水観音堂 ·········· 30 A 2
Kiyose City 清瀬市 ·········· 15 H 1
Kiyose Station 清瀬駅 ·········· 15 H 1
Kiyosu-bashi (bridge) 清洲橋 ·········· 17 G 7
Kiyosumi 1～3 (Kōtō-ku) 清澄1～3丁目(江東区) ··· 17 H 7
Kiyosumi Garden 清澄庭園 ·········· 9 H 5
Kobuchi Station 古淵駅 ·········· 15 F 7
Kodaira Cemetery 小平霊園 ·········· 15 H 2
Kodaira City 小平市 ·········· 15 G 2
Kodaira Station 小平駅 ·········· 15 H 2
Kōdansha 講談社 ·········· 25 G 7
Kodenmachō Station (subway) 小伝馬町駅(地下鉄) ··· 16 E 5
Kōdō 1～2 (Adachi-ku) 弘道1～2丁目(足立区) ··· 8 C 5
Kōdōkan 講道館 ·········· 16 A 2
Kodomono-Kuni (see Nat'l Children's Land) こどもの国 ··· 60 B 2
Kodomono-Shiro (see Nat'l Children's Castle) こどもの城 ··· 54 C 5
Kōenji-Kita 1～4 (Suginami-ku) 高円寺北1～4丁目(杉並区) ··· 10 E 4
Kōenji-Minami 1～5 (Suginami-ku) 高円寺南1～5丁目(杉並区)
·········· 10 E 5
Kōenji Station 高円寺駅 ·········· 10 E 5
Kōgakuin University 工学院大学 ·········· 56 D 5
Kōgakuin Univ. (Hachiōji) 工学院大学(八王子) ··· 14 C 3
Koganei City 小金井市 ·········· 15 H 3
Koganei Park 小金井公園 ·········· 15 H 2
Kohinata 1～4 (Bunkyō-ku) 小日向1～4丁目(文京区) ··· 23 I 1
Kōhoku 1～7 (Adachi-ku) 江北1～7丁目(足立区) ··· 8 C 7
Kōhoku-ku (Yokohama City) 港北区(横浜市) ··· 61 F 2
Koigakubo Station 恋ケ窪駅 ·········· 15 G 2
Koishikawa 1～5 (Bunkyō-ku) 小石川1～5丁目(文京区) ··· 23 I 1
Koishikawa Botanical Garden 小石川植物園 ·········· 25 I 6
Koishikawa Kōrakuen (garden) 小石川後楽園 ··· 16 A 2
Koishikawa Post Office 小石川郵便局 ·········· 23 I 1
Koiwa Station 小岩駅 ·········· 8 E 2
Kojima 1～2 (Taitō-ku) 小島1～2丁目(台東区) ··· 17 F 2
Kōjimachi 1～6 (Chiyoda-ku) 麹町1～6丁目(千代田区) ··· 23 H 6
Kōjimachi Post Office 麹町郵便局 ·········· 69 F 4
Kōjimachi Station (subway) 麹町駅(地下鉄) ··· 23 I 6
Kojima-shinden Station 小島新田駅 ·········· 61 I 2

Kojiya 1～5 (Adachi-ku) 古千谷1～5丁目(足立区) ··· 8 A 7
Kojiyachō (Adachi-ku) 古千谷町(足立区) ··· 8 A 6
Kojiya Station 糀谷駅 ·········· 13 H 6
Kokkai-gijidōmae Station (subway) 国会議事堂前駅(地下鉄) ··· 47 F 5
Kōko Bldg 公庫ビル ·········· 36 B 4
Kokubunji City 国分寺市 ·········· 15 F 3
Kokubunji Station 国分寺駅 ·········· 15 G 3
Kokudō Station 国道駅 ·········· 61 G 4
Kokugakuin University 国学院大学 ·········· 20 E 5
Kokugikan (see Sumo Stadium) 国技館 ··· 17 G 4
Kōkū Kaikan (see Aviation Bldg) 航空会館 ··· 38 A 5
Kokuryō Station 国領駅 ·········· 15 I 4
Kokusai Akasaka Bldg 国際赤坂ビル ·········· 46 D 6
Kokusai Bldg 国際ビル ·········· 37 I 6
Kokusai Bunka Kaikan (see Int'l House of Japan) 国際文化会館 ··· 49 I 4
Kokusai Shin Akasaka Bldg 国際新赤坂ビル ··· 46 C 6
Kokusaitenjijō Station 国際展示場駅 ·········· 7 G 5
Kokushikan Univ. (Setagaya) 国士館(世田谷) ··· 12 E 2
Kokushikan Univ. (Tsurukawa) 国士館(鶴川) ··· 74 C 4
Kōkyo (Imperial Palace) 皇居 ·········· 16 A 7
Kōkyo-gaien (Chiyoda-ku) 皇居外苑(千代田区) ··· 16 B 7
Kōkyo Gaien (see Imperial Palace Outer Garden) 皇居外苑 ··· 37 G 7
Kōkyo Higashi Gyoen (Eastern Garden of the Imperial Palace) 皇居東苑 ··· 36 C 7
Komaba 1～4 (Meguro-ku) 駒場1～4丁目(目黒区) ··· 20 A 5
Komaba Park 駒場公園 ·········· 11 F 7
Komaba-Tōdaimae Station 駒場東大前駅 ·········· 13 F 1
Komae City 狛江市 ·········· 15 I 5
Komae Station 狛江駅 ·········· 12 A 2
Komagata 1～2 (Taitō-ku) 駒形1～2丁目(台東区) ··· 17 G 2
Komagome 1～7 (Toshima-ku) 駒込1～7丁目(豊島区) ··· 25 I 3
Komagome Station 駒込駅 ·········· 25 J 3
Komatsugawa 1～4 (Edogawa-ku) 小松川1～4丁目(江戸川区) ··· 9 G 3
Komazawa 1～5 (Setagaya-ku) 駒沢1～5丁目(世田谷区) ··· 12 E 2
Komazawa-Daigaku Station 駒沢大学駅 ·········· 12 E 2
Komazawa-Kōen (Setagaya-ku) 駒沢公園(世田谷区) ··· 12 E 3
Komazawa Olympic Park 駒沢オリンピック公園 ··· 12 E 3
Komazawa University 駒沢大学 ·········· 12 E 2
Komazawa Univ. (Tamagawa) 駒沢大学(玉川) ··· 12 C 3
Komiya Station 小宮駅 ·········· 14 E 3
Komone 1～5 (Itabashi-ku) 小茂根1～5丁目(板橋区) ··· 11 F 2
Kōnan 1～5 (Minato-ku) 港南1～5丁目(港区) ··· 29 G 1
Kōnan-ku (Yokohama City) 港南区(横浜市) ··· 60 E 7
Kōnodai Station 国府台駅 ·········· 8 E 1
Kōraku 1～2 (Bunkyō-ku) 後楽1～2丁目(文京区) ··· 23 J 2
Kōrakuen Hall 後楽園ホール ·········· 16 A 3
Kōrakuen Station (subway) 後楽園駅(地下鉄) ··· 16 A 2
Kōrakuen Amusement Park 後楽園ゆうえんち ··· 16 A 2
Koremasa Station 是政駅 ·········· 15 H 4
Kōsei Nenkin Hall (kaikan) 厚生年金会館 ··· 22 E 5
Kōsei Nenkin Hosp. 厚生年金病院 ·········· 23 I 3
Kosuge 1～4 (Katsushika-ku) 小菅1～4丁目(葛飾区) ··· 8 D 5
Kosuge Station 小菅駅 ·········· 8 D 5

113

Kotakechō1～2 (Nerima-ku) 小竹町1～2丁目(練馬区) ········· 11 F 3
Kotake-Mukaihara Station (subway) 小竹向原駅(地下鉄) ····· 11 F 3
Kōtōbashi1～5 (Sumida-ku) 江東橋1～5丁目(墨田区) ········· 17 J 4
Kotobuki1～4 (Taitō-ku) 寿1～4丁目(台東区) ············ 17 G 2
Kōtō-ku 江東区 ······ 7 G 4
Kōtō Ward Office 江東区役所 ········· 9 H 5
Kōwa Int'l Bldg 興和インターナショナルビル ········· 21 F 4
Kōyama1～4 (Nerima-ku) 向山1～4丁目(練馬区) ······ 10 D 3
Koyama1～7 (Shinagawa-ku) 小山1～7丁目(品川区) ·· 28 B 5
Koyamadai1～2 (Shinagawa-ku) 小山台1～2丁目(品川区) ·· 28 A 4
Kozukue Station 小机駅 ········· 60 E 3
Kudan Kaikan (hall) 九段会館 ········· 32 A 5
Kudan-Kita1～4(Chiyoda-ku) 九段北1～4丁目(千代田区) · 23 I 5
Kudan-Minami1～4(Chiyoda-ku) 九段南1～4丁目(千代田区) ·· 23 I 5
Kudan Post Office 九段郵便局 ········· 32 A 5
Kudanshita Station (subway) 九段下駅(地下鉄) ········· 32 A 4
Kugahara1～6 (Ōta-ku) 久が原1～6丁目(大田区) ······ 13 F 5
Kugahara Station 久が原駅 ········· 13 F 5
Kugayama1～5 (Suginami-ku) 久我山1～5丁目(杉並区) ·· 10 B 6
Kuhonbutsu Station 九品仏駅 ········· 12 E 4
Kuji Station 久地駅 ········· 12 B 3
Kumagai Morikazu Art Musm 熊谷守一美術館 ········· 24 A 4
Kumagawa Station 熊川駅 ········· 14 D 2
Kumanochō (Itabashi-ku) 熊野町(板橋区) ········· 24 D 2
Kume Art Museum 久米美術館 ········· 28 C 2
Kumegawa Station 久米川駅 ········· 15 G 1
Kunitachi City 国立市 ········· 15 F 3
Kunitachi Coll. of Music 国立音楽大学 ········· 74 C 2
Kunitachi Station 国立駅 ········· 15 G 3
Kuramae1～4 (Taitō-ku) 蔵前1～4丁目(台東区) ······ 17 G 2
Kuramae Station (subway) 蔵前駅(地下鉄) ········· 17 G 3
Kurihara1～4 (Adachi-ku) 栗原1～4丁目(足立区) ······ 8 C 6
Kurihira Station 栗平駅 ········· 15 G 6
Kurita Museum 栗田美術館 ········· 85 G 7
Kurokawa Station 黒川駅 ········· 15 G 5
Kyōbashi 1～3 (Chūō-ku) 京橋1～3丁目(中央区) ······ 18 D 1
Kyōbashi Kaikan (hall) 京橋会館 ········· 39 I 2
Kyōbashi Post Office 京橋郵便局 ········· 39 H 6
Kyōbashi Station (subway) 京橋駅(地下鉄) ········· 35 J 6
Kyōdō1～5 (Setagaya-ku) 経堂1～5丁目(世田谷区) ·· 12 D 1
Kyōdō News Service (Kyōdō Tsūshin) 共同通信社 ······· 21 J 2
Kyōdō Printing (H. O.) 共同印刷(本社) ········· 25 J 7
Kyōdō Station 経堂駅 ········· 12 D 1
Kyōiku Kaikan (hall) 教育会館 ········· 32 B 5
Kyōikuno-mori Park 教育の森公園 ········· 25 H 6
Kyōjima1～3 (Sumida-ku) 京島1～3丁目(墨田区) ······ 9 F 5
Kyōrin Univ. (Health & Social Sci.) 杏林大学(保健、社会) ···· 14 C 3
Kyōrin Univ. (Med.) 杏林大学(医) ········· 74 (D 3)
Kyōritsu Coll. of Pharmacy 共立薬科大学 ········· 18 A 4
Kyōritsu Kōdō (hall) 共立講堂 ········· 32 C 6
Kyōritsu Women's Univ. (Hachiōji) 共立女子大学(八王子) ·· 74 A 4
Kyōritsu Women's Univ. (Kanda) 共立女子大学(神田) ········· 32 B 5

Kyōteijōmae Station 競艇場前駅 ········· 15 H 4
Kyūden1～5 (Setagaya-ku) 給田1～5丁目(世田谷区) ·· 12 B 1
Kyū Furukawa Garden (Fomer Furukawa Garden) 旧古河庭園 ········· 25 J 2
Kyū Shibarikyū Garden 旧芝離宮庭園 ········· 18 B 5
Kyū Yasuda Garden 旧安田庭園 ········· 17 G 4
Landmark Tower ランドマークタワー ········· 62 E 3
Laforet Museum Akasaka ラフォーレミュージアム赤坂 ········· 48 D 2
Laforet Museum Harajuku ラフォーレミュージアム原宿 ········· 54 B 2
Laforet Museum Iigura ラフォーレミュージアム飯倉 ·· 80 D 5
Lion Corp. ライオン ········· 17 H 3
Long-Term Credit Bank of Japan (H. O.) 日本長期信用銀行(本店) ···· 36 C 5
Lumine (Shinjuku) ルミネ(新宿) ········· 57 E 5
Machida City 町田市 ········· 15 F 6
Machida City Musm of Graphic Arts 町田市立国際版画美術館 ·· 86 C 5
Machida Station 町田駅 ········· 60 A 2
Machiya1～8 (Arakawa-ku) 町屋1～8丁目(荒川区) ······ 27 F 1
Machiya Station 町屋駅 ········· 27 F 2
Maenochō1～6 (Itabashi-ku) 前野町1～6丁目(板橋区) ·· 11 F 1
Magazine House マガジンハウス ········· 39 H 4
Magome Station (subway) 馬込駅(地下鉄) ·· 13 G 4
Maihama Station 舞浜駅 ········· 7 I 5
Mainichi Newspapers 毎日新聞社 ········· 32 C 7
Maison Franco-Japonaise (Nichi-Futsu Kaikan) 日仏会館 ·· 32 D 2
Makino Memorial Garden 牧野記念庭園 ········· 10 B 3
Man'yō Garden of Kokubunji 国分寺万葉植物園 ········· 15 G 3
Marine Tower マリンタワー ········· 63 H 5
Marubeni (H. O.) 丸紅(本社) ········· 36 A 6
Marui Fashion Bldg 丸井ファッション館 ········· 57 H 4
Marunouchi1～3 (Chiyoda-ku) 丸の内1～3丁目(千代田区) ···· 16 C 7
Marunouchi Bldg 丸の内ビル ········· 37 G 4
Marunouchi Piccadilly (cinema) 丸の内ピカデリー(映) · 38 (E 2)
Marunouchi Yaesu Bldg 丸の内八重洲ビル ········· 37 H 5
Maruyama1～2 (Nakano-ku) 丸山1～2丁目(中野区) ·· 10 E 4
Maruyamachō (Shibuya-ku) 円山町(渋谷区) ·· 52 B 6
Maruzen (bookstore) (Nihombashi) 丸善(日本橋店) ···· 35 G 5
Masakado Kubizuka (see Hill of Masakado's Head) 将門首塚 ·· 36 C 5
Matsubara1～6 (Setagaya-ku) 松原1～6丁目(世田谷区) ·· 12 E 1
Matsubara Station 松原駅 ········· 12 D 1
Matsuchiyama-Shōden (temple) 待乳山聖天 ········· 27 I 7
Matsudo Station 松戸駅 ········· 8 C 1
Matsue1～7 (Edogawa-ku) 松江1～7丁目(江戸川区) ·· 9 G 2
Matsugaoka1～2 (Nakano-ku) 松が丘1～2丁目(中野区) ·· 11 F 4
Matsugaya1～4 (Taitō-ku) 松が谷1～4丁目(台東区) ·· 17 F 1
Matsumoto1～2 (Edogawa-ku) 松本1～2丁目(江戸川区) ·· 9 F 2
Matsumotochō (Edogawa-ku) 松本町1～4丁目(江戸川区) ·· 9 F 2
Matsunoki1～3 (Suginami-ku) 松ノ木1～3丁目(杉並区) ·· 10 D 6
Matsuoka Art Museum 松岡美術館 ········· 84 D 6
Matsushima1～4 (Edogawa-ku) 松島1～4丁目(江戸川区) ·· 9 F 3
Matsuya Dept Store (Asakusa) 松屋デパート(浅草店) ·· 31 I 5
Matsuya Dept Store (Ginza) 松屋デパート(銀座店) ········· 39 G 3

114

Matsuzakaya Dept Store（Ginza）　松坂屋デパート（銀座店）⋯⋯ *38* E 4
Matsuzakaya Dept Store（Ueno）　松坂屋デパート（上野店）⋯⋯ *30* A 6
Meaka Fudō（temple）　目赤不動 ⋯⋯ *26* A 5
Meguro 1～4（Meguro-ku）　目黒 1～4丁目（目黒区）⋯⋯ *28* B 2
Meguro Fudō（temple）　目黒不動 ⋯⋯ *28* B 3
Meguro-Honchō 1～6（Meguro-ku）　目黒本町 1～6丁目（目黒区）⋯⋯ *13* G 3
Meguro-ku　目黒区 ⋯⋯ *6* E 5
Meguro Musm of Art　目黒区美術館 ⋯⋯ *28* B 2
Meguro Parasitolongical Musm　目黒寄生虫館 ⋯⋯ *28* B 3
Meguro Public Hall（kōkaidō）　目黒公会堂 ⋯⋯ *83* F 4
Meguro Station　目黒駅 ⋯⋯ *28* C 3
Meguro Ward Gym.　目黒区立体育館 ⋯⋯ *28* A 5
Meguro Ward Office　目黒区役所 ⋯⋯ *13* F 2
Meidaimae Station　明大前駅 ⋯⋯ *10* E 7
Meiji Coll. of Pharm.（Setagaya）　明治薬科大学（世田谷）⋯⋯ *13* F 2
Meiji Coll. of Pharm.（Tanashi）　明治薬科大学（田無）⋯⋯ *74* D 2
Meiji Gakuin University　明治学院大学 ⋯⋯ *29* E 2
Meiji Jingū（shrine）　明治神宮 ⋯⋯ *20* C 1
Meiji-jingūmae Station（subway）　明治神宮前駅（地下鉄）⋯⋯ *54* B 2
Meiji Jingū Outer Gardens　明治神宮外苑 ⋯⋯ *21* F 1
Meiji Kinenkan　明治記念館 ⋯⋯ *21* F 1
Meiji Memorial Hall of Tama　多摩聖蹟記念館 ⋯⋯ *15* G 5
Meiji Mem. Picture Gallery　聖徳記念絵画館 ⋯⋯ *21* F 1
Meiji Seika　明治製菓 ⋯⋯ *37* I 2
Meiji Seimei Bldg　明治生命ビル ⋯⋯ *37* H 5
Meiji Univ.（Ikuta）　明治大学（生田）⋯⋯ *74* D 4
Meiji Univ.（Izumi）　明治大学（和泉）⋯⋯ *10* E 7
Meiji Univ.（Surugacai）　明治大学（駿河台）⋯⋯ *32* D 4
Meiji-za（theater）　明治座 ⋯⋯ *17* F 6
Meikai University　明海大学 ⋯⋯ *45* I 4
Meisei University　明星大学 ⋯⋯ *74* C 4
Mejiro 1～5（Toshima-ku）　目白 1～5丁目（豊島区）⋯⋯ *24* C 6
Mejirodai 1～3（Bunkyō-ku）　目白台 1～3丁目（文京区）⋯ *25* F 7
Mejirodai Station　めじろ台駅 ⋯⋯ *14* C 4
Mejiro Fudō（temple）　目白不動 ⋯⋯ *24* E 7
Mejiro Station　目白駅 ⋯⋯ *24* D 6
Mem. Musm of Printing Bureau　大蔵省印刷局記念館 ⋯ *23* G 4
Midori 1～4（Sumida-ku）　緑 1～4丁目（墨田区）⋯⋯ *17* I 4
Midorigaoka 1～3（Meguro-ku）　緑が丘 1～3丁目（目黒区）⋯⋯ *13* F 3
Midorigaoka Station　緑が丘駅 ⋯⋯ *13* F 3
Midori-ku（Yokohama City）　緑区（横浜市）⋯⋯ *60* D 3
Miharadai 1～3（Nerima-ku）　三原台 1～3丁目（練馬区）⋯⋯ *10* C 2
Mikawashima Station　三河島駅 ⋯⋯ *26* E 4
Minami 1～3（Meguro-ku）　南 1～3丁目（目黒区）⋯⋯ *13* F 3
Minami-Aoyama 1～7（Minato-ku）　南青山 1～7丁目（港区）⋯⋯ *21* F 3
Minami Art Musm　ミナミ美術館 ⋯⋯ *33* I 2
Minami-Asagaya Station（subway）　南阿佐ケ谷駅（地下鉄）⋯⋯ *10* D 5
Minami-Azabu 1～5（Minato-ku）　南麻布 1～5丁目（港区）⋯⋯ *21* G 6
Miamichō（Itabashi-ku）　南町（板橋区）⋯⋯ *24* C 2
Miamichō（Shinjuku-ku）　南町（新宿区）⋯⋯ *23* H 4
Minamidai 1～5（Nakano-ku）　南台 1～5丁目（中野区）⋯⋯ *11* E 6
Minamidaira Station　南平駅 ⋯⋯ *15* E 4

Minami-Enokichō（Shinjuku-ku）　南榎町（新宿区）⋯⋯ *23* G 3
Minami-Gyōtoku Station（subway）　南行徳駅（地下鉄）⋯ *9* H 1
Minami-Hanahata 1～5（Adachi-ku）　南花畑 1～5丁目（足立区）⋯ *8* B 5
Minami-Hashimoto Station　南橋本駅 ⋯⋯ *14* D 6
Minami-Ikebukuro 1～4（Toshima-ku）　南池袋 1～4丁目（豊島区）⋯ *24* E 5
Minami-Kamata 1～3（Ōta-ku）　南蒲田 1～3丁目（大田区）⋯⋯ *13*（H 6）
Minami-Karasuyama 1～6（Setagaya-ku）　南烏山 1～6丁目（世田谷区）⋯ *12* B 1
Minami-Kasai 1～7（Edogawa-ku）　南葛西 1～7丁目（江戸川区）⋯ *9* J 2
Minami-Koiwa 1～8（Edogawa-ku）　南小岩 1～8丁目（江戸川区）⋯ *9* F 2
Minami-ku（Yokohama City）　南区（横浜市）⋯⋯ *60* E 6
Minami-Kugahara 1～2（Ōta-ku）　南久が原 1～2丁目（大田区）⋯ *13* F 5
Minami-Machida Station　南町田駅 ⋯⋯ *60* A 3
Minami-Magome 1～6（Ōta-ku）　南馬込 1～6丁目（大田区）⋯⋯ *13* G 4
Minami-Mizumoto 1～4（Katsushika-ku）　南水元 1～4丁目（葛飾区）⋯ *8* C 3
Minamimotomachi（Shinjuku-ku）　南元町（新宿区）⋯⋯ *23* F 7
Minami-Nagasaki 1～6（Toshima-ku）　南長崎 1～6丁目（豊島区）⋯ *24* A 5
Minami-Ogikubo 1～4（Suginami-ku）　南荻窪 1～4丁目（杉並区）⋯ *10* C 5
Minami-Ōi 1～6（Shinagawa-ku）　南大井 1～6丁目（品川区）⋯ *13* H 4
Minami-Ōizumi 1～6（Nerima-ku）　南大泉 1～6丁目（練馬区）⋯ *10* A 3
Minami-Ōsawa Station　南大沢駅 ⋯⋯ *14* E 5
Minami-Ōtsuka 1～3（Toshima-ku）　南大塚 1～3丁目（豊島区）⋯ *25* G 5
Minami-Rinkan Station　南林間駅 ⋯⋯ *60* A 4
Minami-Rokugō 1～3（Ōta-ku）　南六郷 1～3丁目（大田区）⋯ *13* H 7
Minami-Senju 1～8（Arakawa-ku）　南千住 1～8丁目（荒川区）⋯ *27* H 3
Minami-Senju Station　南千住駅 ⋯⋯ *27* H 4
Minami-Senzoku 1～3（Ōta-ku）　南千束 1～3丁目（大田区）⋯ *13*（F 4）
Minami-Shinagawa 1～6（Shinagawa-ku）　南品川 1～6丁目（品川区）⋯ *29* G 6
Minami-Shinjuku Station　南新宿駅 ⋯⋯ *22* B 6
Minami-Shinozakimachi 1～4（Edogawa-ku）　南篠崎町 1～4丁目（江戸川区）⋯ *9* G 1
Minami-Suna 1～7（Kōtō-ku）　南砂 1～7丁目（江東区）⋯ *9* H 4
Minami-Sunamachi Station（subway）　南砂町駅（地下鉄）⋯ *9* I 4
Minami-Tama Station　南多摩駅 ⋯⋯ *15* G 4
Minami-Tanaka 1～5（Nerima-ku）　南田中 1～5丁目（練馬区）⋯ *10* C 3
Minami-Tokiwadai 1～2（Itabasi-ku）　南常盤台 1～2丁目（板橋区）⋯ *11* F 2
Minami-Yamabushichō（Shinjuku-ku）　南山伏町（新宿区）⋯ *23* G 4
Minami-Yukigaya 1～5（Ōta-ku）　南雪谷 1～5丁目（大田区）⋯ *13* F 4
Minato 1～3（Chūō-ku）　湊 1～3丁目（中央区）⋯⋯ *19* F 2
Minatogaoka Futō Park　みなとが丘ふ頭公園 ⋯⋯ *13* J 4
Minato-ku　港区 ⋯⋯ *7* F 4
Minatono-mieruoka Park　港の見える丘公園 ⋯⋯ *63* H 6
Minato Ward Office　港区役所 ⋯⋯ *18* A 4
Minowa 1～2（Taitō-ku）　三ノ輪 1～2丁目（台東区）⋯ *27* G 5
Minowa Station（subway）　三ノ輪駅（地下鉄）⋯⋯ *27* G 4
Misakichō 1～3（Chiyoda-ku）　三崎町 1～3丁目（千代田区）⋯ *16* A 3
Mishuku 1～2（Setagaya-ku）　三宿 1～2丁目（世田谷区）⋯ *13* F 1
Misono 1～2（Itabashi-ku）　三園 1～2丁目（板橋区）⋯ *10* D 1
Misuji 1～2（Taitō-ku）　三筋 1～2丁目（台東区）⋯ *17* F 2
Mita 1～2（Meguro-ku）　三田 1～2丁目（目黒区）⋯ *28* B
Mita 1～5（Minato-ku）　三田 1～5丁目（港区）⋯ *21* I 6
Mitaka City　三鷹市 ⋯⋯ *15* I 3
Mitakadai Station　三鷹台駅 ⋯⋯ *10* B 5
Mitaka Station　三鷹駅 ⋯⋯ *15* I 3

Mita Station (subway)　三田駅(地下鉄)	21	J 7
Mitsubishi Bldg　三菱ビル	37	G 5
Mitsubishi Electric Bldg　三菱電機ビル	37	G 5
Mitsubishi Heavy Industries Bldg　三菱重工ビル	37	G 5
Mitsubishi Shoji Bldg　三菱商事ビル	37	G 5
Mitsubishi Trust Bank (H. O.)　三菱信託銀行(本店)	36	E 4
Mitsui Bussan (Mitsui & Co.) Bldg　三井物産ビル	36	C 5
Mitsuike Park　三ツ池公園	61	G 3
Mitsui Main Bldg　三井本館	34	C 5
Mitsui Marine & Fire Insurance　三井海上火災(本社)	33	F 4
Mitsui Mutual Life Insurance (H. O.)　三井生命(本社)	36	C 5
Mitsui Trust Bank (H. O.)　三井信託銀行(本店)	34	D 5
Mitsukoshi Dept Store (Main Store)　三越デパート(本店)	34	D 4
Mitsukoshi Dept Store (Ginza)　三越デパート(銀座店)	39	F 3
Mitsukoshi Dept Store (Ikebukuro)　三越デパート(池袋店)	59	E 3
Mitsukoshi Dept Store (Shinjuku)　三越デパート(新宿店)	57	G 4
Mitsukoshimae Station (subway)　三越前駅(地下鉄)	34	C 4
Mitsukoshi Theater　三越劇場	34	D 5
Mitsuzawa Park　三ツ沢公園	60	E 5
Miyagi 1〜2 (Adachi-ku)　宮城1〜2丁目(足立区)	11	I 2
Miyagi Michio Mem. Hall　宮城道雄記念館	85	G 3
Miyamae 1〜5 (Suginami-ku)　宮前1〜5丁目(杉並区)	10	C 5
Miyamae daira Station　宮前平駅	12	B 5
Miyamae-ku (Kawasaki City)　宮前区(川崎市)	12	A 4
Miyamotochō (Itabashi-ku)　宮本町(板橋区)	11	G 2
Miyanosaka Station　宮の坂駅	13	D 1
Miyasaka 1〜3 (Setagaya-ku)　宮坂1〜3丁目(世田谷区)	12	D 1
Miyazakidai Station　宮崎台駅	12	B 5
Miyoshi 1〜4 (Kōtō-ku)　三好1〜4丁目(江東区)	19	H 1
Mizue Station (subway)　瑞江駅(地下鉄)	9	G 1
Mizuho Town　瑞穂町	14	D 1
Mizumoto 1〜5 (Katsushika-ku)　水元1〜5丁目(葛飾区)	8	B 3
Mizumoto-Kōen (Katsushika-ku)　水元公園(葛飾区)	8	B 3
Mizumoto Park　水元公園	8	B 2
Mogusa-en (garden)　百草園	15	F 4
Mogusaen Station　百草園駅	15	F 4
Mokuba-kan (theater)　木馬館	31	G 3
Momoi 1〜4 (Suginami-ku)　桃井1〜4丁目(杉並区)	10	C 4
Monzen-nakachō 1〜2 (Kōtō-ku)　門前仲町1〜2丁目(江東区)	19	H 2
Monzen-nakachō Station (subway)　門前仲町駅(地下鉄)	19	H 2
Mōri 1〜2 (Kōtō-ku)　毛利1〜2丁目(江東区)	9	G 6
Morishita 1〜5 (Kōtō-ku)　森下1〜5丁目(江東区)	17	I 6
Morishita Station (subway)　森下駅(地下鉄)	17	H 6
Moto-Akasaka 1〜2 (Minato-ku)　元赤坂1〜2丁目(港区)	21	H 1
Moto-Asakusa 1〜4 (Taitō-ku)　元浅草1〜4丁目(台東区)	17	F 2
Moto-Azabu 1〜3 (Minato-ku)　元麻布1〜3丁目(港区)	21	G 5
Moto-Hasunuma Station (subway)　本蓮沼駅(地下鉄)	11	G 1
Motoki (Adachi-ku)　本木(足立区)	8	D 6
Motomachi (Yokohama City)　元町(横浜市)	63	G 6
Motomachi Park　元町公園	63	H 6
Moto-sumiyoshi Station　元住吉駅	61	G 1
Moto-Yoyogichō (Shibuya-ku)　元代々木町(渋谷区)	20	A 2
Mukaigawara Station　向河原駅	61	G 1
Mukaihara 1〜3 (Itabashi-ku)　向原1〜3丁目(板橋区)	11	F 3
Mukōgaoka 1〜2 (Bunkyō-ku)　向丘1〜2丁目(文京区)	26	B 6
Mukōgaoka Yūen　向ヶ丘遊園	12	A 4
Mukōgaoka-yūen Station　向ヶ丘遊園駅	12	A 3
Mukōjima 1〜5 (Sumida-ku)　向島1〜5丁目(墨田区)	17	J 1
Mukōjima Hyakka-en (garden)　向島百花園	83	G 3
Murauchi Art Museum　村内美術館	86	B 3
Musashi-Hikida Station　武蔵引田駅	14	B 2
Musashi Inst. of Technology　武蔵工業大学	12	E 4
Musashi-Itsukaichi Station　武蔵五日市駅	14	A 2
Musashi-Koganei Station　武蔵小金井駅	15	H 3
Musashi-Kosugi Station　武蔵小杉駅	12	E 5
Musashi-Koyama Station　武蔵小山駅	28	B 5
Musashi-Masuko Station　武蔵増戸駅	14	B 2
Musashi-Mizonokuchi Station　武蔵溝ノ口駅	12	C 4
Musashi-Murayama City　武蔵村山市	14	E 1
Musashi-Nakahara Station　武蔵中原駅	12	D 5
Musashi-Nitta Station　武蔵新田駅	13	F 6
Musashino Academia Musicae (Ekoda)　武蔵野音楽大学(江古田)	11	F 3
Musashino Academia Musicae (Iruma)　武蔵野音楽大学(入間)	74	B 1
Musashino Art University　武蔵野美術大学	74	(C 2)
Musashino City　武蔵野市	15	I 2
Musashino Civic Auditorium　武蔵野市民文化会館	82	D 3
Musashinodai Station　武蔵野台駅	15	H 4
Musashino Mausoleum　武蔵野陵	14	C 4
Musashino Park　武蔵野公園	82	D 3
Musashino Women's Coll.　武蔵野女子大学	74	(D 3)
Musashi-Sakai Station　武蔵境駅	15	I 3
Musashi-Seki Station　武蔵関駅	10	A 4
Musashi-Shinjō Station　武蔵新城駅	12	D 5
Musashi-Shiraishi Station　武蔵白石駅	61	H 4
Musashi-Sunagawa Station　武蔵砂川駅	14	E 2
Musashi University　武蔵大学	11	E 3
Musashi-Yamato Station　武蔵大和駅	15	F 1
Museum of Calligraphy　書道博物館	26	E 5
Museum of Fiber & Tech.　東京農工大付属繊維博物館	86	D 3
Musm of Maritime Sci. (Funeno-Kagakukan)　船の科学館	13	J 3
Musm of Modern Japanese Literature　日本近代文学館	72	B 1
Mutsugi 1〜4 (Adachi-ku)　六木1〜4丁目(足立区)	8	B 4
My City　マイシティ	57	F 4
MYLORD　ミロード	57	F 5
Myōgadani Station (subway)　茗荷谷駅(地下鉄)	25	H 7
Myōhō-ji (temple)　妙法寺	10	E 5
Myōren-ji Station　妙蓮寺駅	61	F 4
MZA Ariake　エムザ　有明	83	G 4
Nagahara Station　長原駅	13	G 4
Naganuma Station　長沼駅	14	E 4
Nagasaki 1〜6 (Toshima-ku)　長崎1〜6丁目(豊島区)	24	A 4
Nagatachō 1〜2 (Chiyoda-ku)　永田町1〜2丁目(千代田区)	21	I 1
Nagatachō Station (subway)　永田町駅(地下鉄)	46	D 3

Nagatsuta Station　長津田駅 ················ *60*　B 3
Naikaku Bunko (see Cabinet Library)　内閣文庫 ········· *36*　D 7
Naitōmachi (Shinjuku-ku)　内藤町(新宿区) ········· *22*　E 6
Nakachō (Itabashi-ku)　仲町(板橋区) ········· *11*　G 2
Nakachō 1～2 (Meguro-ku)　中町1～2丁目(目黒区) ······ *13*　G 2
Nakachō (Shinjuku-ku)　中町(新宿区) ········· *23*　H 4
Nakadai 1～3 (Itabashi-ku)　中台1～3丁目(板橋区) ······ *11*　F 1
Nakagami Station　中神駅 ················ *14*　E 2
Nakagawa 1～5 (Adachi-ku)　中川1～5丁目(足立区) ······ *9*　C 3
Nakagawara Station　中河原駅 ················ *15*　G 4
Nakahara-ku (Kawasaki City)　中原区(川崎市) ········· *61*　F 1
Nakai 1～2 (Shinjuku-ku)　中井1～2丁目(新宿区) ······ *11*　F 4
Naka-Ikegami 1～2 (Ōta-ku)　仲池上1～2丁目(大田区) ····· *13*　G 5
Nakai Station　中井駅 ················ *11*　F 4
Naka-Itabashi (Itabashi-ku)　中板橋(板橋区) ········· *11*　G 2
Naka-Itabashi Station　中板橋駅 ················ *11*　G 2
Naka-Jūjō 1～4 (Kita-ku)　中十条1～4丁目(北区) ······ *11*　H 2
Nakajuku (Itabashi-ku)　仲宿(板橋区) ········· *11*　G 2
Naka-Kasai 1～8 (Edogawa-ku)　中葛西1～8丁目(江戸川区) ··· *9*　I 3
Naka-ku (Yokohama City)　中区(横浜市) ········· *61*　F 6
Nakamachi 1～5 (Setagaya-ku)　中町1～5丁目(世田谷区) ····· *12*　D 3
Naka-Magome 1～3 (Ōta-ku)　中馬込1～3丁目(大田区) ····· *13*　G 4
Nakamaruchō (Itabashi-ku)　中丸町(板橋区) ········· *24*　C 2
Naka-Meguro 1～5 (Meguro-ku)　中目黒1～5丁目(目黒区) ····· *28*　A 1
Naka-Meguro Station　中目黒駅 ················ *13*　G 2
Nakamise Dōri　仲見世通り ················ *31*　H 5
Nakamura 1～3 (Nerima-ku)　中村1～3丁目(練馬区) ······ *10*　D 3
Nakamurabashi Station　中村橋駅 ················ *10*　D 3
Nakamura-Kita 1～4 (Nerima-ku)　中村北1～4丁目(練馬区) ···· *10* (D 3)
Nakamura-Minami 1～3 (Nerima-ku)　中村南1～3丁目(練馬区) ···· *10*　D 3
Nakane 1～2 (Meguro-ku)　中根1～2丁目(目黒区) ······ *13*　F 3
Nakano 1～6 (Nakano-ku)　中野1～6丁目(中野区) ······ *11*　E 5
Nakanobu 1～6 (Shinagawa-ku)　中延1～6丁目(品川区) ····· *28*　B 6
Nakanobu Station (subway)　中延駅(地下鉄) ········· *13*　H 4
Nakano-Fujimichō Station (subway)　中野富士見町(地下鉄) ···· *11*　E 5
Nakano-ku　中野区 ················ *6*　D 2
Nakano-sakaue Station (subway)　中野坂上駅(地下鉄) ····· *11*　F 5
Nakanoshima Station　中野島駅 ················ *15*　I 5
Nakano-Shimbashi Station (subway)　中野新橋駅(地下鉄) ···· *11*　F 5
Nakano Station　中野駅 ················ *11*　E 5
Nakano Sun Plaza　中野サンプラザ ········· *11*　E 5
Nakano Ward Culture Center　中野区文化センター ······ *11*　F 5
Nakano Ward Office　中野区役所 ········· *10*　E 5
Naka-Ochiai 1～4 (Shinjuku-ku)　中落合1～4丁目(新宿区) ···· *24*　A 6
Naka-Okachimachi Station (subway)　仲御徒町駅(地下鉄) ···· *30*　C 6
Naka-Rokugō 1～4 (Ōta-ku)　仲六郷1～4丁目(大田区) ····· *13*　G 7
Nakayama Racecourse　中山競馬場 ········· *83*　I 3
Nakayama Station　中山駅 ················ *60*　C 3
Nakazato 1～3 (Kita-ku)　中里1～3丁目(北区) ······ *26*　A 2
Nakazatochō (Shinjuku-ku)　中里町(新宿区) ········· *23*　H 2
Nandomachi (Shinjuku-ku)　納戸町(新宿区) ········· *23*　H 4
Nanpeidaichō (Shibuya-ku)　南平台町(渋谷区) ········· *20*　B 5

Narihira 1～5 (Sumida-ku)　業平1～5丁目(墨田区) ······ *17*　J 2
Narihirabashi Station　業平橋駅 ················ *17*　J 1
Narimasu 1～5 (Itabashi-ku)　成増1～5丁目(板橋区) ····· *10*　D 1
Narimasu Station　成増駅 ················ *10*　D 1
Narita Airport (see New Tokyo Int'l Airport)　成田空港 ······ *155*
Narita-Higashi 1～5 (Suginami-ku)　成田東1～5丁目(杉並区)　*10*　D 5
Narita-Nishi 1～4 (Suginami-ku)　成田西1～4丁目(杉並区) ···· *10*　D 5
Naruse Station　成瀬駅 ················ *60*　A 2
Nat'l Archives　国立公文書館 ················ *32*　B 7
Nat'l Astronomical Observatory　国立天文台 ········· *6*　A 4
Nat'l Cancer Center　国立がんセンター ········· *39*　G 7
Nat'l Children's Castle (Kodomono-Shiro)　こどもの城 ····· *54*　C 5
Nat'l Children's Hosp.　国立小児病院 ········· *13*　F 1
Nat'l Children's Land　こどもの国 ················ *60*　B 2
Nat'l Diet Bldg (Kokkai-Gijidō)　国会議事堂 ········· *47*　F 4
Nat'l Diet Library　国立国会図書館 ········· *47*　F 3
Nat'l Education Center　国立教育会館 ········· *47*　G 7
Nat'l Hosp. Medical Service Center　国立病院医療センター ···· *23*　E 3
Nat'l Musm of Modern Art, Tokyo　東京国立近代美術館 ···· *32*　B 7
Nat'l Museum of Western Art　国立西洋美術館 ········· *30*　B 1
Nat'l Nakano Hosp.　国立中野病院 ········· *11*　E 4
Nat'l Nishigaoka Stadium　国立西ケ丘競技場 ········· *11*　G 1
Nat'l Noh Theater　国立能楽堂 ················ *80*　D 2
Nat'l Ōkura Hosp.　国立大蔵病院 ········· *12*　C 2
Nat'l Olympic Mem. Youth Center　オリンピック記念青少年総合センター ···· *20*　B 1
Nat'l Park for Nature Study　国立自然教育園 ········· *28*　D 2
Nat'l Saitama Hosp.　国立埼玉病院 ········· *10*　C 1
Nat'l Science Museum　国立科学博物館 ········· *30*　C 1
Nat'l Stadium　国立競技場 ················ *20*　E 1
Nat'l Theater　国立劇場 ················ *46*　E 2
Nat'l Tokyo No. 2 Hosp.　国立東京第二病院 ········· *13*　F 2
Nat'l Yoyogi Gymnasium　国立代々木競技場 ········· *20*　C 3
NCR Japan　日本エヌ・シー・アール ········· *47*　F 7
NEC　日本電気 ················ *21*　J 6
Negishi 1～5 (Taitō-ku)　根岸1～5丁目(台東区) ······ *27*　F 5
Negishi Forest Park　根岸森林公園 ········· *61*　F 6
Negishi Station　根岸駅 ················ *61*　F 7
Nerima 1～4 (Nerima-ku)　練馬1～4丁目(練馬区) ······ *10*　E 3
Nerima-ku　練馬区 ················ *6*　C 1
Nerima Station　練馬駅 ················ *10*　E 3
Nerima Ward Office　練馬区役所 ········· *10*　E 3
New Aoyama Bldg　新青山ビル ········· *21*　G 2
New Kokusai Bldg　新国際ビル ········· *37*　J 5
New Marunouchi Bldg　新丸の内ビル ········· *37*　F 4
New Melsa　ニューメルサ ········· *38*　E 4
New Nat'l Theater Tokyo　東京新国立劇場 ········· *22*　A 6
New Ōtemachi Bldg　新大手町ビル ········· *36*　D 3
New Tokyo Bldg　新東京ビル ········· *37*　I 5
New Tokyo Int'l Airport (Narita)　新東京国際空港(成田) ······ *155*
New Tokyo P. O.　新東京郵便局 ········· *9*　I 4
New Yūrakuchō Bldg　新有楽町ビル ········· *38*　D 1

Nezu 1～2 (Bunkyō-ku) 根津1～2丁目(文京区)･･････ 26 C6

Nezu Art Museum 根津美術館･･････････････････ 55 G5

Nezu Jinja (shrine) 根津神社･･････････････････ 26 B6

Nezu Station (subway) 根津駅(地下鉄)･･･････････ 26 C7

NHK Broadcasting Center NHK放送センター･･･ 52 C1

NHK Broadcast Museum NHK放送博物館･････ 18 A3

NHK Hall NHKホール･･･････････････････････ 80 C2

Nibanchō (Chiyoda-ku) 二番町(千代田区)･･････ 23 H6

Nichidō Fire & Marine Insurance 日動火災海上･･･ 39 G5

Nichi-Futsu Kaikan (see Maison Franco-Japonaise) 日仏会館･･ 32 D2

Nichigeki Tōhō 日劇東宝･････････････････････ 38 E2

Nichirei (H. O.) ニチレイ(本社)････････････ 32 A2

Nihombashi 1～3 (Chūō-ku) 日本橋1～3丁目(中央区) 16 D7

Nihombashi (bridge) 日本橋････････････････ 34 E4

Nihombashi-Bakurochō 1～2 (Chūō-ku) 日本橋馬喰町1～2丁目(中央区)･････ 17 F5

Nihombashi-dōri Post Office 日本橋通郵便局･･･ 35 G5

Nihombashi-Hakozakichō (Chūō-ku) 日本橋箱崎町(中央区)･･･ 19 F1

Nihombashi-Hamachō 1～3 (Chūō-ku) 日本橋浜町1～3丁目(中央区)･･･ 17 G6

Nihombashi-Hisamatsuchō (Chūō-ku) 日本橋久松町(中央区)･･･ 17 F6

Nihombashi-Honchō 1～4 (Chūō-ku) 日本橋本町1～4丁目(中央区)･･･ 16 D5

Nihombashi-Hongokuchō 1～4 (Chūō-ku) 日本橋本石町1～4丁目(中央区)･･･ 16 D6

Nihombashi-Horidomechō 1～2 (Chūō-ku) 日本橋堀留町1～2丁目(中央区)･･･ 17 E6

Nihombashi-Kabutochō (Chūō-ku) 日本橋兜町(中央区)･･･ 35 F2

Nihombashi-Kakigarachō 1～2 (Chūō-ku) 日本橋蠣殻町1～2丁目(中央区)･･･ 17 F7

Nihombashi-Kayabachō 1～3 (Chūō-ku) 日本橋茅場町1～3丁目(中央区)･･･ 18 E1

Nihombashi-Koamichō (Chūō-ku) 日本橋小網町(中央区)･･･ 34 E1

Nihombashi-Kobunachō (Chūō-ku) 日本橋小舟町(中央区)･･･ 16 E6

Nihombashi-Kodenmachō (Chūō-ku) 日本橋小伝馬町(中央区)･･･ 16 E5

Nihombashi-Muromachi 1～4 (Chūō-ku) 日本橋室町1～4丁目(中央区)･･･ 16 D5

Nihombashi-Nakasu (Chūō-ku) 日本橋中洲(中央区)･･･ 17 G7

Nihombashi-Ningyōchō 1～3 (Chūō-ku) 日本橋人形町1～3丁目(中央区)･･･ 17 F6

Nihombashi-Ōdenmachō (Chūō-ku) 日本橋大伝馬町(中央区)･･･ 17 E5

Nihombashi Plaza Bldg 日本橋プラザ･･･ 35 G5

Nihombashi Post Office 日本橋郵便局･･･ 35 E3

Nihombashi Station (subway) 日本橋駅(地下鉄)･･･ 35 F5

Nihombashi-Tomizawachō (Chūō-ku) 日本橋富沢町(中央区)･･･ 17 F6

Nihombashi-Yokoyamachō (Chūō-ku) 日本橋横山町(中央区)･･･ 16 F5

Nihon Keizai Newspapers 日本経済新聞社･･･ 36 B3

Nihon Mingei-kan (see Japan Folk Crafts Museum) 日本民芸館･･･ 13 F1

Nihon Minka-en (see Kawasaki Municipal Park of Japanese Houses) 日本民家園･･･ 12 A3

Nihon Seinen-kan Hall 日本青年館ホール･･･ 80 D3

Nihon Theater (cinema) 日本劇場(映)･･･ 38 E1

Nihon Toshi Center Hall 日本都市センターホール 46 C2

Nihon Unisys (H. O.) 日本ユニシス(本社)･･･ 19 G4

Nihon Univ. (Agr. & Vetn.) 日本大学(農獣医)･･･ 13 F2

Nihon Univ. (Arts) 日本大学(芸術)･･･ 11 F3

Nihon Univ. (Comm.) 日本大学(商)･･･ 74 E4

Nihon Univ. (Dent.) 日本大学(歯)･･･ 32 E3

Nihon Univ. (Econ.) 日本大学(経済)･･･ 32 C2

Nihon Univ. (Hum. & Sci.) 日本大学(文理)･･･ 12 D1

Nihon Univ. (Law) 日本大学(法)･･･ 32 B2

Nihon Univ. (Matsudo Dent.) 日本大学(松戸、歯)･･･ 75 H1

Nihon Univ. (Med.) 日本大学(医)･････････････ 74 F2

Nihon Univ. (Sci. &Engn.) 日本大学(理工)･･･ 33 E4

Nihonzutsumi 1～2 (Taitō-ku) 日本堤1～2丁目(台東区) 27 H5

Niihori 1～2 (Edogawa-ku) 新堀1～2丁目(江戸川区)･･ 9 G2

Niijuku 1～6 (Katsushika-ku) 新宿1～6丁目(葛飾区)･･ 8 D3

Nijūbashi (bridge) 二重橋･･･････････････ 16 A7

Nijūbashimae Station (subway) 二重橋前駅(地下鉄)･･･ 37 H6

Nijukkimachi (Shinjuku-ku) 二十騎町(新宿区)･･･ 23 G4

Nikkan kōgyō Hall 日刊工業ホール･･･ 32 A4

Nikka Whisky ニッカウヰスキー･･･ 55 F6

Nikkei Hall 日経ホール･･･ 36 C3

Nikolai Cathedral ニコライ堂･･･ 33 F3

Ningyōchō Station (subway) 人形町駅(地下鉄)･･･ 17 F6

Ninoechō (Edogawa-ku) 二之江町(江戸川区)･･･ 9 (H2)

Nippon Broadcasting ニッポン放送･･･ 38 C1

Nippon Budōkan 日本武道館･･･ 16 A5

Nippon Bldg 日本ビル･･･ 36 D2

Nippon Bunka Univ. 日本文化大学･･･ 14 D5

Nippon Coll. of Health & P. E. 日本体育大学･･･ 12 D3

Nippon Columbia 日本コロムビア･･･ 46 A6

Nippon Dental Coll. 日本歯科大学･･･ 23 J4

Nippon Fire & Marine Insurance (H. O.) 日本火災海上(本社)･･･ 35 F5

Nippon Ginkō (see Bank of Japan) (H. O.) 日本銀行(本店)･･ 34 D6

Nippon Medical School 日本医科大学･･･ 26 B6

Nippon Medical School (Shin-Maruko) 日本医科大学(新丸子) 75 E5

Nippon Med. Sch. Hosp. 日本医大病院･･･ 26 B6

Nippon N. C. R. (see NCR Japan) 日本エヌ・シー・アール･･･ 47 F7

Nippon Oil (Nisseki) 日本石油(日石)･･･ 38 A5

Nippon Press Center 日本プレスセンター･･･ 47 I7

Nippon Shinpan 日本信販･･･ 16 C2

Nippon Steel Corp. (H. O.) 新日本製鉄(本社)･･･ 36 E1

Nippon Television (NTV) 日本テレビ放送網･･･ 23 H6

Nippon Trust Bank (H. O.) 日本信託銀行(本店)･･･ 35 G5

Nippon Vetn. & Zootech. Coll. 日本獣医畜産大学･･･ 74 (D3)

Nippon Worem's Coll. of P. E. 日本女子体育大学･･･ 74 (E3)

Nippori Station 日暮里駅･･･ 26 D6

Nishiarai 1～7 (Adachi-ku) 西新井1～7丁目(足立区)･･ 8 B7

Nishiarai Daishi (temple) 西新井大師･･･ 8 C6

Nishiarai-Honchō 1～5 (Adachi-ku) 西新井本町1～5丁目(足立区)･･ 8 C7

Nishiarai-Sakaechō 1～3 (Adachi-ku) 西新井栄町1～3丁目(足立区)･･ 8 C6

Nishiarai Station 西新井駅･･･ 8 C6

Nishi-Asakusa 1～3 (Taitō-ku) 西浅草1～3丁目(台東区) 17 G1

Nishi-Ayase 1～4 (Adachi-ku) 西綾瀬1～4丁目(足立区) 8 C5

Nishi-Azabu 1～4 (Minato-ku) 西麻布1～4丁目(港区)･･ 21 F5

Nishi-Chōfu Station 西調布駅･･･ 15 I4

Nishidai 1～4 (Itabashi-ku) 西台1～4丁目(板橋区)･･ 11 E1

Nishidai Station (subway) 西台駅(地下鉄)･･ 11 F1

Nishi-Eifuku Station 西永福駅･･･ 10 D6

Nishigahara 1～4 (Kita-ku) 西ヶ原1～4丁目(北区)･･ 25 I2

Nishigaoka 1～3 (Kita-ku) 西が丘1～3丁目(北区)･･ 11 G1

Nishi-Gokenchō (Shinjuku-ku) 西五軒町(新宿区)･･ 23 H2

Nishi-Gotanda 1～8 (Shinagawa-ku) 西五反田1～8丁目(品川区)･･ 28 C4

Nishi-Hachiōji Station　西八王子駅 …………… 14　C 4
Nishihara 1〜3 (Shibuya-ku)　西原1〜3丁目(渋谷区)… 11　F 6
Nishi-Hokima 1〜4 (Adachi-ku)　西保木間1〜4丁目(足立区)… 8　B 6
Nishi-Hongan-ji (temple)　西本願寺 …………… 18　D 3
Nishi-Ichinoe 1〜4 (Edogawa-ku)　西一之江1〜4丁目(江戸川区) … 9　G 2
Nishi-Ikebukuro 1〜5 (Toshima-ku)　西池袋1〜5丁目(豊島区) … 24　C 5
Nishi-Ikō 1〜4 (Adachi-ku)　西伊興1〜4丁目(足立区)… 8　B 7
Nishi-Kahei 1〜2 (Adachi-ku)　西加平1〜2丁目(足立区)… 8　C 5
Nishi-Kamata 1〜8 (Ōta-ku)　西蒲田1〜8丁目(大田区) … 13　G 5
Nishi-Kameari 1〜4 (Katsushika-ku)　西亀有1〜4丁目(葛飾区)… 8　D 4
Nishi-Kanda 1〜3 (Chiyoda-ku)　西神田1〜3丁目(千代田区) … 16　A 4
Nishi-Kasai 1〜8 (Edogawa-ku)　西葛西1〜8丁目(江戸川区) … 9　I 3
Nishi-Kasai Station (subway)　西葛西駅(地下鉄) … 9　I 3
Nishikata 1〜2 (Bunkyō-ku)　西片1〜2丁目(文京区) … 26　B 7
Nishiki 1〜2 (Nerima-ku)　錦1〜2丁目(練馬区) … 11　E 2
Nishi-Koiwa 1〜5 (Edogawa-ku)　西小岩1〜5丁目(江戸川区) … 8　E 2
Nishi-Kōjiya 1〜4 (Ōta-ku)　西糀谷1〜4丁目(大田区)… 13　H 6
Nishi-Kokubunji Station　西国分寺駅 …………… 15　G 3
Nishi-Komatsugawamachi (Edogawa-ku)　西小松川町(江戸川区) … 9　G 3
Nishi-Koyama Station　西小山駅 …………… 28　A 6
Nishi-ku (Yokohama City)　西区(横浜市) …………… 61　F 6
Nishi-Kunitachi Station　西国立駅 …………… 15　F 3
Nishimachi Int'l School　西町インターナショナルスクール … 21　G 5
Nishi-Magome 1〜2 (Ōta-ku)　西馬込1〜2丁目(大田区) … 13 (G 4)
Nishi-Magome Station (subway)　西馬込駅(地下鉄) …… 13　G 5
Nishi-Minemachi (Ōta-ku)　西嶺町(大田区) …………… 13　F 5
Nishi-Mizue 1〜5 (Edogawa-ku)　西瑞江1〜5丁目(江戸川区) … 9　G 2
Nishi-Mizumoto 1〜6 (Katsushika-ku)　西水元1〜6丁目(葛飾区) … 8　B 3
Nishi-Nakanobu 1〜3 (Shinagawa-ku)　西中延1〜3丁目(品川区) … 28　B 7
Nishi-Nippori 1〜6 (Arakawa-ku)　西日暮里1〜6丁目(荒川区) … 26　D 3
Nishi-Nippori Station　西日暮里駅 …………… 26　C 4
Nishi-Ochiai 1〜4 (Shinjuku-ku)　西落合1〜4丁目(新宿区) … 11　F 4
Nishiogi-Kita 1〜5 (Suginami-ku)　西荻北1〜5丁目(杉並区) … 10　C 5
Nishi-Ogikubo Station　西荻窪駅 …………… 10　B 5
Nishiogi-Minami 1〜4 (Suginami-ku)　西荻南1〜4丁目(杉並区) … 10　C 5
Nishi-Ogu 1〜8 (Arakawa-ku)　西尾久1〜8丁目(荒川区) … 26　B 1
Nishi-Ōi 1〜6 (Shinagawa-ku)　西大井1〜6丁目(品川区) … 13　H 4
Nishi-Ōi Station　西大井駅 …………… 13　H 4
Nishi-Ōizumi 1〜6 (Nerima-ku)　西大泉1〜6丁目(練馬区) … 10　A 2
Nishi-Ōjima Station (subway)　西大島駅(地下鉄) … 9　H 4
Nishi-Rokugō 1〜4 (Ōta-ku)　西六郷1〜4丁目(大田区) … 13　G 7
Nishi-Shimbashi 1〜3 (Minato-ku)　西新橋1〜3丁目(港区) … 18　A 3
Nishi-Shinagawa 1〜3 (Shinagawa-ku)　西品川1〜3丁目(品川区) … 28　E 6
Nishi-Shinjuku 1〜8 (Shinjuku-ku)　西新宿1〜8丁目(新宿区) … 22　B 5
Nishi-Shinjuku Station (subway)　西新宿駅(地下鉄) … 56　B 2
Nishi-Shinkoiwa 1〜5 (Katsushika-ku)　西新小岩1〜5丁目(葛飾区) … 9　F 3
Nishi-Sugamo 1〜4 (Toshima-ku)　西巣鴨1〜4丁目(豊島区) … 25　G 5
Nishi-Sugamo Station (subway)　西巣鴨駅(地下鉄) … 25　G 5
Nishi-Tachikawa Station　西立川駅 …………… 14　E 3
Nishi-Takashimadaira Station (subway)　西高島平駅(地下鉄) … 100
Nishitoyama Tower Homes　西戸山タワーホームズ … 22　C 2
Nishi-Waseda 1〜3 (Shinjuku-ku)　西早稲田1〜3丁目(新宿区) … 22　E 1

Nishiya Station　西谷駅 …………… 6C　D 5
Nishi-Yokohama Station　西横浜駅 …………… 62　A 3
Nishō-Gakusha Univ.　二松学舎大学 …………… 23　J 5
Nissan Fire & Marine Insurance　日産火災海上 … 55　G 1
Nissan Motor Bldg　日産自動車ビル …………… 39　G 6
Nissei Hibiya Bldg　日生日比谷ビル …………… 38　B 2
Nissei Theater　日生劇場 …………… 38　B 2
Nisshin Flour Milling (H. O.)　日清製粉(本社) … 34　E 1
Nisshō Iwai　日商岩井 …………… 46　D 6
Nittsū Bldg　日通ビル(日本通運) …………… 33　H 2
NKK Bldg　NKKビル …………… 36　D 5
Noa Bldg　ノアビル …………… 49　I 1
Noborito Station　登戸駅 …………… 12　A 3
Nogata 1〜6 (Nakano-ku)　野方1〜6丁目(中野区) … 10　E 4
Nogata Station　野方駅 …………… 10　E 4
Nogawa Park　野川公園 …………… 15　H 3
Noge 1〜3 (Setagaya-ku)　野毛1〜3丁目(世田谷区) … 12　D 4
Nogechō (Yokohama City)　野毛町(横浜市) … 62　D 5
Nogeyama Park　野毛山公園 …………… 62　C 5
Nogi Jinja (shrine)　乃木神社 …………… 48　D 6
Nogi Kaikan　乃木会館 …………… 48　D 6
Nogizaka Station (subway)　乃木坂駅(地下鉄) … 21　G 3
Noguchi Mem. Hall　野口英世記念会館 …………… 23　E 6
Nomura Securities　野村証券 …………… 34　E 4
Nozawa 1〜4 (Setagaya-ku)　野沢1〜4丁目(世田谷区) … 13　F 2
NTT Hibiya Bldg　NTT日比谷ビル …………… 38　B 3
Nukui 1〜5 (Nerima-ku)　貫井1〜5丁目(練馬区) … 10　D 3
Numabe Station　沼部駅 …………… 13　F 5
Numabukuro 1〜4 (Nakano-ku)　沼袋1〜4丁目(中野区) … 10　E 4
Numabukuro Station　沼袋駅 …………… 11　E 4

OAG-Haus (see German Culture Center)　ドイツ文化会館 … 48　B 6
OAG-Hall　オーアーゲーホール …………… 48　B 6
O Art Museum　O美術館 …………… 29　F 5
Ōbirin College　桜美林大学 …………… 15　F 6
Ōbunsha　旺文社 …………… 23　H 3
Ochanomizu Station　御茶ノ水駅 …………… 33　F 3
Ochanomizu University　お茶の水女子大学 …………… 25　G 7
Ochiai Central Park　落合中央公園 …………… 22　B 1
Ochiai Station (subway)　落合駅(地下鉄) … 11　F 4
Odai 1〜2 (Adachi-ku)　小台1〜2丁目(足立区) … 11　I 2
Odaiba Kaihin Park　お台場海浜公園 …………… 13　J 2
Odakyū Ace (arcade)　小田急エース …………… 56　E 4
Odakyū Dept Store　小田急デパート …………… 57　F 4
Odakyū Halc　小田急ハルク …………… 56　E 3
Odakyū-Tama Center Station　小田急多摩センター駅 … 15　F 5
Ōdōri Park　大通公園 …………… 62　D 6
Ōgai Mem. Library　鴎外記念図書館 …………… 26　B 5
Ogawamachi Station (subway)　小川町駅(地下鉄) … 33　F 5
Ogawa Station　小川駅 …………… 15　G 2
Ōgi 1〜3 (Adachi-ku)　扇1〜3丁目(足立区) … 8　D 7
Ōgibashi 1〜3 (Kōtō-ku)　扇橋1〜3丁目(江東区) … 9　H 5

Ogikubo 1～5 (Suginami-ku)　荻窪1～5丁目(杉並区)‥‥ *10* C 5
Ogikubo Station　荻窪駅 ‥‥‥‥‥‥‥‥‥‥‥‥‥‥‥ *10* C 5
Ōgimachi Station　扇町駅 ‥‥‥‥‥‥‥‥‥‥‥‥‥‥‥ *61* I 4
Ōguchi Station　大口駅 ‥‥‥‥‥‥‥‥‥‥‥‥‥‥‥‥ *61* F 4
Ohanajaya 1～3 (Katsushika-ku)　お花茶屋1～3丁目(葛飾区)‥‥ *8* D 4
Ohanajaya Station　お花茶屋駅 ‥‥‥‥‥‥‥‥‥‥‥‥ *8* D 4
Ōhara 1～2 (Setagaya-ku)　大原1～2丁目(世田谷区)‥‥ *10* E 7
Ōharachō (Itabashi-ku)　大原町(板橋区) ‥‥‥‥‥‥‥ *11* (G1)
Ōhashi 1～2 (Meguro-ku)　大橋1～2丁目(目黒区) ‥‥ *20* A 5
Ōi 1～7 (Shinagawa-ku)　大井1～7丁目(品川区) ‥‥ *13* H 4
Ōi Futō (wharf)　大井ふ頭 ‥‥‥‥‥‥‥‥‥‥‥‥‥ *13* J 4
Ōi-Keibajōmae Station　大井競馬場前駅 ‥‥‥‥‥‥‥ *13* I 4
Ōimachi Station　大井町駅 ‥‥‥‥‥‥‥‥‥‥‥‥‥‥ *13* H 4
Ōi Racecourse　大井競馬場 ‥‥‥‥‥‥‥‥‥‥‥‥‥ *13* I 4
Ōizumi-Gakuenchō 1～9 (Nerima-ku)　大泉学園町1～9丁目(練馬区)‥‥ *10* B 1
Ōizumi-Gakuen Station　大泉学園駅 ‥‥‥‥‥‥‥‥‥ *10* B 2
Ōizumimachi 1～6 (Narima-ku)　大泉町1～6丁目(練馬区) ‥‥‥ *10* B 2
Ōji 1～6 (Kita-ku)　王子1～6丁目(北区) ‥‥‥‥‥‥ *11* (H2)
Ōji-Honchō 1～3 (Kita-ku)　王子本町1～3丁目(北区) ‥‥ *11* H 2
Ōjima 1～9 (Kōtō-ku)　大島1～9丁目(江東区) ‥‥‥‥ *9* H 4
Ōjima Station (subway)　大島駅(地下鉄) ‥‥‥‥‥‥ *9* H 4
Ōji Paper　王子製紙 ‥‥‥‥‥‥‥‥‥‥‥‥‥‥‥‥ *39* G 3
Ōji Station　王子駅 ‥‥‥‥‥‥‥‥‥‥‥‥‥‥‥‥‥ *11* H 2
Okachimachi Station　御徒町駅 ‥‥‥‥‥‥‥‥‥‥‥‥ *30* B 6
Okamoto 1～3 (Setagaya-ku)　岡本1～3丁目(世田谷区)‥‥‥ *12* C 2
Ōkawabata River City 21　大川端リバーシティ21‥‥‥‥ *19* F 3
Ōkawa Station　大川駅 ‥‥‥‥‥‥‥‥‥‥‥‥‥‥‥‥ *61* H 4
Okino 1～2 (Adachi-ku)　興野1～2丁目(足立区) ‥‥‥ *8* C 7
Okinomiyachō (Edogawa-ku)　興宮町(江戸川区) ‥‥‥ *9* (F2)
Ōkubo 1～3 (Shinjuku-ku)　大久保1～3丁目(新宿区)‥‥ *22* D 3
Ōkubo Station　大久保駅 ‥‥‥‥‥‥‥‥‥‥‥‥‥‥‥ *22* B 3
Okudo 1～9 (Katsushika-ku)　奥戸1～9丁目(葛飾区) ‥‥ *8* E 3
Ōkunitama Jinja (shrine)　大国魂神社 ‥‥‥‥‥‥‥‥ *82* C 3
Ōkura 1～6 (Setagaya-ku)　大蔵1～6丁目(世田谷区) ‥‥ *12* C 2
Ōkura Museum　大倉集古館 ‥‥‥‥‥‥‥‥‥‥‥‥‥ *48* E 1
Ōkurayama Japanese Apricot Garden　大倉山梅林 ‥‥ *61* F 3
Ōkurayama Station　大倉山駅 ‥‥‥‥‥‥‥‥‥‥‥‥‥ *61* F 3
Okusawa 1～8 (Setagaya-ku)　奥沢1～8丁目(世田谷区) ‥‥ *12* E 4
Okusawa Station　奥沢駅 ‥‥‥‥‥‥‥‥‥‥‥‥‥‥‥ *13* F 4
Oku Station　尾久駅 ‥‥‥‥‥‥‥‥‥‥‥‥‥‥‥‥‥ *26* A 1
Olympic Mem. Youth Center　オリンピック記念青少年総合センター‥‥ *20* B 1
Ōme City　青梅市 ‥‥‥‥‥‥‥‥‥‥‥‥‥‥‥‥‥‥ *14* B 1
Ōme-Kaidō Station　青梅街道駅 ‥‥‥‥‥‥‥‥‥‥‥ *15* G 2
Ōmiya 1～2 (Suginami-ku)　大宮1～2丁目(杉並区) ‥‥ *10* D 6
Ōmiya Hachiman (shrine)　大宮八幡 ‥‥‥‥‥‥‥‥‥ *10* D 6
Ōmori-Higashi 1～5 (Ōta-ku)　大森東1～5丁目(大田区)‥‥ *13* I 6
Ōmori-Honchō 1～2 (Ōta-ku)　大森本町1～2丁目(大田区) ‥‥ *13* H 5
Ōmori-Kaigan Station　大森海岸駅 ‥‥‥‥‥‥‥‥‥‥ *13* H 5
Ōmori-Kita 1～6 (Ōta-ku)　大森北1～6丁目(大田区) ‥‥ *13* H 5
Ōmorimachi Station　大森町駅 ‥‥‥‥‥‥‥‥‥‥‥‥ *13* H 5
Ōmori-Minami 1～5 (Ōta-ku)　大森南1～5丁目(大田区) ‥‥ *13* I 6
Ōmori-Naka 1～3 (Ōta-ku)　大森中1～3丁目(大田区)‥‥ *13* H 6

Ōmori-Nishi 1～7 (Ōta-ku)　大森西1～7丁目(大田区)‥‥ *13* H 5
Ōmori Station　大森駅 ‥‥‥‥‥‥‥‥‥‥‥‥‥‥‥‥ *13* H 4
Omotesandō Station (subway)　表参道駅(地下鉄)‥‥‥‥ *54* E 4
Omurai Station　小村井駅 ‥‥‥‥‥‥‥‥‥‥‥‥‥‥ *9* F 4
Onarimon Station (subway)　御成門駅(地下鉄) ‥‥‥‥ *18* A 4
Ongakunotomo Hall　音楽の友ホール ‥‥‥‥‥‥‥‥‥ *81* G 3
Ontakesan Station　御嶽山駅 ‥‥‥‥‥‥‥‥‥‥‥‥‥ *13* F 4
Ōokayama 1～2 (Meguro-ku)　大岡山1～2丁目(目黒区)‥‥ *13* F 3
Ōokayama Station　大岡山駅 ‥‥‥‥‥‥‥‥‥‥‥‥‥ *13* F 4
Orchard Hall　オーチャードホール ‥‥‥‥‥‥‥‥‥‥ *52* B 4
Ōsaki 1～5 (Shinagawa-ku)　大崎1～5丁目(品川区) ‥‥ *28* D 5
Ōsaki-Hirokōji Station　大崎広小路駅 ‥‥‥‥‥‥‥‥ *28* D 5
Ōsaki New City　大崎ニューシティ ‥‥‥‥‥‥‥‥‥‥ *29* E 5
Ōsaki Post Office　大崎郵便局 ‥‥‥‥‥‥‥‥‥‥‥‥ *28* D 4
Ōsaki Station　大崎駅 ‥‥‥‥‥‥‥‥‥‥‥‥‥‥‥‥ *28* E 5
Oshiage 1～3 (Sumida-ku)　押上1～3丁目(墨田区) ‥‥ *9* F 5
Oshiage Station　押上駅 ‥‥‥‥‥‥‥‥‥‥‥‥‥‥‥ *9* F 5
Ōsugi 1～5 (Edogawa-ku)　大杉1～5丁目(江戸川区) ‥‥ *9* F 2
Ōta-ku　大田区 ‥‥‥‥‥‥‥‥‥‥‥‥‥‥‥‥‥‥‥ *6* E 6
Ōta Memorial Museum of Art　太田記念美術館 ‥‥‥‥ *54* B 2
Ōta Ward Office　大田区役所 ‥‥‥‥‥‥‥‥‥‥‥‥‥ *13* H 5
Ōte Center Bldg　大手センタービル ‥‥‥‥‥‥‥‥‥‥ *36* D 5
Ōtemachi 1～2 (Chiyoda-ku)　大手町1～2丁目(千代田区) ‥‥ *16* C 6
Ōtemachi Bldg　大手町ビル ‥‥‥‥‥‥‥‥‥‥‥‥‥‥ *36* D 4
Ōtemachi First Square　大手町ファーストスクエア ‥‥‥ *36* D 4
Ōtemachi Station (subway)　大手町駅(地下鉄) ‥‥‥‥ *16* C 6
Ōtorii Station　大鳥居駅 ‥‥‥‥‥‥‥‥‥‥‥‥‥‥‥ *13* I 6
Ōtori Jinja (shrine) (Adachi-ku)　大鷲神社(足立区) ‥‥ *8* A 5
Ōtori Jinja (shrine) (Meguro-ku)　大鳥神社(目黒区) ‥‥ *28* B 3
Ōtori Jinja (shrine) (Taitō-ku)　鷲神社(台東区) ‥‥‥ *27* G 6
Otowa 1～2 (Bunkyō-ku)　音羽1～2丁目(文京区) ‥‥‥ *25* G 7
Ōtsuka 1～6 (Bunkyō-ku)　大塚1～6丁目(文京区) ‥‥ *25* G 6
Ōtsuka Station　大塚駅 ‥‥‥‥‥‥‥‥‥‥‥‥‥‥‥‥ *25* G 4
Ōtsuma Women's University　大妻女子大学 ‥‥‥‥‥‥ *23* I 5
Ōyaguchi 1～2 (Itabashi-ku)　大谷口1～2丁目(板橋区)‥‥ *24* A 2
Ōyaguchi-Kamichō (Itabashi-ku)　大谷口上町(板橋区) ‥‥ *24* B 1
Ōyaguchi-Kitachō (Itabashi-ku)　大谷口北町(板橋区) ‥‥ *11* F 2
Ōyamachō (Itabashi-ku)　大山町(板橋区) ‥‥‥‥‥‥‥ *11* G 2
Ōyamachō (Shibuya-ku)　大山町(渋谷区) ‥‥‥‥‥‥‥ *11* F 7
Oyamadai 1～3 (Setagaya-ku)　尾山台1～3丁目(世田谷区) ‥‥ *12* E 4
Oyamadai Station　尾山台駅 ‥‥‥‥‥‥‥‥‥‥‥‥‥ *12* E 4
Ōyama-Higashichō (Itabashi-ku)　大山東町(板橋区) ‥‥ *24* C 1
Ōyama-Kanaichō (Itabashi-ku)　大山金井町(板橋区) ‥‥ *24* C 1
Ōyama-Nishichō (Itabashi-ku)　大山西町(板橋区) ‥‥‥ *24* B 1
Ōyama Station　大山駅 ‥‥‥‥‥‥‥‥‥‥‥‥‥‥‥‥ *11* G 2
Ōyata 1～5 (Adachi-ku)　大谷田1～5丁目(足立区) ‥‥‥ *8* C 4
Ozaku Station　小作駅 ‥‥‥‥‥‥‥‥‥‥‥‥‥‥‥‥ *14* C 1

Pacifico Yokohama　横浜国際平和会議場 ‥‥‥‥‥‥‥‥ *63* F 2
Paper Museum　紙の博物館 ‥‥‥‥‥‥‥‥‥‥‥‥‥‥ *87* G 2
Parco Theater　パルコ劇場 ‥‥‥‥‥‥‥‥‥‥‥‥‥‥ *52* D 3
Parliamentary Museum　衆議院憲政記念館 ‥‥‥‥‥‥‥ *47* F 3

Pensee Hall　パンセホール ………………………… 32　A 3
Pentax Gallery (Camera Musm)　ペンタックスギャラリーカメラ博物館 …… 84　C 4
Playguide Bldg　プレイガイドビル …………………… 39　G 2
Prince Arisugawa Mem. Park　有栖川宮記念公園 ……… 21　F 6
Prince Chichibu Mem. Rugby Stadium　秩父宮記念ラグビー場 … 21　F 2
Printemps Ginza Dept Store　プランタン銀座 ………… 39　F 2

Reconstruction Memorial Hall　東京都復興記念館 …… 17　H 3
Reiyūkai Temple　霊友会釈迦殿 ……………………… 49　H 1
RF Radio Nippon　アール・エフ・ラジオ日本 ……… 62　C 5
Riccar Art Museum　リッカー美術館 ………………… 38　D 3
Rikkyō Univ.　立教大学 ……………………………… 24　C 4
Rikugi-en (garden)　六義園 …………………………… 25　J 4
Rinkaichō 1～6 (Edogawa-ku)　臨海町1～6丁目(江戸川区) … 9　J 3
Rinshino-mori Park　林試の森公園 …………………… 28　A 4
Risshō-Kōseikai　立正佼成会 ………………………… 10　E 6
Risshō Univ.　立正大学 ……………………………… 28　D 5
Riverpoint Tower　リバーポイントタワー …………… 19　F 2
Roi Roppongi　ロア六本木 …………………………… 49　H 4
Rokakōen Station　芦花公園駅 ……………………… 10　C 7
Roka Kōshun-en (Roka Kōen) (garden)　芦花恒春園 … 12　C 1
Rokubanchō (Chiyoda-ku)　六番町(千代田区) ……… 23　H 6
Rokuchō 1～4 (Adachi-ku)　六町1～4丁目(足立区) … 8　C 5
Rokugatsu 1～3 (Adachi-ku)　六月1～3丁目(足立区) … 8　B 6
Rokugō-dote Station　六郷土手駅 …………………… 13　G 7
Roppongi 1～7 (Minato-ku)　六本木1～7丁目(港区) … 21　G 3
Roppongi Forum　六本木フォーラム ………………… 49　H 4
Roppongi Station (subway)　六本木駅(地下鉄) ……… 49　G 5
Rox Bldg　ロックスビル ……………………………… 31　F 4
Ryōgoku 1～4 (Sumida-ku)　両国1～4丁目(墨田区) … 17　G 4
Ryōgoku-bashi (bridge)　両国橋 …………………… 17　G 4
Ryōgoku Post Office　両国郵便局 …………………… 17　F 4
Ryōgoku Public Hall　両国公会堂 …………………… 17　G 4
Ryōgoku Station　両国駅 …………………………… 17　G 4
Ryokuen-toshi Station　緑園都市駅 ………………… 60　C 6
Ryūsen 1～3 (Taitō-ku)　竜泉1～3丁目(台東区) …… 27　G 5
Ryūshi Mem. Gallery　竜子記念館 ………………… 13　H 5
Ryūtsū Center Station　流通センター駅 …………… 13　I 5

Sabō Kaikan (hall)　砂防会館 ……………………… 46　D 3
Saga 1～2 (Kōtō-ku)　佐賀1～2丁目(江東区) ……… 19　G 1
Sagamihara Station　相模原駅 ……………………… 14　E 6
Sagami-Ōno Station　相模大野駅 ………………… 60　A 3
Sagami Women's Univ.　相模女子大学 …………… 74　C 5
Saginomiya 1～6 (Nakano-ku)　鷺宮1～6丁目(中野区) … 10　D 4
Saginomiya Station　鷺ノ宮駅 ……………………… 10　D 4
Saginuma Station　鷺沼駅 ………………………… 60　D 1
Saikumachi (Shinjuku-ku)　細工町(新宿区) ……… 23　H 4
Santa Maria Sch.　サンタマリアスクール ………… 10　C 3
St. Ignatius Church　聖イグナチオ教会 …………… 23　H 6
St. Joseph College　セントジョセフカレッジ ……… 63　H 7
St. Luke's Garden　聖路加ガーデン ……………… 18　E 3

St. Luke's Hosp. (Sei Roka Byōin)　聖路加病院 ……… 18　E 3
St. Luke's Nursing Coll.　聖路加看護大学 ………… 73　F 7
St. Marianna Med. Coll.　聖マリアンナ医科大学 …… 74　D 4
St. Mary's Cathedral　東京カテドラル聖マリア大聖堂 ‥ 23　G 1
St. Mary's Int'l Sch.　セントメリーズ インターナショナルスクール ‥ 12　D 3
St. Maur Int'l Sch.　サンモール インターナショナルスクール … 63　H 7
Saiwaichō (Itabashi-ku)　幸町(板橋区) …………… 24　B 2
Saiwai-ku (Kawasaki City)　幸区(川崎市) ………… 61　H 2
Sakaechō (Itabashi-ku)　栄町(板橋区) …………… 11　G 2
Sakaechō (Kita-ku)　栄町(北区) …………………… 25　J 1
Sakaechō (Nerima-ku)　栄町(練馬区) …………… 11　(F 3)
Sakamachi (Shinjuku-ku)　坂町(新宿区) ………… 23　G 5
Sakashita 1～3 (Itabashi-ku)　坂下1～3丁目(板橋区) … 11　F 1
Sakura 1～3 (Setagaya-ku)　桜1～3丁目(世田谷区) … 12　D 2
Sakura Bank (H. O.)　さくら銀行 ………………… 32　A 5
Sakura Bank (M. O.)　さくら銀行東京営業部 …… 38　C 2
Sakura-bashi (bridge)　桜足 ……………………… 27　I 7
Sakuradai 1～6 (Nerima-ku)　桜台1～6丁目(練馬区) … 10　E 3
Sakuradai Station　桜台駅 ………………………… 10　E 3
Sakurada-mon (gate)　桜田門 …………………… 47　I 3
Sakuradamon Station (subway)　桜田門駅(地下鉄) … 47　H 4
Sakuragaoka 1～5 (Setagaya-ku)　桜丘1～5丁目(世田谷区) … 12　D 2
Sakuragaokachō (Shibuya-ku)　桜丘町(渋谷区) … 20　C 5
Sakuragaoka Station　桜ヶ丘駅 ………………… 60　A 5
Sakuragawa 1～3 (Itabashi-ku)　桜川1～3丁目(板橋区) … 11　F 2
Sakuragichō Station　桜木町駅 ………………… 62　E 4
Sakurajōsui 1～5 (Setagaya-ku)　桜上水1～5丁目(世田谷区) … 12　D 1
Sakurajōsui Station　桜上水駅 ………………… 10　D 7
Sakura-Shinmachi 1～2 (Setagaya-ku)　桜新町1～2丁目(世田谷区) … 12　D 2
Sakura-Shinmachi Station　桜新町駅 ………… 12　D 2
Samezu Station　鮫州駅 ………………………… 13　I 4
Samonchō (Shinjuku-ku)　左門町(新宿区) …… 23　F 6
San'ai　三愛 ……………………………………… 39　E 3
Sanbanchō (Chiyoda-ku)　三番町(千代田区) … 23　I 5
Saneatsu Park　実篤公園 ……………………… 82　E 4
San'eichō (Shinjuku-ku)　三栄町(新宿区) …… 23　G 5
Sangenjaya 1～2 (Setagaya-ku)　三軒茶屋1～2丁目(世田谷区) … 13　F 2
Sangenjaya Station　三軒茶屋駅 ……………… 13　F 2
Sangūbashi Station　参宮橋駅 ………………… 20　B 1
Sankei-en (garden)　三渓園 …………………… 61　G 7
Sankei Kaikan (hall)　サンケイ会館 …………… 36　C 3
Sankei Newspapers　産業経済(サンケイ)新聞社 … 36　C 3
Sannō 1～4 (Ōta-ku)　山王1～4丁目(大田区) … 13　H 4
Sannō Grand Bldg　山王グランドビル ………… 46　C 4
Sano 1～2 (Adachi-ku)　佐野1～2丁目(足立区) … 8　B 4
Sanrio Puroland　サンリオピューロランド …… 82　C 4
Sanseidō Bookstore　三省堂書店 ……………… 32　D 4
Santonodai Prehistoric Site　三殿台遺跡 …… 61　F 7
San'yō Akasaka Bldg　サンヨー赤坂ビル …… 46　C 5
Sapporo Breweries　サッポロビール ………… 38　E 5
Saranuma 1～3 (Adachi-ku)　皿沼1～3丁目(足立区) … 8　B 7
Sarue 1～2 (Kōtō-ku)　猿江1～2丁目(江東区) … 9　H 5

Sarugakuchō 1~2 (Chiyoda-ku)　猿楽町1~2丁目(千代田区)‥ *16* B 3
Sarugakuchō (Shibuya-ku)　猿楽町(渋谷区)‥‥‥‥‥‥ *20* C 6
Sasazuka 1~3 (Shibuya-ku)　笹塚1~3丁目(渋谷区)‥ *11* E 6
Sasazuka Station　笹塚駅‥‥‥‥‥‥‥‥‥‥‥‥‥‥ *11* E 6
Satsukidai Station　五月台駅‥‥‥‥‥‥‥‥‥‥‥‥ *15* H 6
Sayama-ko (lake)　狭山湖‥‥‥‥‥‥‥‥‥‥‥‥‥‥ *15* F 1
Scala-za (cinema) (Yūrakuchō)　スカラ座(映)(有楽町)‥ *38* C 2
Science Bldg　サイエンスビル‥‥‥‥‥‥‥‥‥‥‥ *46* D 6
Science Museum (Kagaku Gijutsukan)　科学技術館‥‥‥‥ *32* A 6
Science & Technology Foundation of Japan　国際科学技術財団‥ *92* E 6
Science University of Tokyo　東京理科大学‥‥‥‥‥‥ *23* I 3
Seibijō Station　整備場駅‥‥‥‥‥‥‥‥‥‥‥‥‥ *13* I 16
Seibu Dept Store (Ikebukuro)　西武デパート(池袋店)‥ *58* D 5
Seibu Dept Store (Shibuya)　西武デパート(渋谷店)‥‥ *52* E 4
Seibu Dept Store (Yūrakuchō)　西武デパート(有楽町店)‥‥ *38* E 2
Seibuen (amusement park)　西武園‥‥‥‥‥‥‥‥‥ *15* F 1
Seibuen Station　西武園駅‥‥‥‥‥‥‥‥‥‥‥‥‥ *15* G 1
Seibu-Kyūjōmae Station　西武球場前駅‥‥‥‥‥‥‥‥ *15* F 1
Seibu Lions Stadium　西武ライオンズ球場‥‥‥‥‥‥ *82* C 2
Seibu-Shinjuku Station　西武新宿駅‥‥‥‥‥‥‥‥‥ *57* F 2
Seibu-Tachikawa Station　西武立川駅‥‥‥‥‥‥‥‥ *14* E 2
Seibu-Yagisawa Station　西武柳沢駅‥‥‥‥‥‥‥‥‥ *15* I 2
Seibu-Yūenchi Station　西武遊園地駅‥‥‥‥‥‥‥‥ *15* F 1
Seijō 1~9 (Setagaya-ku)　成城1~9丁目(世田谷区)‥ *12* B 2
Seijō-Gakuenmae Station　成城学園前駅‥‥‥‥‥‥‥ *12* C 2
Seijō University　成城大学‥‥‥‥‥‥‥‥‥‥‥‥‥ *12* B 2
Seikadō Library　静嘉堂文庫‥‥‥‥‥‥‥‥‥‥‥‥ *12* C 3
Seikei University　成蹊大学‥‥‥‥‥‥‥‥‥‥‥‥ *10* A 4
Seikōsha　精工舎‥‥‥‥‥‥‥‥‥‥‥‥‥‥‥‥‥ *9* G 5
Seiroka Garden　聖路加ガーデン‥‥‥‥‥‥‥‥‥‥ *18* E 3
Seiseki-Sakuragaoka Station　聖蹟桜ヶ丘駅‥‥‥‥‥‥ *15* F 4
Seisen Int'l Sch.　清泉インターナショナルスクール‥‥ *12* D 3
Seisen Women's Coll.　清泉女子大学‥‥‥‥‥‥‥‥ *28* E 4
Seishinchō 1~2 (Edogawa-ku)　清新町1~2丁目(江戸川区)‥ *9* I 3
Seishō-ji (temple)　青松寺‥‥‥‥‥‥‥‥‥‥‥‥‥ *18* A 4
Sekai Bōeki Center Bldg (see World Trade Center Bldg)　世界貿易センタービル‥ *18* B 5
Sekiguchi 1~3 (Bunkyō-ku)　関口1~3丁目(文京区)‥ *23* G 1
Sekihara 1~3 (Adachi-ku)　関原1~3丁目(足立区)‥‥ *8* C 6
Sekimachi-Higashi 1~2 (Nerima-ku)　関町東1~2丁目(練馬区)‥ *10* (B 4)
Sekimachi-Kita 1~5 (Nerima-ku)　関町北1~5丁目(練馬区)‥ *10* A 4
Sekimachi-Minami 1~4 (Nerima-ku)　関町南1~4丁目(練馬区)‥ *10* A 4
Senda (Kōtō-ku)　千田(江東区)‥‥‥‥‥‥‥‥‥‥ *9* (H 5)
Sendagaya 1~6 (Shibuya-ku)　千駄ケ谷1~6丁目(渋谷区)‥ *20* D 1
Sendagaya Station　千駄ケ谷駅‥‥‥‥‥‥‥‥‥‥‥ *22* D 7
Sendagi 1~5 (Bunkyō-ku)　千駄木1~5丁目(文京区)‥ *26* B 5
Sendagi Station (subway)　千駄木駅(地下鉄)‥‥‥‥‥ *26* C 5
Sengaku-ji (temple)　泉岳寺‥‥‥‥‥‥‥‥‥‥‥‥ *29* F 2
Sengakuji Station (subway)　泉岳寺駅(地下鉄)‥‥‥‥ *29* G 2
Sengawa Station　仙川駅‥‥‥‥‥‥‥‥‥‥‥‥‥‥ *15* J 4
Sengoku 1~4 (Bunkyō-ku)　千石1~4丁目(文京区)‥ *25* I 5
Sengoku 1~3 (Kōtō-ku)　千石1~3丁目(江東区)‥‥‥ *9* H 5
Sengoku Station (subway)　千石駅(地下鉄)‥‥‥‥‥ *25* J 5

Senju (Adachi-ku)　千住(足立区)‥‥‥‥‥‥‥‥‥ *27* I 1
Senju-Hashidochō (Adachi-ku)　千住橋戸町(足立区)‥‥ *27* H 2
Senju-Kawarachō (Adachi-ku)　千住河原町(足立区)‥‥ *27* H 2
Senju-Midorichō 1~3 (Adachi-ku)　千住緑町1~3丁目(足立区)‥ *27* G 1
Senju-Miyamotochō (Adachi-ku)　千住宮元町(足立区)‥ *27* H 1
Senju-Nakachō (Adachi-ku)　千住仲町(足立区)‥‥‥ *27* H 1
Senju-Nakaichō (Adachi-ku)　千住中居町(足立区)‥‥ *27* H 1
Senju-Ōhashi Station　千住大橋駅‥‥‥‥‥‥‥‥‥‥ *27* H 2
Senju-Sakuragi 1~2 (Adachi-ku)　千住桜木1~2丁目(足立区)‥ *27* G 1
Senju-Sekiyachō (Adachi-ku)　千住関屋町(足立区)‥‥ *27* I 2
Senkawachō 1~2 (Toshima-ku)　千川町1~2丁目(豊島区)‥ *24* B 2
Senkawa Station (subway)　千川駅(地下鉄)‥‥‥‥‥ *24* A 3
Senshū Bunko　千秋文庫‥‥‥‥‥‥‥‥‥‥‥‥‥‥ *85* F 4
Senshū University (Ikuta)　専修大学(生田)‥‥‥‥‥ *74* D 4
Senshū University (Kanda)　専修大学(神田)‥‥‥‥‥ *32* B 4
Sensō-ji (temple)　浅草寺‥‥‥‥‥‥‥‥‥‥‥‥‥ *31* H 3
Senzoku 1~2 (Meguro-ku)　洗足1~2丁目(目黒区)‥ *13* F 3
Senzoku 1~4 (Taitō-ku)　千束1~4丁目(台東区)‥‥ *27* G 5
Senzoku Gakuen Coll.　洗足学園大学‥‥‥‥‥‥‥‥ *74* E 4
Senzoku-ike Station　洗足池駅‥‥‥‥‥‥‥‥‥‥‥ *13* G 4
Senzoku Park　洗足公園‥‥‥‥‥‥‥‥‥‥‥‥‥‥ *13* F 4
Senzoku Station　洗足駅‥‥‥‥‥‥‥‥‥‥‥‥‥‥ *13* G 3
Seta 1~5 (Setagaya-ku)　瀬田1~5丁目(世田谷区)‥ *12* D 3
Setagaya 1~4 (Setagaya-ku)　世田谷1~4丁目(世田谷区)‥ *12* E 2
Setagaya Art Musm　世田谷区立世田谷美術館‥‥‥‥‥ *12* D 2
Setagaya-Daita Station　世田谷代田駅‥‥‥‥‥‥‥‥ *13* E 1
Setagaya-ku　世田谷区‥‥‥‥‥‥‥‥‥‥‥‥‥‥ *6* C 5
Setagaya Station　世田谷駅‥‥‥‥‥‥‥‥‥‥‥‥‥ *12* E 2
Setagaya Ward Office　世田谷区役所‥‥‥‥‥‥‥‥ *12* E 1
Seya-ku (Yokohama City)　瀬谷区(横浜市)‥‥‥‥‥ *60* B 5
Sezon Museum of Art　セゾン美術館‥‥‥‥‥‥‥‥ *58* D 6
Shakujiidai 1~8 (Nerima-ku)　石神井台1~8丁目(練馬区)‥ *10* B 3
Shakujii-Kōen Station　石神井公園駅‥‥‥‥‥‥‥‥ *10* C 3
Shakujiimachi 1~8 (Nerima-ku)　石神井町1~8丁目(練馬区)‥ *10* C 3
Shakujii Park　石神井公園‥‥‥‥‥‥‥‥‥‥‥‥‥ *10* C 3
Shiba 1~5 (Minato-ku)　芝1~5丁目(港区)‥‥‥‥ *21* J 6
Shiba Daijingū (shrine)　芝大神宮‥‥‥‥‥‥‥‥‥ *18* A 5
Shiba-Daimon 1~2 (Minato-ku)　芝大門1~2丁目(港区)‥ *18* B 5
Shiba-Kōen 1~4 (Minato-ku)　芝公園1~4丁目(港区)‥ *18* A 4
Shiba-Kōen Station (subway)　芝公園駅(地下鉄)‥‥‥ *18* A 5
Shibamata 1~7 (Katsushika-ku)　柴又1~7丁目(葛飾区)‥ *8* D 2
Shibamata Station　柴又駅‥‥‥‥‥‥‥‥‥‥‥‥‥ *8* D 2
Shibamata Taishakuten (temple)　柴又帝釈天‥‥‥‥‥ *8* D 2
Shiba Park　芝公園‥‥‥‥‥‥‥‥‥‥‥‥‥‥‥‥ *18* A 5
Shiba Post Office　芝郵便局‥‥‥‥‥‥‥‥‥‥‥‥ *68* D 5
Shibasaki Station　柴崎駅‥‥‥‥‥‥‥‥‥‥‥‥‥ *15* I 4
Shiba Seinenkan Hall　芝青年館ホール‥‥‥‥‥‥‥ *80* C 6
Shibaura 1~4 (Minato-ku)　芝浦1~4丁目(港区)‥‥ *18* A 7
Shibaura-futō Station　芝浦ふとう駅‥‥‥‥‥‥‥‥ *29* I 1
Shibaura Inst. of Technology　芝浦工業大学‥‥‥‥‥ *29* H 1
Shibuto Cinetower　渋東シネタワー‥‥‥‥‥‥‥‥‥ *52* D 5
Shibuya 1~4 (Shibuya-ku)　渋谷1~4丁目(渋谷区)‥ *20* C 4

Shibuya-ku　渋谷区 ································ 6　E 4
Shibuya Parco Store　渋谷パルコ ········ 52　D 3
Shibuya Post Office　渋谷郵便局 ········ 54　B 6
Shibuya Public Hall (kōkaidō)　渋谷公会堂 ········ 52　D 1
Shibuya Station　渋谷駅 ···················· 53　F 5
Shibuya Takarazuka (cinema)　渋谷宝塚 (映) ······ 52　E 4
Shibuya Ward Office　渋谷区役所 ········ 52　D 1
Shiinamachi Station　椎名町駅 ············ 24　B 5
Shikahama 1～8 (Adachi-ku)　鹿浜1～8丁目(足立区) ·· 11　I 1
Shimane 1～4 (Adachi-ku)　島根1～4丁目(足立区) ··· 8　C 6
Shimbashi 1～6 (Minato-ku)　新橋1～6丁目(港区) ··· 18　B 3
Shimbashi Enbujō (theater)　新橋演舞場 ···· 39　G 6
Shimbashi Post Office　新橋郵便局 ······ 38　D 6
Shimbashi Station　新橋駅 ·················· 38　B 6
Shimizu 1～3 (Suginami-ku)　清水1～3丁目(杉並区) ·· 10　C 4
Shimizuchō (Itabashi-ku)　清水町(板橋区) ······ 11　G 2
Shimo 1～5 (Kita-ku)　志茂1～5丁目(北区) ···· 11　H 1
Shimo-Akatsuka Station　下赤塚駅 ········ 10　D 1
Shimo-Igusa 1～5 (Suginami-ku)　下井草1～5丁目(杉並区) ·· 10　C 4
Shimo-Igusa Station　下井草駅 ············ 10　D 4
Shimo-Itabashi Station　下板橋駅 ········ 24　E 2
Shimo-Kamatachō (Edogawa-ku)　下鎌田町(江戸川区) ··· 9 (G 1)
Shimo-Kitazawa Station　下北沢駅 ········ 13　E 1
Shimo-Maruko 1～4 (Ōta-ku)　下丸子1～4丁目(大田区) ·· 13　F 6
Shimo-Maruko Station　下丸子駅 ·········· 13　F 5
Shimo-Meguro 1～6 (Meguro-ku)　下目黒1～6丁目(目黒区) ·· 28　A 3
Shimomiyabichō (Shinjuku-ku)　下宮比町(新宿区) ···· 23　I 3
Shimo-Ochiai 1～4 (Shinjuku-ku)　下落合1～4丁目(新宿区) ·· 24　C 6
Shimo-Ochiai Station　下落合駅 ············ 24　B 7
Shimo-Shakujii 1～6 (Nerima-ku)　下石神井1～6丁目(練馬区) ·· 10　C 3
Shimo-Shinmei Station　下神明駅 ·········· 13　H 3
Shimo-Shinozakimachi (Edogawa-ku)　下篠崎町(江戸川区) ··· 9 (G 1)
Shimo-Takaido 1～5 (Suginami-ku)　下高井戸1～5丁目(杉並区) ·· 10　D 6
Shimo-Takaido Station　下高井戸駅 ······ 10　D 7
Shimouma 1～6 (Setagaya-ku)　下馬1～6丁目(世田谷区) ·· 13　F 2
Shimura 1～3 (Itabashi-ku)　志村1～3丁目(板橋区) ·· 11　F 1
Shimura-sakaue Station (subway)　志村坂上駅(地下鉄) ·· 11　G 1
Shimura-sanchōme Station (subway)　志村三丁目駅(地下鉄) ·· 11　F 1
Shinagawa Futō (wharf)　品川ふ頭 ········ 29　J 3
Shinagawa Jinja (shrine)　品川神社 ········ 29　G 5
Shinagawa-ku　品川区 ······················ 6　E 5
Shinagawa Station　品川駅 ·················· 29　G 3
Shinagawa Ward Office　品川区役所 ······ 29　F 7
Shin-Akitsu Station　新秋津駅 ············ 15　G 1
Shinanomachi (Shinjuku-ku)　信濃町(新宿区) ···· 23　F 6
Shinanomachi Station　信濃町駅 ·········· 23　F 7
Shin-Banba Station　新馬場駅 ·············· 29　G 6
Shin-Daita Station　新代田駅 ·············· 12　E 1
Shinden 1～3 (Adachi-ku)　新田1～3丁目(足立区) ·· 11　I 1
Shin Edogawa Park　新江戸川公園 ········ 23　F 1
Shinhibiya Bldg　新日比谷ビル ············ 38　A 4
Shin-Itabashi Station (subway)　新板橋駅(地下鉄) ······ 25　F 1

Shinjuku 1～7 (Shinjuku-ku)　新宿1～7丁目(新宿区) ··· 22　D 5
Shinjuku Bunka Cinema　新宿文化シネマ (映) ······ 57　I 4
Shinjuku Center Bldg　新宿センタービル ······ 56　C 4
Shinjuku Central Park　新宿中央公園 ······ 56　A 5
Shinjuku Culture Center　新宿文化センター ······ 22　D 4
Shinjuku Dai-Ichi Seimei Bldg　新宿第一生命ビル ······ 56　A 4
Shirjuku Grand Odeon-za (cinema)　新宿グランドオデヲン座(映) ··· 57　F 1
Shirjuku-gyoenmae Station (subway)　新宿御苑前駅(地下鉄) ·· 22　E 6
Shinjuku Historical Musm　新宿歴史博物館 ······ 23　G 5
Shinjuku i-Land　新宿アイランド ·········· 56　C 3
Shinjuku Imperial Gardens (see Shinjuku Gyoen)　新宿御苑 ·· 22　D 6
Shinjuku-Kita Post Office　新宿北郵便局 ······ 69　F 1
Shinjuku Kokusai Bldg　新宿国際ビル ······ 56　A 3
Shinjuku Koma Theater　新宿コマ劇場 ······ 57　G 2
Shinjuku-ku　新宿区 ························ 6　E 3
Shinjuku L Tower　新宿Lタワー ············ 56　D 4
Shinjuku Milano-za (cinema)　新宿ミラノ座(映) ····· 57　F 1
Shinjuku Mitsui Bldg　新宿三井ビル ········ 56　C 4
Shinjuku Monolith　新宿モノリス ·········· 56　C 6
Shinjuku Musashino-kan (cinema)　新宿武蔵野館(映) ·· 57　G 4
Shinjuku Nomura Bldg　新宿野村ビル ······ 56　C 3
Shinjuku NS Bldg　新宿NSビル ············ 56　B 6
Shinjuku Park Tower　新宿パークタワー ······ 22　A 6
Shinjuku Piccadilly (cinema)　新宿ピカデリー(映) ··· 57　H 3
Shinjuku Plaza (cinema)　新宿プラザ(映) ··· 57　G 2
Shinjuku Post Office　新宿郵便局 ·········· 56　D 5
Shinjuku-sanchōme Station (subway)　新宿三丁目駅(地下鉄) ·· 57　I 4
Shinjuku Scala-za (cinema)　新宿スカラ座(映) ··· 57　I 4
Shinjuku Shōchiku (cinema)　新宿松竹(映) ·· 57　H 3
Shinjuku Sports Center　新宿スポーツセンター ······ 22　D 2
Shinjuku Station　新宿駅 ···················· 57　F 4
Shinjuku Subnade　新宿サブナード ·········· 57　G 3
Shinjuku Sumitomo Bldg　新宿住友ビル ······ 56　B 4
Shinjuku Tōei (cinema)　新宿東映(映) ······ 57　I 5
Shinjuku Tōkyū (cinema)　新宿東急(映) ····· 57　F 1
Shinjuku Ward Office　新宿区役所 ·········· 57　G 2
Shin-Kamata 1～3 (Ōta-ku)　新蒲田1～3丁目(大田区) ·· 13　G 6
Shinkawa 1～2 (Chūō-ku)　新川1～2丁目(中央区) ·· 19　F 1
Shin-Kawasaki Station　新川崎駅 ·········· 61　G 2
Shin-Kiba 1～4 (Kōtō-ku)　新木場1～4丁目(江東区) ··· 7　H 5
Shin-Kiba Station (subway)　新木場駅(地下鉄) ··· 9　J 4
Shin-Kodaira Station　新小平駅 ············ 15　G 2
Shin-Kōenji Station (subway)　新高円寺駅(地下鉄) ·· 10　E 5
Shin-Koganei Station　新小金井駅 ·········· 15　H 3
Shin-Koiwa 1～4 (Katsushika-ku)　新小岩1～4丁目(葛飾区) ·· 9　F 3
Shin-Koiwa Station　新小岩駅 ·············· 9　F 3
Shin-Koyasu Station　新子安駅 ············ 61　G 4
Shinmachi 1～3 (Setagaya-ku)　新町1～3丁目(世田谷区) ·· 12　E 2
Shin-Maruko Station　新丸子駅 ············ 12　E 5
Shinmei 1～3 (Adachi-ku)　神明1～3丁目(足立区) ·· 8　B 4
Shinmei-Minami 1～2 (Adachi-ku)　神明南1～2丁目(足立区) ·· 8　B 4
Shin-Mikawashima Station　新三河島駅 ······ 26　D 3

123

Shin-Nakano Station（subway）　新中野駅（地下鉄）······ *11* E 5
Shin-Nihombashi Station　新日本橋駅··············· *34* B 4
Shin Nisseki Bldg　新日石ビル··························· *37* I 5
Shinobazuno-ike（pond）　不忍池······················ *16* D 1
Shin-Ochanomizu Station（subway）　新御茶ノ水駅（地下鉄）···· *33* F 4
Shin-Ogawamachi（Shinjuku-ku）　新小川町（新宿区）····· *23* I 2
Shin-Ōhashi 1～3（Kōtō-ku）　新大橋1～3丁目（江東区）······ *17* G 5
Shin-Ōkubo Station　新大久保駅······················ *22* C 3
Shinonome 1～2（Kōtō-ku）　東雲1～2丁目（江東区）····· *9* J 5
Shin-Ōtsuka Station（subway）　新大塚駅（地下鉄）····· *25* G 5
Shinozakimachi 1～7（Edogawa-ku）　篠崎町1～7丁目（江戸川区）···· *9* G 1
Shinozaki Station（subway）　篠崎駅（地下鉄）······· *9* G 1
Shin-Sakuradai Station　新桜台駅····················· *11* F 3
Shinsenchō（Shibuya-ku）　神泉町（渋谷区）············ *20* B 5
Shinsen Station　神泉駅······························· *20* B 5
Shin Seibijō Station　新整備場駅······················ *13* I 7
Shin-Shibaura Station　新芝浦駅······················ *61* H 4
Shin-Suna 1～3（Kōtō-ku）　新砂1～3丁目（江東区）····· *9* I 4
Shin-Takashimadaira Station（subway）　新高島平駅（地下鉄）·· *100*
Shintomi 1～2（Chūō-ku）　新富1～2丁目（中央区）··· *18* D 2
Shintomichō Station（subway）　新富町駅（地下鉄）··· *18* D 2
Shin-Urayasu Station　新浦安駅······················· *7* J 4
Shin-Yokohama Station　新横浜駅····················· *61* F 3
Shin-Yurigaoka Station　新百合ケ丘駅················· *15* H 6
Shiofune Kannon（temple）　塩船観音··················· *82* A 1
Shiohama 1～2（Kōtō-ku）　塩浜1～2丁目（江東区）····· *19* J 4
Shiomi 1～2（Kōtō-ku）　潮見1～2丁目（江東区）····· *9* I 5
Shiomi Station　潮見駅······························· *9* I 5
Shirakawa 1～4（Kōtō-ku）　白河1～4丁目（江東区）··· *9* G 5
Shirasagi 1～3（Nakano-ku）　白鷺1～3丁目（中野区）··· *10* D 4
Shiratori 1～4（Katsushika-ku）　白鳥1～4丁目（葛飾区）··· *8* D 4
Shirayuri Women's College　白百合女子大学··········· *74* E 3
Shiroganechō（Shinjuku-ku）　白銀町（新宿区）······· *23* H 3
Shirokane 1～6（Minato-ku）　白金1～6丁目（港区）··· *21* G 7
Shirokanedai 1～5（Minato-ku）　白金台1～5丁目（港区）··· *28* E 2
Shiseidō The Ginza　資生堂ザ・ギンザ·············· *38* D 5
Shishibone 1～5（Edogawa-ku）　鹿骨1～5丁目（江戸川区）··· *9* F 2
Shishibonechō（Edogawa-ku）　鹿骨町（江戸川区）··· *9*(G 1)
Shitamachi Museum　下町風俗資料館·················· *30* A 4
Shitaya 1～3（Taitō-ku）　下谷1～3丁目（台東区）··· *24* F 6
Shitaya Jinja（shrine）　下谷神社····················· *17* F 1
Shitte Station　尻手駅······························· *61* G 2
Shōan 1～3（Suginami-ku）　松庵1～3丁目（杉並区）··· *10* B 5
Shōchiku kaikan（hall）　松竹会館····················· *39* H 5
Shōgakukan　小学館································· *32* C 5
Shōin-jinjamae Station　松陰神社前··················· *12* E 2
Shōtō 1～2（Shibuya-ku）　松涛1～2丁目（渋谷区）··· *20* B 4
Shōtō Art Museum　松涛美術館······················· *52* A 5
Shōwa Academia Musicae　昭和音楽大学·············· *74* B 6
Shōwa Coll. of Pharm.　昭和薬科大学················· *12* D 2
Shōwajima 1～2（Ōta-ku）　昭和島1～2丁目（大田区）··· *13* I 6
Shōwajima Station　昭和島駅························· *13* I 6

Shōwamachi 1～3（Kita-ku）　昭和町1～3丁目（北区）···· *11*(I 2)
Shōwa Mem. Park　昭和記念公園····················· *15* E 3
Shōwa Station　昭和駅······························· *61* I 3
Shōwa University　昭和大学························· *13* G 3
Shōwa Women's University　昭和女子大学············· *13* F 2
Shukugawara Station　宿河原駅······················ *12* B 3
Silk Museum　シルク博物館························· *63*(G 4)
Sōgetsu Art Center（hall）　草月会館················· *48* B 6
Sogō Art Museum　そごう美術館······················ *62* D 1
Sogō Dept Store（Tokyo）　そごうデパート（東京店）··· *38* E 1
Sogō Dept Store（Yokohama）　そごうデパート（横浜店）··· *62* D 1
Sōji-ji（temple）　総持寺························· *61* G 3
Sōka Gakkai　創価学会··························· *23* F 7
Sōka University　創価大学························· *14* D 3
Somei Cemetery　染井霊園························· *25* H 3
Sony（H. O.）　ソニー（本社）······················ *29* F 4
Sony Bldg　ソニービル··························· *38* E 3
Sophia（Jōchi）University　上智大学··············· *46* A 1
Sophia Univ.（Theol.）　上智大学（神学）·········· *74* E 2
Soshigaya 1～6（Setagaya-ku）　祖師谷1～6丁目（世田谷区）··· *12* C 1
Soshigaya-Okura Station　祖師ケ谷大蔵駅··········· *12* C 2
Soto-Kanda 1～6（Chiyoda-ku）　外神田1～6丁目（千代田区）··· *16* D 3
Spiral Bldg　スパイラルビル······················· *54* E 5
State Guesthouse（Geihin-kan）　迎賓館············· *21* G 1
Striped House Museum　ストライプハウス美術館······· *49* H 4
Suehirochō Station（subway）　末広町駅（地下鉄）··· *33* H 1
Suehirotei（theater）　末広亭····················· *57* I 4
Sugachō（Shinjuku-ku）　須賀町（新宿区）··········· *23* F 6
Sugamo 1～5（Toshima-ku）　巣鴨1～5丁目（豊島区）··· *25* H 3
Sugamo Post Office　巣鴨郵便局··················· *69* I 2
Sugamo Station　巣鴨駅························· *25* I 4
Suginami-ku　杉並区························· *6* C 3
Suginami Public Hall（kōkaidō）　杉並公会堂········· *10* C 5
Suginami Ward Office　杉並区役所················· *10* D 5
Sugino Kōdō（hall）　杉野講堂··················· *28* D 2
Sugino Women's Coll.　杉野女子大学··············· *28* C 3
Suidō 1～2（Bunkyō-ku）　水道1～2丁目（文京区）··· *23* I 1
Suidōbashi Station　水道橋駅··················· *32* A 1
Suidōchō（Shinjuku-ku）　水道町（新宿区）·········· *23* H 2
Suitengū（shrine）　水天宮······················ *17* F 7
Sukiyabashi Hankyū Dept Store　数寄屋橋阪急デパート··· *38* D 3
Sumida 1～5（Sumida-ku）　墨田1～5丁目（墨田区）··· *8* E 5
Sumida-ku　墨田区························· *7* H 2
Sumida Park　墨田公園························· *17* I 1
Sumida Ward Office　墨田区役所················· *17* I 1
Sumitomo Bank Tokyo H. O. Bldg　住友銀行東京本部ビル··· *36* D 5
Sumitomo Corp.　住友商事······················ *32* C 6
Sumiyoshi 1～2（Kōtō-ku）　住吉1～2丁目（江東区）··· *9* G 5
Sumiyoshichō（Shinjuku-ku）　住吉町（新宿区）······· *23* F 4
Sumiyoshi Jinja（shrine）（Tsukuda）　住吉神社（佃）··· *19* F 3
Sumiyoshi Station（subway）　住吉駅（地下鉄）··· *9* H 5
Summer Land（see Tokyo Summer Land）　サマーランド（東京サマーランド）·· *14* B 2

Sumō Museum　相撲博物館 ……………………… 85　H7
Sumō Stadium (Kokugikan)　国技館 …………… 17　G4
Sun Plaza (Nakano Sun Plaza)　サンプラザ(中野サンプラザ) …… 11　E5
Sunshine-60 Bldg　サンシャイン60 ……………… 59　H4
Sunshine Aquarium　サンシャイン国際水族館 ……… 59　I5
Sunshine City　サンシャインシティ ……………… 59　H4
Sunshine Theater　サンシャイン劇場 …………… 59　I5
Suntory Hall　サントリーホール ………………… 48　E2
Suntory Museum of Art　サントリー美術館 ……… 46　B3
Suzukakedai Station　すずかけ台駅 …………… 60　A3
Suzumoto Engeijō (theater)　鈴本演芸場 ……… 30　A5

Tabata 1〜6 (Kita-ku)　田端1〜6丁目(北区) …… 26　B3
Tabata-Shinmachi 1〜3 (Kita-ku)　田端新町1〜3丁目(北区) ‥ 26　C3
Tabata Station　田端駅 …………………………… 26　C3
Tachiaigawa Station　立会川駅 ………………… 13　I4
Tachibana 1〜6 (Sumica-ku)　立花1〜6丁目(墨田区) … 8　F4
Tachikawa City　立川市 ………………………… 15　E3
Tachikawa Station　立川駅 ……………………… 15　F3
Tagara 1〜5 (Nerima-ku)　田柄1〜5丁目(練馬区) … 10　D2
Taihei 1〜4 (Sumida-ku)　太平1〜4丁目(墨田区) … 17　J3
Thiramachi 1〜2 (Meguro-ku)　平町1〜2丁目(目黒区) … 13　F3
Taishidō 1〜5 (Setagaya-ku)　太子堂1〜5丁目(世田谷区) … 12　E1
Taishō University　大正大学 …………………… 25　G2
Taisō-ji (temple)　大宗寺 ……………………… 22　D5
Taitō 1〜4 (Tatō-ku)　台東1〜4丁目(台東区) … 16　E3
Taitō-ku　台東区 ………………………………… 7　G2
Taitō Traditional Crafts Musm　台東区伝統工芸展示館 ‥ 31　G2
Taitō Ward Office　台東区役所 ………………… 30　E2
Takaban 1〜3 (Meguro-ku)　鷹番1〜3丁目(目黒区) … 13　F2
Takabashi (Kōtō-ku)　高橋(江東区) …………… 17　H6
Takachiho Coll. of Commerce　高千穂商科大学 … 10　D6
Takada 1〜3 (Toshima-ku)　高田1〜3丁目(豊島区) … 22　D1
Takadanobaba 1〜4 (Shinjuku-ku)　高田馬場1〜4丁目(新宿区) … 22　C1
Takadanobaba Station　高田馬場駅 …………… 22　C1
Takahata Fudō (temple)　高幡不動 …………… 15　F4
Takahata-fudō Station　高幡不動駅 …………… 15　F4
Takaido-Higashi 1〜4 (Suginami-ku)　高井戸東1〜4丁目(杉並区) … 10　C6
Takaido-Nishi 1〜3 (Suginami-ku)　高井戸西1〜3丁目(杉並区) … 10　C6
Takaido Station　高井戸駅 ……………………… 10　C6
Takamatsu 1〜6 (Nerima-ku)　高松1〜6丁目(練馬区) ‥ 10　D2
Takamatsu 1〜3 (Toshima-ku)　高松1〜3丁目(豊島区) … 24　B3
Takanawa 1〜4 (Minato-ku)　高輪1〜4丁目(港区) … 29　F2
Takanawadai Station (subway)　高輪台駅(地下鉄) … 29　F3
Takanawa Post Office　高輪郵便局 …………… 68　B6
Takanodai 1〜5 (Nerima-ku)　高野台1〜5丁目(練馬区) … 10　C3
Takanodai Station　鷹の台駅 …………………… 15　G2
Takanodai Station　高野台駅 …………………… 6　C2
Takaosanguchi Station　高尾山口駅 …………… 14　B5
Takaosan Yakuōin (temple)　高尾山薬王院 …… 14　B5
Takao Station　高尾駅 …………………………… 14　C4
Takarachō Station (subway)　宝町駅(地下鉄) … 18　D1

Takarada-Ebisu Jinja (shrine)　宝田恵比寿神社 ……… 34　B3
Takaramachi 1〜2 (Katsushika-ku)　宝町1〜2丁目(葛飾区) … 8　E4
Takasago 1〜8 (Katsushika-ku)　高砂1〜8丁目(葛飾区) … 8　D3
Takashimadaira 1〜9 (Itabashi-ku)　高島平1〜9丁目(板橋区) … 10　E1
Takashimadaira Station (subway)　高島平駅(地下鉄) … 100
Takashimaya Dept Store　高島屋デパート ……… 35　G5
Takashimaya Times Square　高島屋タイムズスクエア ‥ 57　G6
Takatsu-ku (Kawasaki City)　高津区(川崎市) … 12　C3
Takatsu Station　高津駅 ………………………… 12　C4
Takebashi Station (subway)　竹橋駅(地下鉄) … 32　C7
Takenotsuka 1〜7 (Adachi-ku)　竹の塚1〜7丁目(足立区) … 8　B6
Takenotsuka Station　竹ノ塚駅 ………………… 8　B6
Takeshiba Passenger Terminal　竹芝客航ターミナル … 18　C5
Takeshiba Station　竹芝駅 ……………………… 18　C5
Takinogawa 1〜7 (Kita-ku)　滝野川1〜7丁目(北区) … 25　G1
Takushoku Univ. (Hachiōji)　拓殖大学(八王子) … 14　C5
Takushoku Univ. (Myōgadani)　拓殖大学(茗荷谷) … 23　H1
Tama Art University　多摩美術大学 …………… 12　D3
Tamabochimae Station　多磨墓地前駅 ………… 15　H4
Tama Cemetery (reien)　多磨霊園 ……………… 15　H3
Tamachi Station　田町駅 ………………………… 21　J7
Tama City　多摩市 ……………………………… 15　F5
Tama-Dōbutsukōen Station　多摩動物公園駅 … 15　F4
Tamagawa 1〜2 (Ōta-ku)　多摩川1〜2丁目(大田区) … 13　G6
Tamagawa 1〜4 (Setagaya-ku)　玉川1〜4丁目(世田谷区) … 12　D3
Tamagawadai 1〜2 (Setagaya-ku)　玉川台1〜2丁目(世田谷区) … 12　D3
Tamagawa-Denenchōfu 1〜2 (Setagaya-ku)　玉川田園調布1〜2丁目(世田谷区) … 13 (E4)
Tamagawaen Station　多摩川園駅 ……………… 13　F4
Tamagawa-Gakuenmae Station　玉川学園前駅 … 15　G7
Tamagawa-Jōsui Station　玉川上水駅 ………… 15　F2
Tamagawa University　玉川大学 ……………… 15　G7
Tama-ko (lake)　多摩湖 ………………………… 15　F1
Tama-ku (Kawasaki City)　多摩区(川崎市) … 12　A3
Tama New Town　多摩ニュータウン …………… 15　F5
Tama-Plaza Station　たまプラーザ駅 ………… 50　D1
Tamareien Station　多磨霊園駅 ………………… 15　H4
Tama Tech　多摩テック ………………………… 14　E5
Tama Univ.　多摩大学 …………………………… 74　C4
Tama Zoological Park　多摩動物公園 …………… 15　F4
Tamazutsumi 1〜2 (Setagaya-ku)　玉堤1〜2丁目(世田谷区) … 12　E4
Tanashi City　田無市 …………………………… 15　H2
Tanashi Station　田無駅 ………………………… 15　I2
Tana Station　田奈駅 …………………………… 50　B2
Tanmachi Station　反町駅 ……………………… 51　F5
Tansumachi (Shinjuku-ku)　箪笥町(新宿区) … 23　H3
Tateishi 1〜8 (Katsushika-ku)　立石1〜8丁目(葛飾区) … 8　E3
Tatekawa 1〜4 (Sumida-ku)　立川1〜4丁目(墨田区) … 17　I5
Tatenochō (Nerima-ku)　立野町(練馬区) …… 10　B4
Tatsumi 1〜3 (Kōtō-ku)　辰巳1〜3丁目(江東区) … 9　I5
Tatsumi Station (subway)　辰巳駅(地下鉄) … 19　J7
Tatsunuma 1〜2 (Adachi-ku)　辰沼1〜2丁目(足立区) … 8　B4
Tawaramachi Station (subway)　田原町駅(地下鉄) …… 17　G2

TBS Hall　TBSホール	48	B 3
Technoplaza Katsushika　テクノプラザかつしか	8	D 5
Teikoku Gekijō（see Imperial Theater）帝国劇場	37	J 6
Teikyō Univ.（Hachiōji）帝京大学（八王子）	15	F 4
Teikyō Univ.（Itabashi）帝京大学（板橋）	75	F 2
Tekko Bldg　鉄鋼ビル	35	F 6
Telecom Center Station　テレコムセンター駅	7	G 5
Tenjinchō（Shinjuku-ku）天神町（新宿区）	23	H 2
Tenri Gallery　天理ギャラリー	33	F 6
Tenshin Okakura Mem. Park　岡倉天心記念公園	26	C 5
TEPCO Electric Energy Musm　東京電力電力館	53	E 2
Tessenkai Noh Theater　銕仙会能楽研究所	55	F 5
Tetsugakudō Park　哲学堂公園	11	F 4
Tobacco & Salt Museum　たばこと塩の博物館	52	E 2
Tobitakyū Station　飛田給駅	15	H 4
Tōbu Asakusa Station　東武浅草駅	31	I 4
Tōbu Dept Store　東武デパート	58	D 4
Tōbu-Nerima Station　東武練馬駅	10	E 1
Toda Boat Course　戸田ボート場	83	E 2
Todoroki 1〜8（Setagaya-ku）等々力1〜8丁目（世田谷区）	12	E 3
Todoroki Station　等々力駅	12	E 3
Tōgeki（cinema）東劇（映）	39	H 6
Togenuki Jizō（Kōgan-ji）（temple）とげぬき地蔵（高岩寺）	25	H 3
Tōgō Jinja（shrine）東郷神社	54	B 1
Tōgō Seiji Art Museum　東郷青児美術館	56	D 3
Togoshi 1〜6（Shinagawa-ku）戸越1〜6丁目（品川区）	28	D 6
Togoshi-Ginza Station　戸越銀座駅	28	C 6
Togoshi-Kōen Station　戸越公園駅	13	H 3
Togoshi Park　戸越公園	28	D 7
Togoshi Station（subway）戸越駅（地下鉄）	13	H 3
Tōhō Gakuen School of Music　桐朋学園大学	74	E 3
Tōhō Seimei Bldg　東邦生命ビル	53	G 5
Tōhō Seimei Hall　東邦生命ホール	80	C 3
Tōhō University　東邦大学	13	H 5
Tōkai 1〜6（Ōta-ku）東海1〜6丁目（大田区）	13	J 4
Tōkai Bank　東海銀行	36	E 2
Tōkaichiba Station　十日市場駅	60	C 3
Tōkai Univ.（Yoyogi）東海大学（代々木）	20	A 3
Tokiwa 1〜2（Kōtō-ku）常盤1〜2丁目（江東区）	17	H 6
Tokiwadai 1〜4（Itabashi-ku）常盤台1〜4丁目（板橋区）	11	F 2
Tokiwadai Station　ときわ台駅	11	F 2
Tokumaru 1〜8（Itabashi-ku）徳丸1〜8丁目（板橋区）	10	E 1
Tokyo Big Sight　東京ビッグサイト（国際展示場）	7	G 5
Tokyo Broadcasting Station（TBS）東京放送	48	B 4
Tokyo Bldg　東京ビル	37	H 4
Tokyo Budōkan　東京武道館	8	C 4
Tokyo Bunka Kaikan（see Tokyo Met. Festival Hall）東京文化会館	30	B 1
Tokyo Central Musm of Art　東京セントラル美術館	39	G 2
Tokyo Central Post Office　東京中央郵便局	37	H 4
Tokyo Central Wholesale Market（Ōta）東京中央卸売市場（大田）	13	J 4
Tokyo Central Wholesale Market（Tsukiji）東京中央卸売市場（築地）	18	D 4
Tokyo Chamber of Comm. & Ind.　東京商工会議所	37	I 5
Tokyo City Air Terminal（Hakozaki）東京シティエアターミナル（箱崎）	17	G 7
Tokyo Club Bldg　東京倶楽部ビル	47	F 7
Tokyo Coll. of Economics　東京経済大学	74	C 3
Tokyo Coll. of Pharmacy　東京薬科大学	74	B 4
Tokyo Daibutsu　東京大仏	83	E 2
Tokyo Dental Coll.　東京歯科大学	32	B 2
Tokyo Disneyland　東京ディズニーランド	7	I 5
Tokyo Dome　東京ドーム	16	A 2
Tokyo Electrical Engn Coll.　東京電機大学	32	E 5
Tokyo Electric Power Co.（H. O.）東京電力（本社）	38	B 4
Tokyo Engineering Coll.　東京工科大学	14	D 5
Tokyo Expressway Public Corp.　首都高速道路公団	47	H 7
Tokyo Gakugei Univ.　東京学芸大学	15	G 3
Tokyo Gas Bldg　東京ガスビル	18	B 5
Tokyo Globe-za（theater）東京グローブ座	81	F 1
Tokyo Grain Exchange　東京穀物商品取引所	34	E 1
Tokyo Higashi-Hongan-ji（temple）東京東本願寺	17	G 1
Tokyo Int'l Forum　東京国際フォーラム	37	I 4
Tokyo Inst. of Polytechnics　東京工芸大学	74	B 6
Tokyo Inst. of Technology　東京工業大学	13	F 4
Tokyo Int'l Airport（Haneda）東京国際空港（羽田）	13	J 6
Tokyo Int'l Post Office　東京国際郵便局	36	C 2
Tokyo Int'l Trade Center　東京国際貿易センター	18	D 6
Tokyo Jikeikai Idai Univ.（see Jikei Univ. School of Medicine）	18	A 4
Tokyo Jindai Botanical Park（see Jindai Botanical Park）	15	I 4
Tokyo Kaijō Bldg　東京海上ビル	37	F 5
Tokyo Kaikan　東京会館	37	I 6
Tokyo Kasei Gakuin Coll.　東京家政学院大学	74	A 4
Tokyo Kasei Univ.　東京家政大学	75	F 2
Tokyo Kōsei Nenkin Hall（Kaikan）東京厚生年金会館	22	D 5
Tokyo Kōtsū Kaikan　東京交通会館	38	F 1
Tokyo Kyōsai Hosp.　東京共済病院	28	A 1
Tokyo Medical Coll.　東京医科大学	22	E 5
Tokyo Med. Coll. Hosp.　東京医大病院	56	B 2
Tokyo Med. & Dent Univ.　東京医科歯科大学	33	F 2
Tokyo Met. Art Museum　東京都美術館	26	E 7
Tokyo Met. Art Space　東京芸術劇場	58	C 4
Tokyo Met. Central Library　都立中央図書館	21	G 6
Tokyo Met. Children's House　東京都児童会館	54	B 5
Tokyo Met. Festival Hall（Tokyo Bunka Kaikan）東京文化会館	30	B 1
Tokyo Met. Government　東京都庁	56	A 5
Tokyo Met. Hibiya Library　都立日比谷図書館	38	A 3
Tokyo Met. Inst. of Tech.　東京都立科学技術大学	74	B 3
Tokyo Met. Kokusai H. Sch.　東京都立国際高等学校	13	F 3
Tokyo Met. Musm of Modern Literature　東京都立近代文学博物館	84	B 1
Tokyo Met. Musm of Photography　東京都写真美術館	28	C 1
Tokyo Met. Teien Art Museum　東京都庭園美術館	28	D 2
Tokyo Met. Univ.　東京都立大学	14	E 5
Tokyo Met. Yumenoshima Tropical Plant Dome　東京都夢の島熱帯植物館	87	H 4
Tokyo Mosque　東京モスク	11	F 7
Tokyo Music Coll.　東京音楽大学	24	E 6
Tokyo Mutual Life Insurance　東京生命	38	B 4

Tokyo National Museum　東京国立博物館 …… 26　E6
Tokyo Nat'l Univ. of Fine Arts and Music　東京芸術大学 26　D6
Tokyo Newspapers　東京新聞社 29　G3
Tokyo Opera City　東京オペラシティ …… 22　A6
Tokyo Port Wild Bird Park　東京港野鳥公園 …… 13　I5
Tokyo Racecourse　東京競馬場 15　H4
Tokyo Sea Life Park　葛西臨海水族園 9　J3
Tokyo Station　東京駅 …… 37　G3
Tokyo Stock Exchange　東京証券取引所 …… 35　F2
Tokyo Summer Land　東京サマーランド 14　B2
Tokyo Takarazuka Theater　東京宝塚劇場 …… 38　C2
Tokyo Teleport Station　東京テレポート駅 …… 7　G5
Tokyo Tower　東京タワー 21　J4
Tokyo Trade Center　東京産業貿易会館 …… 18　C5
Tokyo Union Theological Seminary　東京神学大学 74 (D3)
Tokyo Univ. of Agriculture　東京農業大学 …… 12　D2
Tokyo Univ. of Agr. & Tech.　東京農工大学 74 (D3)
Tokyo Univ. of Art anc Design　東京造形大学 74　A4
Tokyo Univ. of Fisheries　東京水産大学 29　H4
Tokyo Univ. of Foreign Studies　東京外国語大学 …… 25　H2
Tokyo Univ. of Mercantile Marine　東京商船大学 19　G3
Tokyo Wholesale Center (TOC)　東京卸売センター 28　C5
Tokyo Women's Christan Univ.　東京女子大学 …… 10　B5
Tokyo Women's Medical Coll.　東京女子医科大学 23　F4
Tokyo Women's P. E. Coll.　東京女子体育大学 74　C3
Tōkyū Bunka Kaikan　東急文化会館 53　F4
Tōkyū Dept Store (Main Shop)　東急デパート(本店) … 52　C3
Tōkyū Dept Store (Nihombashi)　東急デパート(日本橋) … 35　F4
Tōkyū Hands Store (Ikebukuro)　東急ハンズ(池袋) 59　G4
Tōkyū Hands Store (Shibuya)　東急ハンズ(渋谷) 52　D3
Tōkyū Plaza Bldg　東急プラザ 52　E5
Tomigaya 1~2 (Shibuya-ku)　富ケ谷1~2丁目(渋谷区) 20　A3
Tomihisachō (Shinjuku-ku)　富久町(新宿区) 22　E5
Tomioka 1~2 (Kōtō-ku)　富岡1~2丁目(江東区) 19　H2
Tomioka Hachimangū (shrine)　富岡八幡宮 19　H2
Toneri 1~6 (Adachi-ku)　舎人1~6丁目(足立区) 8　A7
Tonerichō (Adachi-ku)　舎人町(足立区) 8　B7
Tonogoyato Garden　殿ケ谷戸庭園 15　G3
Toppan Printing (H. O.)　凸版印刷(本社) 16　E3
Toranomon 1~5 (Minato-ku)　虎ノ門1~5丁目(港区) … 21　J3
Toranomon Hall　虎ノ門ホール 47　G7
Toranomon Hosp.　虎の門病院 21　J2
Toranomon Pastoral　虎ノ門パストラル 21　J3
Toranomon Station (subway)　虎ノ門駅(地下鉄) 18　A2
Tōray Bldg　東レビル 34　C4
Torigoe 1~2 (Taitō-ku)　鳥越1~2丁目(台東区) 17　F3
Torigoe Jinja (shrine)　鳥越神社 17　F3
Toritsu-Daigaku Station　都立大学駅 13　F3
Toritsu-Kasei Station　都立家政駅 10　D4
Tōshiba Bldg　東芝ビル 18　B6
Tōshiba Science Inst.　東芝科学館 87　F5
Toshima 1~8 (Kita-ku)　豊島1~8丁目(北区) 11　I1

Toshima-en (amusement park)　としまえん(豊島園) … 1C　D3
Toshimaen Station　豊島園駅 1C　E3
Toshima-ku　豊島区 6　E2
Toshima Post Office　豊島郵便局 59　I4
Toshima Public Hall (Kōkaidō)　豊島公会堂 59　G3
Toshima Ward Office　豊島区役所 59　F3
Tōshinchō 1~2 (Itabashi-ku)　東新町1~2丁目(板橋区)… 11　F2
Tōshōgū (shrine)　東照宮 16　D1
Totsuka-ku (Yokohama City)　戸塚区(横浜市) 60　C7
Totsukamachi 1 (Shinjuku-ku)　戸塚町1丁目(新宿区)… 23　F2
Totsuka Station　戸塚駅 60　C7
Tourist Into. Center (Asakusa)　浅草文化観光センター … 31　H5
Tourist Into. Center (Yūrakuchō)　ツーリストインフォメーションセンター(有楽町) … 38　D2
Tōwa 1~5 (Adachi-ku)　東和1~5丁目(足立区) 8　B4
Toyama 1~3 (Shinjuku-ku)　戸山1~3丁目(新宿区)… 22　E3
Toyama Park　戸山公園 22　D2
Tōyō 1~7 (Kōtō-ku)　東陽1~7丁目(江東区) 9　H5
Tōyō Bunko (library)　東洋文庫 26　A4
Tōyōchō Station (subway)　東陽町駅(地下鉄) 9　I5
Tōyō Eiwa Women's Univ.　東洋英和女学院大学 74　D6
Toyoda Station　豊田駅 14　E4
Toyokawa Inari (temple)　豊川稲荷 21　G1
Toyomichō (Chūō-ku)　豊海町(中央区) 18　D5
Toyosu 1~6 (Kōtō-ku)　豊洲1~6丁目(江東区) 19　G6
Toyosu Station (subway)　豊洲駅(地下鉄) 19　H5
Toyotama-Kami 1~2 (Nerima-ku)　豊玉上1~2丁目(練馬区) 10 (E3)
Toyotama-Kita 1~6 (Nerima-ku)　豊玉北1~6丁目(練馬区) 10　E3
Toyotama-Minami 1~3 (Nerima-ku)　豊玉南1~3丁目(練馬区) 10　E3
Toyotama-Naka 1~4 (Nerima-ku)　豊玉中1~4丁目(練馬区) 10　E3
Tōyō University　東洋大学 26　A6
Tōyō Univ. (Asaka)　東洋大学(朝霞) 74　E1
Tōzen-ji (temple)　東禅寺 29　F2
Transportation Museum　交通博物館 33　G4
Tsubaki 1~2 (Adachi-ku)　椿1~2丁目(足立区) 8　C7
Tsubouchi Mem. Theatre Musm of Waseda Univ.　早稲田大学坪内博士記念演劇博物館 85　G2
Tsuda College　津田塾大学 74　C2
Tsuda Hall　津田ホール 80　D2
Tsudayama Station　津田山駅 12　C4
Tsukiji 1~7 (Chūō-ku)　築地1~7丁目(中央区) 18　D3
Tsukijimachi (Shinjuku-ku)　築地町(新宿区) 23　H2
Tsukiji Shijō　築地市場(東京中央卸売市場) 18　D4
Tsukiji Station (subway)　築地駅(地下鉄) 39　J5
Tsukimino Station　つきみ野駅 60　A3
Tsukishima 1~4 (Chūō-ku)　月島1~4丁目(中央区) 19　F4
Tsukishima Station (subway)　月島駅(地下鉄) 19　F3
Tsukuda 1~3 (Chūō-ku)　佃1~3丁目(中央区) 19　F3
Tsukudochō (Shinjuku-ku)　津久戸町(新宿区) 23　I3
Tsukudo-Hachimanchō (Shinjuku-ku)　筑土八幡町(新宿区) 23　I3
Tsukushino Station　つくし野駅 60　B3
Tsunashima Station　綱島駅 61　F2
Tsurugamine Station　鶴ヶ峰駅 60　C4
Tsurukawa Station　鶴川駅 15　G6

Tsurumaki 1〜5 (Setagaya-ku)　弦巻1〜5丁目(世田谷区) …… *12* D 2
Tsurumi-ku (Yokohama City)　鶴見区(横浜市) ……… *61* G 3
Tsurumi-Ono Station　鶴見小野駅 ……………………… *61* G 4
Tsurumi Station　鶴見駅 …………………………………… *61* G 3
Tsurumi-Tsubasa-bashi　鶴見つばさ橋 ………………… *61* H 5
Tsurumi University　鶴見大学 …………………………… *61* G 4
Tsutsujigaoka Station　つつじケ丘駅 ………………… *15* J 4
Tsutsumidōri 1〜2 (Sumida-ku)　堤通1〜2丁目(墨田区) … *9* E 5
TV Asahi (ANB)　テレビ朝日 …………………………… *49* H 6
TV Kanagawa (TVK)　テレビ神奈川 …………………… *63* H 6
TV Tokyo (TX)　テレビ東京 …………………………… *49* F 1
Twin Tower Bldg (Yūrakuchō)　ツインタワービル(有楽町) …… *38* C 1

Uchi-Kanda 1〜3 (Chiyoda-ku)　内神田1〜3丁目(千代田区) … *16* C 5
Uchisaiwaichō 1〜2 (Chiyoda-ku)　内幸町1〜2丁目(千代田区) ……… *18* B 2
Uchisaiwaichō Station (subway)　内幸町駅(地下鉄) … *38* A 4
Udagawachō (Shibuya-ku)　宇田川町(渋谷区) ……… *20* B 4
Uehara 1〜3 (Shibuya-ku)　上原1〜3丁目(渋谷区) … *20* A 3
Ueno 1〜7 (Taitō-ku)　上野1〜7丁目(台東区) …… *16* D 2
Ueno Gakuen University　上野学園大学 ……………… *17* F 1
Ueno-Hirokōji Station (subway)　上野広小路駅(地下鉄) … *30* A 6
Ueno-Kōen (Taitō-ku)　上野公園(台東区) …………… *26* D 7
Ueno Park　上野公園 ……………………………………… *26* E 7
Ueno Post Office　上野郵便局 ………………………… *69* I 5
Ueno Royal Museum　上野の森美術館 ………………… *30* B 2
Ueno-Sakuragi 1〜2 (Taitō-ku)　上野桜木1〜2丁目(台東区) … *26* E 6
Ueno Shōchiku (cinema)　上野松竹(映) ……………… *30* B 3
Ueno Station　上野駅 …………………………………… *30* C 2
Ueno Takarazuka (cinema)　上野宝塚(映) …………… *30* B 3
Ueno Tōhō (cinema)　上野東宝(映) …………………… *30* B 3
Ueno Zoological Gardens (see Ueno Zoo)　上野動物園 … *26* D 7
Uguisudanichō (Shibuya-ku)　鶯谷町(渋谷区) …… *20* C 5
Uguisudani Station　鶯谷駅 …………………………… *26* E 6
Ukima 1〜5 (Kita-ku)　浮間1〜5丁目(北区) ……… *11* G 1
Ukitachō (Edogawa-ku)　宇喜田町(江戸川区) …… *9* H 3
Umeda 1〜8 (Adachi-ku)　梅田1〜8丁目(足立区) … *8* C 6
Umegaoka 1〜3 (Setagaya-ku)　梅丘1〜3丁目(世田谷区) … *12* E 1
Umegaoka Station　梅ケ丘駅 …………………………… *12* E 1
Umejima 1〜3 (Adachi-ku)　梅島1〜3丁目(足立区) … *8* C 6
Umejima Station　梅島駅 ………………………………… *8* C 6
Umewaka Noh Theater　梅若能楽堂 …………………… *11* F 5
Umeyashiki Station　梅屋敷駅 ………………………… *13* H 6
Umezato 1〜2 (Suginami-ku)　梅里1〜2丁目(杉並区) … *10* D 5
Umibe (Kōtō-ku)　海辺(江東区) ……………………… *9* (H5)
Umi-Shibaura Station　海芝浦駅 ……………………… *61* H 4
Unane 1〜3 (Setagaya-ku)　宇奈根1〜3丁目(世田谷区) … *12* C 3
Univ. of Electro-Communications　電気通信大学 …… *74* D 3
Univ. of Sacred Heart (Seishin)　聖心女子大学 …… *21* F 6
University of Tokyo　東京大学 ………………………… *16* C 1
Univ. of Tokyo (Agr.)　東京大学(農) ………………… *26* B 7
Univ. of Tokyo (Liberal Arts)　東京大学(教養) …… *20* A 4
Univ. of Tokyo Hosp.　東大病院 ……………………… *16* C 1

Unoki 1〜3 (Ota-ku)　鵜の木1〜3丁目(大田区) ……… *13* F 5
Unoki Station　鵜の木駅 ………………………………… *13* F 5
Urayasu Station (subway)　浦安駅(地下鉄) ………… *9* I 1
Urbannet New Ōtemachi Bldg　アーバンネット新大手町ビル … *36* D 3
Ushida Station　牛田駅 …………………………………… *8* E 5
Ushigome Post Office　牛込郵便局 …………………… *23* H 3

Wada 1〜3 (Suginami-ku)　和田1〜3丁目(杉並区) … *10* E 5
Wakaba 1〜3 (Shinjuku-ku)　若葉1〜3丁目(新宿区) … *23* G 6
Wakabadai Station　若葉台駅 …………………………… *15* G 5
Wakabayashi 1〜5 (Setagaya-ku)　若林1〜5丁目(世田谷区) … *12* E 1
Wakabayashi Station　若林駅 …………………………… *12* E 1
Wakagi 1〜3 (Itabashi-ku)　若木1〜3丁目(板橋区) … *11* F 1
Wakamatsuchō (Shinjuku-ku)　若松町(新宿区) …… *23* F 3
Wakamiya 1〜3 (Nakano-ku)　若宮1〜3丁目(中野区) … *10* D 4
Wakamiyachō (Shinjuku-ku)　若宮町(新宿区) …… *23* I 3
Wakasu (Kōtō-ku)　若洲(江東区) …………………… *7* H 5
Wakō (store)　和光 ……………………………………… *39* F 3
Wakō University　和光大学 …………………………… *15* G 7
Wanza Ariake Bay Mall　湾座有明 …………………… *83* G 4
Wasedamachi (Shinjuku-ku)　早稲田町(新宿区) … *23* F 2
Waseda-Minamichō (Shinjuku-ku)　早稲田南町(新宿区) … *23* F 2
Waseda Station (subway)　早稲田駅(地下鉄) ……… *23* F 2
Waseda-Tsurumakichō (Shinjuku-ku)　早稲田鶴巻町(新宿区) … *23* G 2
Waseda University　早稲田大学 ……………………… *23* F 3
Waseda Univ. (Sci. & Engn.)　早稲田大学(理工) …… *22* D 2
Waseda Univ. Memorial Hall　早稲田大学記念会堂 … *23* F 2
Wayō Women's University　和洋女子大学 …………… *75* H 2
Women's Coll. of Fine Arts　女子美術大学 …………… *75* E 3
World Bag Museum　世界のカバン館 …………………… *31* H 7
World Trade Center Bldg　世界貿易センタービル ……… *18* B 5

Yabe Station　矢部駅 …………………………………… *14* E 6
Yabo Tenmangū (shrine)　谷保天満宮 ……………… *82* C 3
Yaesu 1〜2 (Chūō-ku)　八重洲1〜2丁目(中央区) … *16* D 7
Yaesu Book Center　八重洲ブックセンター ………… *37* I 2
Yagawa Station　矢川駅 ………………………………… *15* F 3
Yagōchimachi 1〜2 (Edogawa-ku)　谷河内町1〜2丁目(江戸川区) … *9* G 1
Yaguchi 1〜3 (Ōta-ku)　矢口1〜3丁目(大田区) … *13* G 6
Yaguchinowatashi Station　矢口渡駅 ………………… *13* G 6
Yahara 1〜6 (Nerima-ku)　谷原1〜6丁目(練馬区) … *10* C 2
Yahiro 1〜6 (Sumida-ku)　八広1〜6丁目(墨田区) … *9* F 4
Yahiro Station　八広駅 ………………………………… *9* F 4
Yaho Station　谷保駅 …………………………………… *15* G 3
Yakō Station　矢向駅 …………………………………… *61* G 2
Yakult (H. O.)　ヤクルト(本社) ……………………… *38* C 7
Yakult Hall　ヤクルトホール …………………………… *80* E 6
Yakumo 1〜5 (Meguro-ku)　八雲1〜5丁目(目黒区) … *12* E 3
Yamabukichō (Shinjuku-ku)　山吹町(新宿区) …… *23* I 3
Yamada Station　山田駅 ………………………………… *14* D 4
Yamaha Hall　ヤマハホール …………………………… *38* E 5
Yamashitachō (Yokohama City)　山下町(横浜市) ……… *63* G 5

Yamashita Park　山下公園 ················· 63　G 5
Yamashita Station　山下駅 ················· 12　D 1
Yamatane Musm of Art　山種美術館 ········· 35　G 2
Yamatechō (Yokohama City)　山手町(横浜市)·· 63　G 6
Yamate Church　山手教会 ················· 52　E 3
Yamate Museum　山手資料館 ··············· 63　(H6)
Yamate Park　山手公園 ··················· 63　G 7
Yamate Station　山手駅 ·················· 61　F 6
Yamatochō (Itabashi-ku)　大和町(板橋区)··· 11　G 2
Yamatochō 1～4 (Nakano-ku)　大和町1～4丁目(中野区) ······ 10　D 4
Yamato Mutual Life Insurance (H. O.)　大和生命(本社)·· 38　B 3
Yamato Station　大和駅 ·················· 60　A 5
Yanagibashi 1～2 (Taitō-ku)　柳橋1～2丁目(台東区)·· 17　G 4
Yanagihara 1～2 (Adachi-ku)　柳原1～2丁目(足立区) ···· 8　D 5
Yanaka 1～5 (Adachi-ku)　谷中1～5丁目(足立区) ······ 8　C 4
Yanaka 1～7 (Taitō-ku)　谷中1～7丁目(台東区) ···· 26　D 6
Yanaka Cemetery　谷中霊園 ··············· 26　D 5
Yanokuchi Station　矢野口駅 ·············· 15　H 5
Yaraichō (Shinjuku-ku)　矢来町(新宿区) ···· 23　H 3
Yarai Noh Theater　矢来能楽堂 ············· 81　G 3
Yasaka Station　八坂駅 ·················· 15　G 1
Yashio 1～5 (Shinagawa-ku)　八潮1～5丁目(品川区)·· 29　I 6
Yasuda Kasai-Kaijō Bldg　安田火災海上本社ビル ·· 56　D 3
Yasuda Seimei Bldg　安田生命ビル ········· 56　E 5
Yasuda Seimei Hall　安田生命ホール ········ 56　E 5
Yasukuni Jinja (shrine)　靖国神社 ········· 23　I 5
Yayoi 1～2 (Bunkyō-ku)　弥生1～2丁目(文京区)·· 26　B 7
Yayoi Art Musm　弥生美術館 ·············· 16　C 1
Yayoichō (Itabashi-ku)　弥生町(板橋区) ···· 11　G 2
Yayoichō 1～6 (Nkano-ku)　弥生町1～6丁目(中野区)·· 11　E 6
Yayoiai Station　弥生台駅 ················ 60　C 6
Yazaike 1～3 (Adachi-ku)　谷在家1～3丁目(足立区)·· 8　B 7
YMCA ·································· 33　F 6
Yochōmachi (Shinjuku-ku)　余丁町(新宿区) ··· 22　E 4
Yōga 1～4 (Setagaya-ku)　用賀1～4丁目(世田谷区)·· 12　D 2
Yōga Station　用賀駅 ···················· 12　D 2
Yokoami 1～2 (Sumida-ku)　横網1～2丁目(墨田区)·· 17　H 3
Yokohama Arena　横浜アリーナ ············· 61　F 3
Yokohama Archives of History　横浜開港資料館 ·· 63　(G5)
Yokohama Bay Bridge　横浜ベイブリッジ ····· 61　G 6
Yokohama City　横浜市 ·················· 60　C 4
Yokohama City Air Terminal　横浜シティエアターミナル·· 62　D 1
Yokohama City Univ. (Med.)　横浜市立大(医)·· 62　D 7
Yokohama Coll. of Commerce (Tsurumi)　横浜商科大学(鶴見)·· 61　G 4
Yokohama Cultural Gym.　横浜文化体育館 ····· 63　E 6
Yokohama Doll Musm　横浜人形の家 ········· 63　(H5)
Yokohama Int'l Sch.　横浜インターナショナルスクール·· 63　H 6
Yokohama Marine Science Musm　横浜海洋科学博物館 ·· 63　(H5)
Yokohama Museum of Art　横浜美術館 ········ 62　E 3
Yokohama National University　横浜国立大学 ·· 60　E 5
Yokohama Opening Port Mem. Hall　横浜開港記念会館 ·· 63　(F5)
Yokohama Park　横浜公園 ················· 63　F 5

Yokohama Stadium　横浜スタジアム ········· 63　F 5
Yokohama Station　横浜駅 ················· 62　C 1
Yokokawa 1～5 (Sumida-ku)　横川1～5丁目(墨田区)·· 17　J 3
Yokota Airfield　横田飛行場 ·············· 14　D 1
Yokoteramachi (Shinjuku-ku)　横寺町(新宿区) ·· 23　H 3
Yokoyama Taikan Mem. Cottege　横山大観記念館 ·· 85　H 5
Yomiuri Hall　読売ホール ··············· 38　E 1
Yomiuri Land　よみうりランド ············ 15　H 5
Yomiuri-Landmae Station　読売ランド前駅 ··· 15　H 5
Yomiuri Newspapers　読売新聞社 ··········· 36　C 4
Yonbanchō (Chiyoda-ku)　四番町(千代田区) ·· 23　I 5
Yotsuba 1～2 (Itabashi-ku)　四葉1～2丁目(板橋区)·· 10　E 1
Yotsugi 1～5 (Katsushika-ku)　四つ木1～5丁目(葛飾区)·· 8　E 4
Yotsugi Station　四ツ木駅 ················ 9　E 4
Yatsuya 1～4 (Shinjuku-ku)　四谷1～4丁目(新宿区)·· 23　G 6
Yotsuya Post Office　四谷郵便局 ··········· 68　E 3
Yotsuya-sanchōme Station (subway)　四谷三丁目駅(地下鉄)·· 23　F 6
Yotsuya Station　四ツ谷駅 ················ 23　G 6
Yoyogi 1～5 (Shibuya-ku)　代々木1～5丁目(渋谷区)·· 22　C 6
Yoyogi-Hachiman Station　代々木八幡駅 ····· 20　A 2
Yoyogi-Kamizonochō (Shibuya-ku)　代々木神園町(渋谷区)·· 20　B 2
Yoyogi-Kōen Station (subway)　代々木公園駅(地下鉄)·· 20　A 2
Yoyogi Park　代々木公園 ················· 20　B 2
Yoyogi Station　代々木駅 ················· 22　C 6
Yoyogi-Uehara Station　代々木上原駅 ······· 11　F 7
Yukigaya-Ōtsukamachi (Ōta-ku)　雪谷大塚町(大田区)·· 13　F 4
Yukigaya-Ōtsuka Station　雪が谷大塚駅 ····· 13　F 4
Yumenoshima (Kōtō-ku)　夢の島(江東区) ···· 9　J 4
Yumenoshima Park　夢の島公園 ············ 9　J 5
Yumenoshima Tropical Plant Dome　夢の島熱帯植物館·· 87　H 4
Yūrakuchō 1～2 (Chiyoda-ku)　有楽町1～2丁目(千代田区)·· 38　D 1
Yūrakuchō Bldg　有楽町ビル ·············· 38　D 1
Yūrakuchō Mullion　有楽町マリオン ········· 38　D 2
Yūrakuchō Station　有楽町駅 ·············· 18　C 2
Yurigaoka Station　百合ケ丘駅 ············ 15　H 5
Yūsen Bldg　郵船ビル ··················· 37　F 5
Yushima 1～4 (Bunkyō-ku)　湯島1～4丁目(文京区)·· 16　C 2
Yushima Confucian Shrine (Yushima Seidō)　湯島聖堂·· 33　F 2
Yushima Jinja (shrine)　湯島神社 ·········· 16　C 2
Yushima Station (subway)　湯島駅(地下鉄) ·· 16　D 2
Yutakachō 1～6 (Shinagawa-ku)　豊町1～6丁目(品川区)·· 28　D 7
Yūtenji 1～2 (Meguro-ku)　祐天寺1～2丁目(目黒区)·· 13　F 2
Yūtenji Station　祐天寺駅 ················ 13　F 2

Zempukuji 1～4 (Suginami-ku)　善福寺1～4丁目(杉並区)·· 10　B 4
Zempukuji Park　善福寺公園 ·············· 10　B 4
Zōjō-ji (temple)　増上寺 ················ 18　A 5
Zōshigaya 1～3 (Toshima-ku)　雑司が谷1～3丁目(豊島区)·· 25　F 6
Zōshigaya Cemetery　雑司が谷霊園 ········· 25　F 6
Zōshiki Station　雑色駅 ················· 13　H 7

Japanese Index
各種機関、著名企業、博物館などの五十音順索引

この索引は、英語からでは検索しにくいと思われる各種機関、著名企業、博物館などを、五十音順で収蔵したものです。地名、駅名等は、ABC順の索引をご参照下さい。また、官公庁、外国公館、航空会社、ホテル／旅館は、各種電話番号のページをご参照下さい。

あ

アクシスビル　Axis Bldg ･･････････････････ 49　H 3
アークヒルズ　Ark Hills ･･････････････････ 48　E 2
アジア会館　Asia Center of Japan ････････ 48　C 6
アーバンネット新大手町ビル　Urbannet New Ōtemachi Bldg ･･ 36　D 3
アブアブ　ABAB ･･････････････････････････ 30　B 4
アメヤ横町　Ameya-Yokochō ････････････ 30　B 4
アメリカンクラブ　American Club ･･･････ 49　I 2
アール・エフ・ラジオ日本　RF Radio Nippon ･･ 62　C 5
アルパ専門店街　Alpa Shopping Complex ･･ 59　H 5
あさひ銀行本店　Asahi Bank (H. O.) ･･････ 36　D 5
合気道本部道場　Aikidō World H. Q. ･･････ 22　E 4
葵会館　Aoi Kaikan ･･･････････････････････ 88　E 5
青葉インターナショナルスクール　Aoba Int'l Sch. ･･ 20　B 6
青山円形劇場　Aoyama Round Theater ････ 80　C 3
青山学院大学　Aoyama Gakuin Univ. ･･････ 54　D 6
青山学院大学（厚木）　Aoyama Gakuin Univ. (Atsugi) ･･ 74　A 7
青山学院大学（理工）　Aoyama Gakuin Univ. (Sci. & Engn.) ･･ 74　E 3
青山劇場　Aoyama Theater ････････････････ 54　C 5
青山霊園　Aoyama Cemetery ･･････････････ 55　H 3
赤坂公会堂　Akasaka Public Hall ･･････････ 46　A 5
赤坂御所　Akasaka Palace ････････････････ 21　G 1
赤坂センタービル　Akasaka Center Bldg ･･ 46　A 4
赤坂郵便局　Akasaka Post Office ･･････････ 48　B 7
赤門　Akamon ･････････････････････････････ 16　B 1
秋葉原電気器具街　Akihabara Electrical Stores Street ･･ 33　H 3
浅草演芸ホール　Asakusa Engei Hall ･･････ 31　F 4
浅草観音堂　Asakusa Knnondō ････････････ 31　H 3
浅草公会堂　Asakusa Public Hall ･････････ 31　H 4
浅草巧芸堂　Asakusa Handicrafts Museum ･･ 31　F 3
浅草松竹　Asakusa Shōchiku ･･････････････ 31　G 4
浅草神社　Asakusa Jinja ･･････････････････ 31　I 3
浅草東映　Asakusa Tōei ･･･････････････････ 31　G 2
浅草東宝　Asakusa Tōhō ･･･････････････････ 31　G 3
浅草風俗歴史館　Asakusa Museum ････････ 31　H 3
浅草文化観光センター　Asakusa Tourist Info. Center ･･･ 31　H 5
浅草郵便局　Asakusa Post Office ･････････ 31　F 6
朝倉彫塑館　Asakura Choso Museum ･･････ 85　I 4
朝日新聞社　Asahi Newspapers ････････････ 18　C 3
朝日生命（本社）　Asahi Mutual Life Insurance (H. O.) ･･ 56　D 4

朝日生命ホール　Asahi Seimei Hall ･･･････ 56　D 4
麻布グリーン会館　Azabu Green Kaikan ･･ 49　G 1
麻布大学（獣医）　Azabu Univ. (Veterinary) ･･ 74　B 5
麻布郵便局　Azabu Post Office ･･･････････ 49　H 1
亜細亜大学　Asia Univ. ･･･････････････････ 74　D 3
味の素（本社）　Ajinomoto (H. O.) ･･･････ 37　I 1
飛鳥山公園　Asukayama Park ･･････････････ 25　I 1
愛宕神社　Atago Jinja ･･････････････････････ 80　D 5
足立区役所　Adachi Ward Office ･････････ 8　C 5
厚木飛行場　Atsugi Airfield ･･･････････････ 60　A 5
跡見学園女子大学　Atomi Gakuen Women's Univ. ･･ 74　D 1
穴八幡神社　Ana-Hachiman Jinja ･･････････ 23　E 2
新井薬師　Arai Yakushi ･･･････････････････ 83　F 3
荒川区役所　Arakawa Ward Office ･･･････ 27　F 3
荒川自然公園　Arakawa Natural Park ･･････ 27　F 2
荒川総合スポーツセンター　Arakawa Sports Center ･･ 27　G 3
有明コロシアム　Ariake Colosseum ･･････ 83　G 4
有明テニスの森公園　Ariake Tennis-no-mori Park ･･ 7　G 5
有栖川宮記念公園　Prince Arisugawa Mem. Park ･･ 21　F 6

い

イイノホール　Iino Hall ･･･････････････････ 47　I 7
飯野ビル　Iino Bldg ･･･････････････････････ 47　I 7
医学文化館　House of Medical Treasures ･･ 86　A 1
井草八幡宮　Igusa Hachimangū ･･･････････ 10　B 4
生田緑地　Ikuta Green ････････････････････ 82　D 4
池袋スカラ座　Ikebukuro scala-za ･･･････ 59　E 3
池袋東急　Ikebukuro Tōkyū ･･･････････････ 59　E 3
池袋東宝　Ikebukuro Tōhō ････････････････ 59　G 5
池袋パルコ　Ikebukuro Parco ･･･････････ 58　E 4
石橋メモリアルホール　Ishibashi Memorial Hall ･･ 17　F 1
伊勢丹デパート　Isetan Dept Store ･･････ 57　H 4
伊勢丹美術館　Isetan Museum of Art ･･････ 57　H 3
板橋区役所　Itabashi Ward Office ･･･････ 24　D 1
板橋区立郷土資料館　Folk Musm of Itabashi Ward ･･ 87　E 2
板橋郵便局　Itabashi Post Office ･･･････････ 24　E 1
市谷八幡神社　Ichigaya-Hachiman Jinja ･･ 23　H 5
一葉記念館　Ichiyō Mem. Hall ･･･････････ 27　G 5
出光美術館　Idemitsu Art Gallery ･･･････ 37　J 6
井の頭公園　Inokashira Park ･･･････････････ 10　A 5

井の頭自然文化園　Inokashira Natural Cultural Garden‥ 10　A5
岩崎博物館　Iwasaki Museum ‥‥‥‥‥‥‥‥‥‥‥ 63　H6
岩波ホール　Iwanami Hall ‥‥‥‥‥‥‥‥‥‥‥‥ 32　C4

う

上野学園大学　Ueno Gakuen Univ. ‥‥‥‥‥‥‥‥‥ 17　F1
上野公園　Ueno Park ‥‥‥‥‥‥‥‥‥‥‥‥‥‥ 26　E7
上野郵便局　Ueno Post Office ‥‥‥‥‥‥‥‥‥‥ 69　I5
上野松竹　Ueno Shōchiku ‥‥‥‥‥‥‥‥‥‥‥‥ 30　B3
上野宝塚　Ueno Takarazuka ‥‥‥‥‥‥‥‥‥‥‥ 30　B3
上野動物園　Ueno Zoo (Ueno Zoological Gardens) ‥‥ 26　D7
上野東宝　Ueno Tōhō ‥‥‥‥‥‥‥‥‥‥‥‥‥‥ 30　B3
上野の森美術館　Ueno Royal Museum ‥‥‥‥‥‥‥ 30　B2
牛込郵便局　Ushigome Post Office ‥‥‥‥‥‥‥‥ 23　H3
梅若能楽堂　Umewaka Noh Theater ‥‥‥‥‥‥‥‥ 11　F5

え

abc会館ホール　abc Kaikan Hall ‥‥‥‥‥‥‥‥‥ 80　D6
AIU赤坂ビル　AIU Akasaka Bldg ‥‥‥‥‥‥‥‥‥ 46　B4
AIGビル　AIG Bldg ‥‥‥‥‥‥‥‥‥‥‥‥‥‥ 36　E5
FM東京ホール　FM Tokyo Hall ‥‥‥‥‥‥‥‥‥ 47　E1
NHK放送センター　NHK Broadcasting Center ‥‥‥ 20　B3
NHK放送博物館　NHK Broadcast Museum ‥‥‥‥ 18　A3
NHKホール　NHK Hall ‥‥‥‥‥‥‥‥‥‥‥‥ 80　C2
NKKビル　NKK Bldg ‥‥‥‥‥‥‥‥‥‥‥‥‥ 36　D5
NTT日比谷ビル　NTT Hibiya Bldg ‥‥‥‥‥‥‥‥ 38　B3
エムザ有明　MZA Ariake ‥‥‥‥‥‥‥‥‥‥‥‥ 83　G4
永代橋　Eitai-bashi ‥‥‥‥‥‥‥‥‥‥‥‥‥‥ 19　F1
回向院（南千住）　Ekō-in (Minami-senju) ‥‥‥‥‥ 27　H4
回向院（両国）　Ekō-in (Ryōgoku) ‥‥‥‥‥‥‥‥ 17　G5
越中島公園　Etchūjima Park ‥‥‥‥‥‥‥‥‥‥‥ 19　G2
江戸川区役所　Edogawa Ward Office ‥‥‥‥‥‥‥ 9　G3
江戸川総合レクリエーション公園　Edogawa Recreation Park‥ 9　J2
江戸・東京博物館　Edo-Tokyo Musm ‥‥‥‥‥‥‥ 17　H4
荏原神社　Ebara Jinja ‥‥‥‥‥‥‥‥‥‥‥‥‥ 29　G5
恵比寿ガーデンプレイス　Ebisu Garden Place ‥‥‥ 51　F3
炎天寺　Enten-ji ‥‥‥‥‥‥‥‥‥‥‥‥‥‥‥ 8　B6
円融寺　En'yū-ji ‥‥‥‥‥‥‥‥‥‥‥‥‥‥‥ 13　F3

お

O美術館　O Art Musm ‥‥‥‥‥‥‥‥‥‥‥‥ 29　F5
オーアーゲーホール　OAG Hall ‥‥‥‥‥‥‥‥‥ 48　B6
オーチャードホール　Orchard Hall ‥‥‥‥‥‥‥‥ 52　B4
オリンピック記念青少年総合センター　Nat'l Olympic Mem. Youth Center‥ 20　B1
鷗外記念図書館　Ōga Mem. Library ‥‥‥‥‥‥‥‥ 26　B5
王子製紙　Ōji Paper ‥‥‥‥‥‥‥‥‥‥‥‥‥‥ 39・F3
桜美林大学　Ōbirin Coll. ‥‥‥‥‥‥‥‥‥‥‥‥ 15　F6
旺文社　Ōbunsha ‥‥‥‥‥‥‥‥‥‥‥‥‥‥‥ 23　H3
大井競馬場　Ōi Racecourse ‥‥‥‥‥‥‥‥‥‥‥ 13　J4
大井ふ頭　Ōi Futō ‥‥‥‥‥‥‥‥‥‥‥‥‥‥ 13　J4
大川端リバーシティ2　Ōkawabata River City 21 ‥‥ 19　F3
大国魂神社　Ōkunitama Jinja ‥‥‥‥‥‥‥‥‥‥ 82　C3

大倉集古館　Ōkura Museum ‥‥‥‥‥‥‥‥‥‥ 48　E1
大蔵省印刷局記念館　Mem. Museum of Printing Bureau ‥‥‥ 23　G4
大倉山梅林　Ōkurayama Japanese Apricot Garden‥‥‥ 61　F3
大崎ニューシティ　Ōsaki New City ‥‥‥‥‥‥‥ 29　F5
大崎郵便局　Ōsaki Post Office ‥‥‥‥‥‥‥‥‥ 28　D4
太田記念美術館　Ōta Mem. Musm of Art ‥‥‥‥‥ 54　B2
大田区役所　Ōta Ward Office ‥‥‥‥‥‥‥‥‥‥ 13　H5
大妻女子大学　Ōtsuma Women's Univ. ‥‥‥‥‥‥ 23　I5
大手センタービル　Ōte Center Bldg ‥‥‥‥‥‥‥ 36　D5
大手町ファーストスクエア　Ōtemachi First Square ‥‥‥ 36　D4
大手町ビル　Ōtemachi Bldg ‥‥‥‥‥‥‥‥‥‥‥ 36　D4
大通公園　Ōdōri Park ‥‥‥‥‥‥‥‥‥‥‥‥‥ 62　D6
大鷲神社（足立区）　Ōtori Jinja (Adachi-ku) ‥‥‥ 8　A5
鷲神社（台東区）　Ōtori Jinja (Taitō-ku) ‥‥‥‥‥ 27　G6
大鳥神社（目黒区）　Ōtori Jinja (Meguro-ku) ‥‥‥ 28　B3
大宮八幡　Ōmiya Hachiman ‥‥‥‥‥‥‥‥‥‥‥ 10　D6
岡倉天心記念公園　Tenshin Okakura Mem. Park ‥‥‥ 26　C5
大仏次郎記念館　Jirō Osaragi Mem. Museum ‥‥‥ 63 (H6)
お台場海浜公園　Odaiba Kaihin Park ‥‥‥‥‥‥‥ 13　J2
小田急エース　Odakyū Ace ‥‥‥‥‥‥‥‥‥‥‥ 56　E4
小田急デパート　Odakyū Dept Store ‥‥‥‥‥‥‥ 57　F4
小田急ハルク　Odakyū Halc ‥‥‥‥‥‥‥‥‥‥‥ 56　E3
落合中央公園　Ochiai Central Park ‥‥‥‥‥‥‥‥ 22　B1
お茶の水女子大学　Ochanomizu Univ. ‥‥‥‥‥‥ 25　H7

か

カザルスホール　Casals Hall ‥‥‥‥‥‥‥‥‥‥ 32　E4
ガスの科学館　Gas Science Center ‥‥‥‥‥‥‥‥ 87　G4
ガスホール　Gas Hall ‥‥‥‥‥‥‥‥‥‥‥‥‥ 38　E5
がす資料館　Gas Museum ‥‥‥‥‥‥‥‥‥‥‥ 86　D2
かっぱ橋道具街　Kappabashi Kitchenware Town ‥‥‥ 17　G1
絵画館（聖徳記念絵画館）　Meiji Mem. Picture Gallery‥ 21　F1
外交史料館　Diplomatic Record Office ‥‥‥‥‥‥ 49　H2
花王（本社）　Kaō Corp. (H. O.) ‥‥‥‥‥‥‥‥‥ 35　G1
科学技術館　Science Museum ‥‥‥‥‥‥‥‥‥‥ 16　A5
学士会館　Gakushi Kaikan ‥‥‥‥‥‥‥‥‥‥‥ 32　D6
学習院大学　Gakushūin Univ. ‥‥‥‥‥‥‥‥‥‥ 24　D6
家具の博物館　Furniture Museum ‥‥‥‥‥‥‥‥‥ 18　E5
葛西臨海公園　Kasai-rinkai Park ‥‥‥‥‥‥‥‥‥ 7　I5
葛西臨海水族園　Tokyo Sea Life Park ‥‥‥‥‥‥‥ 87　H4
鹿島ビル　Kajima Bldg ‥‥‥‥‥‥‥‥‥‥‥‥‥ 46　B4
霞が関ビル　Kasumigaseki Bldg ‥‥‥‥‥‥‥‥‥ 47　F6
勝鬨橋　Kachidoki-bashi ‥‥‥‥‥‥‥‥‥‥‥‥ 18　D4
葛飾区役所　Katsushika Ward Office ‥‥‥‥‥‥‥ 8　E4
神奈川県近代文学館　Kanagawa Pref. Musm of Modern Literature‥ 63　I6
神奈川県民ホール　Kanagawa Kenmin Hall ‥‥‥‥ 63　G5
神奈川県立音楽堂　Kanagawa Pref. Concert Hall ‥‥ 62　D4
神奈川県立青少年センター　Kanagawa Pref. Youth Center‥ 62　D4
神奈川県立図書館　Kanagawa Pref. Library ‥‥‥‥ 62　D4
神奈川県立博物館　Kanagawa Pref. Museum ‥‥‥‥ 63　E4
神奈川県立武道館　Kanagawa Pref. Budōkan Gym. ‥ 83　E6
神奈川工科大学　Kanagawa Inst. of Tech. ‥‥‥‥‥ 74　A6

神奈川大学　Kanagawa Univ. ……………… 61　F4
歌舞伎座　Kabuki-za……………………… 39　G4
歌舞伎町東映　Kabukichō Tōei …………… 57　F2
雷門　Kaminarimon ………………………… 31　H5
紙の博物館　Paper Museum ……………… 87　G2
亀戸天神　Kameido Tenjin ………………… 9　G5
掃部山公園　Kamon'yama Park …………… 62　D3
川崎球場　Kawasaki Stadium ……………… 61　H3
川崎競馬場　Kawasaki Racecourse ……… 83　F5
川崎市民ミュージアム　Kawasaki City Museum … 86　E5
川崎大師　Kawasaki Daishi ………………… 61　I3
寛永寺　Kan'ei-ji …………………………… 26　E6
癌研究会付属病院　Cencer Institute Hosp.… 25　F3
観世能楽堂　Kanze Noh Theater ………… 52　A2
神田外語学院　Kanda Inst. of Foreign Languages … 33　G6
神田書店街　Kanda Bookshops Area …… 32　C4
神田明神　Kanda Myōjin …………………… 33　G1
神田郵便局　Kanda Post Office …………… 33　G4
関内ホール　Kannai Hall …………………… 63　F5

き

キリンビール（本社）　Kirin Breweries(H. O.) … 54　A3
紀尾井町ビル　kioichō Bldg ………………… 46　B1
岸記念体育館　Kishi Mem. Gym. ………… 20　C3
鬼子母神堂（下谷）　Kishimojin-dō(Shitaya) … 27　F6
鬼子母神堂（雑司が谷）　Kishimojin-dō(Zōshigaya) … 24　E6
北区役所　Kita Ward Office ………………… 11　H2
北里大学　Kitasato Univ. …………………… 21　G7
北里大学（相模原）　Kitasato Univ.(Sagamihara) … 74　B5
北の丸公園　Kitanomaru Nat'l Garden …… 16　A5
喜多六平太記念能楽堂　Kita Roppeita Mem. Noh Theater … 80　A5
砧公園　Kinuta Park ………………………… 12　C2
紀ノ国屋（スーパーマーケット）　Kinokuniya International … 54　D5
紀伊国屋書店　Kinokuniya Bookstore …… 57　G4
紀伊国屋ホール　Kinokuniya Hall ………… 57　G4
旧芝離宮庭園　Kyū Shibarikyū Garden … 18　B5
旧古河庭園　Kyū Furukawa Garden……… 25　J2
旧安田庭園　Kyū Yasuda Garden ………… 17　G4
教育会館　Kyōiku Kaikan …………………… 32　B5
教育の森公園　Kyōikuno-mori Park ……… 25　H6
共同印刷（本社）　kyōdō Printing(H. O.) … 25　J7
共同通信社　Kyōdō News Service ……… 21　I2
京橋会館　Kyōbashi Kaikan ……………… 39　I2
京橋郵便局　Kyōbashi Post Office ……… 39　H6
共立講堂　Kyōritsu Kōdō …………………… 32　C6
共立女子大学（神田）　Kyōritsu Women's Univ.(Kanda) … 32　B5
共立女子大学（八王子）　Kyōritsu Women's Univ.(Hachiōji) … 74　A4
共立薬科大学　Kyōritsu Coll. of Pharm. … 18　A4
杏林大学（医学）　Kyōrin Univ.(Med.) …… 75　I5
杏林大学（保健、社会）　Kyōrin Univ.(Health, Social Sciences) … 14　C3
清澄庭園　Kiyosumi Garden ……………… 9　H5
清水観音堂　Kiyomizu Kannondō ………… 30　A2

銀座コア　Ginza Core ……………………… 39　F4
銀座小松　Ginza Komatsu ………………… 38　E4
銀座みゆき館劇場　Ginza Miyuki-kan Theater … 38　D3
銀座能楽堂　Ginza Noh Theater ………… 38　D4
銀座メルサ　Ginza Melsa …………………… 39　G2

く

グランドヒル市ケ谷　Grand Hill Ichigaya … 23　H5
クリスチャンアカデミー　Christian Academy … 15　I1
グリーンタワービル　Green Tower Bldg …… 56　A4
グリーンホール　Green Hall ………………… 82　D4
九段会館　Kudan Kaikan …………………… 32　A5
九段郵便局　Kudan Post Office …………… 32　A5
国立音楽大学　Kunitachi Coll. of Music … 74　C2
熊谷守一美術館　Kumagai Morikazu Art Museum … 24　A4
弘明寺　Gumyō-ji …………………………… 60　E7
久米美術館　Kume Art Museum ………… 28　C2
栗田美術館　Kurita Museum ……………… 85　G7

け

KDD（国際電信電話）ビル　KDD Bldg …… 56　C6
けやきホール　Keyaki Hall ………………… 82　D3
慶応大学（日吉）　Keiō Univ.(Hiyoshi) … 61　G2
慶応大学（三田）　Keiō Univ.(Mita) ……… 21　I6
慶応大学（四ツ谷）　Keiō Univ.(Yotsuya) … 23　F7
京王デパート　Keiō Dept Store …………… 57　E5
慶応病院　Keiō(Univ.)Hosp. ……………… 23　F7
京王モール　Keiō Mall ……………………… 56　E5
芸術座　Geijutsu-za ………………………… 38　C3
恵泉女学園大学　Keisen Jogakuen Univ. … 74　C4
経団連　Federation of Economic Orgs …… 36　B3
迎賓館　State Guesthouse ………………… 21　G1
源空寺　Genkū-ji …………………………… 17　F1
建設共済会館　Kensetsu Kyōsai Kaikan … 55　F5
健保会館　Kenpo Kaikan …………………… 48　E7

こ

こどもの国　Nat'l Children's Land ………… 60　B2
こどもの城　Nat'l Children's Castle ……… 54　C5
こまばエミナース　Komaba Eminence …… 88　B2
小石川後楽園　Koishikawa Kōrakuen …… 12　A2
小石川植物園　Koishikawa Botanical Garden … 25　I6
小石川郵便局　Koishikawa Post Office … 69　H3
工学院大学　Kōgakuin Univ. ……………… 56　D5
工学院大学（八王子）　Kōgakuin Univ.(Hachiōji) … 14　C3
皇居　Imperial Palace ……………………… 16　A7
皇居外苑　Imperial Palace Outer Garden … 37　G7
皇居東御苑　Eastern Garden of the Imperial Palace … 16　B6
航空会館　Aviation Bldg …………………… 38　A5
公庫ビル　Kōko Bldg ……………………… 36　B4
麹町郵便局　Kōjimachi Post Office ……… 69　F4
厚生年金会館　Kōsei Nenkin Hall ……… 22　D5

厚生年金病院　Kōsei Nenkin Hosp. ……………………… 23　I3
講談社　Kōdansha ……………………………………… 25　G7
交通博物館　Transportation Museum ………………… 33　G4
講道館　Kōdōkan ………………………………………… 16　A2
江東区役所　Kotō Ward Office ……………………… 9　H5
合同庁舎（大手町）　Common Gov't Bldg（Ōtemachi）…… 36　B5
合同庁舎（霞ケ関）　Common Gov't Bldg（Kasumigaseki）… 47　G6
豪徳寺　Gōtoku-ji ……………………………………… 12　E1
後楽園ホール　Kōrakuen Hall ………………………… 16　A3
後楽園ゆうえんち　Kōrakuen Amusement Park ……… 16　A2
興和インターナショナルビル　Kōwa Int'l Bldg ……… 21　F4
小金井公園　Koganei Park …………………………… 15　H2
国会議事堂　Nat'l Diet Bldg ………………………… 47　F4
国学院大学　Kokugakuin Univ. ……………………… 20　E5
国技館　Sumō Stadium ………………………………… 17　G4
国際赤坂ビル　Kokusai Akasaka Bldg ……………… 46　D6
国際科学技術財団　Science & Technology Foundation of Japan … 92　E6
国際基督教大学　Int'l Christian Univ. ……………… 75　H6
国際交流基金　Japan Foundation …………………… 48　E2
国際新赤坂ビル　Kokusai Shin Akasaka Bldg ……… 46　C6
国際電信電話ビル　KDD Bldg ………………………… 56　C6
国際ビル　Kokusai Bldg ……………………………… 37　I6
国際文化会館　Int'l House of Japan ………………… 49　I4
国際文化フォーラム　Japan Forum …………………… 93　F4
（東京）国際貿易センター　Tokyo Int'l Trade Center … 18　D6
国士館大学（世田谷）　Kokushikan Univ.（Setagaya）… 12　E2
国士館大学（鶴川）　Kokushikan Univ.（Tsurukawa）… 74　C4
国分寺万葉植物園　Man'yō Garden of Kokubunji …… 15　G3
国立大蔵病院　Nat'l Ōkura Hosp. …………………… 12　C2
国立科学博物館　Nat'l Science Museum …………… 30　C1
国立がんセンター　Nat'l Cancer Center …………… 39　G7
国立教育会館　Nat'l Education Center ……………… 47　G7
国立競技場　Nat'l Stadium …………………………… 20　E1
国立劇場　National Theater ………………………… 46　E2
国立公文書館　Nat'l Archives ………………………… 32　B7
国立国会図書館　Nat'l Diet Library ………………… 47　F3
国立埼玉病院　Nat'l Saitama Hosp. ………………… 10　C1
国立自然教育園　Nat'l Park for Nature Study ……… 28　D2
国立小児病院　Nat'l Children's Hosp. ……………… 13　F1
国立西洋美術館　Nat'l Musm of Western Art ……… 30　B1
国立天文台　Nat'l Astronomical Observatory ……… 6　A4
国立東京第二病院　Nat'l Tokyo No. 2 Hospital …… 13　F2
国立中野病院　Nat'l Nakano Hosp. ………………… 11　E4
国立西が丘競技場　Nat'l Nishigaoka Stadium ……… 11　G1
国立能楽堂　Nat'l Noh Theater ……………………… 80　D2
国立病院医療センター　Nat'l Hosp. Medical Service Center … 22　E3
国立代々木競技場　Nat'l Yoyogi Gymnasium ……… 20　C3
護国寺　Gokoku-ji ……………………………………… 25　G6
古代オリエント博物館　Ancient Orient Museum …… 59　I5
小平霊園　Kodaira Cemetery ………………………… 15　H2
国会議事堂　National Diet Bldg ……………………… 47　F5
御殿山ヒルズ　Gotenyama Hills ……………………… 29　F5

五島美術館　Gotoh Art Museum …………………… 12　D3
五島プラネタリウム　Gotoh Planetarium …………… 53　G5
五百羅漢寺　Gohyaku-Rakan-ji ……………………… 28　B3
駒沢大学　Komazawa Univ. ………………………… 12　E2
駒沢大学（玉川）　Komazawa Univ.（Tamagawa）… 12　C3
駒沢オリンピック公園　Komazawa Olympic Park …… 12　E3
駒場公園　Komaba Park ……………………………… 11　F7

さ
サイエンスビル　Science Bldg ………………………… 46　D6
サッポロビール　Sapporo Breweries ………………… 38　E5
サンケイ会館　Sankei Kaikan ………………………… 36　C3
サンケイ（産業経済）新聞社　Sankei Newspapers … 36　C3
サンシャイン劇場　Sunshine Theater ……………… 59　I5
サンシャイン国際水族館　Sunshine Aquarium ……… 59　I5
サンシャインシティ　Sunshine City ………………… 59　H4
サンシャインプラネタリウム　Sunshine Planetarium … 59　I5
サンシャイン60　Sunshine 60 ……………………… 59　H4
サンタマリアスクール　Santa Maria Sch. …………… 10　C3
サントリー美術館　Suntory Musm of Art …………… 46　B3
サントリーホール　Suntory Hall ……………………… 48　E2
サンプラザ　Sun Plaza ………………………………… 11　E5
サンモールインターナショナルスクール　St Maur Int'l Sch. … 63　H7
サンヨー赤坂ビル　San'yō Akasaka Bldg …………… 46　C5
サンリオ・ピューロランド　Sanrio Puroland ………… 82　C4
さくら銀行（本店）　Sakura Bank（H. O.）…………… 32　A5
さくら銀行（東京営業部）　Sakura Bank（M. O.）… 38　C2
相模女子大学　Sagami Women's Coll. ……………… 74　C5
桜田門　Sakuradamon ………………………………… 47　I3
桜橋　Sakura-bashi …………………………………… 27　I7
実篤公園　Saneatsu Park …………………………… 82　E4
砂防会館　Sabō Kaikan ……………………………… 46　D3
狭山湖　Sayama-ko …………………………………… 15　F1
三愛　San'ai …………………………………………… 39　E3
産業安全技術館　Industrial Safety & Technical Musm … 84　C6
三渓園　Sankei-en …………………………………… 61　G7
三省堂書店　Sanseidō Bookstore …………………… 32　D4
三殿台遺跡　Santonodai Prehistoric Site ………… 61　F6
山王グランドビル　Sannō Grand Bldg ……………… 46　C4

し
シネヴィヴァン　Cine Vivant ………………………… 49　H6
ジャパンインターナショナルスクール　Japan Int'l Sch. … 20　D3
ジャパンタイムズ　The Japan Times ………………… 29　H1
シルク博物館　Silk Museum ………………………… 63　(G4)
JAビル　JA Bldg ……………………………………… 36　C3
JBPオーバル　JBP Oval ……………………………… 54　D5
JR（本社）　JR（H. O.）……………………………… 22　C6
JTB日本交通公社（本社）　JTB（H. O.）…………… 36　E3
塩船観音　Shiofune Kannon ………………………… 82　A1
慈恵医大病院　Jikei Univ. Hosp. …………………… 18　A4
時事通信社　Jiji Press ………………………………… 47　J7

資生堂ザ・ギンザ　Shiseidō The Ginza ……… 38　D5
下町風俗資料館　Shitamachi Museum ……… 30　A4
下谷神社　Shitaya Jinja ……… 17　F1
自転車文化センター　Bicycle Culture Center ……… 84　D5
実践女子大学　Jissen Women's Univ. ……… 74　B3
品川区役所　Shinagawa Ward Office ……… 29　F7
品川神社　Shinagawa Jinja ……… 29　G5
品川ふ頭　Shinagawa Wharf ……… 29　J3
不忍池　Shinobazuno-ike ……… 16　D1
芝浦工業大学　Shibaura Inst. of Tech. ……… 29　H1
芝公園　Shiba Park ……… 18　A5
芝青年館ホール　Shiba Seinenkan Hall ……… 80　C6
芝大神宮　Shiba Daijingū ……… 18　A5
柴又帝釈天　Shibamata Taishakuten ……… 8　D2
芝郵便局　Shiba Post Office ……… 68　D5
渋谷区役所　Shibuya Ward Office ……… 52　D1
渋谷公会堂　Shibuya Public Hall ……… 52　D1
渋谷宝塚　Shibuya Takarazuka ……… 52　E4
渋谷東映　Shibuya Tōei ……… 53　F4
渋谷東急　Shibuya Tōkyu ……… 53　F5
渋谷パルコ　Shibuya Parco ……… 52　D3
渋谷郵便局　Shibuya Post Office ……… 54　B6
石神井公園　Shakujii Park ……… 10　C3
衆議院憲政記念館　Parliamentary Museum ……… 47　F3
自由劇場　Jiyū Theater ……… 21　F4
首都高速道路公団　Tokyo Expwy Public Corp. ……… 47　H7
順天堂医院　Juntendō Hosp. ……… 32　E1
順天堂大学　Juntendō Univ. ……… 32　D1
小学館　Shōgakukan ……… 32　C5
浄真寺（九品仏）　Jōshin-ji (Kuhonbutsu) ……… 12　E3
松竹会館　Shōchiku Kaikan ……… 39　H5
上智大学　Sophia Univ. ……… 46　A1
上智大学（神学）　Sophia Univ. (Theol.) ……… 74　E2
松涛美術館　Shōtō Art Museum ……… 52　A5
城北中央公園　Jōhoku Central Park ……… 11　F2
昭和音楽大学　Shōwa Academia Musicae ……… 74　B6
昭和記念公園　Shōwa Mem. Park ……… 15　E3
昭和女子大学　Shōwa Women's Univ. ……… 13　F2
昭和大学　Shōwa Univ. ……… 13　G3
昭和薬科大学　Shōwa Coll. of Pharm. ……… 15　G7
女子栄養短大　Kagawa Nutrition Junior Coll. ……… 25　J3
女子美術大学　Women's Coll. of Fine Arts ……… 75　E3
書道博物館　Musm of Calligraphy ……… 26　E6
白百合女子大学　Shirayuri Women's College ……… 74　E3
新青山ビル　New Aoyama Bldg ……… 76　D4
新江戸川公園　Shin Edogawa Park ……… 23　F1
新大手町ビル　New Ōtemachi Bldg ……… 36　D3
神宮外苑　Meiji Jingū Outer Gardens ……… 21　F1
神宮球場　Jingū Stadium ……… 21　F2
新国際ビル　New Kokusai Bldg ……… 37　J5
新宿アイランド　Shinjuku i-Land ……… 56　C3
新宿Lタワー　Shinjuku L Tower ……… 56　D4

新宿NSビル　Shinjuku NS Bldg ……… 56　D6
新宿北郵便局　Shinjuku-Kita Post Office ……… 69　F1
新宿御苑　Shinjuku Imperial Gardens ……… 22　D6
新宿区役所　Shinjuku Ward Office ……… 57　G2
新宿グランドオデヲン座　Shinjuku Grand Odeon-za ……… 57　F1
新宿国際ビル　Shinjuku Kokusai Bldg ……… 56　A3
新宿コマ劇場　Shinjuku Koma Theater ……… 57　G2
新宿サブナード　Shinjuku Subnade ……… 57　G3
新宿松竹　Shinjuku Shōchiku ……… 57　H3
新宿スカラ座　Shinjuku Scala-za ……… 57　I4
新宿スポーツセンター　Shinjuku Sports Center ……… 22　D2
新宿住友ビル　Shinjuku Sumitomo Bldg ……… 56　B4
新宿センタービル　Shinjuku Center Bldg ……… 56　C4
新宿第一生命ビル　Shinjuku Daiichi Seimei Bldg ……… 56　A4
新宿中央公園　Shinjuku Central Park ……… 56　A5
新宿東映　Shinjuku Tōei ……… 57　I5
新宿東急　Shinjuku Tōkyu ……… 57　F1
新宿野村ビル　Shinjuku Nomura Bldg ……… 56　C3
新宿パークタワー　Shinjuku Park Tower ……… 22　A6
新宿ピカデリー　Shinjuku Piccadilly ……… 57　H3
新宿プラザ　Shinjuku Plaza ……… 57　G2
新宿文化シネマ　Shinjuku Bunka Cinema ……… 57　I4
新宿文化センター　Shinjuku Culture Center ……… 22　D4
新宿三井ビル　Shinjuku Mitsui Bldg ……… 56　C4
新宿ミラノ座　Shinjuku Milano-za ……… 57　F1
新宿武蔵野館　Shinjuku Musashino-kan ……… 57　G4
新宿モノリス　Shinjuku Monolith ……… 56　C6
新宿郵便局　Shinjuku Post Office ……… 56　D5
新宿歴史博物館　Shinjuku Historical Musm ……… 23　G5
神代植物公園　Jindai Botanical Park ……… 15　I4
深大寺　Jindai-ji ……… 15　I4
新東京国際空港（成田）　New Tokyo Int'l Airport (Narita) ……… 155
新東京ビル　New Tokyo Bldg ……… 37　I5
新東京郵便局　New Tokyo P. O. ……… 9　I4
新日石ビル　Shin Nisseki Bldg ……… 37　I5
新日本製鉄（本社）　Nippon Steel Corp. (H. O.) ……… 36　E1
新橋演舞場　Shimbashi Enbujō ……… 39　G6
新橋郵便局　Shimbashi Post Office ……… 38　D6
新日比谷ビル　Shinhibiya Bldg ……… 38　A4
新丸の内ビル　New Marunouchi Bldg ……… 37　F4
新有楽町ビル　New Yūrakuchō Bldg ……… 38　D1

す

スカラ座　Scala-za ……… 38　C2
ストライプハウス美術館　Striped House Musm ……… 49　H4
スパイラルビル　Spiral Bldg ……… 54　E5
水天宮　Suitengū ……… 17　F7
末広亭　Suehiro-tei ……… 57　I4
巣鴨郵便局　Sugamo Post Office ……… 69　I2
杉並区役所　Suginami Ward Office ……… 10　D5
杉並公会堂　Suginami Public Hall ……… 10　C5
杉野学園衣裳博物館　Costume Museum ……… 28　C3

杉野講堂　Sugino Kōdō ……………………… 28　D2
杉野女子大学　Sugino Women's Coll. ……… 28　C3
数寄屋橋阪急デパート　Sukiyabashi Hankyū Dept Store …… 38　D3
鈴本演芸場　Suzumoto Engeijō ……………… 30　A5
墨田区役所　Sumida Ward Office……………… 17　I1
隅田公園　Sumida Park ……………………… 17　I1
住友銀行東京本部ビル　Sumitomo Bank Tokyo H. O. Bldg …… 36　D5
住友商事　Sumitomo Corp. …………………… 32　C6
住吉神社（佃）　Sumiyoshi Jinja …………… 19　F3
相撲博物館　Sumō Museum ………………… 85　H7

せ

セゾン美術館　Sezon Museum of Art……… 58　D6
セントジョセフカレッジ　St. Joseph College … 63　H7
セントメリーズインターナショナルスクール　St. Mary's Int'l Sch. …… 12　D3
聖イグナチオ教会　St. Ignatius Church …… 23　H6
静嘉堂文庫　Seikadō Library ……………… 12　C3
成蹊大学　Seikei Univ. ……………………… 10　A4
精工舎　Seikōsha ……………………………… 9　G5
青松寺　Seishō-ji …………………………… 18　A4
成城大学　Seijō Univ.………………………… 12　B2
聖心女子大学　Univ. of Sacred Heart …… 21　F6
清泉インターナショナルスクール　Seisen Int'l Sch. …… 12　D3
清泉女子大学　Seisen Women's Coll. ……… 28　E4
聖徳記念絵画館　Meiji Mem. Picture Gallery … 21　F1
聖路加ガーデン　St. Luke's Garden ……… 18　E3
西武園　Seibuen ……………………………… 15　F1
西武デパート（池袋店）　Seibu Dept Store (Ikebukuro) … 58　D5
西武デパート（渋谷店）　Seibu Dept Store (Shibuya) … 52　E4
西武デパート（有楽町店）　Seibu Dept Store (Yūrakuchō) … 38　E2
西武ライオンズ球場　Seibu Lions Stadium…… 82　C2
聖マリアンナ医科大学　St. Marianna Med. Coll. … 74　D4
聖路加看護大学　St. Luke's Nursing Coll. … 73　F7
聖路加病院　St. Luke's Hosp. ……………… 18　E3
世界のカバン館　World Bag Museum ……… 31　H7
世界貿易センタービル　World Trade Center Bldg … 18　B5
世田谷区役所　Setagaya Ward Office ……… 12　E1
世田谷区立世田谷美術館　Setagaya Art Museum … 12　D2
泉岳寺　Sengaku-ji …………………………… 29　F2
全国伝統的工芸品センター　Japan Traditional Crafts Center … 55　F2
千秋文庫　Senshū Bunko …………………… 85　F4
専修大学（生田）　Senshū Univ. (Ikuta) … 74　D4
専修大学（神田）　Senshū Univ. (Kanda) … 32　B4
浅草寺　Sensō-ji …………………………… 31　H3
洗足学園大学　Senzoku Gakuen Univ. …… 74　E4
洗足公園　Senzoku Park …………………… 13　F4
全特会館　Zentoku Kaikan ………………… 49　G2
全日本空手道連盟　Japan Karatedō Federation …… 92　(E5)
全日本剣道連盟　All Japan Kendō Federation … 93　H7
善福寺公園　Zempukuji Park ……………… 10　B4

そ

ソニー（本社）　Sony (H. O.) ……………… 29　F4
ソニービル　Sony Bldg ……………………… 38　E3
そごうデパート（東京店）　Sogō Dept Store (Tokyo) … 38　E1
そごうデパート（横浜店）　Sogō Dept Store (Yokohama) … 62　D1
そごう美術館　Sogō Art Museum ………… 86　E6
創価学会　Sōka Gakkai ……………………… 23　F7
創価大学　Sōka Univ. ……………………… 14　D3
草月会館　Sōgetsu Art Center ……………… 48　B6
雑司が谷霊園　Zōshigaya Cemetery ……… 25　F6
総持寺　Sōji-ji ……………………………… 61　G3
増上寺　Zōjō-ji ……………………………… 18　A5
染井霊園　Somei Cemetery ………………… 25　H3

た

たばこと塩の博物館　Tabacco & Salt Museum … 52　E2
第一勧業銀行（本店）　Dai-ichi Kangyō Bank (H. O.) … 38　B4
第一生命（本社）　Dai-ichi Mutual Life Insurance (H. O.) … 38　C1
大円寺　Daien-ji ……………………………… 28　C3
太鼓館　Drum Museum ……………………… 31　F5
大正大学　Taishō Univ. ……………………… 25　G2
大宗寺　Taisō-ji ……………………………… 22　D5
台東区伝統工芸展示館　Taitō Traditional Crafts Musm … 31　G2
台東区役所　Taito Ward Office …………… 30　E2
大東文化大学　Daitō Bunka Univ. ………… 11　E1
大日本印刷（本社）　Dai Nippon Printing (H. O.) … 23　H4
大丸デパート　Daimaru Dept Store ……… 35　G7
大名時計博物館　Daimyō Clock Museum … 26　C6
太陽生命（本社）　Taiyō Mutual Life Insurance (H. O.) … 35　G4
高尾山薬王院　Takaosan Yakuō-in ……… 14　B5
高島屋デパート　Takashimaya Dept Store … 35　G5
高島屋タイムズスクエア　Takashimaya Times Square … 57　G6
高千穂商科大学　Takachiho Coll. of Comm. … 10　D6
高輪郵便局　Takanawa Post Office ……… 29　G1
高幡不動　Takahata Fudō …………………… 15　F4
宝田恵比寿神社　Takarada Ebisu Jinja …… 34　B3
拓殖大学（八王子）　Takushoku Univ. (Hachiōji) … 14　C5
拓殖大学（茗荷谷）　Takushoku Univ. (Myōgadani) … 23　H1
竹芝客船ターミナル　Takeshiba Passenger Terminal … 18　C5
凧の博物館　Kite Museum ………………… 35　F3
玉川大学　Tamagawa Univ. ………………… 15　G7
多摩湖　Tama-ko …………………………… 15　F1
多摩聖蹟記念館　Meiji Mem. Hall of Tama … 15　G5
多摩川　Tama-gawa ………………………… 74　C4
多摩テック　Tama Tech ……………………… 14　E5
多摩動物公園　Tama Zoological Park ……… 15　F4
多摩美術大学　Tama Univ. of Art ………… 12　D3
多磨霊園　Tama Cemetery ………………… 15　H3

ち

秩父宮記念ラグビー場　Prince Chichibu Mem. Rugby Stadium … 21　F2
千鳥ヶ淵戦没者墓苑　Chidorigafuchi Nat'l Mem. Garden … 23　J5

中央区役所　Chūō Ward Office ……… 39　I 4
中央信託銀行（本店）　Chūō Trust Bank (H. O.) … 35　I 6
中央大学　Chūō Univ. ……… I5　F 5
中央大学（理工学部）　Chūō Univ. (Sci. & Engn.) ……… I6　A 2
中華街（横浜）　China Town (Yokohama) ……… 63　G 5
長泉院　Chōsen-in ……… 28　A 2
長命寺　Chōmei-ji ……… I0　C 3
千代田区役所　Chiyoda Ward Office ……… 32　A 5
千代田生命（本社）　Chiyoda Mutual Life Insurance (H. O.) … 28　A I
千代田区総合体育館　Chiyoda Ward Gym. ……… 36　B 3
千代田ビル　Chiyoda Bldg ……… 35　I 6
椿山荘　Chinzan-sō ……… 23　G I

つ
ツインタワービル（有楽町）　Twin Tower Bldg (Yūrakuchō) … 38　C I
ツーリストインフォメーションセンター（有楽町）　Tourist Info. Center … 38　D 2
築地市場（東京中央卸売市場）　Tsukiji Shijō ……… I8　D 4
津田塾大学　Tsuda Coll. ……… 74　C 2
津田ホール　Tsuda Hall ……… 80　D 2
坪内博士記念演劇博物館　Tsubouchi Mem. Theatre Waseda Univ. … 85　G 2
鶴見つばさ橋　Tsurumi-Tsubasa-bashi ……… 61　H 5
鶴見大学　Tsurumi Univ. ……… 61　G 4

て
TBSホール　TBS Hall ……… 48　B 3
テクノプラザかつしか　Technoplaza Katsushika ……… 8　D 5
テレビ朝日　TV Asahi (ANB) ……… 49　H 6
テレビ神奈川　TV Kanagawa (TVK) ……… 63　H 6
テレビ東京　TV Tokyo ……… 49　F I
帝京大学（板橋）　Teikyo Univ. (Itabashi) ……… 75　F 2
帝京大学（八王子）　Teikyo Univ. (Hachiōji) … I5　F 4
帝国劇場　Imperial Theater ……… 37　J 6
逓信総合博物館　Communications Museum ……… 36　C 3
帝都高速度交通営団　Teito Rapid Transit Authority … 30　D 3
哲学堂公園　Tetsugakudō Park ……… I I　F 4
鉄鋼ビル　Tekko Bldg ……… 35　F 6
銕仙会能楽研究所　Tessenkai Noh Theater ……… 55　F 5
電気通信大学　Univ. of Electro-Communications ……… 74　D 3
電通（本社）　Dentsū Inc. (H. O.) ……… 39　H 5
伝通院　Denzū-in ……… 23　J I
伝法院　Denbō-in ……… 31　H 4
天理ギャラリー　Tenri Gallery ……… 33　F 6
DNタワー21　DN Tower21 ……… 38　D I

と
ドイツ文化会館　German Culture Center ……… 48　B 6
とげぬき地蔵（高岩寺）　Togenuki Jizō (Kōgan-ji) … 25　H 3
としまえん（豊島園）　Toshimaen ……… I0　D 3
東海銀行　Tōkai Bank ……… 36　E 2
東海大学（代々木）　Tōkai Univ. (Yoyogi) … 20　A 3
東急デパート（日本橋店）　Tōkyū Dept Store (Nihombashi) … 35　F 4
東急デパート（本店）　Tōkyū Dept Store (Main Shop) … 52　C 3

東急ハンズ（池袋）　Tōkyū Hands Store (Ikebukuro) … 59　G 4
東急ハンズ（渋谷）　Tōkyū Hands Store (Shibuya) … 52　D 3
東急プラザ　Tōkyū Plaza ……… 52　E 5
東急文化会館　Tōkyū Bunka Kaikan ……… 53　F 4
東京文化村　Bunkamura ……… 52　B 4
東京ビッグサイト（国際展示場）　Tokyo Big Sight ……… 7　G 5
東京医科歯科大学　Tokyo Med. & Dent. Univ. ……… 33　F 2
東京医科大学　Tokyo Medical Coll. ……… 22　E 5
東京医大病院　Tokyo Med. Coll. Hosp. ……… 56　B 2
東京オペラシティ　Tokyo Opera City ……… 22　A 6
東京卸売センター（TOC）　Tokyo Wholesale Center … 28　C 5
東京音楽大学　Tokyo Music Coll. ……… 24　E 6
東京会館　Tokyo Kaikan ……… 37　I 6
東京外国語大学　Tokyo Univ. of Foreign Studies ……… 25　H 2
東京海上ビル　Tokyo Kaijō Bldg ……… 37　F 5
東京学芸大学　Tokyo Gakugei Univ. ……… I5　G 3
東京ガスビル　Tokyo Gas Bldg ……… I8　B 5
東京家政学院大学　Tokyo Kasei Gakuin Coll. ……… 74　A 4
東京家政大学　Tokyo Kasei Univ. ……… 75　F 2
東京カテドラル聖マリア大聖堂　St. Mary's Cathedral … 23　G I
東京共済病院　Tokyo Kyōsai Hosp. ……… 28　A I
東京倶楽部ビル　Tokyo Club Bldg ……… 47　F 7
東京グローブ座　Tokyo Globe-za ……… 81　F I
東京経済大学　Tokyo Coll. of Economics ……… 74　C 3
東京芸術劇場　Tokyo Met. Art Space ……… 58　C 4
東京芸術大学　Tokyo Univ. of Fine Arts and Music … 26　D 6
東京競馬場　Tokyo Racecourse ……… I5　H 4
東京工科大学　Tokyo Engineering Coll. ……… I4　D 5
東京工業大学　Tokyo Inst. of Technology ……… I3　F 4
東京工芸大学　Tokyo Inst. of Polytechnics ……… 74　B 6
東京交通会館　Tokyo Kōtsū Kaikan ……… 38　F I
東京港野鳥公園　Tokyo Port Wild Bird Park ……… I3　I 5
東京国際空港（羽田）　Tokyo Int'l Airport (Haneda) ……… I3　J 6
東京国際フォーラム　Tokyo Int'l Forum ……… 37　I 4
東京国際貿易センター　Tokyo Int'l Trade Center … I8　D 6
東京国際郵便局　Tokyo Int'l Post Office ……… 36　C 2
東京穀物商品取引所　Tokyo Grain Exchange ……… 34　E I
東京国立近代美術館　Nat'l Musm of Modern Art, Tokyo … 32　B 7
東京国立博物館　Tokyo Nat'l Museum ……… 26　E 6
東京サマーランド　Tokyo Summer Land ……… I4　B 2
東京歯科大学　Tokyo Dental Coll. ……… 32　B 2
東京シティエアターミナル（箱崎）　Tokyo City Air Teminal (Hakozaki) … I7　G 7
東京慈恵会医科大学　Jikei Univ. Sch. of Medicine … I8　A 4
東京慈恵会医大病院　Jikei Univ. Hosp. ……… I8　A 4
東京証券取引所　Tokyo Stock Exchange ……… 35　F 2
東京商工会議所　Tokyo Chamber of Comm. & Ind. … 37　I 5
東京商船大学　Tokyo Univ. of Mercantile Marine … I9　G 3
東京女子医科大学　Tokyo Women's Medical Coll. … 23　F 4
東京女子体育大学　Tokyo Women's P. E. Coll. … 74　C 3
東京女子大学　Tokyo Women's Christian Univ. … I0　B 5
東京神学大学　Tokyo Union Theological Seminary … 75　H 6
東京新国立劇場　New Nat'l Theater Tokyo ……… 22　A 6

東京新聞社　Tokyo Newspapers ················· 29　G 3
東京水産大学　Tokyo Univ. of F sheries ········· 29　H 4
東京生命（本社）　Tokyo Mutual Life Insurance(H. O.) ·· 38　B 4
東京セントラル美術館　Tokyo Central Musm of Art ····· 39　G 2
東京造形大学　Tokyo Univ. of Art and Design ····· 74　A 4
東京相和銀行（本店）　Tokyo Sŏwa Bank(H. O.) ········· 48　D 1
東京大学　Univ. of Tokyo ··················· 16　C 1
東京大学（教養）　Univ. of Tokyo(Liberal Arts) ········· 20　A 4
東京大学（農）　Univ. of Tokyo(Agr.) ········· 26　B 7
東京大学病院　Univ. of Tokyo Hosp. ········· 16　C 1
東京大仏　Tokyo Daibutsu ··················· 83　E 2
東京宝塚劇場　Tokyo Takarazuka Theater ········· 38　C 2
東京タワー　Tokyo Tower ··················· 21　J 4
東京中央卸売市場（大田）　Tokyo Central Wholesale Market(Ōta) 13　J 5
東京中央卸売市場（築地）　Tokyo Central Wholesale Market(Tsukiji) ··· 18　D 4
東京中央郵便局　Tokyo Central Post Office ········· 37　H 4
東京ディズニーランド　Tokyo Disneyland·············· 7　I 5
東京電機大学　Tokyo Electrical Engn. Coll. ········· 32　E 5
東京電力（本社）　Tokyo Electric Power Co.(H. O.) ········· 38　B 4
東京電力電力館　TEPCO Electric Energy Museum ········· 53　E 2
東京ドイツ文化センター　German Culture Center ····· 48　B 6
東京都産業貿易会館　Tokyo Trade Center ········· 18　C 5
東京都児童会館　Tokyo Met. Children's House·········· 54　B 5
東京都写真美術館　Tokyo Met. Musm of Photography ·· 28　C 1
東京都庁　Tokyo Met. Government ············· 56　A 5
東京都庭園美術館　Tokyo Met. Teien Art Museum ··· 28　D 2
東京都美術館　Tokyo Met. Art Museum ········· 26　E 7
東京都復興記念館　Reconstruction Mem. Hall ····· 85　H 7
東京ドーム　Tokyo Dome ··················· 16　A 2
東京都夢の島熱帯植物館　Tokyo Met. Yumenoshima Tropical Plant Dome ·· 87　H 4
東京都立科学技術大学　Tokyo Met. Inst. of Tech. ········· 74　B 3
東京都近代文学博物館　Tokyo Met. Musm of Modern Literature ··· 84　B 1
東京都立国際高等学校　Tokyo Met. Kokusai H. Sch. ··· 13　F 1
東京都立大学　Tokyo Met. Univ. ··············· 14　E 5
東京都立中央図書館　Tokyo Met. Central Library········· 21　G 6
東京都立日比谷図書館　Tokyo Met. Hibiya Library········· 38　A 3
東京農業大学　Tokyo Univ. of Agriculture ········· 12　D 2
東京農工大学　Tokyo Univ. of Agr. & Tech. ········· 75　I 6
東京東本願寺　Tokyo Higashi-Hongan-ji ········· 17　G 1
東京武道館　Tokyo Budŏkan ··················· 8　C 4
東京ビル　Tokyo Bldg ··················· 37　H 4
東京文化会館　Tokyo Met. festival Hall ········· 30　B 1
東京放送　Tokyo Broadcasting Station(TBS) ········· 48　B 4
東京三菱銀行（本店）　Bank of Tokyo-Mitsubishi(H. O.) ··· 37　H 5
東京モスク　Tokyo Mosque ··················· 11　F 7
東京薬科大学　Tokyo Coll. of Pharmacy ········· 74　B 4
東京理科大学　Science Univ. of Tokyo ········· 23　I 3
東京労災病院　Tokyo Rōsai Hosp. ············· 13　I 6
東劇　Tōgeki ··························· 39　H 6
刀剣博物館　Japanese Sword Museum ········· 22　A 7
東郷記念館　Tōgō Mem. Hall ··················· 54　C 1
東郷神社　Tōgō Jinja ··················· 54　B 1

東郷青児美術館　Tōgō Seiji Art Museum ··········· 56　D 3
東芝科学館　Tōshiba Science Inst. ·············· 87　F 5
東芝ビル　Tōshiba Bldg ··················· 18　B 6
東条会館　Tōjo Kaikan ··················· 47　E 3
東照宮　Tōshōgū ··························· 16　D 1
東禅寺　Tōzen-ji ··························· 29　F 2
東武デパート　Tōbu Dept Store·············· 58　D 4
桐朋学園大学　Tōhō Gakuen School of Music ··· 74　E 3
東邦生命ビル　Tōhō Seimei Bldg ············· 53　G 5
東邦生命ホール　Tōhō Seimei Hall ············· 80　C 3
東邦大学　Tōhō Univ. ····················· 13　H 5
東洋英和女学院大学　Tōyō Ejwa Women's Univ. ··· 74　D 6
東洋信託銀行（本店）　Tōyō Trust Bank(H. O.) ········· 36　E 4
東洋大学　Tōyō Univ. ····················· 26　A 6
東洋大学（朝霞）　Tōyō Univ.(Asaka) ········· 74　E 1
東洋文庫　Tōyō Bunko ··················· 26　A 4
東レ　Toray ··························· 34　C 4
戸越公園　Togoshi Park ··················· 28　D 7
豊島区役所　Toshima Ward Office ············· 59　F 3
豊島公会堂　Toshima Public Hall·············· 59　G 3
豊島郵便局　Toshima Post Office ············· 59　I 4
戸田ボート場　Toda Boat Course ············· 83　E 2
独協大学　Dokkyo Univ. ··················· 75　G 1
凸版印刷（本社）　Toppan Printing(H. O.) ········· 16　E 3
殿ヶ谷戸庭園　Tonogayato Garden ··········· 15　G 3
富岡八幡宮　Tomioka Hachimangū ············· 19　H 2
戸山公園　Toyama Park ··················· 22　D 2
豊川稲荷　Toyokawa Inari ··················· 21　G 1
虎の門病院　Toranomon Hosp. ··············· 21　J 2
虎ノ門パストラル　Toranomon Pastoral ········· 21　J 3
虎ノ門ホール　Toranomon Hall ············· 47　G 7
鳥越神社　Torigoe Jinja ··················· 17　F 3

な
内閣文庫　Cabinet Library ··················· 36　D 7
中野区役所　Nakano Ward Office ············· 10　E 5
（中野）サンプラザ　Nakano Sun Plaza ········· 11　E 5
中野区文化センター　Nakano Ward Culture Center ···· 11　F 5
仲見世通り　Nakamise Dōri ··················· 31　H 5
中山競馬場　Nakayama Racecourse ··········· 83　I 3
成田空港　New Tokyo Int'l Airport(Narita) ················· 155

に
ニコライ堂　Nikolai Cathedral ··············· 33　F 3
ニチレイ（本社）　Nichirei(H. O.) ············· 32　A 2
ニッカウ井スキー　Nikka Whisky ············· 55　F 6
ニッポン放送　Nippon Broadcasting ··········· 38　C 1
ニューメルサ　New Melsa ··················· 38　E 4
肉筆浮世絵美術館　Autographic Ukiyoe Museum ··· 84　C 5
西新井大師　Nishiarai Daishi ··············· 8　C 6
西本願寺　Nishi-Hongan-ji ··················· 18　D 3
西町インターナショナルスクール　Nishimachi Int'l Sch. ····· 21　G 5

西戸山タワーホームズ　Nishitoyama Tower Homes ······· 22　C 2
二重橋　Nijū-bashi ··· 16　A 7
二松学舎大学　Nishō-Gakusha Univ. ····················· 23　J 5
日劇東宝　Nichigeki Tōhō ···································· 38　E 2
日動火災海上（本社）　Nichidō Fire & Marine Insurance (H. O.) ····· 39　G 5
日仏会館　Maison Franco-Japonaise ·················· 32　D 2
日刊工業ホール　Nikkan Kōgyō Hall ··················· 81　G 4
日経ホール　Nikkei Hall ······································ 36　C 3
日産火災海上　Nissan Fire & Marine Insurance ······ 55　G 1
日産自動車ビル　Nissan Motor Bldg ···················· 39　G 6
日商岩井　Nisshō Iwai ·· 46　D 6
日清製粉（本社）　Nisshin Flour Milling (H. O.) ········· 34　E 1
日生劇場　Nissei Theater ····································· 38　B 2
日生日比谷ビル　Nissei Hibiya Bldg ···················· 38　B 2
日赤医療センター　J. R. C. Medical Service Center ··· 21　F 5
日通ビル（日本通運）　Nittsū Bldg ······················· 33　H 2
日本IBM（本社）　IBM Japan (H. O.) ····················· 49　F 3
日本医科大学　Nippon Medical School ················· 26　B 6
日本医大（新丸子）　Nippon Medical Sch. (Shin-Maruko) ··· 75　E 5
日本医大病院　Nippon Med. Sch. Hosp. ··············· 26　B 6
日本エヌ・シー・アール　N. C. R Japan ·················· 47　F 7
日本開発銀行　Japan Development Bank ·············· 36　B 4
日本学術振興会　Japan Society for the Promotion of Science ··· 93　F 4
日本火災海上ビル　Nippon Fire & Marine Insurance Bldg ··· 35　F 5
日本近代文学館　Musm of Modern Japanese Literature ········· 84　B 1
日本銀行（本店）　Bank of Japan (H. O.) ················ 34　C 6
日本経済新聞社　Nihon Keizai Newspapers ··········· 36　B 3
日本劇場（映）　Nihon Theater ····························· 38　E 1
日本興業銀行（本店）　Industrial Bank of Japan (H. O.) ··· 36　E 4
日本工業倶楽部　Industry Club of Japan ·············· 37　E 4
日本コロムビア　Nippon Columbia ······················· 46　A 6
日本歯科大学　Nippon Dental Coll. ····················· 23　J 4
日本社会事業大学　Japan Coll. of Social Work ······· 74　D 2
日本獣医畜産大学　Nippon Vetn. & Zootech. Coll. ··· 75　H 5
日本酒センター　Japanese Sake Center ················ 39　F 4
日本女子体育大学　Nippon Women's Coll. of P. E. ··· 75　I 4
日本女子大学　Nippon Women's Univ. ·················· 25　F 7
日本書道美術館　Japan Calligraphy Museum ········· 87　F 2
日本信託銀行（本店）　Nippon Trust Bank (H. O.) ····· 35　G 5
日本信販　Nippon Shinpan ·································· 16　C 2
日本青年館ホール　Nihon Seinenkan Hall ············· 80　D 3
日本赤十字看護大学　Japan Red Cross Coll. of Nursing ··· 72　C 4
日本赤十字社　Japan Red Cross Society ·············· 18　A 4
日本石油（日石）　Nippon Oil ······························· 38　A 5
日本体育大学　Nippon Coll. of Health & P. E. ········ 12　D 3
日本大学（医）　Nihon Univ. (Med.) ······················ 74　F 2
日本大学（経済）　Nihon Univ. (Econ.) ··················· 32　C 2
日本大学（芸術）　Nihon Univ. (Art) ······················ 11　F 3
日本大学（歯）　Nihon Univ. (Dent.) ····················· 32　E 3
日本大学（商）　Nihon Univ. (Comm.) ··················· 74　E 4
日本大学（農獣医）　Nihon Univ. (Agr. & Vetn.) ········ 13　F 2
日本大学（文理）　Nihon Univ. (Huma. & Sci.) ········· 12　D 1
日本大学（法）　Nihon Univ. (Law) ······················· 32　B 2
日本大学（松戸歯）　Nihon Univ. (Matsudo Dent.) ········· 75　H 1
日本大学（理工）　Nihon Univ. (Sci. & Engn.) ·········· 33　E 4
日本長期信用銀行　Long-Term Credit Bank of Japan ··· 36　C 5
日本テレビ放送網　Nippon Television (NTV) ··········· 52　H 6
日本電気（本社）　NEC (H. O.) ····························· 21　J 6
日本点字図書館　Braille Library ·························· 22　D 1
日本都市センターホール　Nihon Toshi Center Hall ··· 46　C 2
日本橋　Nihombashi ··· 34　E 4
日本ビル　Nippon Bldg ·· 36　D 2
日本橋通郵便局　Nihombashi-dōri Post Office ········ 35　G 5
日本橋プラザ　Nihombashi Plaza Bldg ················· 35　G 5
日本橋郵便局　Nihombashi Post Office ················ 35　E 3
日本プレスセンター　Nippon Press Center ············· 47　I 7
日本武道館　Nippon Budōkan ······························ 16　A 5
日本文化大学　Nippon Bunka Univ. ····················· 14　D 5
日本貿易振興会　Japan External Trade Orgn (JETRO) ··· 21　J 2
日本民家園　Kawasaki Municipal Park of Japanese Houses ··· 12　A 3
日本民芸館　Japan Folk Crafts Museum ·············· 13　F 1
日本輸出入銀行　Export-Import Bank of Japan ······· 36　A 6
日本ユニシス（本社）　Nippon Unisys (H. O.) ··········· 19　G 4
日本ルーテル学院大学　Japan Lutheran Theol. Coll. ··· 75　H 6

ね
根岸森林公園　Negishi Forest Park ····················· 61　F 6
根津神社　Nezu Jinja ··· 26　B 6
根津美術館　Nezu Art Museum ··························· 55　G 5
練馬区役所　Nerima Ward Office ························· 10　E 3

の
ノアビル　Noa Bldg ·· 49　I 1
農工大付属繊維博物館　Musm of Fiber & Tech. ······ 87　I 3
野川公園　Nogawa Park ······································ 15　H 3
乃木会館　Nogi Kaikan ······································ 48　D 6
乃木神社　Nogi Jinja ··· 48　D 6
野口英世記念会館　Noguchi Mem. Hall ··············· 23　E 6
野毛山公園　Nogeyama Park ······························ 62　C 5
野村証券　Nomura Securities ······························ 34　E 4

は
ハイジア（東京都健康プラザ）　Hygeia (Tokyo Met. Health Plaza) ··· 57　F 1
ハザマビル　Hazama Bldg ···································· 55　G 1
ハナエ・モリビル　Hanae Mori Bldg ····················· 54　D 4
パルコ劇場　Parco Theater ·································· 52　D 3
パンセホール　Pensee Hall ·································· 32　A 3
拝島大師　Haijima Daishi ··································· 14　D 3
俳優座劇場　Haiyū-za Theater ···························· 49　G 5
博品館劇場　Hakuhinkan Theater ······················· 38　D 6
博報堂（本社）　Hakuhōdō (H. O.) ························· 32　D 6
箱崎エアターミナル　Tokyo City Air Terminal (Hakozaki) ··· 17　G 7
馬事公苑　Baji Kōen ·· 12　D 2
芭蕉記念館　Bashō Mem. Hall ···························· 17　H 6

畠山記念館　Hatakeyama Collection ············· 28　E 3
八王子こども科学館　Hachiōji Science Center ······ 86　B 4
八王子市郷土資料館　Hachiōji City Museum ········ 86　A 3
花園神社　Hanazono Jinja ······················ 57　H 3
花やしき　Hanayashiki ························· 31　G 2
羽田空港　Tokyo Int'l Airport (Haneda) ·········· 13　J 6
浜町公園　Hamachō Park ······················ 17　G 6
浜離宮朝日ホール　Hamarikyu Ashi Hall ········· 18　C 4
浜離宮恩賜庭園　Hamarikyū Onshi Garden ······· 18　C 4
原美術館　Hara Mus. of Contemporary Art ········ 29　F 5
原宿クエスト　Harajuku Quest ·················· 54　B 2
晴海ふ頭　Harumi Futō ······················· 18　E 6
阪急デパート（有楽町店）　Hankyū Dept Store (Yūrakuchō) ··· 38　D 2
半蔵門会館　Hanzōmon Kaikan ················· 46　E 1

ひ
ビッグボックスビル　Big Box Bldg ·············· 22　D 1
日枝神社　Hie Jinja ·························· 46　D 5
東日本銀行（本店）　Higashi-Nippon Bank (H. O.) ··· 35　H 4
光が丘公園　Hikarigaoka Park ·················· 10　D 1
氷川神社（赤坂）　Hikawa Jinja ················ 48　D 3
毘沙門天（神楽坂）　Bishamonten ··············· 23　I 3
日立（本社）　Hitachi (H. O.) ················· 33　F 3
一ッ橋ホール　Hitotsubashi Hall ··············· 32　B 5
一ッ橋講堂　Hitotsubashi Kōdō ················ 32　C 6
一橋大学　Hitotsubashi Univ. ·················· 74　C 3
一橋大学（小平）　Hitotsubashi Univ. (Kodaira) ···· 15　G 2
日の出桟橋　Hinode Sanbashi ·················· 18　B 7
日比谷映画　Hibiya Cinema ···················· 38　C 2
日比谷公園　Hibiya Park ······················ 38　A 1
日比谷公会堂　Hibiya Public Hall ··············· 38　A 3
日比谷国際ビル　Hibiya Kokusai Bldg ··········· 38　A 4
日比谷図書館　Hibiya Library ·················· 38　A 3
日比谷シティ　Hibiya City ···················· 38　A 4
日比谷シャンテ　Hibiya Chanter ··············· 38　C 2
日比谷ダイビル　Hibiya Dai Bldg ··············· 38　B 4
日比谷パークビル　Hibiya Park Bldg ············ 38　C 1
広尾病院　Hiro-o Hosp. ······················ 21　F 6

ふ
フェリス女学院大学　Ferris Women's Coll. ········ 63　G 7
フジテレビジョン　Fuji Television ·············· 23　F 2
プランタン銀座　Printemps Ginza Dept Store ······ 39　F 2
ブリヂストン美術館　Bridgestone Musm of Art ····· 35　H 5
プレイガイドビル　Playguide Bldg ·············· 39　F 4
深川江戸資料館　Fukagawa Edo Museum ········· 87　G 3
深川不動　Fukagawa Fudō ····················· 19　H 2
富国生命（本社）　Fukoku Mutual Life Insurance (H. O.) ··· 38　A 4
富士銀行（本店）　Fuji Bank (H. C.) ············ 36　D 4
富士銀行資料館　Fuji Bank Museum ············· 34　D 2
富士神社　Fuji Jinja ························· 26　A 4
富士通ゼネラル（本社）　Fujitsu General (H. O.) ··· 12　D 5

富士フィルム（本社）　Fuji Photo Film (H. O.) ····· 55　H 6
府中市郷土の森　Fuchū Municipal Musm Kyōdonomori ··· 86　C 4
武道館　Nippon Budōkan ······················ 16　A 5
船の科学館　Musm of Maritime Science ··········· 13　J 3
普門ホール　Fumon Hall ······················ 83　F 3
古河総合ビル　Furukawa Sōgō Bldg ············· 37　H 5
文化学園服飾博物館　Bunka Gakuen Costume Musm ··· 22　B 6
文化女子大学　Bunka Women's Univ. ············ 22　B 6
文化放送　Bunka Broadcasting (NCB) ············ 23　F 6
文京ふるさと歴史館　Bunkyo Museum ··········· 16　B 2
文京区役所　Bunkyō Ward Office ··············· 16　A 2
文京総合体育館　Bunkyō Ward Gym. ············ 16　C 2
文芸座　Bungei-za ··························· 59　F 2

へ
ベルビー赤坂　Belle Vie Akasaka ··············· 46　B 4
ペンタックス ギャラリー カメラ博物館　Pentax Gallery (Camera Musm) ····· 84　C 4

ほ
防衛医科大学校　Defense Medical Coll. ··········· 74　C 1
宝生能楽堂　Hoshō Noh Theater ················ 32　B 1
法政大学（市ヶ谷）　Hōsei Univ. (Ichigaya) ······ 23　I 4
法政大学（小金井）　Hōsei Univ. (Koganei) ······· 15　H 3
法政大学（多摩）　Hōsei Univ. (Tama) ··········· 74　A 4
法華経寺　Hokekyō-ji ························ 83　I 3
星薬科大学　Hoshi Coll. of Pharm. ·············· 13　G 3
保土ヶ谷公園　Hodogaya Park ················· 60　E 5
堀切菖蒲園　Horikiri Shōbuen (iris garden) ········· 8　E 4
本郷郵便局　Hongō Post Office ················· 69　H 4
本州製紙　Honshū Paper ······················ 39　F 5
本田技研（本社）　Honda Motor (H. O.) ·········· 55　I 1
本牧市民公園　Honmoku Cltizen's Park ··········· 61　G 7
本門寺　Honmon-ji ·························· 13　G 5

ま
マイシティ　My City ························· 57　F 4
マガジンハウス　Magazine House ·············· 39　H 4
マリンタワー　Marine Tower ·················· 63　H 5
毎日新聞社　Mainichi Newspapers ·············· 32　C 7
牧野記念庭園　Makino Mem. Garden ············ 10　B 3
将門首塚　Masakado Kubizuka (Hill of Masakado's Head) ··· 36　C 5
町田市立国際版画美術館　Machida City Musm of Graphic Arts ··· 86　C 5
松岡美術館　Matsuoka Art Museum ············· 84　D 6
松坂屋デパート（上野店）　Matsuzakaya Dept Store (Ueno) ··· 30　A 6
松坂屋デパート（銀座店）　Matsuzakaya Dept Store (Ginza) ··· 38　E 4
待乳山聖天　Matsuchiyama Shōden ············· 27　I 7
松屋デパート（浅草店）　Matsuya Dept Store (Asakusa) ··· 31　I 5
松屋デパート（銀座店）　Matsuya Dept Store (Ginza) ··· 39　G 3
丸井ファッション館　Marui Fashion Bldg ········· 57　H 4
丸善（日本橋店）　Maruzen (Nihombashi) ········· 35　G 5
丸の内ピカデリー　Marunouchi Piccadilly ········ 38　E 2
丸の内ビル　Marunouchi Bldg ················· 37　G 4

丸の内八重洲ビル　Marunouchi Yaesu Bldg･･････････ 37　H 5
丸紅　Marubeni Corp.････････････････････････････ 36　A 6

み

ミナミ美術館　Minami Art Museum ･･････････････ 33　I 2
ミロード　MYLORD ･･････････････････････････ 57　F 5
みなとが丘埠頭公園　Minatogaoka Futo Park ････････ 13　J 4
水元公園　Mizumoto Park ･･････････････････････ 8　B 2
三ツ池公園　Mitsuike Park ･･････････････････････ 61　G 3
三井海上火災（本社）　Mitsui Marine & Fire Insurance ･･ 33　F 4
三井信託銀行（本店）　Mitsui Trust Bank (H. O.) ･･････ 34　D 5
三井生命（本社）　Mitsui Mutual Life Insurance (H. O.) ･･ 36　C 5
三井物産ビル　Mitsui Bussan Bldg ･･････････････ 36　C 5
三井本館　Mitsui Main Bldg ････････････････････ 34　C 5
三越劇場　Mitsukoshi Theater ･･････････････････ 34　D 5
三越デパート（池袋店）　Mitsukoshi Dept Store (Ikebukuro) ････ 59　E 3
三越デパート（銀座店）　Mitsukoshi Dept Store (Ginza) ････････ 39　F 3
三越デパート（新宿店）　Mitsukoshi Dept Store (Shinjuku) ････ 57　G 4
三越デパート（本店）　Mitsukoshi Dept Store (Main Store) ････ 34　D 4
三ツ沢公園　Mitsuzawa Park ･･････････････････ 60　E 5
三菱重エビル　Mitsubishi Heavy Industries Bldg ･･････ 37　G 5
三菱商事ビル　Mitsubishi Shōji Bldg･･････････････ 37　H 5
三菱信託銀行（本店）　Mitsubishi Trust Bank (H. O.) ････ 36　E 4
三菱電機ビル　Mitsubishi Electric Bldg ････････････ 37　G 5
港区役所　Minato Ward Office････････････････････ 18　A 4
港の見える丘公園　Minatono-mieruoka Park ････････ 63　H 6
宮城道雄記念館　Miyagi Michio Mem. Hall ･･･････ 85　G 3
妙法寺　Myōhō-ji ････････････････････････････ 10　E 5

む

向ヶ丘遊園　Mukōgaoka-Yūen ････････････････ 12　A 4
向島百花園　Mukōjima Hyakkaen ････････････････ 83　G 3
武蔵工業大学　Musashi Inst. of Tech. ･･････････････ 12　E 4
武蔵大学　Musashi Univ. ･･････････････････････ 11　E 3
武蔵野音楽大学（入間）　Musashino Academia Musicae (Iruma) ･･････ 74　B 1
武蔵野音楽大学（江古田）　Musashino Academia Musicae (Ekoda) ･･ 11　F 3
武蔵野公園　Musashino Park ･･････････････････ 82　D 3
武蔵野市民文化会館　Musashino Civic Auditorium ･･････ 82　D 3
武蔵野女子大学　Musashino Women's Univ. ･･････ 75　H 5
武蔵野美術大学　Musashino Art Univ. ･･････････ 75　H 4
武蔵野陵　Musashino Mausoleum ･･････････････ 14　C 4
村内美術館　Murauchi Art Museum･･････････････ 86　B 3

め

目赤不動　Meaka Fudō ････････････････････････ 26　A 5
明海大学　Meikai Univ. ････････････････････････ 75　I 4
明治学院大学　Meiji Gakuin Univ.････････････････ 29　E 2
明治記念館　Meiji Kinenkan ････････････････････ 21　F 1
明治座　Meiji-za ････････････････････････････ 17　F 6
明治神宮　Meiji jingū ･･････････････････････････ 20　C 1
明治神宮外苑　Meiji jingū Outer Gardens ････････ 21　F 1
明治製菓　Meiji Seika ･･････････････････････････ 37　I 2

明治生命ビル　Meiji Seimei Bldg ･･････････････ 37　H 5
明治大学（生田）　Meiji Univ. (Ikuta) ･･････････ 74　D 4
明治大学（和泉）　Meiji Univ. (Izumi) ･･････････ 10　E 3
明治大学（駿河台）　Meiji Univ. (Surugadai) ････ 32　D 4
明治薬科大学（世田谷）　Meiji Coll. of Pharm. (Setagaya) ･･････ 13　F 2
明治薬科大学（田無）　Meiji Coll. of Pharm. (Tanashi) ･･ 74　D 2
明星大学　Meisei Univ. ････････････････････････ 74　C 4
目黒寄生虫館　Meguro Parasitological Museum ････ 28　B 3
目黒区立体育館　Meguro Ward Gym. ････････････ 28　A 5
目黒区美術館　Meguro Musm of Art ････････････ 28　B 2
目黒区役所　Meguro Ward Office ････････････････ 13　F 2
目黒公会堂　Meguro Public Hall ････････････････ 83　F 4
目黒不動　Meguro Fudō ････････････････････････ 28　B 3
目白不動　Mejiro Fudō ････････････････････････ 24　E 7

も

百草園　Mogusa-en ･･････････････････････････ 15　F 4
木馬館　Mokuba-kan ･･････････････････････････ 31　G 3
元町公園　Motomachi Park ････････････････････ 63　H 6

や

ヤクルト（本社）　Yakult (H. O.) ････････････････ 38　C 7
ヤマハホール　Yamaha Hall ････････････････････ 38　E 5
八重洲ブックセンター　Yaesu Book Center ････････ 37　I 2
野球体育博物館　Baseball Hall of Fame & Museum･･･ 85　G 4
靖国神社　Yasukuni Jinja ････････････････････ 23　I 5
安田火災海上本社ビル　Yasuda Kasai-Kaijo Bldg ････ 56　D 3
安田信託銀行（本店）　Yasuda Trust Bank (H. O.) ････ 34　E 5
安田生命ビル　Yasuda Seimei Bldg ････････････ 57　E 5
安田生命ホール　Yasuda Seimei Hall ････････････ 56　E 5
谷中霊園　Yanaka Cemetery ･･････････････････ 26　D 5
谷保天満宮　Yabo Tenmangū ････････････････ 82　C 3
山一証券　Yamaichi Securities ････････････････ 35　F 2
山下公園　Yamashita Park ････････････････････ 63　G 5
山種美術館　Yamatane Museum of Art ･･････････ 35　G 2
山手教会　Yamate Church ････････････････････ 52　E 3
山手公園　Yamate Park･･････････････････････ 63　G 7
山手資料館　Yamate Museum ･･････････････････ 63　(H6)
大和生命（本社）　Yamato Mutual Life Insurance (H. O.) ･･････ 38　B 3
弥生美術館　Yayoi Art Museum ････････････････ 16　C 1
矢来能楽堂　Yarai Noh Theater ･･･････････････ 81　G 3

ゆ

ゆうぽうと簡易保険ホール　U-Port Kan'l Hoken Hall ･･･ 28　D 4
郵船ビル　Yūsen Bldg ････････････････････････ 37　F 5
有楽町朝日ホール　Yūrakuchō Asahi Hall ････････ 38　E 2
有楽町ビル　Yūrakuchō Bldg ････････････････ 38　D 1
有楽町マリオン　Yūrakuchō Mulion ･･････････････ 38　D 2
湯島神社　Yushima Jinja ･･････････････････････ 16　C 2
湯島聖堂　Yushima Confucian Shrine ･･････････ 33　F 2
夢の島公園　Yumenoshima Park･･････････････ 9　J 5

よ

よみうりランド　Yomiuri Land ················· 15　H 5
横田飛行場　Yokota Airfield ················· 14　D 1
横浜アリーナ　Yokohama Arena ················· 61　F 3
横浜インターナショナルスクール　Yokohama Int'l Sch. ········ 63　H 6
横浜ベイブリッジ　Yokohama Bay Bridge ········· 61　G 6
横浜開港記念会館　Yokohama Opening Port Mem. Hall········ 63　(F 5)
横浜開港資料館　Yokohama Archives of History ··········· 63　(G 5)
横浜海洋科学博物館　Yokohama Marine Science Musm ········· 63　(H 5)
横浜公園　Yokohama Park ················· 63　F 5
横浜国際平和会議場　Pacifico Yokohama ·········· 63　F 2
横浜国立大学　Yokohama Nat'l Univ. ··········· 60　E 5
横浜商科大学（鶴見）　Yokohama Coll. of Comm.(Tsurumi) ····· 61　G 4
横浜市立大学（医）　Yokohama City Univ.(Med.) ········· 62　D 7
横浜スタジアム　Yokohama Stadium ··········· 63　F 5
横浜人形の家　Yokohama Doll Musm ··········· 63　(H 5)
横浜美術館　Yokohama Musm of Art········· 62　E 3
横浜文化体育館　Yokohama Cultural Gym.········· 63　E 6
横山大観記念館　Yokoyama Taikan Mem. Cottege ········ 85　H 5
吉田苞竹記念館　Hōchiku Yoshida Mem. Hall············· 49　G 2
四谷郵便局　Yotsuya Post Office ··········· 68　E 3
読売新聞社　Yomiuri Newspapers··········· 36　C 4
読売ホール　Yomiuri Hall ················· 38　E 1
代々木公園　Yoyogi Park············· 20　B 2

ら

ライオン（本社）　Lion Corp.(H. O.) ················· 17　H 3
ラフォーレミュージアム赤坂　Laforet Museum Akasaka ········ 48　D 2
ラフォーレミュージアム飯倉　Laforet Museum Iigura ·· 80　D 5
ラフォーレミュージアム原宿　Laforet Museum Harajuku ······· 54　B 2
ランドマークタワー　Landmark Tower ················· 62　E 3

り

リッカー美術館　Riccar Art Museum ················· 38　D 3
リバーポイントタワー　Riverpoint Tower ·············· 19　F 2
六義園　Rikugi-en ················· 25　J 4
立教大学　Rikkyō Univ.· ················· 24　C 4
立正佼成会　Risshō Kōseikai··········· 10　E 6
立正大学　Risshō Univ. ··········· 28　D 5
竜子記念館　Ryūshi Mem. Gallery··········· 13　H 5
両国公会堂　Ryōgoku Public Hall··········· 17　G 4
両国橋　Ryōgoku-bashi················· 17　G 4
両国郵便局　Ryōgoku Post Office ············· 17　F 4
林試の森公園　Rinshino-mori Park ············· 28　A 4

る

ルミネ（新宿）　Lumine(Shinjuku) ··········· 57　E 5

れ

霊友会釈迦殿　Reiyūkai Temple ················· 49　H 1

ろ

ロア六本木　Roi Roppongi ················· 49　H 4
ロックスビル　Rox Bldg ················· 31　F 4
芦花恒春園（芦花公園）　Roka Kōshun-en(Roka Kōen) ·· 12　C 1
六郷橋　Rokugō-bashi ················· 61　H 2
六本木フォーラム　Roppongi Forum ················· 49　H 4

わ

YMCA ················· 33　F 6
和光　Wakō ················· 39　F 3
和光大学　Wakō Univ. ················· 15　G 7
早稲田大学　Waseda Univ. ················· 23　F 3
早稲田大学（理工）　Waseda Univ.(Sci. & Engn.) ····· 22　D 2
早稲田大学記念会堂　Waseda Univ. Memorial Hall ····· 23　F 2
和洋女子大学　Wayō Women's Univ. ················· 75　H 2
湾座有明　Wanza Ariake Bay Mall ················· 83　G 4

141

Government Offices

官公庁

Agency for Cultural Affairs　文化庁	3581-4211		
Agency of Natural-Resources & Energy	3501-1511		
資源エネルギー庁			
Board of Audit　会計検査院	3581-3251	47	G 5
Defense Agency　防衛庁	3408-5211	48	E 6
Defense Facilities Administration Agency	3408-5211	49	E 6
防衛施設庁			
Economic Planning Agency　経済企画庁	3581-0261		
Environment Agency　環境庁	3581-3351	47	I 6
Fair Trade Commission　公正取引委員会	3581-5471		
Fire Defense Agency　消防庁	5574-7111		
Fisheries Agency　水産庁	3502-8111		
Food Agency　食糧庁	3502-8111		
Foreign Service Training Institute	3943-5481	25	H 7
外務省研修所			
Forestry Agency　林野庁	3502-8111		
Hokkaido Development Agency	3581-9111	47	G 6
北海道開発庁			
House of Councillors　参議院	3581-3111	47	F 4
House of Representatives　衆議院	3581-5111	47	F 5
Imperial Household Agency　宮内庁	3213-1111	47	I 1
Institute of Public Health　国立公衆衛生院	3441-7111	28	E 1
Japan Academy　日本学士院	3822-2101	67	I 5
Japan Art Academy　日本芸術院	3821-7191	16	E 1
Management & Coordination Agency	3581-6361		
総務庁			
Maritime Safety Agency　海上保安庁	3591-6361	47	H 4
Meteorological Agency　気象庁	3212-8341	36	A 6
Metropolitan Police Dept.　警視庁	3581-4321	47	H 4
Ministry of Agriculture Forestry & Fisheries	3502-8111	47	H 5
農林水産省			
Ministry of Construction　建設省	3580-4311	47	H 4
Ministry of Education　文部省	3581-4211	47	G 6
Ministry of Finance　大蔵省	3581-4111	47	G 6
Ministry of Foreign Affairs　外務省	3580-3311	47	G 5
Ministry of Health & Welfare　厚生省	3503-1711	47	I 5
Ministry of Home Affairs　自治省	5574-7111		
Ministry of Int'l Trade & Industry	3501-1511	47	H 6
通商産業省			
Ministry of Justice　法務省	3580-4111	47	I 4
Ministry of Labor　労働省	3593-1211	47	I 6
Ministry of Posts & Telecommunications	3504-4411	47	H 6
郵政省			
Ministry of Transport　運輸省	3580-3111	47	H 4
National Diet　国会議事堂		47	F 4
National Diet Library　国立国会図書館	3581-2331	47	F 3
National Institute of Health			
国立予防衛生研究所	3444-2181	28	C 2
National Land Agency　国土庁	3593-3311	47	I 6
National Personnel Authority　人事院	3581-5311	47	J 4
National Police Agency　警察庁	3581-0141	47	H 4
National Public Safety Commission	3581-0141		
国家公安委員会			
National Tax Administration Agency	3581-4161		
国税庁			
Okinawa Development Agency　沖縄開発庁	3581-2361	47	F 6
Patent Office　特許庁	3581-1101	47	F 7
Prime Minister's Office　総理府	3581-2361	47	F 6
Prime Minister's Official Residence	3581-0101	46	E 6
内閣総理大臣官邸			
Printing Bureau　大蔵省印刷局	3582-4411	21	J 3
Public Prosecutor's Office　検察庁	3592-5611	47	I 5
Science & Technology Agency　科学技術庁	3581-5271	47	G 5
Science Council of Japan　日本学術会議	3403-6291	21	G 3
Small & Medium Enterprise Agency	3501-1511		
中小企業庁			
Social Insurance Agency　社会保険庁	3503-1711		
Supreme Court　最高裁判所	3264-8111	46	E 2
Tokyo Customshouse　東京税関	3472-7000	29	I 3
Tokyo District Court　東京地方裁判所	3581-5411	47	I 5
Tokyo High Court　東京高等裁判所	3581-5411	47	I 5
Tokyo Regional Immigration Bureau	3286-5241	36	B 5
東京入国管理局			
Tokyo Metropolitan Government	5321-1111	56	A 5
東京都庁			
Yokohama Customshouse　横浜税関	(045)201-4981	63	G 4

Embassies
外国公館

Country	電話	地図		Country	電話	地図	
Afghanistan　アフガニスタン	3407-7900	66	C 2	Guinea　ギニア	3443-8211	66	B 5
Algeria　アルジェリア	3711-2661	66	A 4	Haiti　ハイチ	3486-7096		
Argentina　アルゼンチン	5420-7101	21	G 6	Honduras　ホンジュラス	3409-1150	66	C 4
Australia　オーストラリア	5232-4111	21	I 6	Hungary　ハンガリー	3798-8801	20	B 6
Austria　オーストリア	3451-8281	21	H 5	India　インド	3262-2391	23	J 4
Bangladesh　バングラデシュ	5704-0216	66	A 3	Indonesia　インドネシア	3441-4201	28	D 3
Belgium　ベルギー	3262-0191	23	H 6	Iran　イラン	3446-8011	21	H 6
Belarus　ベラルーシ	0065-3839	67	F 4	Iraq　イラク	3423-1727	66	D 4
Bolivia　ボリビア	3499-5441	66	C 4	Ireland　アイルランド	3263-0695	67	F 4
Brazil　ブラジル	3404-5211	55	F I	Israel　イスラエル	3264-0911	23	I 6
Britain (see United Kingdom)	3265-5511	23	J 6	Italy　イタリア	3453-5291	21	I 6
Brunei　ブルネイ	3447-7997	66	A 6	Jamaica　ジャマイカ	3435-1861	66	A 4
Buigaria　ブルガリア	3465-1021	20	A 2	Jordan　ヨルダン	3580-5856	46	D 4
Burkina Faso　ブルキナファソ	3400-7919	66	C 3	Kenya　ケニア	3723-4006		
Burundi　ブルンジ	3443-7321	66	A 6	Korea (South)　大韓民国	3452-7611	21	H 6
Cambodia　カンボジア	3478-0861	66	D 4	Kuwait　クウェート	3455-0361	21	I 7
Cameroon　カメルーン	5430-4985			Laos　ラオス	5411-2291	49	I 7
Canada　カナダ	3408-2101	48	B 6	Lebanon　レバノン	3580-1227	46	D 4
Chile　チリ	3452-7561	21	J 5	Liberia　リベリア	3726-5711		
China　中華人民共和国	3403-3380	49	J 7	Libya　リビア	3477-0701	66	B 3
Colombia　コロンビア	3440-6491	66	A 5	Luxembourg　ルクセンブルク	3265-9621	67	F 4
Congo　コンゴ民主共和国	3423-3981			Madagascar　マダガスカル	3446-7252	66	C 4
Costa Rica　コスタリカ	3486-1812	66	C 4	Malawi　マラウイ	3449-3010	66	A 6
Côte d'Ivoire　コートジボアール	5454-1401			Malaysia　マレーシア	3476-3840	20	B 6
Croatia　クロアチア	5478-8481	66	B I	Marshall Is　マーシャル諸島	5379-1701	66	E 3
Cuba　キューバ	3716-3112	29	F 4	Mauritania　モーリタニア	3449-3810	66	A 6
Czechoslovakia　チェコ	3400-8122	66	A 4	Mexico　メキシコ	3581-1131	46	D 7
Denmark　デンマーク	3496-3001	20	C 6	Micronesia　ミクロネシア	3585-5456	66	D 5
Djibouti　ジブティ	3496-6135	66	B 2	Mongolia　モンゴル	3469-2088	20	A 4
Dominican Rep.　ドミニカ	3499-6020	66	C 4	Morocco　モロッコ	3478-3271	21	D I
EU-Delegation　駐日EU委員会	3239-0441	67	F 4	Mozambique　モザンビーク	3485-7621	66	C I
Ecuador　エクアドル	3499-2800	66	C 4	Myanmar　ミャンマー	3441-9291	29	F 5
Egypt　エジプト	3770-8022	20	B 6	Nepal　ネパール	3705-5558		
El Salvador　エルサルバドル	3499-4461	66	C 2	Netherlands　オランダ	5401-0411	21	J 4
Ethiopia　エチオピア	3718-1003			New Zealand　ニュージーランド	3467-2271	20	A 4
Fiji　フィジー	3587-2038	49	I I	Nicaragua　ニカラグア	3499-0400	66	C 4
Finland　フィンランド	3422-2231	21	G 6	Nigeria　ナイジェリア	5721-5391	66	A 4
France　フランス	5420-8800	21	G 6	Norway　ノルウェー	3440-2611	21	F 5
Gabon　ガボン	3448-9540	66	A 5	Oman　オマーン	3402-0877	20	D 1
Germany　ドイツ連邦共和国	3473-0151	21	G 6	Pakistan　パキスタン・	3454-4861	21	G 5
Ghana　ガーナ	5706-3201			Panama　パナマ	3499-3741	66	C 4
Greece　ギリシア	3403-0871	49	I 7	Papua New Guinea　パプア・ニューギニア	3454-7801	66	C 5
Guatemala　グアテマラ	3400-1830	66	C 4	Paraguay　パラグアイ	5485-3101	66	A 2

Peru　ペルー	3406-4240	20	E 5		Syria　シリア	3586-8977	48	E 4
Philippines　フィリピン	3496-2731	20	B 5		Tanzania　タンザニア	3425-4531		
Poland　ポーランド	3280-2881	66	A 5		Thailand　タイ	3441-7352	28	D 3
Portugal　ポルトガル	3400-7907	66	C 2		Tunisia　チュニジア	3353-4111	66	E 5
Qatal　カタール	3224-3911	66	D 4		Turkey　トルコ	3470-5131	20	D 2
Romania　ルーマニア	3479-0311	66	C 4		Uganda　ウガンダ	3465-4552	66	C 1
Russia　ロシア	3583-4224	49	I 1		Ukraina　ウクライナ	3432-0917	66	E 6
Rwanda　ルワンダ	3486-7800	66	C 4		U. A. E　アラブ首長国連邦	5486-0604	66	C 4
Saudi Arabia　サウジアラビア	3589-5241	49	I 3		United Kingdom　イギリス	3265-5511	23	J 6
Senegal　セネガル	3464-8451	20	B 6		Uruguay　ウルグアイ	3486-1888	66	C 4
Singapore　シンガポール	3586-9116	49	I 4		U. S. A　アメリカ合衆国	3224-5000	48	D 1
Slovakia　スロバキア	3400-8122	66	C 4		Vatican City　ローマ法王庁	3263-6851	23	I 5
Sloveniya　スロベニア	5570-6275	66	D 4		Venezuela　ベネズエラ	3409-1501	66	C 4
South Africa　南アフリカ	3265-3366	67	E 4		Viet Nam　ベトナム	3466-3313	20	A 2
Spain　スペイン	3583-8531	49	,E 1		Yemen　イエメン	3499-7151	66	C 4
Sri Lanka　スリランカ	3585-7431	48	E 1		Yugosiavia　ユーゴスラビア	3447-3571	29	F 5
Sudan　スーダン	3476-0811	66	B 2		Zambia　ザンビア	3491-0121		
Sweden　スウェーデン	5562-5050	49	F 1		Zimbabwe　ジンバブエ	3280-0331	66	B 4
Swizerland　スイス	3473-0121	21	F 5					

Airlines
航空会社

Aeroflot Russian Intl Airlines (SU)	3434-9681			キャセイ・パシフィック航空			
アエロフロート・ロシア航空				China Airlines (CI)　中華航空	3436-1501		
Air Canada　エア・カナダ	3585-4635			China Eastern Airlines　中華東方航空	5251-0711		
Air China (CA)　中国国際航空	5251-0711			Continental Micronesia Airlines	3508-6421		
Air France (AF)　エールフランス	3475-2211			コンチネンタル・ミクロネシア航空			
Air India (AI)　エア・インディア	3214-7631			Delta Air Lines (DL)　デルタ航空	5275-7500		
Air Lanka (UL)　エアランカ	3573-4263			Deutsche Lufthansa (LH)	3578-6770	47	F 7
Air New Zealand (TE)	3213-0968			ルフトハンザ・ドイツ航空			
ニュージーランド航空				Dragon Air HongKong　香港ドラゴン航空	3506-8361		
Air Pacific (FJ)　エア・パシフィック航空	3435-1377			Egypt Air (MS)　エジプト航空	3211-4524	36	D 6
Alitalia Airlines (AZ)　アリタリア航空	3592-3970	47	F 7	Finnair (AY)　フィンエアー	3222-6992		
All Nippon Airways (NH)　Int'l 国際	5489-8800			P. T. Garuda Indonesia (GA)	3595-3451	47	F 6
全日空　Domestic 国内	3272-1212			ガルーダ・インドネシア航空			
American Airlines (AA)　アメリカ航空	3214-2111			Iberia Airlines of Spain (IB)　イベリア・スペイン航空	3578-3555		
Ansett Australian Airlines　アンセット・オーストラリア航空	5210-0791			The Airline of the Islamic Republic of Iran (IR)	3586-2567	47	E 7
Asiana Airlenes (OZ)　アシアナ航空	5572-7660			イラン航空			
Austrian Airlines　オーストリア航空	3597-6100			Japan Airlines (JL)　Int'l 国際	3457-1181		
Biman Bangladesh Airlines (BG)	3502-7922			日本航空　Domestic 国内	3456-2111		
ビーマン・バングラディシュ航空				Japan Air System (JD)　日本エアシステム			
British Airways (BA)　英国航空	5401-5701	38	C 1	Int'l 国際	3438-1155		
Canadian Airlines Int'l (CP)	3212-5811			Domestic 国内	3432-6111		
カナディアン航空				Japan Asia Airways (EG)　日本アジア航空	3455-7511		
Cathay Pacific Airways (CX)	3504-1531			KLM Royal Dutch Airlines (KL)	3216-5330		

KLMオランダ航空			
Korean Air (KE)　大韓航空	5443-3343	*37*	J 5
Malaysia Airlines　マレーシア航空	3432-8502	*78*	E 7
Nothwest Airlines (NW)	5400-7230		
ノースウエスト航空			
Olympic Airways	3201-0251		
オリンピック航空			
Pakistan Int'l Airlines (PK)	3216-4641		
パキスタン国際航空			
Philippine Airlines (PR)　フィリピン航空	3580-1574	*46*	C 4
Qantas Airways (QF)	3597-5576		
カンタス・オーストラリア航空			
Royal Nepal Airlines　ロイヤル・ネパール航空	3369-3317		
Sabena Belgian World Airlines (SN)	3585-6551	*46*	E 6
サベナ・ベルギー航空			
Scandinavian Airlines System (SK)	3503-3155		
スカンジナビア航空			
Singapore Airlines (SQ)	3213-1158		
シンガポール航空			
Swiss Air Transport (SR)　スイス航空	3212-1011		
Thai Airways Int'l (TG)　タイ国際航空	3593-0522		
Turkish Airlines　トルコ航空	5251-1511		
United Airlines (UA)　ユナイテッド航空	3817-4411		
Valig Brazilian Airlenes (RG)	3211-6761	*35*	D 6
ヴァリグ・ブラジル航空			
Virgin Atlantic Airways (VS)	3499-8831		
ヴァージンアトランティック航空			

Hotel and Inns
ホテル，旅館

Akasaka Prince Hotel	3234-1111	*46*	C 3
赤坂プリンスホテル			
Akasaka Tōkyū Hotel　赤坂東急ホテル	3580-2311	*46*	C 4
Akasaka Yōkō Hotel　赤坂陽光ホテル	3586-4050	*48*	D 4
Akihabara Washington Hotel	3255-3311	*33*	I 4
秋葉原ワシントンホテル			
ANA Hotel Tokyo　東京全日空ホテル	3505-1111	*20*	E 1
Asakusa View Hotel　浅草ビューホテル	3847-1111	*31*	F 2
Asia Center of Japan (Hotel Asia Kaikan)	3402-6111	*48*	C 6
ホテルアジア会館			
Atagoyama　Tōkyū Inn　愛宕山東急イン	3431-0109	*88*	E 5
Bund Hotel　バンドホテル	(045)621-1101	*63*	H 5
Capitol Tōkyū Hotel	3581-4511	*46*	D 5
キャピトル東急ホテル			
Center Hotel Tokyo　センターホテル東京	3667-2711	*89*	F 6
Chisan Hotel Tokyo　チサンホテル東京	3785-3211	*91*	F 4
Chisan Hotel Hamamatsuchō	3452-6511	*41*	G 1
チサンホテル浜松町			
Dai-ichi Hotel Annex	3503-5611	*38*	B 5
第一ホテルアネックス			
Daiichi Hotel Tokyo　第一ホテル東京	3501-4411	*68*	B 5
Daiichi Hotel Tokyo Bay	(0473)55-3333	*91*	H 4
第一ホテル東京ベイ			
Dai-ichi Hotel Tokyo Seafort	5460-4411	*88*	A 7
第一ホテル東京シーフォート			
Diamond Hotel　ダイヤモンドホテル	3263-2211	*23*	I 6
Fairmont Hotel　フェヤーモントホテル	3262-1151	*89*	F 4
Four Seasons Hotel Chinzansō Tokyo	3942-2222	*89*	G 2
フォーシーズンズホテル椿山荘東京			
Ginza Capital Hotel	3543-8211	*39*	J 4
銀座キャピタルホテル			
Ginza Dai-ichi Hotel　銀座第一ホテル	3542-5311	*38*	E 6
Ginza Nikkō Hotel　銀座日航ホテル	3571-4911	*38*	C 5
Ginza Tōbu Hotel　銀座東武ホテル	3546-0111	*39*	F 5
Ginza Tōkyū Hotel　銀座東急ホテル	3541-2411	*39*	G 5
Gotenyama Hills Hotel Tokyo	5488-3911	*29*	F 5
御殿山ヒルズホテルラフォーレ東京			
Grand Central Hotel	3256-3211	*33*	G 6
グランドセントラルホテル			
Haneda Tōkyū Hotel　羽田東急ホテル	3747-0311	*91*	G 5
Harumi Grand Hotel	3533-7111		
晴海グランドホテル			
Hill Port Hotel　ヒルポートホテル	3462-5171	*52*	E 6

Hilltop (Yamanoue) Hotel　山の上ホテル	3293-2311	*32*	D 3
Holiday Inn Tokyo　ホリディ・イン東京	3553-6161	*89*	F 7
Hotel Century Hyatt	3349-0111	*56*	A 4
ホテルセンチェリーハイアット			
Hotel Cosmo Yokohama	(045)314-3111	*62*	B 1
ホテルコスモ横浜			
Hotel East21 Tokyo	5683-5683	*91*	G 3
ホテルイースト21東京			
Hotel Edmont　ホテルエドモント	3237-1111	*89*	G 4
Hotel Ginza Dai-ei　ホテル銀座ダイエー	3545-1111	*39*	H 4
Hotel Grand City	3984-5121	*59*	G 3
ホテルグランドシティ			
Hotel Grand Palace	3264-1111	*16*	A 4
ホテルグランドパレス			
Hotel Happo-kaku　ホテル八峰閣	3982-1181	*58*	E 6
Hotel Holiday Inn Yokohama	(045)681-3311		
ホテルホリデイ・イン横浜			
Hotel Ibis　ホテルアイビス	3403-4411	*49*	G 5
Hotel Kizankan　ホテル機山館	3812-1211	*89*	H 4
Hotel Daiei　ホテルダイエー	3813-6271	*89*	H 4
Hotel Kokusai Kankō　ホテル国際観光	3215-3281	*37*	F 2
Hotel Lungwood　ホテルラングウッド	3803-1234	*26*	D 5
Hotel Metropolitan	3980-1111	*58*	C 5
ホテルメトロポリタン			
Hotel New Grand	(045)681-1841	*63*	H 5
ホテルニューグランド			
Hotel New Meguro　ホテルニューメグロ	3719-8121	*91*	F 4
Hotel New Ōtani　ホテルニューオータニ	3265-1111	*46*	B 2
Hotel New Ōkura　ホテルニューオークラ	3582-0111	*21*	J 3
Hotel Pacific Meridien Tokyo	3445-6711	*29*	F 3
ホテルパシフィックメリディアン東京			
Hotel Park Lane Nishikasai	3675-8900	*91*	H 3
ホテルパークレーン西葛西			
Hotel Park Side　ホテルパークサイド	3836-5711	*89*	H 5
Hotel President Aoyama	3497-0111	*21*	F 2
ホテルプレジデント青山			
Hotel Rich Yokohama	(045)312-2111	*62*	C 1
ホテルリッチ横浜			
Hotel Satoh　ホテルサトー	3815-1133	*32*	B 1
Hotel Sunlite Shinjuku	3356-0391	*57*	I 2
ホテルサンライト新宿			
Hotel Sunroute Ikebukuro	3980-1911	*59*	F 3
ホテルサンルート池袋			

Hotel Sunroute Plaza Tokyo	(0473)55-1111	91	H 4
ホテルサンルートプラザ東京			
Hotel Sunroute Shibuya	3464-6411	52	D 6
ホテルサンルート渋谷			
Hotel Sunroute Tokyo	3375-3211	56	E 7
ホテルサンルート東京			
Hotel Tokiwa　ホテルときわ	3202-4321	89	F 2
Hotel Kaiyō　ホテル海洋	3368-1121	89	F I
Hotel Tōkyū Kankō　ホテル東急観光	3582-0451	48	D 2
Hotel Tōyō　ホテル東陽	3615-1041	91	G 3
Hotel Yokohama Garden	(045)641-1311	91	I 3
ホテル横浜ガーデン			
Hotel Yokohama, The	(045)662-1321	63	G 5
ザ・ホテルヨコハマ			
Ikebukuro Center city Hotel	3985-1311	58	D I
池袋センターシティホテル			
Ikebukuro Hotel Thatre	3988-2251	59	G 4
池袋ホテルテアトル			
Ikenohata Bunka Center	3822-0515	89	H 5
池之端文化センター			
Imperial Hotel(Teikoku Hotel)	3504-1111	38	B 3
帝国ホテル			
Inabasō Ryokan　旅館稲葉荘	3341-9581	88	E 2
Inn Shin-Nakano Lodge　新中野ロッヂ	3381-4886		
Isezakichō Washington Hotel	(045)243-1111	91	H 7
伊勢佐木町ワシントンホテル			
Kawasaki Grand Hotel	(044)244-2111	91	I 5
川崎グランドホテル			
Kawasaki Hotel Park	(044)211-5885	91	I 4
川崎ホテルパーク			
Kawasaki Nikkō Hotel	(044)244-5841	91	H 5
川崎日航ホテル日航			
Kayabachō Pearl Hotel	3553-2211	89	F 7
茅場町パールホテル			
Keiō Plaza(Inter-Continental) Hotel	3344-0111	56	C 5
京王プラザホテル			
Kikuya Ryokan　菊久屋旅館	3841-4051	89	I 6
MaRRoad Inn Akasaka	3585-7611	48	D 5
マロウド・イン赤坂			
Mitsui Garden Hotel Kamata	5710-1131	91	F 5
三井ガーデンホテル蒲田			
Mitsui Urban Hotel Ginza	3572-4131	38	C 5
三井アーバンホテル銀座			
Miyako Hotel Tokyo　都ホテル東京	3447-3111	29	E I
Miyako Inn Tokyo　都イン東京	3454-3111	29	G I
New Ōtani Inn Tokyo	3779-9111	88	A 6
ニューオータニイン東京			
New Ōtani Inn Yokohama	(045)252-1311	90	E 7
ニューオータニイン横浜			
New Sanno U. S. Forces Center, The	3440-7871	88	B 4
ニューサンノー米軍センター			
New Satellite Hotel Shibaura	5444-0202		
ニューサテライトホテル芝浦			
New Takanawa Prince Hotel	3442-1111	29	F 3
新高輪プリンスホテル			
Nihon Seinenkan Hotel　日本青年館ホテル	3401-0101	83	D 3
Omori Tōkyū Inn　大森東急イン	3768-0109	91	F 5
Ours Inn Hankyū　アワーズイン阪急	3775-6121	91	F 4
Palace Hotel　パレスホテル	3211-5211	36	D 6
Richmond Hotel Tokyo	3565-4111	89	G I
リッチモンドホテル東京			
Rihga Loyal Hotel Waseda		5285-1121	
リーガロイヤルホテル早稲田			
Roppongi Prince Hotel	3587-1111	49	F 3
六本木プリンスホテル			
Royal Park Hotel　ロイヤルパークホテル	3667-1111	89	G 7
Ryckan Asakusa Shigetsu (Mikawaya Bekkan)		3843-2345	
旅館浅草指月(旧三河屋別館)			
Ryokan Katsutarō　旅館勝太郎	3821-9808	26	D 7
Ryokan Toki　旅館都貴	3657-1747		
Ryokan Sansuisō　旅館山水荘	3441-7475	88	A 5
Ryōgoku Pearl Hotel　両国パールホテル	3626-3211	89	H 7
Ryōgoku River Hotel　両国リバーホテル	3634-1711	89	H 7
Sakura Ryokan　桜旅館	3876-8118		
Satellite Hotel Yokohama	(045)641-0202	63	G 5
サテライトホテルヨコハマ			
Sawanoya Ryokan　澤の屋旅館	3822-2251	26	C 6
Shanpia Hotel Akasaka	3586-0811	48	C 5
シャンピアホテル赤坂			
Shanpia Hotel Aoyama	3407-2111	53	H 4
シャンピアホテル青山			
Shanpia Grande Tokyo Bay Hotel	(0473)55-5555	91	H 4
シェラトングランデトーキョウベイホテル			
Shiba Park Hotel　芝パークホテル	3433-4141	88	D 6
Shibuya Tōbu Hotel　渋谷東武ホテル	3476-0111	52	D 2
Shibuya Tōkyū Inn　渋谷東急イン	3498-0109	53	F 4
Shinagawa Prince Hotel　品川プリンスホテル			
	3440-1111	29	F 4
Shin.uku New City Hotel	3375-6511	88	E 2
新宿ニューシティホテル			
Shinjuku Prince Hotel	3205-1111	57	F 2
新宿プリンスホテル			
Shinjuku Sunpark Hotel	3362-7101	89	F I
新宿サンパークホテル			
Shinjuku Washington Hotel	3343-3111	56	B 7
新宿ワシントンホテル			
Shin Yokohama Fuji View Hotel	(045)473-002I	90	D 6
新横浜フジビューホテル			
Shin Yokohama Hotel　新横浜ホテル	(045)471-6011	90	E 6
Shin Yokohama Kokusai Hotel	(045)473-1311	90	E 6
新横浜国際ホテル			
Shin Yokohama Prince Hotel	(045)471-1111	90	E 5
新横浜プリンスホテル			
Star Hotel Tokyo　スターホテル東京	3361-1111	56	E 2

Star Hotel Yokohama スターホテル横浜	(045)651-3111	63	H 5
Suidōbashi Grand Hotel 水道橋グランドホテル	3816-2101	89	H 4
Suigetsu Hotel/Ohgaisō 水月ホテル／鷗外荘	3822-4611	26	D 7
Sunshine City Prince Hotel サンシャインプリンスホテル	3988-1111	59	I 4
Taishō Central Hotel 大正セントラルホテル	3232-0101	89	G 1
Takanawa Prince Hotel 高輪プリンスホテル	3447-1111	29	F 3
Takanawa Tōbu Hotel　高輪東武ホテル	3447-0111	88	A 6
Teikoku Hotel (see imperial Hotel)	3504-1111	38	B 3
Tōkō Hotel　東興ホテル	3494-1050	88	A 5
Tokyo Bay Hillton 東京ベイヒルトン	(0473)55-5555	91	H 4
Tokyo Bay Hotel Tokyū 東京ベイホテル東急	(0473)55-2411		
Tokyo City Hotel　東京シティーホテル	3270-7671	34	C 3
Tokyo Grand Hotel　東京グランドホテル	3456-2222	88	D 6
Tokyo Green Hotel Ochanomizu 東京グリーンホテルお茶ノ水	3255-4161	33	G 4
Tokyo Green Hotel Kōrakuen 東京グリーンホテル後楽園	3816-4161	32	A 1
Tokyo Green Hotel Suidōbashi 東京グリーンホテル水道橋	3295-4161	32	C 6
Tokyo Hilton International 東京ヒルトンインターナショナル	3344-5111	56	A 3
Tokyo Hotel Urashima　東京ホテル浦島	3533-3111	19	F 5
Tokyo Int'l Youth Hostel 東京国際ユースホステル	3235-1107	89	G 4
Tokyo Marunouchi Hotel 東京丸の内ホテル	3215-2151	36	E 3
Tokyo Ochanomizu Hotel Juraku 東京お茶の水ホテル聚楽	3251-7222	33	G 3
Tokyo Prince Hotel　東京プリンスホテル	3432-1111	18	A 4
Tokyo Shinhankyū Hotel　東京新阪急ホテル	5550-5700		
Tokyo Station Hotel 東京ステーションホテル	3231-2511	37	G 3
Tokyo Sunny Side Hotel 東京サニーサイドホテル	3649-1211	91	G 3
Tokyo YMCA Hotel　東京YMCAホテル	3293-1911	33	F 6
Tokyo YMCA Hostel 東京YMCAホステル	3293-5421	32	E 3
Tokyo YMCA Sadohara Hostel 東京YMCA砂土原ホステル	3268-7313	89	F 3
Toyochō Bista Hotel　東陽町ビスタホテル	3699-0333	91	H 3
Westin Hotel Tokyo ウエスティンホテル東京	5423-7000	51	F 3
Yaesu Fujiya Hotel　八重洲富士屋ホテル	3273-2111	37	J 3
Yamanoue Hotel　山の上ホテル (see Hilltop Hotel)			
YMCA Asia Youth Center YMCAアジア青少年センター	3233-0631	93	G 4
Yokohama Grand Intercontinental Hotel ヨコハマグランドインターコンチネンタルホテル	(045)223-2222	91	E 7
Yokohama Isezakichō Washington Hotel 横浜伊勢佐木町ワシントンホテル	(045)243-7111	91	H 7
Yokohama Grand Intercontinental Hotel 横浜国際ホテル	(045)311-1311	62	B 1
Yokohama Prince Hotel 横浜プリンスホテル	(045)751-1111	90	E 7
Yokohama Royal Park Hotel Nikko 横浜ロイヤルパークホテルニッコー	(045)221-1111	91	E 7
Yokohama Tōkyū Hotel 横浜東急ホテル	(045)311-1682	62	C 1

Others
その他

Police 警察への急報 110
Fire and Ambulance (calls answered in Japanese) 火事・救急車 119
Telephone：電話
    Long Distance Calls (operator-assisted) 市外通話 100
    Collect/Credit Calls コレクト/クレジット通話 106
    Number Inquiries 電話番号案内 5295-1010 (English) or 104
    Repair Service 電話の故障 113
International Telephone：国際電話
    Booking (operator-assisted calls) 申し込み 0051
    Inquiries (operator-assisted calls) 問い合わせ 0057
Domestic Telegram：国内電報 115
International Telegram：国際電報 3344-5151
Time 時報 117
Weather 天気予報 (045) 319-8100 and (0425) 52-2511 Ext. 4181 (English), or 177
Tourist Information Centers：ツーリスト・インフォメーション・センター
    Tokyo (Yurakucho) 東京 (有楽町) 3502-1461
    Asakusa 浅草 3842-5566
    New Tokyo International Airport (Narita) 新東京国際空港 (成田) (0476) 32-8711
    Yokohama 横浜 (045) 641-5824
Japan Travel-Phones (toll free)：旅行相談
    Eastern Japan 東日本 0120-222800
    Weastern Japan 西日本 0120-444800
Teletourist Service (English tape) 観光案内 (英語) 3503-2911
    〃 (French tape) 〃 (仏語) 3503-2926
Flight Information：フライト案内
    Narita 成田 (0476) 32-2800
    Haneda 羽田 3747-8010
Airport Baggage Service (ABC) 空港荷物サービス 3545-1131
Airport Limousine Bus Information 空港リムジンバス案内 3665-7251
Keisei Skyliner (Ueno-Narita) 京成スカイライナー (上野－成田) 3831-0131
Railway Information Center (Japan Railways) 鉄道案内 (JR) 3212-4441
JAF (car breakdown service) 日本自動車連盟 (車故障サービス) 3463-0111
Japan Travel Bureau 日本交通公社 3276-7777
Hospital Information 病院案内 3212-2323
American Pharmacy (English spoken) アメリカン・ファーマシー 3271-4034
Tokyo English Life Line (TELL) 東京イングリッシュ・ライフ・ライン 3264-4347
Tokyo Regional Immigration Bureau 東京入国管理局 3286-5241
Foreign Residents' Advisory Center (Tokyo) 東京都庁外国人相談センター 5320-7744
Tokyo International Post Office 東京国際郵便局 3241-4891

Useful Phrases
道のたずね方

Occassionally the romaji phrases differ slightly in translation from the literal Japanese.

GENERAL

Excuse me.
すみません。
Sumimasen.

Thank you.
ありがとう。
Arigatō.

train
電車/列車
densha/ressha

subway
地下鉄
chikatetsu

station
駅
eki

bus
バス
basu

bus stop
バス停
basu-tei

ticket
切符
kippu

entrance
入口
iriguchi

exit
出口
deguchi

straight
まっすぐ
massugu

turn
まがる
magaru

right
右
migi

left
左
hidari

stop
止まる
tomaru

back
うしろ
ushiro

How much?
料金は、いくら？
Ikura?

I want to go to (place name).
私は、(場所名)に行きたい。
Watashi wa, (place name) ni ikitai.

Where is the toilet?
トイレはどこですか?
Toile wa, doko desu ka?

Is there anyone here who speaks English?
英語のできる人はいますか?
Eigo no dekiru hito wa, imasu ka?

Please telephone (number/name).
(電話番号/人・機関名)に、電話をかけて下さい。
(number/name) ni, denwa o kakete kudasai.

ASKING THE WAY

Is this (place name)?
ここは(場所名)ですか?
Koko wa, (place name) desu ka?

Where is (place name)?
(場所名)は、どこですか?
(place name) wa, doko desu ka?

Where is (place name) on this map?
(場所名)は、この地図のどこにありますか?
(place name) wa, kono chizu no, doko ni arimasu ka?

How long will it take to go to (place name)?
(場所名)に行くには、どのくらい時間がかかりますか?
(place name) ni iku ni wa, dono kurai jikan ga kakarimasu ka?

TAKING A TAXI

(destination), please.
(行き先)まで、行って下さい。
(destination) made, itte kudasai.

Please stop here.
ここで、止めて下さい。
Koko de, tomete kudasai.

How much is it?
料金は、いくらですか?
Ikura desu ka?

TAKING A TRAIN/SUBWAY

Which line should I take to go to (station name)?
(駅名)に行くには、何線ですか？
(station name) wa, nanisen desu ka ?

Which train should I take to go to (station name)?
(駅名)に行くには、どの電車に乗ればよいですか？
(station name) wa, dono densha ni noreba yoi desu ka?

Where do I buy a ticket?
切符は、どこで買えますか？
Kippu wa, doko de kaemasu ka?

How much is a ticket to (station name)?
(駅名)まで、料金はいくらですか？
(station name) made, ikura desu ka?

What is the platform number for (station name)?
(駅名)行きは、何番線ですか？
(station name)-iki wa, nanbansen desu ka?

Is this the right platform for (station name)?
(駅名)行きは、このホームですか？
(station name)-iki wa, kono hōmu desu ka?

Is this the right train to (station name)?
この電車は、(駅名)に行きますか？
Kore wa, (station name) ni ikimasu ka?

Does this train stop at (station name)?
この電車は、(駅名)に停まりますか？
Kore wa, (station name) ni tomarimasu ka?

How many more stops to (station name)?
(駅名)は、いくつ目ですか？
(station name) wa, ikutsume desu ka?

Where should I change trains to go to (station name)?
(駅名)に行くには、どこで乗り換えですか？
(station name) wa, doko de norikae desu ka?

Please let me know when we arrive at (station name).
(駅名)に着いたら、教えて下さい。
(station name) ni tsuitara, oshiete kudasai.

What time is the next train to (station name)?
次の(駅名)行きの電車は、何時ですか？
Tsugi no (station name)-iki wa, nanji desu ka?

本書の基図は（株）人文社版使用。
京葉地区－「この地図の作成に当たっては、建設省国土地理院発行の20万分の１地勢図
を使用しました。（測量法第30条に基づく成果使用承認　平５　関使、第69号）」

ザ　ニユウ　トウキヨウ　バイリンガル　アトラス
The New Tokyo Bilingual Atlas　新東京二ヵ国語地図　第二版
しんとうきよう に こくごちづ だいにはん

| 1993年 8 月 5 日 | 第 1 版第 1 刷発行 |
| 1997年 8 月20日 | 第 2 版第 1 刷発行 |

定価はカバーに表示してあります

編著者　梅田　厚
うめだ あつし
　　　　〒183　東京都府中市多磨町 2 － 3 － 6
　　　　電話　（0423）63 － 4643
発行者　野間佐和子
発行所　株式会社 講談社
　　　　〒112－01 東京都文京区音羽2丁目12－21
　　　　電話　編集部　（03）5395 － 3575
　　　　　　　販売部　（03）5395 － 3622
　　　　　　　製作部　（03）5395 － 3615
印刷所　凸版印刷株式会社
製本所　株式会社 国宝社

本書の無断複写（コピー）は著作権法
上での例外を除き、禁じられています。

落丁本・乱丁本は、ご面倒ですが、講談社書籍
製作部あてにお送りください。送料小社負担に
てお取り替えいたします。なお、この本につい
てのお問い合わせは、国際室あてにお願いいた
します。

Ⓒ梅田　厚　1997　Printed in Japan
ISBN4-06-208828-2（国 A）